The Evolutionary Biology of Human Body Fatness:
Thrift and Control

This comprehensive synthesis of current medical and evolutionary litera-ture addresses key questions about the role body fat plays in human biol-ogy. It explores how body energy stores are regulated, how they develop over the life-course, what biological functions they serve, and how they may have evolved. There is now substantial evidence that human adiposity is not merely a buffer against the threat of starvation but also a resource for meeting the energy costs of growth, reproduction and immune func-tion. Furthermore, the hormonal secretions of adipose tissue play a key regulatory role in allocating energy between these competing functions. As such, it may be considered as important in our species' evolution as other traits such as bipedalism, large brains, and long life spans and devel-opmental periods. Indeed, adiposity is integrally linked with these other traits and with our capacity to colonise and inhabit diverse ecosystems. It is because human metabolism is so sensitive to environmental cues that manipulative economic forces are now generating the current obesity epidemic.

JONATHAN C. K. WELLS is a Reader in Paediatric Nutrition at the University College London (UCL) Institute of Child Health. He conducts research on paediatric energetics and body composition, using anthropo-logical and evolutionary approaches to inform biological understanding.

Cambridge Studies in Biological and Evolutionary Anthropology

Series editors

HUMAN ECOLOGY
C. G. Nicholas Mascie-Taylor, University of Cambridge
Michael A. Little, State University of New York, Binghamton
GENETICS
Kenneth M. Weiss, Pennsylvania State University
HUMAN EVOLUTION
Robert A. Foley, University of Cambridge
Nina G. Jablonski, California Academy of Science
PRIMATOLOGY
Karen B. Strier, University of Wisconsin, Madison

Also available in the series

41 *Macaque Societies – A Model for the Study of Social Organization* Bernard
   Thierry, Mewa Singh & Werner Kaumanns (eds.) 0 521 81847 8
42 *Simulating Human Origins and Evolution* Ken Wessen 0 521 84399 5
43 *Bioarchaeology of Southeast Asia* Marc Oxenham & Nancy Tayles (eds.)
   0 521 82580 6
44 *Seasonality in Primates* Diane K. Brockman & Carel P. van Schaik 0 521 82069 3
45 *Human Biology of Afro-Caribbean Populations* Lorena Madrigal 0 521 81931 8
46 *Primate and Human Evolution* Susan Cachel 0 521 82942 9
47 *The First Boat People* Steve Webb 0 521 85656 6
48 *Feeding Ecology in Apes and Other Primates* Gottfried Hohmann, Martha Robbins
   & Christophe Boesch (eds.) 0 521 85837 2
49 *Measuring Stress in Humans: A Practical Guide for the Field* Gillian Ice & Gary
   James (eds.) 0 521 84479 7
50 *The Bioarchaeology of Children: Perspectives from Biological and Forensic
   Anthropology* Mary Lewis 0 521 83602 6
51 *Monkeys of the Ta'i Forest* W. Scott McGraw, Klaus Zuberbühler & Ronald Noe
   (eds.) 0 521 81633 5
52 *Health Change in the Asia-Pacific Region: Biocultural and Epidemiological
   Approaches* Ryutaro Ohtsuka & Stanley I. Ulijaszek (eds.) 978 0 521 83792 7
53 *Technique and Application in Dental Anthropology* Joel D. Irish & Greg C. Nelson
   (eds.) 978 0 521 870 610
54 *Western Diseases: An Evolutionary Perspective* Tessa M. Pollard
   978 0 521 61737 6
55 *Spider Monkeys: The Biology, Behavior and Ecology of the Genus Ateles*
   Christina J. Campbell 978 0 521 86750 4
56 *Between Biology and Culture* Holger Schutkowski (ed.) 978 0 521 85936 3
57 *Primate Parasite Ecology: The Dynamics and Study of Host-Parasite
   Relationships* Michael A. Huffman & Colin A. Chapman (eds.) 978 0 521 87246 1

The Evolutionary Biology of Human Body Fatness

Thrift and Control

Jonathan C. K. Wells
UCL Institute of Child Health

CAMBRIDGE
UNIVERSITY PRESS

CAMBRIDGE UNIVERSITY PRESS
Cambridge, New York, Melbourne, Madrid, Cape Town, Singapore,
São Paulo, Delhi, Dubai, Tokyo

Cambridge University Press
The Edinburgh Building, Cambridge CB2 8RU, UK

Published in the United States of America by Cambridge University Press, New York

www.cambridge.org
Information on this title: www.cambridge.org/9780521884204

First published 2010

Printed in the United Kingdom at the University Press, Cambridge

A catalog record for this publication is available from the British Library

Library of Congress Cataloging in Publication data
Wells, Jonathan C. K.
The evolutionary biology of human body fatness / Jonathan C. K. Wells.
    p.   cm. – (Cambridge studies in biological and evolutionary anthropology ; 58)
Includes bibliographical references and index.
ISBN 978-0-521-88420-4 (hardback)
1. Adipose tissues – Evolution.   2. Human evolution.   3. Obesity.   I. Title.
II. Series.
QP88.15.W45   2009
599.9′4 – dc22   2009037302

ISBN 978-0-521-88420-4 Hardback

This book is dedicated to W. Andy Coward
(1941–2007)

Contents

Preface *page* ix

1 **Introduction**   1

2 **Human fatness in broad context**   16

3 **Proximate causes of lipid deposition and oxidation**   49

4 **The ontogenetic development of adiposity**   92

5 **The life-course induction of adiposity**   118

6 **The fitness value of fat**   153

7 **The evolutionary biology of adipose tissue**   195

8 **Adiposity in hominin evolution**   215

9 **Adiposity in human evolution**   244

10 **The evolution of human obesity**   270

References   302
Index   363

Preface

In 1995 I undertook a brief period of fieldwork in the heart of the tropical forests of Sarawak, Malaysia. The intention had been to measure the energy metabolism of undernourished Iban babies using state-of-the-art stable isotope probes, but in the event the babies proved thoroughly healthy and the research aim was abandoned. Instead, I spent a month living in a long-house and made some simpler anthropometric measurements of children and adults. What I really learnt on this trip had very little to do with formal research and was much more about how the Iban live, work and enjoy themselves. Though formerly headhunters, still with skulls hanging down outside the long-house rooves, they offered unstinting warmth and hospitality throughout our visit.

Many of my strongest memories are about the range of foods we were offered. Steamed fish; tender fern shoots; pleasantly bitter vegetables; many varieties of wonderful red rice that I have never found since; curly-shelled snails, which the children gathered for us every day and which you had to suck out of a gash at the end of the shell with a suitable slurping noise; a duck, which I was obliged to select from the pond myself and carry home in a bag, quacking forlornly; rice wine, broken open at 10 a.m. and knocking me off my feet for the rest of the day. And one day, some men came back from a hunting trip with a pair of bush pig.

Naturally we were invited to the barbecue, and soon the smell of roasting meat filled the air. Two plates were passed around, one of meat and one of fat: large cubes of fat, with the coarse bristles of the skin slightly crisped. We never tried the meat, because the fat was reserved for us. It was clear at the time that we visitors were being offered the delicacy, yet at that time I had no idea why fat, rather than the meat, should have been considered more special. Meat has conventionally been portrayed by anthropologists as a luxury food item, as well as a key source of protein.

I never asked any Iban about this, and so I can only assume that they show consistency with many other societies that eat the meat of wild animals. Since that visit, I have become aware that lean meat has such a low ratio of energy to protein that a diet based on it can impose significant energy stress on the body – the 'rabbit malnutrition' known to polar populations. Fat is not just a delicacy but an important source of energy and fat-soluble vitamins. In western industrialised populations, experiencing an epidemic of obesity in both adults and younger age groups, fat is routinely portrayed as a 'bad' food. Things must have been very different until recent decades, and it is likely that the Iban like many other societies consider pork fat a tasty luxury food. I remember few other sources of lipid in their diet other than cooking oil (and the aforementioned duck).

This book aims to illustrate how adipose tissue is one of the most important components of human biology. Most will be familiar with the notion of body fatness as embodying the strategy of 'thrift' – a store of energy, providing the calories to accommodate starvation. Many other functions also benefit from these energy stores, but more importantly adipose tissue also acts as a 'control centre', allocating energy between different biological processes. Adipose tissue is now known to secrete numerous chemicals which act on the brain and other tissues, and it is this combined role in thrift and control that makes adiposity such an interesting trait. Most research on human body fat has been conducted by the biomedical community, showing how high levels of fat increase cardiovascular risk. An evolutionary perspective is urgently required to clarify why humans became so good at acquiring fat, given plentiful food and low activity demands.

This book has built on a considerable amount of work by others. In the literature, Caroline Pond has long been the main expert on adipose tissue, and her monograph *The fats of life* was a key source of material. I am extremely grateful to her for reading the entire draft of this book and providing many valuable suggestions for improvement. Previous reviews by Nick Norgan and Christopher Kuzawa have also proved stimulating and valuable. These authors are especially notable because few others have given the beneficial functions of adipose tissue much attention.

During my academic career, I was first stimulated in evolutionary ecology by the teaching of Robert Foley and Phyllis Lee, at the University of Cambridge. I then worked for seven years at the Medical Research Council's Dunn Nutrition Unit, also in Cambridge. Here, Peter Davies initiated my interest in infant body composition and energetics. I was extremely fortunate to be surrounded by a number of world experts in nutritional techniques. Andy Coward, to whom this book is dedicated, pioneered stable isotope probes for measuring energy expenditure and breast-milk intake in free-living individuals. Almost all my current collaborations are the result of Andy's efforts, and he was always extremely supportive of my evolutionary approach. Tim Cole, a specialist in the statistics of growth and metabolism, has for 15 years helped me tease out the independent associations of body size, fat mass and lean mass with numerous other biological variables. Empirical work on human body composition has been conducted at the UCL Institute of Child Health, London, in collaboration with

Mary Fewtrell, Jane Williams, Dalia Haroun, Sirinuch Chomtho and Russell Viner, and their collective expertise and hard work has been greatly appreciated. Work on the life-course induction of body composition has involved a long-running, and especially enjoyable, collaboration with Cesar Victora and Pedro Hallal at the University of Pelotas, Brazil.

Many others, including a number of anonymous reviewers, have either provided critical feedback on prior publications around which this book was based, co-authored some of the articles, or commented on ideas or individual chapters. Special thanks are due to Mario Siervo, Jay Stock, Ken Ong and David Dunger of the University of Cambridge; Carlos Grijalva-Eternod of UCL Institute of Child Health; Dave Leon and Kristina Stanfield of the London School of Hygiene and Tropical Medicine; Hinke Haisma of the University of Groenigen; Leslie Aiello of UCL Anthropology and the Wenner Gren Foundation; Akanksha A. Marphatia of Action Aid; and members of the evolutionary 'Work in Progress' seminar group at the London School of Economics, including Tom Dickins, Rebecca Sear, Nick Humphrey, Max Steuer, Andy Wells and Richard Webb. Despite the assistance of so many individuals, the following chapters doubtless contain many errors which are entirely my own responsibility. This is a book involving substantial speculation, and it is inevitable that some of it will prove incorrect. 'Some unkind critic once defined prehistory as "the study of the unverifiable to prove the unwarrantable about what never happened anyway"' (Cockburn 1971), and longer-term evolutionary reconstructions are ideal material for such inadequacies. Nevertheless, what I strongly believe *is* true is that without substantial refinement of hominin adipose tissue biology, modern humans would never have come to exist.

1 *Introduction*

The tendency to associate high body weight and adiposity primarily with ill-health is a relatively new perspective in the history of nutrition. A fundamental theme throughout the human historical record has been preoccupation with the threat of food insecurity, hunger, under-nutrition and disease-induced anorexia. References to frequent famine, plague and other instances of malnutrition are evident in the earliest world literature, and many aspects of the first urban communities represented efforts to consolidate agricultural productivity and food supplies through systems of crop irrigation, food storage and redistribution, and social organisation (Newman et al. 1990). Historical records from Mesopotamia from 3000 to 1400 BC, for example, describe the rations given to workers in return for their labour on projects such as irrigation systems, which can be used to estimate approximate dietary energy intake. These data suggest 'that Mesopotamians knew what it took to feed an adult and for the most part attempted to provide it' (Newman et al. 1990).

How well early civilisations addressed periods of food shortage was strongly correlated with their persistence over time. Free food distribution during times of scarcity was practised in the late Roman Republic, not for humanitarian reasons but in order to suppress popular unrest (Newman et al. 1990). Numerous authors have documented collapses of civilisations because of climatic stress or wars undermining agricultural production or the availability of wild foods, as reviewed previously (Fagan 1999). Others have observed the fundamental breakdown of human relationships that may result from severe starvation, most notably Colin Turnbull's account of the Ik, a population in eastern Africa, during the 1960s (Turnbull 1972).

The 'stele of famine', recovered from Ptolemaic Egypt and vividly recounting the Pharaoh's laments, is an early record of the social impact of agricultural failure:

> I am mourning on my high throne for the vast misfortune, because the Nile flood in my time has not come for seven years. Light is the grain; there is lack of crops and of all kinds of food. Each man has become a thief to his neighbour. They desire to hasten and cannot walk. The child cries, the youth creeps along, and the old man; their souls are bowed down, their legs are bent together and drag along the ground, and their hands rest in their

bosoms. The counsel of the great ones in the court is but emptiness. Torn
open are the chests of provisions, but instead of contents there is air.
Everything is exhausted.

(Keys et al. 1950)

Given such frequent reference to and concern with famine, it may seem
slightly paradoxical that nutritionists frequently refer to the idea that, prior to the
origins of agriculture, humans endured recurring cycles of 'feast and famine'.
This idea emerged in particular through a much-cited conceptual paper by the
geneticist Neel (1962), which attempted to explain the origins of vulnerability
to diabetes in some populations. The words chosen may be unfortunate, for
anthropologists generally consider a feast to be a particular kind of ritualised
occasion (Wiessner and Schiefenhovel 1996), whereas famine is a concept
linked strongly with the failure of agricultural productivity (Dando 1980). For
example, archaeological studies suggest that the emergence of agriculture was
initially associated with significant falls in average population health (Cohen
1977; Cohen and Armelagos 1984), and comparison of more contemporary
foragers and farmers indicates that the farmers are more prone to food shortages
(Benyshek and Watson 2006). Preagricultural humans, like any other organism,
undoubtedly experienced ecological fluctuations, as demonstrated by evidence
from the bioarchaeological record (Roy et al. 1996), but nonsedentary foraging
populations are able to use migration to relieve the stress of famine (Fagan
1999).

Over what time-span fat stores were accumulated in our evolutionary past,
how large they were and how they related to patterns of gaining and expending
energy remain difficult to reconstruct, and the notion of 'feast and famine'
requires comprehensive reexamination. In contemporary foraging societies,
for example, the inherent relationship between physical effort and dietary food
intake acts as a constraint on the accumulation of excess body weight. What
is however clear is that famines have been common throughout the historical
period, and under-nutrition has been the primary concern for most of the time
in most populations.

During the nineteenth century, public health efforts in industrialising populations remained directed primarily at improving the nutrition of the poor, for
example, by improving food availability, and by providing appropriate dietary
advice. These efforts were arguably less altruistic than they might appear, given
the powerful impact of the consolidating capitalist system on human demography, living conditions and health. The emerging industrial capitalism required
workers, who in turn must be healthy enough to work. Yet contrary to popular
wisdom, the early effect of the industrial revolution was to worsen living conditions because of economic instability (Komlos 1998), and the secular trend

in height attributable to improvements in population health occurred primarily during the twentieth century. Thus, regardless of the underlying motivation, addressing under-nutrition continued to represent the primary challenge until well into the mid-twentieth century.

In the late nineteenth century, pioneering scientists began to identify with greater specificity the dietary components that are essential for good health, including vitamins, minerals and adequate intakes of protein and energy. At the beginning of the twentieth century, increasing interest was directed towards the notion of nutrient adequacy. Early metabolic experiments assessed basal energy expenditure and its association with a variety of diseases (Atwater and Benedict 1903). Considerable attention was directed to the nutrition of infants and children in relation to their performance at school and their physical growth. Obesity has been documented throughout the historical record and has attracted clinical interest in relation to individual patients from the ancient Greeks onwards, but its relatively low prevalence capped public health interest. It was only in the 1940s that life insurance companies began to take serious interest in mortality data that demonstrated negative effects of high body weight on life expectancy. Soon afterwards, governments began formally to address the issue of excess body weight and its negative impact on cardiovascular health.

The development of interest in body fatness may further have been hampered by the difficulty of evaluating the trait. Adipose tissue is distributed within the human body in a number of depots which merge into one another and are difficult to differentiate (Pond 1998). Early scientific investigation into human body composition (reviewed previously (Wang, Wang, and Heymsfield 1999)) identified fat as a key body component, with, for example, values for the amount of body fat per unit weight reported by Moleschott in 1859. However, the majority of early research focused on the composition of lean mass and its components, for example, by determining the chemical composition of muscle (Katz 1896), or the total body volumes of water, plasma and blood through dilution studies (Keith, Rowntree, and Gerachty 1915; von Hevesy and Hofer 1934). Formal attention to adiposity commenced in the 1940s, with Stuart and colleagues (Stuart, Hill, and Shaw 1940) using two-dimensional standard radiography to estimate adipose tissue mass in vivo, and Behnke and colleagues (Behnke, Feen, and Welham 1942) first applying Archimedes' principle to estimate the relative proportion of fat and lean tissues. In the 1950s, this densitometric approach was given a firm scientific basis by Keys and Brozek (Keys and Brozek 1953), and hydrometry also progressed with appreciation of the relative constancy of the hydration of lean tissue (Pace and Rathburn 1945).

The 1960s saw the development of a suite of further body composition methods, including whole body potassium counting (Forbes and Hursh 1961), dual photon absorptiometry (Mazess, Cameron, and Sorenson 1970), and in vivo neutron activation analysis (Anderson et al. 1964). Theoretical multicomponent models were also developed, combining different measurement technologies so as to improve overall accuracy (Siri 1961; Brozek et al. 1963). Collectively, this research produced reliable and valuable data on whole body composition from the 1960s onwards, but it was only in the 1980s that sophisticated in vivo techniques for discerning internal fat distribution emerged, in the form of computed tomography (CT) scanning (Heymsfield et al. 1979) and magnetic resonance imaging (MRI) (Foster et al. 1984). In view of the relatively late development of body composition methodologies, the vast majority of scientific research and clinical practice since the beginning of the twentieth-century has remained based on very simple outcomes, either weight relative to height (body mass index, see Chapter 2) as originally proposed by Quetelet (1871) and now formally used to categorise obesity (Garrow and Webster 1985), or measurement of regional skinfold thicknesses.

Even as scientific and public health interest in body fatness increased, the Second World War and its aftermath prompted renewed interest in the biology of famine, starvation and global food poverty. Many Western nations were undoubtedly familiar with the detrimental nutritional status of the poor, especially in rapidly industrialising cities, but were relatively ignorant of conditions in other global regions. This oversight is undoubtedly ironic given the major contribution of imperialist economic policies to sustained malnutrition in colonial populations, but as argued by Rodney (1972), imbalanced intercountry economic relationships were a primary means of dissipating and concealing the stresses of capitalism outside western populations themselves. Frequent severe famines in colonial India may have had their crude origins in climate oscillations, but their impact on the indigenous population was substantially exacerbated by economic policies that undermined local food security while directing agricultural productivity to overseas export markets (Davis 2002). The contribution of centuries of imperialist and colonial economic policies to widespread malnutrition in African populations is likewise well established (Rodney 1972). Such mass starvation and malnutrition escaped the notice of the vast majority within Western populations (and indeed many of those enjoying privileged lifestyles within colonial regions), allowing them to be ignored in political policies. When allied troops uncovered the reality of concentration camps in Nazi-occupied Europe, the extreme expression of coerced starvation appeared to be a relative novelty. Indirectly, this experience promoted interest in under-nutrition worldwide and inspired the role of international agencies in relieving famine and food insufficiency.

Even before the full horror of concentration camps emerged, the potential for the international conflict to expose millions of people to starvation had been formally recognised. In the United States, such awareness provided the motivation for the classic Minnesota Starvation Experiment, which involved the experimental under-nutrition of conscientious objectors during 1944 and 1945. In this study, 36 men aged 22 to 33 years were first observed for 12 weeks, then severely under-nourished for 24 weeks, followed by their undergoing a restricted recovery period of 12 weeks and a further eight week period during which diet was unrestricted. In addition to describing in detail the effect of under-nutrition on body composition, appetite and energetics, the study also elucidated the profound impact of starvation on mood and psychological performance. The findings were reported in a comprehensive two-volume work that remains a landmark in nutritional research (Keys et al. 1950), but preliminary findings were already available for guiding postwar rehabilitation efforts in Europe and Asia. More broadly, considerable effort was directed in the postwar era to nutritional aid provision and to investment in the capacity for nutritional rehabilitation in the clinical setting, along with nutritional education and public health promotion. This biomedical progress was complemented by the Green Revolution, using scientific technology to alter radically the productivity of agricultural systems (especially staple crops) in order to achieve the aim of global food security.

In the 1950s, marasmus and kwashiorkor dominated nutritional research (Beaton 1989). The term 'protein-energy' malnutrition was coined in 1959 (Jelliffe 1959; Beaton 1989), and during the 1960s and 1970s much effort was directed to identifying children in the 'prekwashiorkor' stage, in other words undernourished but without specific clinical signs of malnutrition (Beaton 1989). Differentiation of stunted versus wasted children was considered crucial for identifying those currently in need of nutritional rehabilitation.

Alongside this new global effort for tackling population malnutrition, the year 1948 saw the start of the internationally renowned Framingham Heart Study (Dawber, Meadors and Moore, Jr. 1951), a longitudinal investigation into the risk factors for the cardiovascular diseases that were increasingly accounting for mortality in industrialised countries. Similar large cohort studies were initiated in other countries, such as the 1946 UK birth cohort study. By the 1960s, excess body weight was sufficiently common for an American housewife to initiate Weight Watchers International, formalising the notion of dieting in order to constrain body weight and promote health.

The United States saw a rapid escalation in the prevalence of obesity during the second half of the twentieth century. Few data are available for accurately quantifying changes in the prevalence of obesity within populations, and any such efforts are further confounded by the lack of confidence that the relationship between BMI and adiposity has remained constant (Wells et al. 2002). In a comparison of 12,312 white Union Army veterans from the United States measured between 1890 and 1900, and 4059 white middle-aged males from National Health and Nutrition Examination Surveys conducted between 1976 and 2000 in the same nation, the prevalence of obesity categorised as BMI >30 kg/m^2 had increased from 3.4 to 35% (Helmchen and Henderson 2004). These data emphasise that the obesity epidemic comprises changes in its prevalence rather than the emergence of a new disease. Equivalent data for other populations are lacking, but it is generally accepted that the United States has merely been marginally ahead of other industrialised nations in this regard.

More recent studies indicate the prevalence of obesity increasing from 12% to 17.9% over the period from 1991 to 1998 in the United States (Mokdad et al. 1999). The epidemic is readily discerned in modernising countries (Wang, Monteiro, and Popkin 2002), and at the beginning of the twenty-first century, more people are now categorised as overweight than underweight in the global population (Popkin 2007). Obesity is considered a major risk factor for cardiovascular disease – heart attacks, strokes, type 2 diabetes and hypertension – as well as other diseases such as many cancers and reproductive problems. The strong association of obesity with such diseases has led to a prevailing medical view that body fat is harmful to health. Public health messages to restrict body weight and waist circumference, to improve diet and to exercise more are now ubiquitous throughout both the developed and modernising world. The onset of the obesity epidemic has been so rapid that in many developing countries, obesity and under-nutrition manifest as simultaneous health problems. In the most extreme form, a combination of overweight and underweight children can be encountered within a single household (Doak et al. 2005).

There is absolutely no doubt that the world is experiencing a major obesity epidemic and that its consequences for health are extremely serious. Nonetheless, our understanding of obesity remains surprisingly simplistic. Physiological studies increasingly attribute the health risks of obesity primarily to central abdominal fat, and in particular to deep-lying adipose depots such as those around the viscera. Paradoxically, obesity remains formally categorised on the basis of weight relative to height, using the body mass index (BMI; expressed in kg/m^2) (Garrow and Webster 1985). As will become clearer in subsequent chapters, BMI has a relatively poor capacity to rank individuals accurately in terms of body fat level. Human body composition is notoriously difficult to measure with accuracy, and it is only in the last decade or so that nutritional science has developed techniques for widespread application that are also sufficiently accurate to begin understanding the biology of human adipose tissue and its distribution. Currently, we know a great deal more about population trends in BMI than about fatness per se, and much that is written about 'obesity' may have only a tenuous basis in the biology of adipose tissue.

Biological anthropologists have likewise directed interest to body fat only relatively recently. Energy availability has long been considered a critical resource in any organism's ecology and is well understood to have been a major selective pressure during human evolution (Foley and Lee 1991b; Leonard and Robertson 1994; Aiello and Wells 2002). Once again, however, remarkably little attention has been paid to human energy stores. Soft tissue is very poorly preserved in the fossil record or cemeteries and hence cannot provide a material historical record in the same way as skeletal tissue. As biological anthropological research expanded worldwide following the Second World War, investigations of body size and shape were directed primarily towards assessing the adaptation of physique to stresses such as thermal load, physical labour and malnutrition. For example, Roberts (1953) proposed that climatic stresses were the primary factor contributing to population variability in height and physique, although subsequent analyses have demonstrated that nutritional supply is also important (Katzmarzyk and Leonard 1998). Similar work, with a clear basis in colonial economics, addressed the determinants of physical work capacity in tropical environments (Collins and Roberts 1988).

By the 1970s, appreciation of the role of energy stores in funding pregnancy and lactation encouraged anthropologists to conduct widespread field measurements of adiposity using simple methodologies such as skinfold thicknesses. A few pioneers adopted more sophisticated technologies, for example, the transportation of underwater weighing instrumentation to Papua New Guinea (Norgan, Ferro-Luzzi, and Durnin 1982). Interest in adiposity was further fuelled by recognition that many nonindustrialised countries were profoundly affected by exposure to the increasingly globalised economy. The so-called 'coca-colonisation' of populations was reflected in dramatic changes in adult body composition within one or two decades in populations such as Western Samoa (McGarvey 1991).

In the 1970s, the British scientist Caroline Pond found the biology of adipose tissue to be a severely neglected field. She collected carcasses from a variety of sources, including road kills, in order to dissect them and characterise discrete adipose depots. Her work indicated both considerable variability between species in adipose tissue distribution and a broadly common basic pattern in all mammals. Despite such indications of different functional roles of energy stores, and despite increasing awareness that physiological models lacked a mechanistic understanding of energy store regulation, many medical scientists were taken by surprise by the discovery of the hormone leptin in 1994 (Zhang et al. 1994). The functions of leptin are complex, but there is little doubt that a key role is to signal the level of adipose energy stores to the brain. For the first time, adipose tissue was emerging as an active tissue with significant hormonal and regulatory functions rather than an inert store of calories. Numerous other secretory products, hormones and cytokines have since been discovered. Indeed it could be argued that the last decade has seen a radical shift in our appreciation of the relative roles of lean and fat mass. Until recently, adipose

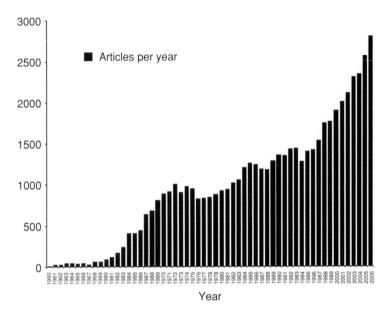

Figure 1.1. Secular trend in the number of scientific publications on the topic of obesity, based on records in the Pubmed database.

tissue had been considered an inert store of lipid – a fuel dump available for exploitation by metabolically active and functional lean tissues. Increasingly, however, adipose tissue, especially the small depots, is considered to emit a range of biochemical factors exerting powerful effects on lean mass, and to integrate diverse physiological functions within a composite regulatory system.

Trends in the publication of articles listing amongst their keywords 'adipose tissue', 'body fat' and 'obesity' are clearly evident in the medical literature. Figure 1.1, for example, illustrates temporal trends in reference to the keyword 'body fat' over the last six decades. There was an initial surge of interest in the 1960s that reflected both pioneering work in the technical capacity to measure human adipose tissue or total fat mass and a general interest in the properties and possible functions of these traits in wild mammals. During the 1960s and 1970s, brown adipose tissue with its enhanced metabolic activity for thermogenesis received considerable attention, but this research declined following recognition that it appeared to contribute little to the biology of obesity in adult humans. Since the 1980s, there has been a second, more steady increase in interest reflecting both a medical concern with the increasing prevalence of overweight and obesity in many populations and the strengthening of evidence linking obesity and ill-health. Adiposity is also increasingly researched by zoologists who explore how species are adapted to survive and breed in unpredictable environments.

Body fat is now a major topic of medical investigation, a major target of the pharmaceutical industry, a primary public health issue and a subject familiar to the vast majority of people in industrialised and modernising populations. Such 'demonising' of body fat is inevitably associated with extreme responses. In the first decade of the twenty-first century, Hollywood appears to favour the size 00 in female actresses – a body shape virtually stripped of all visible adipose depots. Many people attempt to consume diets low in lipid or at least energy content in order to restrict their fat deposition. Eating disorders in industrialised populations are increasingly observed in girls prior to puberty and may derive in part from a fear of undergoing the normal increase in adiposity that accompanies pubertal maturation. Others have rebelled against such scrutiny, arguing that body fatness is the consequence of lifestyle choices and should not be subject to political or societal regulation. This debate is fuelled in part by a long-standing perspective which considers protection from pathogens as the primary rationale of medicine. As the disease spectrum of Western industrialised populations shifts towards 'lifestyle diseases' induced at least partly by behavioural choices and constraints, the contribution of personal responsibility for health is emerging as a controversial area of debate with major implications for the economics of health care.

Amidst such concern, in some instances bordering on panic, remarkably little attention has been directed to the functions of adipose tissue and the beneficial components of its biology. It is often suggested that modern humans are a relatively fat animal, and hence unusually susceptible to the harmful consequences of obesity. From an evolutionary perspective, this susceptibility indicates significant roles of body fat stores in human and hominin biology. Far from humans being 'naturally' obesity-prone, we appear instead to be an animal in whom adipose tissue biology is an integral aspect of our evolutionary adaptation. Some authors now consider that it is the 'unnaturalness' of the modern urbanised environment, rather than anything about humans themselves, that accounts for the high prevalence of obesity (Egger and Swinburn 1997).

The aim of this book is to elucidate in greater detail these roles of adipose tissue, and to identify both the functions and the evolutionary history of human body fat. For the medical profession, body fat stores represent a physical trait that can be measured and intervened on. From an evolutionary perspective, however, body fat represents a strategy – the strategy of storing lipid rather than oxidising it on an immediate basis, and of using these stores to regulate a set of competing biological functions. The evolutionary biology of human fatness refers to the strategy of manipulating the relationship between lipid supply and demand in order to allocate energy and other materials more effectively to specific functions at specific time periods.

Reconstructing the evolutionary biology of a strategy that can neither fossilise nor even maintain consistency within individuals over time is certainly not easy. However, this problem has long occupied evolutionary biologists interested in behaviour, which is likewise generically absent from the fossil record. In the 1960s, the ethologist Nikolaas Tinbergen pioneered a classic solution to this dilemma, adapting the metaphysical model of the philosopher Aristotle to modern biological enquiry.

Aristotle had distinguished four separate components of causality, each of which could be investigated for a given phenomenon. He identified the material causes (constituent materials), the formal cause (form or essence), the efficient cause (predisposing agents) and the final cause (the purpose or end). Tinbergen used this metaphysical model to derive four fundamental questions for biologists, intended to provide discrete categories of explanation for any given behaviour (Tinbergen 1963). He proposed two questions concerning proximate mechanisms underlying behaviour – first, which stimuli elicit the behavioural response, and second, how does the behaviour change across the lifespan of the organism. He then proposed a further two questions concerning ultimate mechanisms – first, what is the function of the behaviour in relation to the organism's survival and reproductive fitness, and second, how does the behaviour vary across different species exposed to differing selective environments. Tinbergen's approach enabled integration of the contributions from a number of behavioural biological subdisciplines (ethology, behavioural ecology, sociobiology and evolutionary psychology), each of which exploits an evolutionary paradigm in the investigation of animal behaviour.

Tinbergen's model is broadly applicable to any biological trait, whether behavioural or not, although the nature of proximate causation differs markedly between physical traits, such as skeletal structure, and behavioural traits. Traditionally, many biologists have modelled the evolution of physical traits such as size, structure or functional output. Increasingly, however, it is recognised that natural selection is better considered to act not on the physical characteristic itself, but on the strategy of developing that characteristic (Houston and McNamara 1999). Thus selection favours not height, but growing; not a brain, but the strategy of investing in cognitive capacities. From this perspective, Tinbergen's approach is ideal for conducting an evolutionary analysis of human body fat. Human adiposity is, as discussed above, the result of the strategy of storing energy in adipose depots. We can then utilise the ethological model to review the proximate causes of fat deposition, the ontogenetic pattern of body development, and the functions of energy stores, before attempting to reconstruct a plausible evolutionary history of the strategy of energy storage.

This book is intended neither to focus on obesity, nor to address the detailed biology of lipids or adipose tissue. Numerous books are now addressing the former topic, and Pond's excellent monograph targeted the latter (Pond 1998). Nevertheless it is necessary to have a good understanding of the causes of fat deposition in order that subsequent reconstructions of function and evolutionary history are well based in physiological reality. An understanding of ontogeny likewise aids in the differentiation of different selective pressures in favouring more or less adipose tissue at different periods in the life course.

The structure of this book is thus broadly based around the approach of Tinbergen but also addresses further related issues, in particular population variability in body composition and the ways in which we can measure it.

Chapter 2 begins with a very brief description of the methods available for acquiring information on body composition both in humans and in mammals more generally. It will quickly become clear that the measurement of body composition presents a number of difficulties that vary according to the species being considered and other factors such as age and condition. Measurements of body fat are particularly difficult in the large number of species which display plasticity in adiposity, as no single measurement may be considered to summarise that organism's biology. Further critical issues concern the optimal approach for expressing data. By convention, adiposity is often expressed as a percentage of fat, that is, the proportion of fat in body weight. This approach has major limitations for comparisons both within and between species, as the proportion of fat is a function not only of variability in adiposity, but also of variability in lean tissue. More sophisticated statistical approaches are therefore required for such comparisons. Despite these challenges, the adiposity profile of humans may be put into a broader mammalian context in order to consider the extent to which we are consistent with, or differ from, other species. This chapter also reviews variability within the human species, focusing on adult body composition in populations occupying a wide variety of physical environments. Although such comparative data are restricted to the simplest body composition methodologies, they are sufficient to indicate the approximate magnitude of between-population variability, and to identify broad secular trends deriving from environmental changes.

Chapter 3 explores a range of proximate causes of fat deposition. Such causes are distributed across the entire range of biology, including at one extreme genetic predisposition and at the other societal ecological factors acting on the organism. Biologists increasingly appreciate the fallacy of attempting to categorise any trait as genetically versus environmentally determined. For each trait, genetic factors are exposed to a vast range of environmental influences, and this interaction is further compounded by the one-way process of ontogeny, which causes the factors acting at any one time point to be associated both with those acting in prior periods, and those likely to act in future periods. As will be reiterated in subsequent chapters, the fact that many genetic factors are strongly associated with adipose tissue biology in no way contradicts the prevailing view that current increases in the prevalence of obesity owe much to environmental change. Our rapidly improving understanding of the biology of adipose tissue increases the validity of models of function and evolutionary history, and furthermore it aids the generation of scenarios by which such hypotheses may be tested.

Chapter 4 discusses the ontogenetic development of body composition, emphasising again that adiposity, lean tissue and size/physique must all be addressed in order to evaluate developmental changes. Recent decades have seen a profusion of studies applying relatively high-quality body-composition techniques across the human life-course, although unsurprisingly data on the fetus remain sparse. Such data allow assessment both of total tissue masses and their regional distribution. Regional adiposity is arguably of greatest importance in both evolutionary and biomedical contexts, as we increasingly appreciate metabolic and functional differences between discrete adipose depots. Integral to such developmental changes in adipose tissue mass and distribution is a life-course pattern of sexual dimorphism, strongly indicative of differing selective pressures acting on the two sexes. At the broadest level, human adiposity might be considered to vary in relation to two key factors – first, the characteristic human developmental profile of body composition which is most evident prior to adulthood; and second, the increasing impact of local environmental factors which generate variability in adult body composition through the cumulative influence of ecological and lifestyle factors.

Whilst Chapter 4 describes the generic developmental profile of human body composition, Chapter 5 focuses in detail on developmental processes through which experience during one period of the life-course influences body composition in subsequent periods. Such developmental consistency is the product of two complementary processes, termed 'phenotypic induction' and 'tracking'. Phenotypic induction refers to a set of mechanisms whereby early-life experience generates long-term effects on subsequent phenotype. For example, growth rate during fetal life and infancy is unusually sensitive to nutritional influence, generating associations between dietary exposures during such periods and subsequent body composition. Towards the end of infancy, phenotype increasingly becomes canalised or 'self-righting', such that the impact of many environmental factors becomes more transient. Under these conditions, many components of childhood body composition appear to track within individuals over time in adulthood. The most recent research is exploring the multigenerational transmission of phenotype, suggesting that the strategy of storing energy is a form of risk management subject to a very complex set of trade-offs.

Chapter 6 reviews evidence for the functions of adipose tissue in human biology. At the time when Tinbergen first presented his model, such functions were attributed to the survival of the organism. Subsequent developments of evolutionary theory have emphasised the concept of reproductive fitness and genetic replication, and indeed inclusive fitness – the concept that the optimal strategy of one organism is dependent not only on its own reproductive achievements, but also on those of kin who share a proportion of the same genes. This chapter builds on a rapidly emerging literature emphasising that adipose tissue is much more than simply a store of energy buffering against the risk of under-nutrition. The role of adipose tissue as a regulatory endocrine organ illustrates the complexity of adipose tissue biology, highlighting how reproductive biology is intricately integrated with other functions such as immune status, developmental schedule and sexual attractiveness.

Chapter 7 is the first of three that attempt to review the evolutionary history of adiposity. The capacity to store energy in adipose tissue, unique to vertebrates, has been argued to play a key role in permitting adaptation to diverse ecological niches and accommodating selective pressures. This chapter considers adipose tissue from a broad perspective, illustrating how different species benefit from adipose tissues to 'solve' specific ecological problems such as lactation, seasonality and migration. Of particular relevance are two 'biological models of thrift', which are fundamental to understanding differences within and between species. Genetic variability in thrift reflects ancestral exposure to specific selective pressures, and between-species or within-species adaptation therein. Within-lifetime plasticity offers a second mode of adaptation of a more transient nature. The biology of adipose tissue is the product of both levels of adaptation, whereby the combination maximises the capacity of energy stores to confer flexibility in relation to local ecological pressures.

Chapter 8 continues this evolutionary review, focusing specifically on hominin evolution. The aim is to attempt a reconstruction of the selective pressures acting on past hominin populations in order to understand the likely evolution of adiposity. This period of evolutionary history is necessarily the most prone to speculation owing to the absence of material fossil evidence and of archaeological evidence indicative of related behaviours. Nevertheless, it is valuable to propose such models in order to integrate the available evidence and generate hypotheses for testing as further data emerge. Furthermore, biologists increasingly utilise dynamic models to simulate optimal trade-offs between sets of benefits and costs. Thus future work may probe reconstructions of hominin adiposity using a number of different approaches. One factor clearly critical in the adipose tissue biology of our species is the large human brain; however, other factors are also suggested as of importance. Increasingly, the genus *Homo* is considered as a 'colonising ape' (Wells and Stock 2007), and human adiposity may owe much to a colonising reproductive strategy.

Chapter 9 completes the reconstruction of the evolutionary history of human adiposity, focusing on the emergence of variability between and within populations of *Homo sapiens*. Such variability relates both to adipose tissue mass per se and also its regional distribution in different body depots. A trade-off model of adipose tissue biology is presented and used to propose a hierarchy of selective pressures acting across the range of ecological environments occupied by human populations. According to this approach, I suggest that regional variability in disease load is a plausible selective pressure generating population differences in adipose tissue biology at the genetic level. Such a model may prove of interest in evolutionary analyses, but it also has significant implications for understanding ethnic variability in the health risks of obesity. Other factors, such as nutritional ecology and climate, may also be relevant but may impact more strongly on physique and energy metabolism rather than on adipose tissue biology itself. However, some ethnic variability may derive from more recent environmental exposures and may reflect the transgenerational transmission of phenotype by nongenetic biological mechanisms.

Chapter 10 concludes by emphasising two apparently contrasting but in fact closely associated perspectives. First, I suggest that human adipose tissue biology is as much a hallmark of our species as are other traits long considered peculiarly human, such as bipedalism, large brain size, and complex social behaviour. According to this argument, natural selection has favoured extraordinary sophistication in the strategy of acquiring and exploiting energy stores, illustrated by the wide range of variability between the genders, across the lifespan, and across different ecological environments. Second, the rapid emergence of the global obesity epidemic highlights the interaction of a complex adipose tissue biology with a set of ecological changes which are rapidly manufacturing an environment very different from that in which human evolution occurred. If humans had not been selected so strongly to exploit energy storage as an adaptive strategy, they would not be so sensitive to these environmental changes. Human technology and behaviour are transforming the ecology of our planet at an unprecedented rate, but the vast majority of species are predicted to respond through demographic dynamics rather than changes in the body composition of individuals. Our species is characterised by an integral connection between adipose tissue biology, reproductive strategy, and niche construction. As we alter our niche and constrain our reproductive effort, our bodies increasingly express these changes in energy dynamics.

I therefore argue that although an evolutionary perspective on human body fatness can make an important contribution to anthropology and the related fields of behavioural ecology and evolutionary demography, it is likely to prove of particular value in elucidating the sensitivity of human adiposity to environmental change. Up to the present period, efforts to halt the global obesity epidemic have been markedly unsuccessful, and pharmacological treatment and surgery have proven more robust in achieving weight loss in obese individuals than have attempts to alter behaviour. An evolutionary approach clarifies the argument that the behaviour of individuals may be an inappropriate level at which to attempt intervention, implying instead that larger scale environmental change is likely to be essential.

2　*Human fatness in broad context*

Any appraisal of human fatness requires consideration of the spectrum of adiposity across mammals in general. Humans have often been described as a relatively fat mammal (Brown and Konner 1987), yet until recently empirical data on a wide variety of species were sparse. In this chapter the body composition of human adults is compared with that of other mammals, addressing both the total mammalian range and also the body composition characteristic of other primate species. It is equally important to consider the variability within the human species by reviewing data on between-population variability. At this stage, these analyses will be restricted to adult data, as the ontological development of body composition is addressed specifically in Chapter 4.

The gold standard for body composition analysis remains cadaver dissection. For the majority of studies both on non-human animals, and particularly on humans themselves, this approach is clearly inappropriate. Assessment of body composition therefore generally requires the measurement of whole-body properties such as density, and the use of theoretical assumptions and mathematical models to convert those raw data into final body composition values. A variety of different approaches have been developed, ranging from simple measurements to extremely sophisticated internal imaging techniques (Ellis 2000; Wells 2007b). Different models of body composition are also invoked that quantify body constituents at atomic, molecular or tissue levels (Wang, Pierson, Jr., and Heymsfield 1992).

The choice of which method to use depends on the species being investigated and the outcomes desired, as well as convenience and cost. Techniques vary in both accuracy and precision, and inevitably the best techniques are the most expensive, time-consuming and specialised. For both within-species and between-species comparisons, the available data derive from a heterogeneous range of technologies. Any review of the body composition literature must therefore take into account the fact that the vast majority of data are not collected using gold standard methodology, and hence have varying degrees of imperfection.

For comparisons between humans and other animals, a further difficulty comprises representivity of the individuals sampled. A fundamental characteristic

16

of adiposity is that it tends to vary within individuals over time, in response to ecological stresses and behavioural activities. Fatness in some species varies drastically between seasons, examples including migrating birds or mammals which lactate during hibernation. Comparisons between species are thus complicated by the difficulty of standardising for ecological fluctuations. Is the adiposity of a bear, for example, best described as the high level encountered at the start of winter hibernation, the low level encountered at the end, or an intermediate level in between?

Despite these difficulties, it is possible to draw broad conclusions about differences within species, and also to identify broad trends within and between human populations. This area is likely to progress substantially in the coming years owing to the growing interest in adipose tissue and fatness, and this chapter offers a very preliminary view.

2.1   Body composition techniques

In vivo measurements of body composition involve the measurement of one or more body properties and the interpretation of such data on the basis of theoretical assumptions about specific tissues, especially those with approximate constancy in a given set of individuals. However, it is now well established that the body undergoes a process of chemical 'maturation' during growth (Widdowson 1950), characterised by a decrease in relative water content in lean tissue, and an increase in relative protein and mineral content (Fomon et al. 1982). These ontogenetic changes generate significant variability in the properties of lean mass, such as its hydration, density and chemical constitution. Thus, accurate measurement of body composition requires detailed information about how tissue properties alter with age in order to ensure appropriate values are used in subsequent calculations.

Two long-standing approaches to the measurement of body composition have comprised hydrometry (Schoeller 1996) and densitometry (Siri 1961; Brozek et al. 1963). The first involves quantification of the amount of water in the body by stable isotope dilution. Total body water can then be converted to an estimate of lean tissue mass by assuming a certain water content of lean tissue. Data on the water content of lean tissue throughout the life-course are available (Fomon et al. 1982; Haschke 1989), making this approach one of the simplest for body composition assessment. It is appropriate for application in all age groups from neonates to the elderly, and it is readily conducted both in the laboratory and in field studies. The main factor limiting its widespread application is the cost of the mass spectrometry analyses; however, in the last decade its utilisation has increased substantially. Furthermore, the hydration of lean tissue is similar across a wide variety of adult mammals, allowing this technique to be used in cross-species comparisons (Wang et al. 1999).

Densitometry is based on the principle of Archimedes, namely, that measurement of body density allows discrimination of the proportion of two constituent tissues of known and constant density. Early work identified approximate constant densities of fat (0.9007 kg/L) and lean tissue (1.10 kg/L) (Brozek et al. 1963), making densitometry a second relatively robust approach to the measurement of human body composition. The technique has been widely used in adults, the main limitation being the impracticality of the traditional apparatus required, that is, underwater weighing (also known as hydrodensitometry). Within the last decade, substantially improved technology has become available for the measurement of body density, namely, whole-body air displacement plethysmography (Dempster and Aitkens 1995). This equipment is currently available for children aged four years and over, and for infants in the first six months of life (Urlando, Dempster, and Aitkens 2003).

Other technologies, such as radiographic and imaging techniques, have high accuracy but have historically been used only in specialised contexts, and they have less to contribute to between-species and between-population comparisons at the current time. Imaging techniques such as CT scanning and MRI are potentially particularly valuable because of their capacity to distinguish regional adipose depots, and hence to enable scientific study of adipose tissue biology. Most body composition techniques, including those discussed above, provide a molecular level of measurement and quantify total body lipid, generally termed fat mass. Total adipose tissue is not directly equivalent to total fat mass because of its containing water and small blood vessels. The water content of adipose tissue is generally at least 10%, and may be much greater in naturally lean wild mammals, and when the tissue is depleted (Pond, personal communication). Hence, measurements of adipose tissue and fat mass are complementary rather than interchangeable. A detailed summary of body composition techniques and their underlying methodological assumptions is given elsewhere (Ellis 2000). However, at the current time, large-scale comparisons require access to relatively simple techniques.

Bioelectrical impedance analysis has proven suitable for field studies, but it has major limitations for between-population analyses of body fatness. The technique uses the body's resistance to a small current to estimate the volume of water (and hence lean tissue mass), using a well-established physical theory which treats the body like a single conducting cylinder (Kushner et al. 1992). Although in all human populations, impedance data adjusted for height show a strong association with body water content (Kushner et al. 1992), the slope of the regression equation relating these two variables differs systematically between populations. The technique can be used only after population-specific validation, using isotope dilution as the reference technique. Few studies have undertaken such validation work, and a further limitation of the technique is that accuracy in individuals is influenced by body geometry (for example, limb length relative to trunk length) (Fuller et al. 2002).

Any large-scale between-population evaluation of human body composition is therefore currently limited to anthropometric data. Owing to its adoption as the criterion on which obesity catergorisation is based (Garrow and Webster 1985), body mass index has often been used as an index of adiposity across the whole range of relative weight. As discussed at length below, however, BMI has serious limitations for comparing both individuals and populations in terms of body composition. The only type of data referring directly to adiposity, and routinely collected in a wide variety of human populations, is measurements of skinfold thickness. The principle of this approach is that measurements of several skinfolds may be added together to provide a 'sum index' of subcutaneous fatness, which may be used to predict body density using regression equations derived from research samples. Body density may then be used to estimate body fatness using Archimedes' principle as discussed above (Siri 1961; Brozek et al. 1963).

Any predictive technique is subject to two types of error. The first error, common to all physical measurements, comprises inaccuracy or imprecision of the measurements themselves. Skinfold measurements are widely considered to present challenges in this context; however, this issue may have been overestimated. Whilst it is undeniable that skinfold measurements are difficult to obtain in obese individuals because of difficulties in identifying the correct measurement site and in obtaining access to an appropriate fold of skin, across the normal range of weight the imprecision within individuals is moderately small relative to variability in skinfold thicknesses between individuals. Hence, raw skinfold measurements tend to rank individuals with high accuracy relative to others within the population, as indicated by consistently high correlations between these raw data and reference measurements (Fuller et al. 1992; Wells et al. 1999).

The second error is of greater importance and derives from the use of raw data in equations predicting an outcome. Figure 2.1 shows a plot of body density against the sum of four skinfolds. Whilst a clear population-association is present between these two variables, indicated by the regression line, most individual data points do not lie along the line. The use of such regression equations to predict body density from raw skinfold data therefore introduces a degree of error (Wells 2007b), given by the standard error of the estimate of the regression equation. This error is often equivalent after extrapolation to around plus or minus 5% fat (Wells et al. 1999).

These limitations were noted previously by Norgan (1994b) and are readily acknowledged here. Nevertheless, the estimation of body fatness using skinfold equations is the only plausible technique available for large-scale population

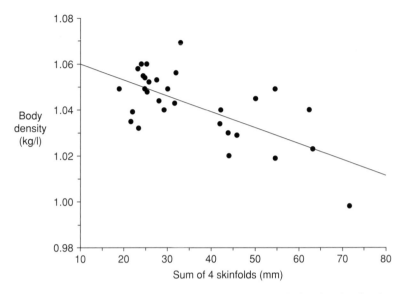

Figure 2.1. Body density determined by underwater weighing plotted against the sum of four skinfold thicknesses, using data from Wells and colleagues (1999). The regression line can be used to predict the body density for any magnitude of sum of skinfolds, but the scatter of the points around the line indicates the error in individuals inherent in this approach.

comparisons in view of the fact that anthropometry offers the only large-scale database. Estimates of total body fatness for groups may at least have greater accuracy than equivalent data in individuals, although there is likely to be significant ethnic variability in the association between the sum of skinfolds and body density. Broadly, the magnitude of differences between populations must inevitably be subject to error, but the relative *ranking* of populations across the range of adiposity and lean size is likely to be more robust, enabling trends between global regions to be considered. This approach is therefore explored here, after first describing the broader mammalian range of adiposity.

2.2   Cross-species comparisons

Data from non-human animals have been collected using a variety of body composition techniques. In some cases, particularly for small species, gold standard carcass analysis has been used, but still with different protocols. Typically, carcasses are dried to constant weight and then ground to a powder. Samples of this powder are then analysed for fat content, non-fat organic matter, and ash content. More sophisticated studies have also identified regional anatomical depots of adipose tissue (Pond 1998) and have furthermore differentiated specific components of lean mass such as organ and muscle mass (Schoenemann 2004). Such dissection is time consuming and difficult, particularly in relation to anatomical depots that are hard to define with precision across species. For this reason, the majority of studies have extracted fat chemically and have not attempted to define its regional distribution. The lack of regional data is one reason why the biology of adipose tissue remains so poorly understood (Pond 1998), a particular limitation of current understanding given our growing awareness that different adipose depots contribute to different biological functions.

Other techniques include hydrometry using isotope dilution, diluting the body water pool with tritium, deuterium or 18-oxygen labelled water, or measurements of body electrical conductivity. Laboratory studies have been conducted using dual energy x-ray absorbtiometry, a technique also used extensively in humans, but cross-species databases remain small. As pointed out by Pond (1998), variability between species in size and shape precludes the derivation of a simple index of relative weight, as provided by BMI in humans. Isotope dilution potentially represents an extremely valuable approach, as studies indicate relative homogeneity in the hydration of lean tissue across species (Wang et al. 1999). This technique has the added benefit that, providing sufficient control of the animal is possible, it can be applied *in vivo* and repeated at regular intervals to quantify changes in adiposity or lean mass.

The largest single database, obtained through applying one technique uniformly across a range of species, is that of Pitts and Bullard (1968), based on gross dissection and the determination of fat content by ether extraction in 39 species. However, below I discuss data combined from several different techniques in order to enhance the range of species considered. A major limitation of these data is that body fat content in many mammal species is strongly influenced by season, since, as discussed in Chapter 7, the primary role of energy stores is to accommodate variability in energy supply. For example, in bears which fast and sleep during the winter months, declines in fat content equivalent to a 25% loss of body weight can occur (Hellgren et al. 1990). More generally, ecological conditions influence the body fat content of the population at any given time. Using the data currently available, collected from a variety of different studies in different circumstances, it is possible to identify only broad trends. As discussed by Schoenemann (2004), the aim here is to benefit from the advantages of a larger dataset while assuming that errors in individual measurements are relatively minor.

Figure 2.2 illustrates data on the proportion of fat in body weight in three orders of mammals. Bats tend to have relatively low proportions of body weight as fat, regardless of their size. Rodents vary markedly in their level of

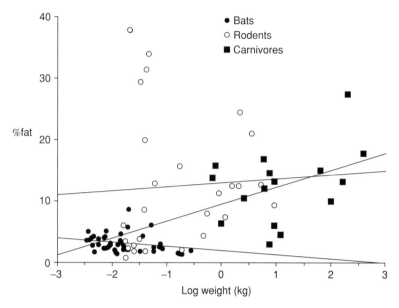

Figure 2.2. The association between log transformed body weight, and the proportion of fat in weight (percentage fat), in three families of mammal. In bats, there is little tendency for percentage fat to change across the scale of weight, although slightly higher values tend to be found in smaller bats. Similarly, in rodents there is no systematic trend for increasing or decreasing percentage fat content across the weight range, rather fatness is highly variable at all weights. In contrast, in carnivores percentage fat increases systematically with increasing body weight (Pond and Mattacks 1985; Pond and Mattacks 1985; Pond and Ramsay 1992; Pond, Mattacks, and Ramsay 1994; Schoenemann 2004; Wirminghaus and Perrin 1993; Studier, Sevick, and Wilson 1994).

fat, but again they show no clear trend towards increasing or decreasing fat with greater weight. Carnivores have an intermediate level of fatness and show a trend towards greater adiposity with increasing weight. This figure indicates substantial variability across species and orders in the level of adiposity across the range of body size. Despite this variability within and between orders, there is nevertheless a clear association between lean mass and fat mass as shown in Figure 2.3. Here, in each order, the absolute amount of fat is strongly associated with the absolute amount of lean, indicating relatively tight constraints on energy stores in relation to size-ranking of the animal. These two trends, both of variability but also of consistency, remain apparent if a wider selection of mammals is considered, intended to highlight the full range of body size and adiposity. Figure 2.4 presents data from 23 species ranging in size from the Yuma bat weighing 6.8 grams to the elephant seal weighing 1920 kilograms, and ranging in percent body fat from virtually zero in the grey kangaroo to above

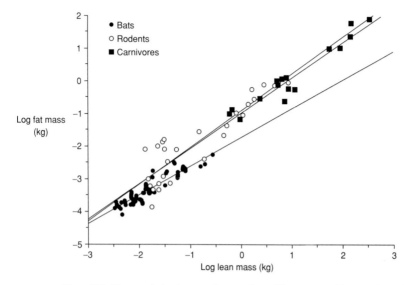

Figure 2.3. The association between log transformed lean mass and log transformed fat mass in the same mammal families as those described in Figure 2.2. In each mammal family, there is a strong positive association between fat mass and lean mass.

40% in the ringed seal. In Figure 2.4, humans can be seen to have intermediate values relative to other mammals of similar size. Thus, considering mammals overall, there is little that identifies humans as of either high or low body fatness. It is therefore necessary to make more specific comparisons addressing phylogenetic issues.

If we consider the type of organism and the environment it occupies, humans emerge as relatively fat for an animal that evolved in the tropical savannah environment. Most other mammals with both high body weight and high levels of body fat tend to be marine species such as seals or whales, or to occupy highly seasonal and cold environments such as the brown bear or polar bear (Pond 1998). Human females in particular, averaging around 24% fat, stand out as extraordinarily fat for a tropical savannah mammal.

Unfortunately, relatively few body composition data are available on other primate species, particularly non-human apes. In a recent review, Dufour and Sauther (2002) discussed data on those few species which have been considered. The main limitation of such data is that the majority derives from captive animals, which tend to accumulate weight above typical levels observed in the wild. Whilst this observation illustrates the general capacity for primates to accumulate energy stores, itself of interest, 'natural' levels of adiposity remain very poorly understood in primates. Captive lemurs were reported to range

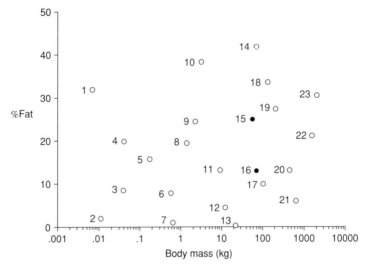

Figure 2.4. Values for the proportion of fat (percentage fat) in weight, across a wide range of body mass, for a selected sample of mammals. The data indicate that across the entire range of body weight, mammal species vary substantially in body fat content. Data points are: (1) Yuma bat (Ewing, Studier, and O'Farrell 1970); (2) Velvety free-tailed bat (Schoenemann 2004); (3) Spiney mouse (Pond and Mattacks 1985); (4) Dwarf hamster (Pond and Mattacks 1985); (5) Cotton rat (Pond and Mattacks 1985); (6) Stoat (Schoenemann 2004) (7) Grey squirrel (Pond and Mattacks 1985); (8) Potoroo (Denny and Dawson 1975); (9) Woodchuck (Schoenemann 2004); (10) Crab-eating macaque (Kamis and Latif 1981); (11) Badger (Pond and Mattacks 1985); (12) Wolverine (Pond, Mattacks, and Ramsay 1994); (13) Grey kangaroo (Tribe and Peel 1963); (14) Ringed seal (Ryg et al. 1990); (15) Human female (Norgan 1994b); (16) Human male (Norgan 1994b); (17) Tiger (Pond and Ramsay 1992); (18) Grey seal (Pond and Mattacks 1985); (19) Brown bear (Pond and Ramsay 1992); (20) Moose (Stephenson et al. 1998); (21) Bactrian camel (Pond 1998); (22) Beaked whale (Mead 1989); (23) Elephant seal male (Bryden 1972). Reproduced with permission from (Wells 2006).

from 8 to 41% fat (Pereira and Pond 1995), captive baboons from 5 to 16% (Rutenberg et al. 1987) and captive gorillas from 19 to 44% (Zihlman and McFarland 2000). In contrast, baboons in the wild are typically only 2% fat (Altmann et al. 1993). Data on wild chimpanzee, bonobo, gorilla, orang-utan and gibbon species are notably lacking, and a comprehensive evaluation of human adiposity in comparative context remains extremely difficult while such data are unavailable.

One particularly informative study, discussed in greater detail in Chapter 6, involved assessment of fat metabolism in orang-utans (Knott 1998). This study clearly demonstrated seasonal metabolism of fat stores during times of energy stress, and hence illustrates that humans are by no means the only ape species utilising energy stores to address ecological perturbations. Overall, therefore, comparison of humans with other species suggests that body fat content is relatively high for non-marine mammals, particularly in females; however, it remains possible that other apes may show some concordance with this pattern. The characteristics of the life history profile of adiposity, and the extent to which they differ from those of other primate species, are discussed in greater detail in Chapter 8.

Most adipose tissue in the human body is white adipose tissue, a storage depot for lipid which can be released in to the bloodstream as required. However, mammals as a group of animals also possess brown adipose tissue, a thermogenic organ distributed in specific anatomical locations for any given species (Cannon and Nedergaard 2004). Brown adipose tissue decouples the process of heat production from the production of the molecule ATP, which is the primary means of storing energy in cells. This allows biochemical substrates to be converted directly into heat (Cannon and Nedergaard 2004). Brown fat is found in particular in newborn mammals, though in varying amounts. In many species, it appears to disappear with maturation, though it plays a key role in the termination of torpor in species which hibernate (Dark 2005). Around 5% of adipose tissue is brown adipose tissue in human neonates, and recent work suggests that many adults still contain some active brown adipose tissue (Nedergaard, Bengtsson, and Cannon 2007). Inter-species differences between white and brown adipose tissue have not been addressed here, as they refer to the functions rather than amount of fatness, but such variability is of course an important component of between-species biological variability, and the issue is revisited for humans in Chapter 6 and for the evolution of adiposity more generally in Chapter 7.

2.3   Comparisons within humans: Body mass index

Anthropologists and human biologists are well aware of significant variability between populations in body size and shape (Roberts 1953; Katzmarzyk and Leonard 1998). Comparison of body composition between populations requires adjustment for such variability in size; however, few studies have addressed this problem comprehensively, which has led to serious inaccuracies in conclusions.

The use of data on weight and height to provide a proxy for adiposity dates back to the late nineteenth century, when the physical scientist Quetelet compiled information about human anthropometrics and proposed that the relative weight of individuals could be evaluated by dividing weight in kilograms by the square of height in meters (Quetelet 1871). Quetelet's index is now known as the body mass index or BMI (Garrow and Webster 1985) and is merely one of several indices intended to adjust weight (W) for height (H) in order to improve the ability to compare within and between individuals. It is helpful to conceptualise this approach using the model of a cylinder, in which the volume of the cylinder acts as a proxy for W. Since individuals vary in H (cylinder length), adjustment for that parameter is required in order to evaluate between-individual variability in volume.

Closely related to BMI is the Benn index (Benn 1971), calculated in similar format but intended to address a slightly different statistical issue. Both BMI and the Benn index are expressed in the format W/H^n; however, whereas the value of n is 2 in the case of BMI, it can vary in the Benn index. A further index, simply W/H, may be considered to belong to the same family where the value of n is 1. However, it is generally accepted that W/H remains too strongly correlated with height to provide an effective means of comparing individuals of different height (Cole 1986).

The statistical rationale for BMI aims to address this issue by generating an index minimally correlated with height, such that variability in BMI reflects variability in weight that is not due to height. Although there are some periods of the life-course when BMI does correlate with height, such as the neonatal period, this correlation is generally of modest magnitude, such that the vast majority of variability in BMI cannot be attributed to height (Wells and Cole 2002a). In this sense BMI is broadly successful at evaluating relative weight throughout the human life-course. The Benn index, in contrast, is intended to identify the value of n at which the correlation between the index and body fatness is maximised. This need not be the same value of n that minimises a correlation with height. The relative utility of these two approaches remains debated, but partly for historical reasons, partly for convenience, and partly due to lack of obvious limitations in its statistical basis, BMI has become the primary index of relative weight in humans of all ages except newborns.

In the 1980s, Garrow and Webster (1985) proposed a simple categorisation for clinical practice, intended to differentiate different degrees of excess weight. They defined the normal range of weight as a BMI of 20 to 25 kg/m², overweight as a BMI of 25 to 30 kg/m², and obesity as a BMI >30 kg/m². Chronic energy deficiency was subsequently further defined using a cut-off of 18.5 kg/m² (James, Ferro-Luzzi, and Waterlow 1988). This categorisation remains fundamental to adult clinical practice and research. In children, such an approach is not possible owing to natural changes in the relationship between weight and height that occur during the process of growth. This gives rise to a wave shaped relationship between BMI and age in each sex, as shown in Figure 2.5.

Childhood obesity has therefore by convention been categorised using BMI cut-offs, for example, by using the 85th or 90th percentile (Cole, Freeman,

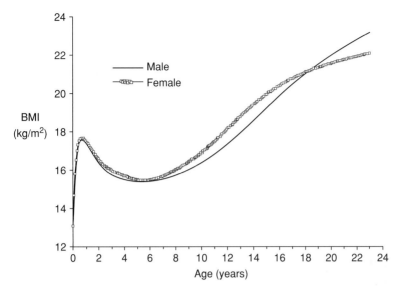

Figure 2.5. The association between body mass index (BMI) and age in children of both sexes. In general, children's values are lower than those in adults, however there is also a systematic curvilinear association, with BMI increasing in early infancy, falling in early childhood and an increasing once again during puberty. The data are from the 1995 UK growth reference (Cole, Freeman, and Preece 1995).

and Preece 1995). This approach has proven problematic as the distribution of BMI values varies substantially between populations and within populations over time. For example, population BMI has tended to increase systematically in European and American populations with the developing obesity epidemic, though the greatest increases have occurred in the upper part of the BMI range. To address this issue, the International Obesity Task Force elected to develop a set of fundamental cut-offs suitable for use in all populations. These cut-offs were developed by identifying BMI values throughout childhood statistically equivalent to the values of 25 and 30 kg/m² used to categorise overweight and obesity in adults (Cole et al. 2000). These new children's cut-offs, calculated as BMI centiles or standard deviation scores, provide a static international benchmark against which the emerging obesity epidemic can be measured.

The popularity of BMI is not difficult to understand. Given the difficulty of measuring body composition as discussed above, weight and height represent readily obtainable data in the vast majority of individuals. They are not considered particularly invasive and are suitable for monitoring over the short- and long-term. Data are available for large population samples, or indeed national surveys in screening programmes, and are furthermore available over lengthy historical time periods. The use of data expressed as standard deviation scores facilitates analyses involving both sexes and different ages.

Despite these advantages, there are clear limitations to the use of BMI as an index of fatness. Paradoxically, as interest in human body fat increases, and awareness of its impact on health and reproductive function grows, many researchers and clinicians remain extraordinarily uncritical of BMI. Yet as is increasingly evident, BMI is a surprisingly poor index of adiposity in individuals. Because of the widespread continued use of BMI for assessing fatness, this chapter will describe the limitations of BMI in detail. In order to address this topic comprehensively, it is also necessary to criticise the main statistical approach to expressing data on adiposity, namely, percentage fat.

For many researchers, the utility of BMI as an index of adiposity is demonstrated by correlations between BMI and percentage fat. For example, Pietrobelli and colleagues (1998) observed correlations between BMI and percentage fat of 0.79 and 0.83 in boys and girls respectively in a sample of children aged 5 to 19 years, indicating that BMI explains 63% of the variance of percentage fat in boys, and 69% in girls. These values nevertheless require interpretation with caution. The high correlations derive primarily from data points at the two ends of the spectrum, in other words a small number of individuals who are both very heavy and very fat, and a second set of individuals who are very light and very lean. Within the main part of the range, agreement between the two indices is substantially poorer – in children with BMI of 20 kg/m^2, adiposity could range from 10 to 40% fat in boys, and from 20 to 50% fat in girls. The notion that individuals with a single BMI value can vary to such an extreme degree in their percentage fat surely precludes confidence in it as a measure of adiposity in individuals; however, this point has been remarkably difficult to get across to many clinical practitioners and researchers.

Other limitations of BMI include inconsistency between populations in its association with fatness. As discussed by Norgan (1994a), the relative proportion of height attributable to the limbs versus the trunk influences physique and body composition, such that tall populations may have low BMI values despite normal levels of subcutaneous fat. In a large sample of human populations, the regression coefficient of BMI on sitting height (SH) divided by total height (H) was 0.90 kg/m^2 per 0.01 SH/H. Given that average SH/H tends to range between 0.50 and 0.55 in most populations, variability in this parameter generates BMI variability in the order of 5 kg/m^2, confounding its interpretation as an index of adiposity (Norgan 1994c). This issue is made all the more complex in view of the fact that there is as much variation in SH/H within groups as there is between groups (Norgan 1994c).

Norgan's analyses were based on skinfold data; however, whole-body data available for a few populations can illustrate more clearly ethnic variability in the association between BMI and fatness. Figure 2.6 shows the adjustment in

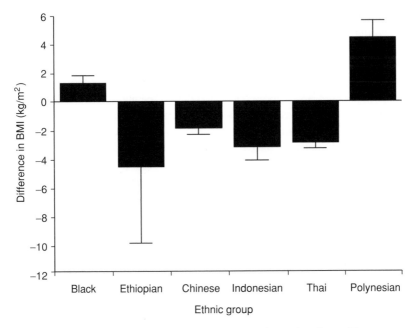

Figure 2.6. Data on six non-European adult populations and a reference European population (zero line), illustrating the adjustment in BMI that is required in order to standardise their percentage fat. Groups above the zero line tend to have less fat than predicted for their BMI, with the converse for those below the line. Based on data from Deurenberg, Yap, and van Staveren (1998). Reprinted by permission from MacMillan Publishers Ltd: International Journal of Obesity 22(12): 1164–71, copyright (1998).

BMI that is required in order to standardise percentage fat between six non-European populations and a reference European population of adults (Deuren-berg, Yap, and van Staveren 1998). Groups above the zero line tend to have less fat than predicted for their BMI, with the converse for those below the line. However, this statistical approach has its own limitations – whilst demonstrating inconsistency between populations in the proportion of fat in weight, it does not reveal whether this variability derives directly from variability in fatness or variability in lean mass. This issue, as mentioned above, derives from the limitations of expressing adiposity in such ratio format.

2.4 The limitations of percentage fat

Traditionally, individuals and populations have been compared on the basis of the proportion of fat mass in body weight, termed percentage body fat. The logic of dividing body fat by weight is that such an index is assumed to adjust for variability in body size. However, there are both conceptual and statistical problems with this approach. Conceptually, it is inappropriate to derive an index adjusting one variable (the numerator) for another (the denominator), when the denominator in fact includes the numerator (Wells and Victora 2005). In this case, body weight itself includes fat mass. As a consequence, increases in the numerator are partially concealed due to the equivalent increase in the denominator. If fat mass is divided by lean mass rather than body weight, this concealment is avoided. Figure 2.7 illustrates the difference between these approaches. Using data from a large survey of young male Brazilian adults, Figure 2.7-a plots fat mass divided by weight against weight, whereas Figure 2.7-b plots fat mass divided by lean mass against lean mass. It can be seen that the slope of the line in the second figure is substantially steeper. Thus the first problem with the outcome percentage of fat is that it fails to express adequately the relationship between increasing body size and relative adiposity.

A second problem with the outcome percentage fat is that it is rarely appropriate to divide one biological variable by another in order to adjust the first for the second. Such ratios are appropriate only given certain allometric conditions, which are now known not to apply for human body composition (Heymsfield et al. 2007). Most human biologists will be familiar with this issue through BMI. If weight is divided only by height, the resulting index weight/height remains strongly correlated with height. This index incorrectly gives the impression that taller people tend to be relatively heavier. In contrast, an appropriate adjustment of weight for height would demonstrate that the average tall person has the same relative weight as the average short person.[1] Once this average relationship has been established, it is then possible to consider whether any given short or tall individual has a high or low relative weight. Most biological indices likewise require the denominator to be raised to a power other than one. Whether fat mass is adjusted for weight, height or lean mass, the power by which the denominator should be raised is unlikely to be 1.

A more appropriate approach for adjusting one variable (A) for another (B) is to plot the two variables against each other, after log-transforming both variables. The aim is to establish an index A/B^n in which the power n is selected such that the index has zero correlation with B. The appropriate value for n is given by the slope of the regression line. Figure 2.7, using data from the same population of young Brazilian male adults, shows that *Fat mass/weight*

---

[1] This proposition assumes that there is no tendency for those of short or tall height to differ in their risk of obesity. In fact there are some indications that shorter men do have an increased risk of obesity (Wells, Treleaven, and Cole 2007) attributable either to genetic factors or the long-term effects of early growth patterns on later adiposity; however, it remains true that the vast majority of variability in BMI can be attributed to variability in weight rather than height.

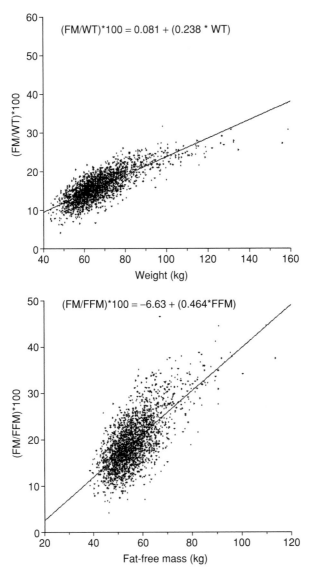

Figure 2.7. Associations between fat mass (FM), lean mass (shown here as fat-free mass, FFM) and weight (WT) in adult male Brazilians, using measurements obtained by bioelectrical impedance analysis. FM/WT plotted against weight (upper panel) shows a relatively shallow slope, indicating that the presence of FM in both numerator and denominator conceals the actual increase in adiposity. FM/FFM plotted against FFM (lower panel) shows a steeper slope, indicating with greater sensitivity the absolute increase in fatness associated with increased FFM. Reproduced with permission from Wells and Victora (2005).

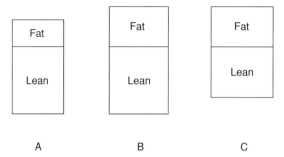

Figure 2.8. Schematic diagram representing three individuals of identical age, sex and height. Individual A has the same lean mass as individual B, but less fat mass, and hence has lower percent fat. Individual C has the same fat mass as individual B, but less lean mass, and likewise has lower percent fat value despite not having less fat mass. Differences in percent fat may be due to variability in lean mass rather than adiposity *per se*. Redrawn with permission from Wells and Cole (2002a).

(FM/WT), and *Fat mass/lean mass* (FM/LM), remain significantly correlated with the denominator and therefore represent inappropriate statistical adjustments. The appropriate indices in this population are $FM/WT^{2.1}$ and $FM/LM^{2.3}$ (Wells and Victora 2005).

A third problem with expressing body composition data in the format of percentage fat is that only variability in adiposity is evaluated. In addition to variation in body size, variability in lean mass is also significant within and between populations. Figure 2.8 is a schematic diagram representing three individuals of the same age, sex and height. Individual A has the same lean mass as individual B, but less fat mass, and hence has a lower percentage fat value. However, individual C has the same fat mass as individual B, but less lean mass, and likewise has a lower percentage fat value despite not having less fat mass. This diagram illustrates that the differences in percentage fat may be due to lean mass rather than adiposity (Wells and Cole 2002a).

Ideally, both lean mass and fat mass should be adjusted for variability in height and considered as independent variables. VanItallie and colleagues (1990) proposed that since:

$$\text{Weight} = \text{Lean mass} + \text{Fat mass}$$

and since:

$$\text{BMI} = \text{Weight/height}^2$$

these two equations can be combined in the format

$$\text{BMI} = \text{Lean mass/height}^2 + \text{Fat mass/height}^2$$

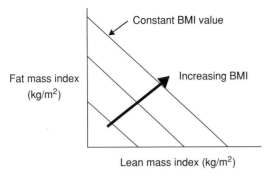

Figure 2.9. Format of the graph generated by Hattori (Hattori, Tatsumi, and Tanaka 1997), in which fat mass index (FMI, calculated as fat mass divided by height squared) is plotted against lean mass index (LMI, calculated as lean mass divided by height squared). Since FMI and LMI add up to BMI, it is possible to add diagonal lines of constant BMI value. It is also possible to incorporate nonparallel lines of constant percentage fat value (see Figure 2.10). Increases in BMI (relative weight) can be entirely due to increased FMI, or entirely due to increased LMI, or to increases in both components (diagonal arrow).

These two variables, known as the lean mass index (LMI) and the fat mass index (FMI), represent discrete measures of relative lean and fat masses, independently adjusted for size (height) (VanItallie et al. 1990).

A major advantage of these indices is that they are presented in the same units as BMI. Hattori and collagues (1997) devised an informative graph, plotting FMI on the y-axis against LMI on the x-axis. Since these two variables must add up in all individuals to BMI, the graph contains a set of parallel lines with negative gradients of constant BMI value. It is also possible to add further lines, which are not parallel to each other, expressing constant percentage fat value. These graphs are ideal for simultaneously comparing the ratio of fat to lean in individuals while also adjusting for variability in body size. Figure 2.9 illustrates the format of these graphs, emphasising that movement in the vertical plane represents variability in relative body fat, movement in the horizontal plane represents variability in relative lean mass, and movement in the positive diagonal plane represents variability in relative weight (i.e., a summary of the variability in relative fat and lean), or BMI.

Strictly speaking, the approach of VanItallie and colleagues (1990) is based on a conceptual splitting of BMI rather than a comprehensive statistical adjustment of fat mass and lean mass for height. It is not necessarily the case that both lean mass and fat mass are adjusted for height when height is raised to the power of 2. This issue can be resolved using the same log-log regression analyses described above, in order to determine the appropriate power by which height should be raised. Empirical analyses suggest that adjustment of fat mass

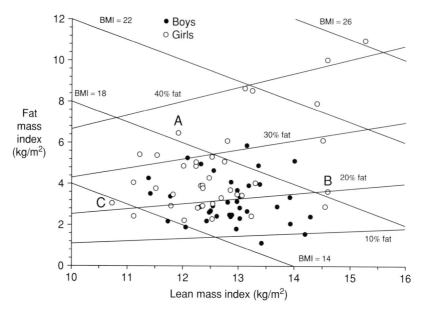

Figure 2.10. A Hattori chart for a sample of children aged eight years, measured by isotope dilution. The arrows identify three boys, A, B and C. A and B have a similar BMI value but differ substantially in their adiposity. C has a similar percentage fat value to B, despite differing substantially in BMI, and is simply smaller than B rather than less fat. Reproduced with the authors' permission from Wells, Chomtho, and Fewtrell (2007).

often requires raising height to a higher power than does adjustment of lean mass (Wells and Cole 2002a). Nevertheless, it is also clear that both fat mass index and lean mass index retain a low correlation with height, such that less than 2% of the variability in these indices can be attributed to insufficient height adjustment (Wells and Cole 2002a). The indices LMI and FMI therefore offer a powerful framework for evaluating within- and between-population variability in body composition, addressing physique (LMI) as well as relative adiposity (FMI).

Whilst expression of adiposity data in the format of fat mass index overcomes the limitations of percentage fat, it is also particularly revealing with reference to the association between BMI and adiposity. Figure 2.10 presents a Hattori chart for a sample of children aged eight years. The arrows identify three boys, A, B and C. Individuals A and B have a similar BMI value but differ substantially in their adiposity. A has twice the FMI of B, which is accounted for by the fact that B has substantially greater LMI than A. Individual C has a similar percentage fat value to B, despite differing substantially in BMI. Here,

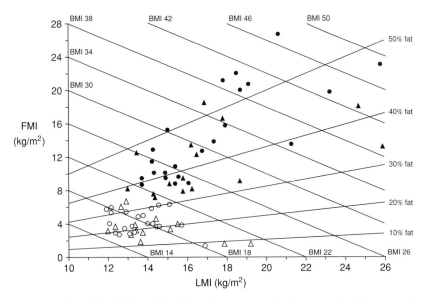

Figure 2.11. A Hattori chart illustrating the range of body composition in both normal weight (boys: △, girls: ○) and obese children (boys: ▲, girls: ●). In both populations, there is substantial variability in relative lean mass as well as relative fat mass. Hence, the additional weight in obesity varies between children in its relative fat content. Reproduced with permission from Wells and colleagues (2006).

individual C is simply smaller than B in both fat and lean masses but has a similar ratio of one to the other.

This scenario is evident across most of the entire spectrum of body composition, although there are biological reasons why it is less apparent for those with very low weights, in whom between-individual variability in body fatness is reduced. Thus Figure 2.11 presents a Hattori chart for both normal weight and obese children, highlighting substantial variability in relative lean mass as well as relative fat mass in those obese.

These charts clearly identify the main limitation of BMI in that it reflects lean mass as well as fat. Indeed, BMI is strongly correlated with percentage fat and fat mass, lean mass, bone mass, head circumference, waist girth, and hip girth, but not with waist-hip ratio (Molarius et al. 1999). Precisely because it is correlated with many body composition outcomes, it is not a particularly sensitive index of any of them. Recent research has highlighted particular limitations of BMI for epidemiological analyses, where it is widely assumed to reveal trends in adiposity. Contrary to this view, the association between birth weight and later BMI appears to be attributable to lean mass rather than fat mass (Wells, Chomtho, and Fewtrell 2007). Likewise, whilst physical activity is inversely associated with adiposity, it is directly associated with muscularity (Ness et al. 2007). Failure to recognise the relationship between BMI and lean mass has left some researchers puzzling as to why habitual vigorous activity appears to '*increase*' the risk of obesity if the condition is categorised by BMI (Andersen et al. 1998).

In highlighting these limitations of BMI, it is important to be specific where the problem lies. As discussed above, BMI is statistically robust and is extremely valuable for clarifying population or individual variability in relative weight. Although BMI increases during growth may be due to lean mass as well as fat mass, rapid changes in BMI z-score are generally attributable to changes in body fatness, as gains in lean mass manifest relatively slowly except during puberty. Large changes in population BMI z-score over time are also indicative of increases in mean body fat content, although the association between these trends may not be exact. A comparison of children measured in the 1990s in the United Kingdom with those measured in the 1960s in America suggests there has been a decline in the relative amount of lean mass per unit height (Wells et al. 2002). The most likely explanation for this proposed decline is reductions in physical activity level, as regular exercise is known to promote the accumulation of muscle mass (Torun and Viteri 1994).

Thus, at a broad level, variability in BMI provides valuable information about relative weight on the basis of a global index of nutritional status. However, to assess variability in body composition, it is critical to use more direct measurements. On the one hand, these data can reveal trends in adiposity, whilst on the other, they can also indicate differences within and between populations in relative lean mass.

2.5   Between-populations comparisons based on skinfolds

Despite the limitations discussed above, the main advantage of predicting total body fat from skinfold data is thus the ability to estimate lean mass as the difference between weight and fat mass. In this chapter I have adopted an approach previously used by Norgan (1990), making the best use of the only source of raw data widely available for between-population comparisons. Data on weight, height and skinfold thicknesses are available for a large variety of populations worldwide and have the further advantage that they are often collected on quite large samples of individuals. The most commonly available data are the triceps and subscapular skinfold thicknesses. These data can be combined with the equation of Durnin and Wormsley (1974) for prediction of body density, and hence percent fat (Siri 1961). In combination with data on weight and height, it is then possible to calculate fat mass and lean mass, and then adjust for height as described above. Wherever possible, this approach was used, although in some datasets only final values for percent fat are provided, and in some cases they were calculated using four rather than two skinfolds.

It is widely accepted that whilst data on raw skinfold thicknesses successfully rank individuals in terms of fatness, absolute values generated from predictive equations have varying accuracy between populations. In their original paper, Durnin and Wormersley (1974) suggested that the accuracy of their approach predicting whole-body fat would depend on the proportion of adipose tissue located in the subcutaneous compartment. Reviewing the literature available at that time, they encountered major inconsistency between studies, with some suggesting up to 70% of fat being subcutaneous, and others proposing only 10% in women (Durnin and Womersley 1974). More recent analyses based on imaging techniques suggest that the subcutaneous component is the largest fat depot across the entire range of BMI, accounting for around 80% of total adipose tissue at the lower end of the spectrum of normal weight and 50% in those morbidly obese (Thomas et al. 1998). Clearly the data presented below should be considered with caution, but they are probably adequate for discerning broad trends between the sexes and between the populations of different global regions.

A literature search was conducted focusing on human biology and nutrition journals over the last five decades. Data on Western populations were not included owing to the powerful impact of urbanisation and obesogenic factors on body composition during the last century. The aim of the exercise was not to provide a definitive review of human body composition but rather to illustrate common characteristics between human populations from different global regions whilst also highlighting the capacity of human body composition to vary in relation to ecological factors. The review therefore focused on the following areas: Africa, Asia, Australasia, the Pacific, South America, and the Arctic region. Data on 74 and 61 populations were compiled for males and females, respectively, focusing on young adults, with data for both sexes available in 48 of these populations. Although a few studies did not provide information on the sample size, the total number of measurements included was derived from approximately 16,000 individuals. Initial analyses describe variability in height and BMI, whereas subsequent analyses describe variability in FMI and LMI.

2.6   Sexual dimorphism

Sexual dimorphism may be most evident in terms of height. All human populations measured to date exhibit a significant greater mean height in adult males

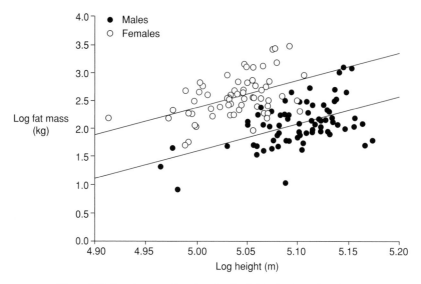

Figure 2.12. Log fat mass plotted against log height for the series of populations analysed in this chapter, demonstrating significant associations in both sexes, but with greater female fatness at any given height.

compared to females, although there is significant variability in the height of individual males and females, and also in the magnitude of this dimorphism between populations. Nevertheless, it is clear that it is a universal human trait for the average male to be larger than the average female, with dimorphism in height typically ranging from 5 to 9% (Stini 1978). In the sample used here, average height was 1.64 (SD 0.06) meters and 1.54 (SD 0.05) meters in males and females, respectively, equivalent to a mean difference of 6 percent. Figure 2.12 plots log fat mass against log height in both sexes in the sample of human populations, demonstrating significant associations and justifying the adjustment of adiposity for height. Figure 2.13 is the equivalent plot for log fat mass against log lean mass.

Figure 2.14 illustrates the mean and standard deviation of BMI in six global regions. In all regions, there is either no significant difference or a relatively small difference between males and females, with females tending to be slightly heavier, especially in Pacific and Arctic populations. The average sex difference was 0.38 kg/m^2 (range of -3.6 to 2.3 kg/m^2). Mean BMI values were relatively similar between African, Asian, Australasian and South American populations, but significantly higher in Arctic and Pacific populations. Figure 2.15 provides similar data for LMI. In almost all populations, males had significantly higher values than females, averaging around 2.2 kg/m^2 more (range zero to

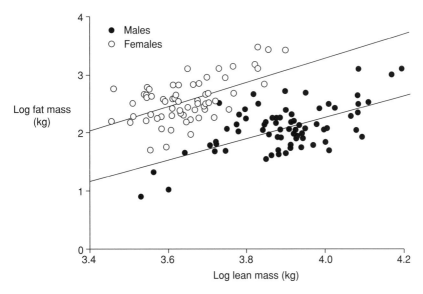

Figure 2.13. Log fat mass plotted against log lean mass for the series of populations analysed in this chapter, demonstrating significant associations in both sexes, but with greater female fatness at any given lean mass.

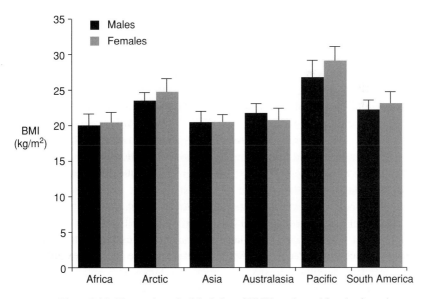

Figure 2.14. Mean and standard deviation of BMI in males and females from six global regions. Females tended to be heavier than males in Arctic and Pacific populations. In both sexes, BMI tended to be greater in Arctic and Pacific populations versus populations in other regions.

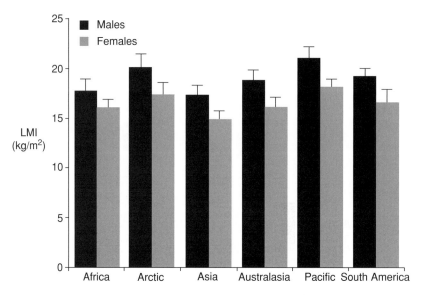

Figure 2.15. Mean and standard deviation of lean mass index (LMI) in males and females from six global regions. Males had significantly higher mean values than females in all regions (p<0.001). Values were lowest in African and Asian populations, and highest in Arctic and Pacific populations.

4.5 kg/m^2). African and Asian populations had the lowest values, Australasian and South American populations marginally higher values, and Arctic and Pacific populations had the highest values, especially in males.

Figure 2.16 provides equivalent data for FMI. Here, mean values in the females were invariably substantially greater than those in males, with the average difference 2.6 kg/m^2 (range 0.7 to 5.8 kg/m^2). Differences between populations were greater for women than for men. In men, African, Arctic, Asian, Australasian and South American men all had relatively similar values, whereas the Pacific men had substantially greater values. In women, African and Australasian populations had the lowest levels of fat, Asian and South American populations intermediate values, Arctic populations high values and Pacific populations extreme values. In proportional terms, males averaged 14% fat (range of 7 to 27%), and females 26% (range of 14 to 41%). Only six populations, from Australasia and Africa, had mean female percentage fat values less than 18%, and the lowest values may well derive from an inappropriateness of the skinfold equations rather than genuine low adiposity. The mean values changed little if Arctic and Pacific populations were omitted from the analysis. Pacific populations have been exposed for several decades to an obesogenic environment, but arctic populations were protected from this effect

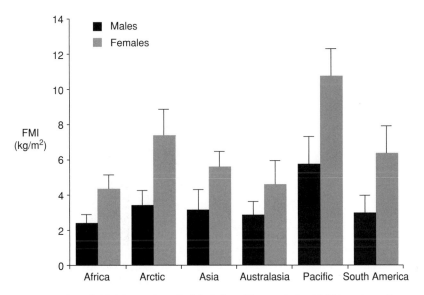

Figure 2.16. Mean and standard deviation of fat mass index (FMI) in males and females from six global regions. Females had significantly higher values than males in all regions (p<0.001). Values were lowest in African and Australian populations, and greatest in Arctic and Pacific populations.

until relatively recently, and notably have substantially less fat than the Pacific populations.

The extent to which population variability in body composition derives from genetic factors is unknown. As discussed in Chapter 3, adiposity has a degree of heritability, and ethnic genetic variability in both physique and body fat distribution is certainly plausible. However, the impact of environmental factors on body composition, particularly on growth rates during early life, complicates the examination of this issue. Multigenerational exposure to particular environmental conditions may generate 'heritability' of body composition without operating through genetic mechanisms. Whatever the genetic contribution to population variability in body composition, it is clear that there are important differences between global regions.

The relationship between population differences in LMI and those in FMI are illustrated more clearly by plotting them on Hattori graphs as scatters (Figures 2.17 and 2.18). These graphs illustrate that in both men and women, the ratio of fat to lean tends to be greater in Asian and Pacific populations, and lowest in Australasian populations. This analysis therefore provides a different perspective, in demonstrating that whereas Asian populations are not notable for large absolute values of FMI or LMI (Figures 2.17 and 2.18), they are often relatively adipose for their size.

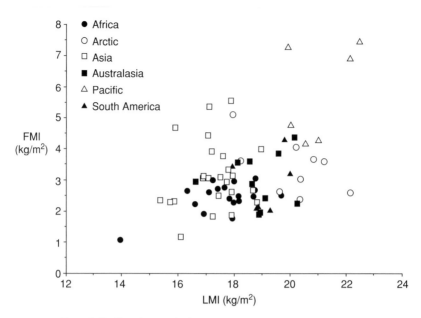

Figure 2.17. Hattori chart plotting fat mass index (FMI) against lean mass index (LMI) in male populations from six global regions. The ratio of fat to lean tends to be greatest in some Asian and Pacific populations, and lowest in Arctic and Australian populations.

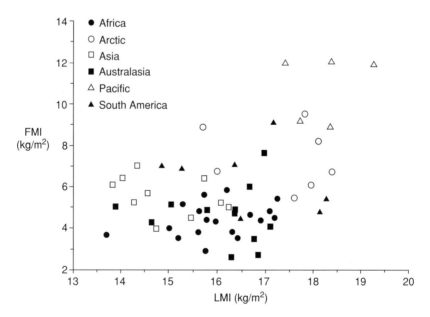

Figure 2.18. Hattori chart plotting fat mass index (FMI) against lean mass index (LMI) in female populations from six global regions. The ratio of fat to lean tends to be greatest in Asian and Pacific populations, and lowest in African and Australian populations.

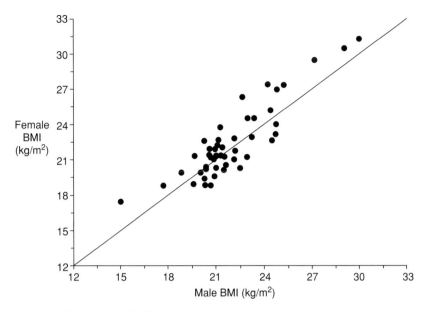

Figure 2.19. BMI of females plotted against that of males in 48 populations, showing no systematic trend for one gender to be heavier than the other.

Despite such population variability, differences between the sexes are universally shown for both relative lean mass and fat mass. Figure 2.19 shows that in 48 populations with data for both sexes, there is no systematic trend for either sex to be heavier than the other, although at higher and lower BMI values there is a tendency for females to be heavier. Figure 2.20 illustrates dimorphism in LMI. Four data points lying close to the line of identity came from African populations, in which the sex difference approximates zero. However, in the vast majority of populations, males have greater LMI than females, and no extant population reverses this trend. Likewise, Figure 2.21 illustrates dimorphism in FMI. In all populations, females have higher values than males, with the difference least in Australasian populations.

2.7 Population variability in shape

Although body composition measurements are increasingly applied in diverse populations, it is not possible to improve substantially on the skinfold data using existing measurements obtained by other techniques. Figure 2.22 plots mean subscapular skinfold against triceps skinfold in the six regional groups in each sex. In women, values of the two skinfolds are very similar, whereas

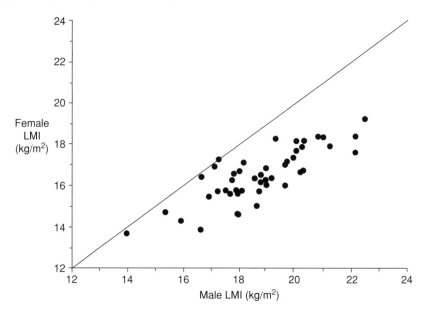

Figure 2.20. Lean mass index of females plotted against that of males in 48 populations, showing a systematic trend for males to have greater levels than females, although in four populations no such difference was apparent. The mean difference was 2.2 (SD 1.0) kg/m².

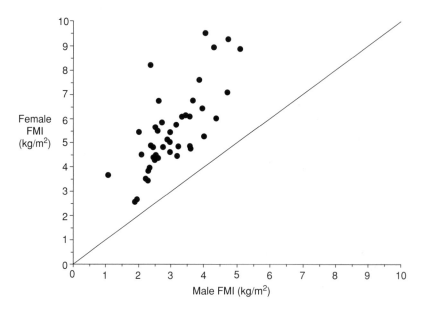

Figure 2.21. Fat mass index of females plotted against that of males in 48 populations, showing a systematic trend for females to have greater levels than males. The mean difference was 2.6 (SD 1.3) kg/m².

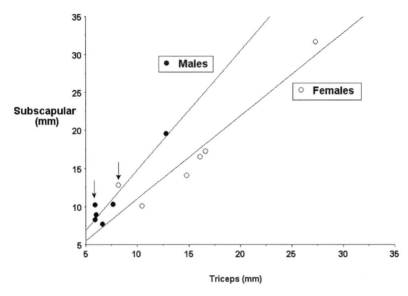

Figure 2.22. Subscapular skinfold plotted against triceps skinfold in six regional population groups in each sex. In women, values of the two skinfolds are very similar, whereas in men the subscapular value is invariably greater. Australasians (indicated by arrows) have a more central fat distribution, due more to having low triceps than high subscapular values.

in men the subscapular value is invariably greater. In both sexes, Australasians have a more central fat distribution as indicated by these simple ratios, due more to having low triceps value than high subscapular values.

Within the last half decade a new approach for the measurement of body shape has emerged, following technological progress by the clothing industry. Three-dimensional photonic body scanning has now been applied in two large sizing surveys in the United Kingdom and United States (Wells, Treleaven, and Cole 2007; Wells et al. 2008a). Collectively, these surveys provide data on over 18,000 adults from industrialised societies. Information about body shape can, like skinfold data, be used to infer broad trends and variability in body fatness. Table 2.1 describes differences in key body measurements between males and females in four ethnic groups. Males tend to have greater arm, chest and waist girths, but smaller hip and thigh girths.

Figures 2.23 and 2.24 further illustrate sex-specific variability between ethnic groups, indicative of ethnic variability in regional fat distribution. In men, after adjusting for differences in height and other social confounding factors, Hispanic men had significantly greater arm, chest, waist and hip girths compared to white men, whereas African American men had significantly greater

Table 2.1. *Gender variability in body shape in adults aged 20 to 30 years of four different ethnic populations*

	UK White		UK Asian		US Black		US Hispanic	
	Male	Female	Male	Female	Male	Female	Male	Female
N	3988	4827	166	178	709	1106	639	839
Weight (kg)	80.2	66.6	70.1	57.1	86.9	79.0	81.2	68.8
Height (m)	1.77	1.64	1.72	1.60	1.77	1.64	1.70	1.58
BMI (kg/m^2)	25.6	25.0	23.6	22.3	27.9	29.3	28.0	27.4
Arm girth (cm)	31.1	28.8	28.9	25.9	34.5	33.1	33.0	30.8
Waist girth (cm)	94.8	87.3	87.0	80.3	95.0	92.7	96.5	90.1
Hip girth (cm)	103.2	104.0	97.4	96.7	104.1	111.9	103.1	106.8
Thigh girth (cm)	48.4	49.2	46.6	46.8	51.2	55.3	49.6	50.1

Data from the UK and US Sizing Surveys. See Wells, Treleaven, and Cole 2007; Wells et al. 2008a.

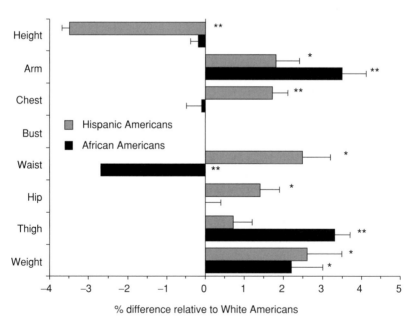

Figure 2.23. Percentage difference in height, body girths and weight of African American and Hispanic American men relative to white American men. All outcomes adjusted for age, income and education and (except height) height. * $p<0.01$; ** $p<0.001$.

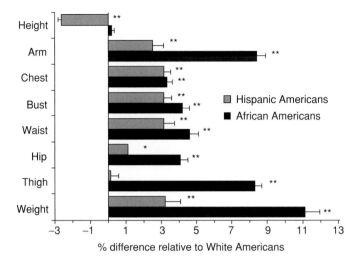

Figure 2.24. Percentage difference in height, body girths and weight of African and Hispanic American women relative to white American men. All outcomes adjusted for age, income and education and (except height) height. * p<0.01; ** p<0.001.

arm and thigh girths but significantly smaller waist girth. In women, Hispanic and African Americans had significantly greater girths of the arm, chest, bust, waist and hip than white women, with thigh girth also being greater in African American but not Hispanic women (Wells et al. 2008a).

Interpretation of the biological nature of these differences is challenging. European, Hispanic and African Americans, for example, differ in the number of generations which have occupied the industrialised niche that they now all share. The factors accounting for ethnic variability in body shape might therefore be genetic, or environmental, and within the latter category, transgenerationally transmitted or arising afresh within each generation. Nevertheless, these shape data provide support for the skinfold data in suggesting significant population variability in body fat content and distribution. These differences may be extremely important both for basic biological functions and for the risk of disease in the current obesity epidemic. This topic is addressed further in Chapter 9.

Summary

Though necessarily limited to data obtained using more rudimentary measurement techniques, the above review highlights three important themes regarding human adiposity.

First, humans may be considered a fat species not in relation to mammals *per se*, but in terms of a land-dwelling mammal that evolved in the tropical savannah niche. Almost all other species of comparable size with more than moderate adiposity occupy temperate habitats where energy-stress is significant, and in many cases such species are marine mammals, where larger body size is more readily accommodated. Across the entire range of BMI, females in particular tend to maintain a relatively high proportion of weight as fat, such that even populations at the lower end of the weight range tend to average greater than 20% fat. Despite being thinner than females, males also average around 14% fat, substantially greater than the vast majority of non-marine male mammals. Clearly this human characteristic requires explanation from an evolutionary perspective.

Second, within the human species, lean mass, fat mass and regional fat distribution all differ between populations, with such variability likely to reflect both genetic adaptations to ancestral environments and exposure to more contemporary ecological stresses. Third, despite such variability, relatively consistent patterns of sexual dimorphism are observed in a variety of traits, including height, relative lean and fat masses, and fat distribution. Despite having similar BMI to males in most populations, females systematically have less lean mass and greater fat mass, and a more peripheral fat distribution. Again, the sexual dimorphism in body composition requires an evolutionary analysis. The remainder of this book therefore attempts to clarify why humans as a species should have high levels of adiposity, and why individuals should vary therein.

3 Proximate causes of lipid deposition and oxidation

According to Tinbergen's approach, proximate causation refers to environmental stimuli that induce the formation and enlargement or depletion of adipose tissue. Many such factors are associated with lipid deposition and oxidation in humans, operating across a wide range of biological levels and indicating that body fatness is a phenotype intricately connected with many other aspects of biology. The aim of this chapter is to review the range of proximate factors and elucidate their underlying mechanisms and interrelationships. Figure 3.1 offers a schematic diagram of the different levels of biology relevant to this issue. At one extreme are the genetic and epigenetic factors that influence energy balance and so alter adiposity, acting through a number of physiological mechanisms which are themselves sensitive to environmental factors that act on them through behaviour. At the other extreme, therefore, is the impact of the broader socio-ecological niche, acting on groups of humans.

Proximal mechanisms distributed across these different levels are fundamental to evolutionary models of the functions of body fat, allowing broader hypotheses to be both generated and tested at physiological or behavioural levels. Ultimately, speculations concerning the value of energy stores during human evolution, or imputed functions of body fat for 'funding' specific functions, can be considered plausible only if they are consistent with the biology of these proximate mechanisms.

3.1   The energy balance equation

The energy balance equation is derived from the physical sciences and the field of thermodynamics, the branch of science that uses energy functions to describe the state of a material system and prescribe rules that govern transitions from one state to another.

The concept of energy balance is a product of the principles embodied by the first law of thermodynamics. This law states that in all processes in an isolated system, the energy of the system remains constant (von Helmholtz 1847). Thus, energy can be neither created nor destroyed, only redistributed in different forms. The same law can be applied to living organisms by taking

49

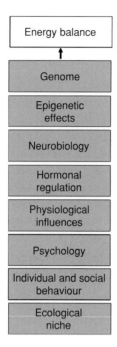

Figure 3.1. Levels of biology implicated in the ability to gain or lose energy stores.

into account energy entering and leaving the system, which is represented by the body. If energy entering the system is not equal to that leaving, the energy content of the system changes proportionately:

Energy in = Energy out ± Energy content of the system

A further extrapolation of this law is also important for understanding energy balance. It states that, in any system, the value of the work done by the system is independent of the pathways involved and is dependent only, and totally, on the state at start and end points (Hess 1838). Thus the conversion of energy from one form to another within the system does not affect the energy content of the system. Together these models enable the scientific study of energy metabolism.

The living organism requires energy to sustain life by supporting metabolic function in all living cells. In animals, the energy is ingested in chemical form as foodstuffs comprising molecules of carbohydrate, fat, protein or alcohol, some of which are then oxidised to provide a metabolic pool of chemical energy. This metabolic pool provides chemical energy for chemical work within the system, and for storage in new tissue during growth and tissue maintenance. Alternatively, the chemical energy may be transformed into other forms of energy to be used in different types of work such as mechanical work or heat.

The expenditure of energy in work is accompanied by heat production. Taking into account efficiency, such heat production is directly proportional to the amount of work being performed in the system, and measurement of heat production can therefore be used to quantify metabolic energy expenditure. This approach, derived directly from the first and second laws of thermodynamics, represents one side of the heat production equation. The other side refers to the metabolic processes involved in expending energy. This approach derives from an awareness that animal heat production arises from the oxidation of carbon, hence energy expenditure can also be estimated by quantifying the oxygen consumed and the carbon dioxide produced.

Energy expenditure can therefore be assessed in two ways – the quantification of heat production (direct calorimetry) or the measurement of respiratory gas exchange (indirect calorimetry). By the end of the nineteenth century, agreement closer than 1% had been demonstrated between these two methodological approaches (Rubner 1894; Atwater and Benedict 1903). Calorimetric apparatus has since undergone continual revision, promoting increased accuracy, precision and ease-of-use. A major advance was the progression from closed-circuit to open-circuit indirect calorimetry, whereby only samples of air rather than the total output are analysed for gaseous content, and gas exchange is calculated rather than measured.

Calorimetry underlies one of the two units of energy that are used in energetic models. Although the SI unit of energy is the joule (J), defined as work done and expressed as $kg/m^2/s^2$, another unit is the calorie (usually referred to in thousands or 'kcals'), broadly defined as the amount of heat required to increase the temperature of 1 gram of water by $1°C$ (Blaxter 1989). This amount of heat is not a constant because the specific heat of water varies with temperature. The calorie used in physiological studies is therefore defined as the $15°C$ calorie, or the heat required to increase the temperature of 1 gram of water from 14.5 to $15.5°C$ (Weast 1975). This definition of the calorie presents no problems in the inter-conversion of data expressed in joules or calories, since 1 calorie equals 4.184 joules.

Energy balance concerns nothing more than the difference between the intake and expenditure of energy. If the two are not equal, then a change in body energy content follows, as expressed in the above equation. The energy balance equation can be expanded to include a number of components into which energy expenditure can be divided:

$$E_i = E_m + E_a + E_g + E_t + E_w$$

where $i =$ intake
         $m =$ basal metabolism
         $a =$ physical activity
         $g =$ growth
         $t =$ thermogenesis
         $w =$ waste losses in faeces, urine and gases

The costs of growth can be further subdivided into energy expended on tissue synthesis and energy stored in new tissue. It is also possible to differentiate between gross energy intake, and metabolisable energy intake which does not incorporate the energy lost in faeces, urine and waste gases and therefore represents energy directly captured by the organism.

According to the logic of the energy balance equation, fat deposition arises from positive energy balance. However, changes in the energy content of a biological system reflect not only the acquisition or loss of body fat, but equivalent changes in other components of weight, such as glycogen, protein and mineral. Of these, fat and protein represent the main energy-containing body components, with each of them characterised by a specific energy content per gram, and a specific energy cost per gram for tissue synthesis. The energy content of fat is substantially greater than that of protein (9.25 vs. 5.65 kcal/g), whereas the costs of tissue synthesis are greater for protein than for fat (7.65 vs. 3.25 kcal/g) (Roberts and Young 1988). In terms of the total energy cost of tissue deposition, these discrepancies broadly cancel out, such that the cost per gram of tissue gained is approximately 5 kcal/g regardless of the fat versus protein content (WHO 1985). However, gram for gram, weight gain in the form of fat represents a markedly greater increase in the energy content of the body compared to weight gain in the form of protein.

The energy balance equation has proven very valuable in research on human energetics. The principles of the energy balance equation underpin all metabolic techniques for the measurement of energy intake and expenditure, and they allow conversion of body composition data into caloric values. However, as an explanation for between-individual variability in weight gain, the energy balance equation is of zero value, precisely because of its mathematical logic and the fact that it expresses a truism (Wells 1998b). Furthermore, little attention has been given to the possibility that energy imbalance might be a consequence, rather than a cause, of weight gain (Taubes 2008).

During early research into the aetiology of obesity, many researchers assumed that fat deposition must be attributable either to *high energy intake* or to *low energy expenditure* (Ravussin et al. 1988; Roberts et al. 1988). The fact that few studies were successful in supporting these hypotheses was attributed

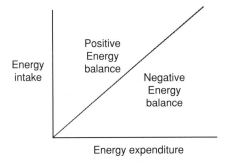

Figure 3.2. Schematic diagram of energy balance, shown by the diagonal line where energy intake is exactly equal to energy expenditure. All individuals lying above the line are in positive energy balance and must gain weight, whereas all those below the line are in negative balance and must lose weight. Positive or negative energy balance may occur across the entire spectra of energy intake or energy expenditure.

to insufficient accuracy of the metabolic techniques utilised for identifying the degree of energy imbalance responsible. The year 1988 saw publication of a scientific article purporting to demonstrate reduced energy expenditure in infants who subsequently demonstrated a high degree of weight gain (Roberts et al. 1988). This publication, though highly cited, has been criticised for relying on an extremely small sample size, and for discounting data showing that those infants gaining most weight by one year also consumed more energy at six months (Wells 1998b). The issue remains controversial, with some well-controlled studies not supporting the hypothesis of low energy expenditure constituting a risk factor for obesity (Weinsier et al. 2003). More importantly, however, there is no need to invoke high energy intake or low energy expenditure in order to account for weight gain.

Figure 3.2 presents a schematic diagram of the energy balance equation. The diagonal line indicates energy balance, where energy intake is exactly equal to energy expenditure. All individuals lying above the line are in positive energy balance and must gain weight, whereas all those below the line are in negative balance and must lose weight. Being above or below that line need have no connection with the magnitude of energy intake or expenditure. Professional sports players often have very high energy intake as well as high energy expenditure, and hence maintain their body weight. Many bed-bound patients have extremely low levels of physical activity, but also have reduced appetite and therefore have low energy intake too. Thus, on a population basis, there is no reason to assume that groups of people with high energy intake or low expenditure must be those showing the greatest change in body energy content.

Rather, weight gain can simply be attributed to energy imbalance, and this imbalance can occur across the entire range of energy expenditure and energy intake. Most researchers still consider that energy imbalance drives weight gain and have ignored the possibility that the process of energy accumulation might itself invoke energy imbalance, by generating inconsistent effects on appetite and activity level. In a provocative book, Taubes (2008) has argued that positive energy balance may be merely a symptom of fattening, whereby the metabolic processes driving triglyceride accumulation may increase hunger whilst promoting lethargy. Taubes' theory should be taken seriously and is discussed elsewhere in this chapter and volume.

In many contexts, the degree of positive energy balance is very small, such that weight gain proceeds slowly and at an undetectable level. However, there are periods in the life course when weight gain is substantially faster and more 'visible' to the individual or to those caring for them. In the first months of life, for example, infants typically gain around 30 g per day, whilst adolescents can also gain 15 g per day (WHO 1985). In Chapter 6, reference is made to a ritual fattening session in a West African population where daily weight gain is around 270 g, equivalent to a positive energy balance of 15 MJ per day (Pasquet et al. 1992). In all these cases, the positive energy balance may be considered driven by hormones responding to behaviour, either those regulating growth, or those responding to the glycemic load of the diet.

Energy imbalance is equally relevant to weight loss as well as weight gain. During weight loss, the energy content of fat and protein stores is released into the metabolic pool and can be used amongst the components of energy expenditure. The total content is not necessarily recaptured owing to any metabolic costs of breaking down existing tissue, for example, the thermal energy released in doing so. Fat and glycogen are substantially more efficient material for energy storage than protein and minimise such losses.

The weakness of the energy balance approach is most apparent when total energy expenditure is considered. Variability in specific components of energy metabolism, such as basal metabolism or the costs of physical activity, might demonstrate more robust associations with weight change, in the first case mediated through some derangement of metabolic control or in the second case mediated through specific behaviours. Large-scale studies have, for example, been able to demonstrate associations between variability in behaviour and subsequent weight gain (Johannsen et al. 2008). These studies essentially indicate a degree of 'thrift' in some individuals, which, given a common environment, translates into additional weight gain. There is little indication however that variability in basal metabolism is a key factor in the predisposition to obesity, and it is more likely to be of importance at the lower end of the spectrum of nutritional intake, providing a buffer against malnutrition. For example, a 0.2 MJ reduction in BMR is likely to negligibly impact on the energetics of an overweight adult, but it may have considerable significance for an underweight individual limited to an energy intake of 4 MJ per day. Furthermore, the thrift itself may be located at the level of the cell, such that apparent alterations in appetite or behaviour might be symptoms rather than causes of the weight gain or loss.

3.2   Genetic factors

It is commonly recognised that adiposity phenotype runs in families, indicating that genes contribute to individual differences in adiposity via a number of different metabolic and behavioural pathways.

Heritability

At the broadest level, heritability in the classic sense refers to the sum of genetic contributions to the variance in phenotype. This definition incorporates the effects of allelic variation (termed 'additive variance'), dominance variation and parental effects, whereby the development of individuals is influenced by genetically determined components of the parental phenotype. Separating out the genetic and environmental contributions to heritability is extremely complex, since only the environmental component can be directly measured. In non-human animal species a variety of experimental approaches can be used, such as crossbreeding. Clearly in humans the available approaches are more limited and are essentially confined to within-family correlations, twin studies and adoption studies. In general, families tend to experience common environments as well as common genes, hence twin and adoption studies are considerably more robust study designs for investigating heritability. Familial correlations in adult body mass index average around 0.2 between parents and offspring, 0.3 between non-twin siblings, and around 0.6 between twins (Schousboe et al. 2004).

Twin studies suggest that around half of inter-individual variation in total fatness and adipose tissue distribution can be attributed to genetic factors. The classic approach, comparing monozygous twins who share 100% of their genes with dizygous twins sharing 50% of their genes, has now been used in a number of studies addressing a variety of body composition outcomes. Table 3.1 presents data from 325 female and 299 male twin pairs, illustrating

Table 3.1. *Heritability of body composition variables in adult twins*

	Men	Women
BMI	0.63	0.58
%fat	0.63	0.59
Sum of skinfolds[1]	0.65	0.61
Limb skinfolds[2]	0.62	0.65
Truncal skinfolds[3]	0.69	0.50
Waist girth	0.61	0.48
Hip girth	0.58	0.52
Height	0.69	0.81
Lean mass	0.56	0.61

Data from Schousboe and colleagues (2004), describing 299 male and 325 female twin pairs, average age 38 years, from Denmark
[1] sum of biceps, triceps, subscapular and suprailiac skinfolds
[2] sum of biceps and triceps skinfolds
[3] sum of subscapular and suprailiac skinfolds

reasonable consistency in the heritability of a variety of indices of body fat, but also indicating heritability of lean mass as well (Schousboe et al. 2004). Three twin studies in particular have been proposed to provide strong evidence for a heritable predisposition to gain or lose body fat during conditions of positive or negative energy balance. In each of these studies, identical twins were either overfed (Bouchard et al. 1990; Bouchard et al. 1994; Bouchard et al. 1996) or underfed (Hainer et al. 2000). In each case, the studies showed substantial intra-pair resemblance in the degree of, and composition of, weight gain or loss. The authors interpreted these findings as suggestive of a strong genetic effect acting on each twin pair. Whilst this interpretation is plausible, it is not the only one. Each monozygous twin pair experiences a common environment in utero, although even monozygous twins are often discordant for birth weight. Maternal programming of offspring phenotype, for example, in relation to her metabolic control during pregnancy, may therefore contribute to intra-pair similarity and between-pair difference in response to positive or negative energy balance. It is also notable that some twin studies indicate greater heritability of lean mass than fatness (Forbes, Sauer, and Weitkamp 1995).

More generally, twin studies using the classic approach suffer from the limitation that the relative importance of environmental versus genetic impact on phenotype depends on the population studied. Where environmental conditions are similar, heritability tend to be over-estimated. Conversely, when a population is recruited from a more homogenous population, the individuals may have many genetic factors in common, which tends to produce over-estimation of the influence of the environment (Bateson and Martin 1999).

Adoption studies can resolve some of the difficulties described above, as they weaken any tendency for genetic and post-natal environmental factors to co-vary. In general, adoption studies have revealed that the body mass index of adoptees shows similarity with that of both their biological parents and siblings, but not with that of either adoptive parent (Stunkard et al. 1986), with this effect apparent across the entire range of body fatness. One study explored similarities between adoptees and both their full siblings and half siblings, enabling differentiation between those sharing only a biological mother or a biological father (Sorensen et al. 1989). There was little evidence that similarities between adoptees and their half siblings differed according to which biological parent they had in common, thus decreasing the likelihood that the resemblances could be attributed to a shared in utero environment (Sorensen et al. 1989). Likewise, the resemblance between adoptees and their siblings was stronger if the biological father was shared, which again implicates an effect of paternal genes (Sorensen et al. 1989). Similar findings were obtained from a study of twins reared apart. In the monozygous twins, intra-pair correlations in body mass index were essentially the same in both men and women, regardless of whether the pairs had been reared apart or together (Stunkard et al. 1990). Equivalent correlations were substantially reduced in dizygous twins, indicating additional non-additive genetic variance.

Collectively, these studies provide strong support for the notion that a significant proportion of the variability in body fatness, across the entire range of fatness, is associated with genetic factors. This scenario is consistent with that in other primate species – for example, studies of baboons have indicated significant heritability of fat mass (0.41), adipocyte cell volume (0.37) and leptin concentration (0.21) (Comuzzie et al. 2003). Nevertheless, the broader implications remain complex. First, almost all the studies conducted to date are from Western populations, with plentiful food supplies and a tendency towards lower activity levels. Such ecological conditions may favour the expression of genetic effects. The coefficient of variation in body mass index tends to be lower in harsher environments, suggesting that in such conditions the common environment exerts a strong effect on phenotype.

Those who have conducted these twin and adoption studies have usually concluded that the family environment exerts negligible effect on variability in fatness. For example, Stunkard and colleagues (1986) proposed that the 'childhood family environment has little or no effect' on variability in adult BMI, while in another study (Stunkard et al. 1990) the same authors attributed less than 1% of the variance in BMI to a shared environment in both male and female twins. This interpretation fits poorly with the overwhelming evidence demonstrating secular trends in body fatness within a relatively constant gene pool. A more appropriate interpretation is that environmental factors exert powerful effects on BMI, but that whatever the state of the environment, genetic factors contribute to individual variability in fatness. In western populations exposed to obesogenic conditions in recent decades, the entire spectrum of nutritional status has shifted to the right. This effect has been strongest in those at the upper end of the weight range, such that there has been a greater increase in the number of individuals classified as overweight or obese than expected for the increase in median or mean BMI (Kromeyer-Hauschild and Zellner 2007).

With populations such as the United States demonstrating such high preva-lences of obesity, some authors have suggested that it may be more valuable to consider the genetics of thinness rather than fatness, and to consider why a minority of individuals appear protected against obesity (Bulik and Allison 2001). Research on animals has identified recessive genes for extreme thinness, whilst human studies including those on twin pairs have demonstrated that her-itability of thinness is as strong as that for obesity. Furthermore, thinness like obesity tracks within individuals over time (Bulik and Allison 2001).

Body fatness as a polygenic trait

The studies discussed above provide strong evidence that fatness is polygenic (Sorensen et al. 1989), although certain genes may exert specific detectable effects. A small number of single-trait conditions have been identified, such as rare mutations in the genes that regulate leptin metabolism, described in patients with severe obesity (O'Rahilly et al. 2003). Importantly, these factors tend to affect appetite control rather than altering metabolism. Although the rarity of such genes precludes them from accounting for current obesity levels, they play an important role in investigating potential treatment strategies (O'Rahilly et al. 2003). The genetic predisposition of 'thinness' is investigated for similar reasons.

In the vast majority of people, body fatness cannot be strongly associated with any particular gene and is rather the result of interplay between multiple genetic and environmental factors. The role of genetic factors is complex, involving the interaction of many genes which individually may have relatively minor effects. Such 'susceptibility' genes work in combination with each other and with environmental factors such as diet, activity level, disease and specific behaviours such as smoking (Froguel and Boutin 2001).

Recently, Bouchard (2007) analysed the map of genes contributing to human obesity in order to clarify how genetic factors are implicated in the biology of adipose tissue. Bouchard found 127 genes demonstrating association with body fatness, of which 22 had positive findings in at least five studies. Bouchard then categorised five 'major classes' of genes acting on adiposity. These were distinguished as acting on metabolic rate or thermogenesis, appetite, physical activity, lipid oxidation rate, and adipocyte lipid storage capacity. In many cases these genes appear to act on or during growth and development.

Nevertheless, it is becoming increasingly difficult to pinpoint the level at which genetic factors are implicated in phenotypic variability. Genetic variability is now known to derive both from variation in DNA sequence and also in the level of DNA expression. Epigenetic processes which modify DNA expression therefore link life-course experience with genotype and make it harder to differentiate whether phenotypic variability derives from genetic predisposition or lifetime experience. For example, monozygous twins are genetically very similar in early life, but they show genetic differences attributable to epigenetic mechanisms by middle age (Fraga et al. 2005).

This issue is particularly relevant when considering population differences in body fatness. As discussed in Chapter 9, population variability may plausibly derive from heritable or ecological factors, or indeed interactions between the two. Population variability in adipose tissue biology may emerge through differential nutritional experience, commencing in utero or even prior to conception. Whatever level of heritability is suggested from twin and adoption studies, individuals can vary markedly within their own lifetimes in fat content.

Imprinted genes

Genomic imprinting refers to the fact that some genes are imprinted, or differentially expressed in the offspring, according to parent of origin. This results either in only the gene from the mother being expressed, and the paternal gene being imprinted (silenced), or vice versa. Genomic imprinting appears to have evolved in mammals to fine-tune growth of the offspring in early life. In general, paternal genes enhance offspring growth whereas maternal genes suppress it, in accordance with parent-offspring conflict theory which predicts an evolutionary 'conflict of interest' between the two parental genomes over the optimal level of maternal investment in each offspring (Haig 1993). However, other theoretical bases for genomic imprinting have also been offered, and not all the findings concerning imprinted genes fit with the parental conflict hypothesis.

Insulin genes, which play a critical role in the regulation of fetal growth, are characterised by antagonistic imprinting, with paternal expression of the INS and Insulin-like growth factor 2 (IGF2) genes and maternal expression of the IGF2 receptor gene. The common VNTR polymorphism in the paternally expressed INS gene influences the level of insulin secretion and has been linked to the development of obesity in childhood (Le, Fallin, and Bougneres 2001).

Because of the growth-promoting role of paternally expressed (maternally imprinted) genes, their polymorphisms may be of particular importance in the genetics of childhood adiposity.

Failure to express genes that are normally inherited from only one parent causes major abnormalities of growth and body composition. Prader-Willi syndrome, where the paternal copy of a gene on chromosome 15 is missing, is characterised by poor appetite in infancy, but with massive hyperphagia from early childhood onwards. It has been hypothesised that the effects of fetal starvation on the developing brain gives rise to an abnormal satiety response, which programmes inappropriate appetite following infancy (Haig and Wharton 2003). If the same segment of this gene is missing or disrupted by maternal inheritance, the consequence is Angelman syndrome, characterised by hyperactivity, mental retardation and the inability to control physical movements (Walter and Paulsen 2003). A further condition attributable to disruption in imprinting is Beckwith-Wiedemann syndrome, characterised by embryonic and placental overgrowth, and a predisposition to childhood tumours (Polychronakos and Kukuvitis 2002).

Collectively, these studies implicate imprinted genes as making a major contribution to the ontogenetic development of body composition. Imprinted genes interact with the process of developmental plasticity such that disruptions of their expression profoundly affect body composition. A variety of imprinted genes have been shown to modulate placental development and fetal growth (Reik et al. 2001), a period of ontogenesis strongly associated with long-term effects on body composition.

Whilst the vast majority of studies of the genetics of body composition have focused on heritability, or on the association between specific genetic factors and body composition traits, a further important issue comprises the differential regional expression of genes in adipose tissue. Several studies have now demonstrated increased levels of gene expression in visceral abdominal adipose tissue compared to other depots (Gabrielsson et al. 2003). Such studies highlight a greater metabolic activity of these adipose tissue depots and help understand the associations between genotype, regional adiposity and functional outcomes.

Epigenetic effects

Within the last decade, an entire new perspective has emerged within genetics, following recognition that variability in DNA expression may be as important for phenotypic variability as variation in DNA content. Alterations in chromatin structure, induced by environmental factors, regulate the expression of genes and indicate a link between life-course experience and gene activity. Epigenetic effects are likely to be of particular importance during early sensitive periods of development, and therefore are highly relevant to the life-course perspective on adiposity presented in Chapter 5.

The first clear evidence of epigenetic effects in the offspring being generated by maternal diet emerged from work on mice, whereby methyl-supplementation of the maternal diet altered indices of metabolism in the offspring (Wolff et al. 1998). Subsequent work using a high-fat diet has demonstrated similar effects on the fetal epigenome in primates (Agaard-Tillery et al. 2008). Whilst the contribution of epigenetic effects to human adiposity remains to be clarified, this latter study clearly shows that indices of adiposity phenotype in the maternal generation act on the offspring. This work emphasises that there is likely to be an optimal, rather than a minimal, level of maternal dietary intake in relation to optimising offspring fitness (Cooney, Dave, and Wolff 2002), consistent with work at other biological levels. Research on the epigenetic profile is likely to expand significantly in the coming decade, and although little is known as yet, the mechanism is clearly fundamental to life-course development.

Extra-somatic contributions

Whilst the human genome is clearly the primary genetic determinant of body fatness, the genetics of other species should not be ignored. Of particular importance here may be bacterial colonisers of the human gut, in particular the Bacteroidetes and the Firmicutes; hence it is necessary to consider the human 'metagenome' (Turnbaugh et al. 2006).

Gut microbes contribute to the digestion of foods, providing metabolic capacities beyond those deriving directly from our own genome (Turnbaugh et al. 2006). Studies in mice show that the relative proportion of Bacteroidetes is reduced in obese compared with lean animals (Ley et al. 2006), while the exchange of gut microbial communities between mice is associated with changes in body fat content. This effect can be attributed to an enhanced capacity of the gut microbiota of obese mice to harvest dietary energy. These findings imply that the microbiota of individual organisms differ systematically according to characteristics such as immune status and nutritional status (Turnbaugh et al. 2006).

These findings have now been replicated in humans, with the relative proportion of Bacteroidetes increasing when obese individuals experience dietary-induced weight loss (Ley et al. 2006). Significantly, the change in the relative proportion of Bacteroidetes was correlated not with dietary intake itself, but with the magnitude of weight loss (Ley et al. 2006). These findings are important not only for elucidating the totality of the genetics of human body composition, but also for highlighting how genetic factors interact with lifestyle changes to induce within-lifespan effects. Clearly these findings are also highly relevant to potential treatments for obesity.

Summary

In sum, therefore, it is clear that genetic factors make an important contribution to between-individual variability in body fatness, and genes and their epigenetic variability are increasingly implicated in a variety of physiological mechanisms underlying differential weight gain or loss. Such genetic variability indicates a variety of selective pressures having operated during human evolution, as discussed in greater detail in Chapter 9. Many such genetic effects appear to be particularly important during development.

3.3   Neurobiology of appetite

The brain makes a key contribution to adiposity by coordinating short- and long-term signals of energy availability and energy needs and converting them into appetite (Schwartz and Morton 2002). Our understanding of this area remains incomplete owing to the key signalling pathways only recently having been discovered. The discovery of leptin stimulated interest in the signalling of energy stores directly to the brain; however, prior work had already emphasised the role of visual, olfactory and auditory signals in appetite stimulation, the role of digestion in generating indices of satiety, and the role of other hormones such as insulin. Current research is unravelling the full complexity of such signalling systems, while also identifying the parts of the brain targeted and demonstrating significant variability in brain morphology related to nutritional status. However, the extent to which the brain actually regulates adiposity remains contentious.

The gastro-intestinal tract generates a variety of signals of mechanical or chemical content. These then convey information to the brain via either primary afferent nerves or hormones (Morrison and Berthoud 2007). Following absorption, macronutrients can further impact on the nervous system through hormonal mechanisms, which thus predispose to a homeostatic system regulating energy balance through effects on both appetite and energy expenditure (Morrison and Berthoud 2007; Schwartz and Morton 2002).

Studies of rats in whom parts of the brain had been surgically removed have shown that the caudal brainstem, the most 'primitive' part of the brain, contains the fundamental neural circuitry required to orchestrate ingestion, digestion and some degree of energy sensing (Morrison and Berthoud 2007). However, other parts of the brain are required for full homeostatic regulation of energy stores, with neurons in the hypothalamus appearing particularly important (Morrison and Berthoud 2007). Neurons within the arcuate nucleus (ARC) of the hypothalamus are sensitive to a variety of signals generated by circulating metabolites, hormones or neural inputs (Morrison and Berthoud 2007). ARC neurons, for example, are sensitive to the adipose-tissue-secreted hormone leptin (see below), and also express appetite-enhancing peptides such as neuoropeptide Y and agouti-related protein. Other ARC neurons express pro-opiomelanocortin (POMC). The balance between different neuronal subsets controls the braking versus accelerating of appetite stimulation (Schwartz and Morton 2002). Thus these neurons collectively respond to the availability of fuels contained in different parts of the body, including plasma-circulating nutrients, those being absorbed from the digestive tract, and those stored in glycogen or adipose tissue (Morrison and Berthoud 2007).

For example, gut peptides such as ghrelin signal the near immediate availability of fuels emerging from the process of digestion, while insulin conveys information about both adipose tissue and circulating glucose levels, and leptin signals longer-term energy status (Schwartz and Morton 2002). A member of the neuropeptide Y protein family known as PYY_{3-36} appears to represent an intermediate signal, inhibiting appetite for up to 12 hours following a meal (Batterham et al. 2002). It may therefore integrate the signals responding to individual meals versus long-term energy balance. Direct administration of these hormones to the brain illustrates their regulatory effect (Morrison and Berthoud 2007). As discussed above, a variety of genes known to impact on obesity status have been shown to regulate or disrupt this appetite regulatory system.

A variety of other signalling mechanisms, targeting in particular the orbitofrontal cortex via intermediate brain regions, convey information about the quality, taste and palatability of foods, and they enable connections between dietary experience and eating preferences to emerge (Morrison and Berthoud 2007). These systems thus allow the individual to learn about food, integrating personal and social experience into a psychological profile. Recent work has elucidated the neuronal basis of expectation and reward in the orbitofrontal cortex of the vertebrate brain, with particular focus on primates (Schultz, Tremblay, and Hollerman 2000; Watson and Platt 2008). Whilst many studies illustrate the role of food as a primary reward stimulus, work on primates further demonstrates the importance of social experience and interaction (Ghazanfar and Santos 2004). Such work has made possible the direct testing of evolutionary game theory in 'games of economic rationality' (Barraclough, Conroy, and Lee 2004). In humans, brain-imaging studies have identified differences in the brain morphology of obese versus non-obese individuals (Pannacciulli et al.

2007), while brain activity also appears altered in patients with the compulsive eating disorder anorexia nervosa (Kaye 2008), suggesting that there may be fundamental neurobiological variability in appetite regulation across the range of nutritional status.

Research on the neurobiology of appetite is critical for understanding the link between physiological mechanisms of weight regulation and behaviour, in terms both of discerning the 'natural' basis of foraging behaviour and also of understanding how behavioural variability, or behavioural change, impacts on nutritional status. It will prove particularly important in understanding the link between human sociality and body weight regulation, and it also has implications for understanding human brain evolution. Yet the notion that the brain is the ultimate regulator of adiposity merits critical appraisal given the persistent chronic energy imbalance that leads to obesity or anorexia.

An alternative approach considers that energy balance takes place ultimately at the level of the cell, and that while the brain responds to multiple signals emanating from cellular metabolism, it can also to some extent be driven by them (Taubes 2008). Experimental studies on animals, wherein specific parts of the brain are removed, have shown that obesity can be induced through hormonal injections without increasing energy intake, as energy expenditure decreased (Lee and Schaffer 1934). Such studies indicate that hormonal perturbations may disrupt the maintenance of stable weight, and they suggest that the brain regulation of appetite may not be the fundamental level at which energy stores are regulated. The brain and cellular approaches may prove to be competing as complementary explanations of appetite regulation.

3.4   Endocrine and paracrine factors

A wide variety of messenger molecules influence, and are influenced by, body fat, operating at a number of different metabolic levels. These may be broadly differentiated into (1) endocrine factors, comprising hormones released into the bloodstream where they target cells, tissue, organs or the entire organism; or (2) paracrine factors which represent the chemical transmission of information through the intercellular space. Owing to their not being released into the bloodstream, paracrine factors exert much more local effects.

Chemical signals may emanate from the brain and act on the cells, or emanate from the cells and act on the brain. If the brain is considered the primary regulatory organ, then metabolism will appear to be driven by brain-regulatory processes. This is the position widely held by obesity researchers, who increasingly consider the condition a problem of appetite dysregulation in the brain. However, if energy balance is considered to occur at the level of cells, then greater attention must be paid to how cellular metabolic signals act on the brain (Taubes 2008).

Endocrine regulation

Endocrine factors include satiety signals and adiposity signals acting on the brain, with these hormones reflecting both long-term state and also the immediate metabolic response to food ingestion. Short-term satiety signals, such as cholecystokinin and ghrelin, are produced by the gut in response to food ingestion and combine with nonhormonal factors such as gastric distension to terminate eating (Schwartz and Morton 2002). In themselves, however, such hormones have little long-term influence on fat stores (Woods and Seeley 2000). Appetite is driven by a variety of orexigenic and anorectic peptides, which respond to both peripheral hormones and circulating levels of carbohydrate, lipid and amino acids (Dhillo 2007). These peptides act on the brain, in particular the hypothalamus, and regulate among other factors the relationship between energy intake, energy stores and energy utilisation. However, adipocytes and associated cells are now known to secrete around 100 multifunctional proteins, which perform a much wider range of functions than the regulation of fuel stores (Atanassova et al. 2007). Examples include inflammatory and immune responses, angiogenesis (blood vessel formation) and wound healing (Atanassova et al. 2007).

Of particular significance for the regulation of fat stores are signals which circulate in the blood proportional to cellular metabolism and body fat content and are transported into the brain, where they regulate energy balance. These include leptin, secreted directly by adipose tissue, and insulin and amylin, secreted by beta cells in the pancreas. Each of these hormones is secreted in direct proportion to the amount of fat in the body, although the rate of secretion is altered in disease states such as type 2 diabetes (Woods and Seeley 2000). However, insulin in particular is also highly sensitive to short-term metabolic status, reflecting dietary intake and cellular energy metabolism. The central nervous system integrates signals of adiposity and ongoing metabolism to regulate food intake and fat stores across a wide range of tissues and functions.

Insulin and other pancreatic hormones

Insulin, deriving from the Latin word *insula* (island), is the main hormone controlling blood-glucose levels and carbohydrate and lipid homeostasis. Its secretion by islets of Langerhans cells in the pancreas is largely determined by blood-glucose concentration. Increased concentrations of insulin induce the storage of glucose in insulin-sensitive muscle and liver cells in the form of glycogen, and the storage of fatty acids in adipocytes through the stimulation of triglyceride synthesis (Ganong 1999). Low concentrations of insulin reverse these processes, causing liver cells to convert glycogen back to glucose so as to increase blood-glucose content and stimulating the release of fatty acids from adipocytes by lipolysis. Counterbalancing the effects of insulin, low blood-glucose levels induce the secretion of glucagon by the pancreas, which causes the liver to increase conversion of glycogen to glucose for release into the blood circulation (Ganong 1999). Amylin acts as an inhibitor of glucagon secretion and then contributes to the stability of blood-glucose levels. This pancreatic regulatory mechanism tightly controls blood-glucose content within a narrow range, except for the transient increase in glucose level following ingestion. Insulin is the only anabolic hormone capable of decreasing blood-glucose content. It acts in opposition to a number of catabolic hormones which increase blood-glucose content. For example, stress hormones such as noradrenaline inhibit the action of insulin and hence raise blood-glucose levels during periods of stress (Ganong 1999).

Some organs, such as the brain, have obligatory energy requirements and are considered insulin insensitive, as the hormone is not required for them to absorb glucose. Other tissues have greater flexibility regarding fuel supply and can readily meet their energy requirements from alternative sources such as fatty acids. As a consequence, muscle and adipose tissue can fluctuate in mass and status as a means of buffering the brain. A key mechanism contributing to this flexibility comprises differential tissue sensitivity or resistance to insulin, along with metabolic flexibility in the fuels used (Galgani, Moro, and Ravussin 2008). Adipose tissue and muscle can be considered as competing tissues for insulin, with muscle clearing more glucose, but less so if a state of insulin resistance develops.

Cellular energy supply derives not merely from glucose, but also from free fatty acids which are released into the blood stream from triglycerides in adipose tissue when insulin levels fall (Randle et al. 1963). Because fatty acid release is inhibited when insulin level is increased, high circulating insulin levels render energy stores temporarily 'invisible' and prevent lipolysis, therefore potentially upsetting cellular energy balance. Indeed, the action of all other hormones on lipid metabolism is suppressed by insulin and high blood-sugar levels (Gordon 1970). Paradoxically, the role of insulin in removing glucose from the blood stream is that it increases hunger (LeMagne 1971). Thus, metabolic flexibility allows the organism to draw on different fuel sources during activities such as sleep or exercise, and insulin helps integrate feeding behaviour with this homeostatic process through its stimulation of appetite and the promotion of lipogenesis. Of significance for understanding human obesity is that chronically high levels of insulin, induced by a diet high in refined carbohydrates (in particular, sucrose), disrupt many aspects of cellular metabolism (Taubes 2008).

Although insulin secretion is closely associated with blood-glucose content, the responsiveness of pancreatic beta cells to glucose is a function of fatness, with fatter individuals secreting proportionally more insulin for a given increase in blood-glucose level (Woods and Seeley 2000). Insulin levels therefore reflect both fat stores and ongoing metabolic needs. The upper end of this range in insulin production is known as insulin resistance, a condition where a tissue fails to respond normally to blood insulin. The pancreas therefore increases the level of insulin production in order to achieve glucose absorption by muscle and adipocytes. If the pancreas is unable to meet these additional demands, blood-glucose-content regulation fails and hyperglycaemia results, leading to diabetes.

Obese individuals are therefore characterised not only by insulin resistance, in that they are less sensitive to circulating insulin, but also by compensatory increased insulin sensitivity. These two traits may be related through a positive feedback process, with obesity worsening insulin resistance, and the resulting hyperinsulinaemia exacerbating obesity (Girod and Brotman 2003). Increasing evidence suggests a role for the inflammatory load of adipose tissue, particularly deep-lying abdominal adipose tissue, in inducing insulin resistance in those obese (Shoelson, Lee, and Goldfine 2006).

The fundamental role of insulin in diverse biological processes such as growth, reproduction and immune function means that this hormone, like leptin, is critical in the allocation of energy between competing functions. Because it is also strongly associated with the comorbidities of obesity, insulin is also fundamental for understanding the trade-offs between the costs and benefits of acquiring and maintaining large energy stores.

Cortisol

Cortisol is a hormone produced by the adrenal gland in response to a variety of types of stress, including illness, trauma, fear, pain and psychological stress. Its actions broadly include the suppression of immune function, increased blood pressure and increased blood sugar levels. It therefore acts antagonistically to insulin by increasing the breakdown of glycogen and lipid in adipose tissue (Cavagnini et al. 2000). Cortisol also acts on lipoprotein lipase, especially within visceral fat which accounts for the disproportionate effect of the hormone on this adipose depot (Bjorntorp 1997). Although it is commonly referred to as the 'stress hormone', it is best considered another regulatory factor modifying metabolism, but one which is particularly responsive to signals of stress and especially relevant for understanding how psychological pressures impact on adipose tissue biology.

Leptin

Leptin differs from insulin and amylin in acting as an adiposity signal that does not track acute metabolic changes (Woods and Seeley 2000). Secreted by adipose tissue, it is often considered to represent a signal of the magnitude of lipid energy stores, but it is more appropriately considered a 'starvation signal', as many energy-requiring physiological processes do not operate in its absence (Prentice et al. 2002). However, its role in signalling energy stores remains debated because of relatively poor correlations being apparent in males in relatively lean populations (Bribiescas 2001; Kuzawa, Quinn, and Adair 2007; Sharrock et al. 2008), and longitudinal analyses suggest that it may fulfil this function more in females in relation to reproductive function (Sharrock et al. 2008).

Leptin acts on a number of receptors in the hypothalamus, the region of the brain responsible for appetite control. By inhibiting the activity of neurons involved in appetite stimulation, leptin acts to constrain energy intake whilst also increasing energy expenditure. Obese individuals tend to have high levels of leptin, suggesting that they have become resistant to its effects and hence do not down-regulate appetite as expected for the high circulating concentration (Woods and Seeley 2000).

Increasingly, leptin is understood to represent a key molecular component of numerous metabolic regulatory pathways whereby adiposity is integrated with other physiological functions. Leptin modifies the availability of oxidisable fuels, which in turn play the fundamental role in the regulation of female reproductive biology (Schneider 2004), and is produced by the placenta during pregnancy and secreted in breast-milk during lactation. Influencing both the hypothalamus-pituitary-gonadal axis and its target tissues (endometrium, placenta and mammary gland), leptin is broadly associated with all the major components of human reproduction in females, including the onset of puberty, the likelihood of conception, and (at the lower end of the nutritional status scale) the capacity for lactation. Maternal adiposity appears less strongly associated with pregnancy physiology per se, which may be attributed to the fact that lactation is substantially more costly than gestation and represents the principal drain on energy stores during reproduction (Clutton-Brock, Albon, and Guinness 1989). However, leptin also has other non-reproductive functions, for example, promoting wound healing in mice (Atanassova et al. 2007). Its role in signalling therefore varies across tissues and between functions, as described in Chapter 6.

Sex hormones

Sex hormones influence both fat and lean components of body composition and are particularly important in terms of their regional impact. The endocrine event termed adrenarche represents an increase in the secretion of adrenal androgen hormones, which accelerate linear growth prior to puberty and initiate the development of secondary sexual characteristics including fat distribution (Bogin 1988). Sex steroid hormones similarly play important roles in the accumulation, metabolism and distribution of adipose tissue. For example, testosterone and oestrogen facilitate fat deposition in the abdomen and gluteo-femoral regions, respectively (Norgan 1997), and are critical in engineering the profound sex differences in fat distribution that emerge during puberty. The effects of oestrogen may be mediated by androgen levels and the enzyme lipoprotein lipase, which, in combination with regional differential tissue sensitivity, contributes to sex-differences in fat distribution (Norgan 1997). Testosterone is also important for the increase in lean mass that occurs in puberty, especially in boys, and therefore is critical for mediating the relative allocation of stored energy to protein versus adipose tissue (Bogin 1988). Differential expression of sex hormone receptors in internal versus subcutaneous adipose tissue depots underlies their site-specific effects (Rosenbaum and Leibel 1999). Androgen receptors are more dense in visceral than peripheral adipose tissue in both sexes, whereas oestrogen receptors are reduced in the visceral tissue in males but not females. Oestrogen is strongly implicated in both the increased fatness, and its gynoid distribution, in females.

Whilst sex steroid hormones exert their strongest effects during puberty, there is growing evidence that exposure to them in fetal life may have long-term effects on phenotype. Studies using the ratio of second to fourth digit as a proxy for fetal exposure to sex hormones have shown associations between this ratio and markers of fat distribution in adulthood (Fink, Neave, and Manning 2003; Fink, Manning, and Neave 2006). As adulthood progresses, sex steroid levels decline owing to an increase in sex hormone binding proteins which reduce the concentration of the free form. Furthermore, with the cessation of gonadal oestrogen production at menopause, the gynoid fat distribution of females reverts to the android one characteristic of males (Rosenbaum and Leibel 1999). In general, within each sex, the variation in the sex hormone profile accounts for differences in body shape, with implications for both reproductive function and health profile.

Cytokines

Many of the products secreted by adipose tissue are cytokines, a group of signalling proteins contributing to cellular communication. It is our increasing awareness of the production of such messenger molecules by adipose tissue, combined with an understanding of the presence of diverse receptor sites on the adipocytes, that has revealed the regulatory role of this tissue.

Many cytokines (e.g., tumour necrosis factor-α, resistin, oncostatin, and interleukins) are pro-inflammatory, promoting inflammation and contributing to the immune system, as discussed in the following section of this chapter. However, other cytokines are anti-inflammatory and contribute to wound healing and recovery from deeper-lying tissue damage (Permana and Reardon 2007). Adiponectin, for example, is an anti-atherogenic, anti-diabetic and anti-inflammatory protein which antagonises pro-inflammatory cytokines such as tumour necrosis factor-α (Atanassova et al. 2007). Angiotensin aids control local blood flow in newly formed blood vessels, while nerve growth factor promotes the growth of nerves, which usually accompanies the growth of blood vessels (Permana and Reardon 2007). The balance between pro- and anti-inflammatory factors therefore regulates the utilisation of energy in immune response and systems of tissue repair. Cytokines are not directly implicated in differential fat deposition, but as products of adipose tissue they are fundamental to its functions as addressed in Chapter 6.

Paracrine regulation

Lymphoid tissue aggregations (e.g., lymph nodes, the omentum, thymus gland and bone marrow) are associated with local adipose tissue, though the tendency for anatomists to dissect away adipose tissue when exploring the lymphatic system has long obscured this connection (Pond 2007). Indeed, adipose tissue is always found adjacent to lymph nodes, regardless of the nutritional status of the individual (Rockson 2004). The division of lymph vessel into numerous small ducts is considered to increase the area of contact between lymphatic system components and the local adipose tissue in which they are embedded (Mattacks, Sadler, and Pond 2004).

It is now clear that this results in paracrine interactions, whereby the adipose tissue provides precursors for immune response to the lymphoid tissue. In turn, perinodal lymph nodes do not respond to fasting but rather activate lipolysis when stimulated by the lymph nodes. It has been argued that the paracrine nature of these associations 'emancipates lymphoid tissues from competition with muscle, liver and other lipid-consuming tissue for blood-borne nutrients' (Pond 2003b). Coupled with the partitioning of adipose tissue into a number of regional depots of varying size, this indicates a sophistication of the immune system in relation to local lymphoid tissue needs (Pond 2003b). Associations between adipose tissue and lymph nodes are strongest in the intra-abdominal and omental regions, which are also the frontline defence against gut infections (Pond 2003a). The importance of the link is further emphasised by their highly localised nature, with perinodal adipose tissue immediately adjacent (within 2 mm) to the lymph node responding most strongly (Pond 2003a).

Fatty acid messenger molecules, such as prostaglandins and leukotrines, are derived from unsaturated fatty acids such as arachidonic acid or n-3 polyunsaturated fatty acids. These messenger molecules act locally on dendritic cells in the lymphatic system, which process antigen material and present it to other cells of the immune system. Cytokine-stimulated lipolysis in perinodal adipocytes releases fatty acids, thereby allowing the dendritic cells to incorporate dietary fatty acids into lipid droplets and also into the cell membrane. Studies in rats have shown that variation in the fatty acid content of specific adipose depots translates into differential availability of fatty acids for the dendritic cells (Mattacks, Sadler, and Pond 2004). Studies on guinea pigs have also demonstrated the effect of dietary fatty acid composition on localised adipocyte take-up of lipid. Collectively, this indicates that perinodal adipose tissue acts as a 'lipid manager', buffering the cellular fatty acid demand of the immune system against perturbations in dietary fatty acid supply (Pond 2003a).

Other paracrine interactions are characteristic of epicardial adipose tissue, located on the myocardium and major blood vessels of the heart. This adipose depot represents a local store of energy targeted at the heart, which may buffer it during sudden shifts from physical inactivity to high energy demand. Epicardial adipose tissue has been shown to be highly metabolically active, with higher rates of fatty acid synthesis and breakdown than in other adipose depots (Iacobellis, Pond, and Sharma 2006). Inter-muscular adipose depots may likewise be characterised by paracrine interactions, further aiding control over the allocation of energy between competing tissues and functions (Pond 2003a).

Whilst paracrine interactions are essentially adaptive, the impairment of lymphatic-adipose tissues is associated with diseases in various organs and tissues. For example, persistent signals of insufficient fatty acid availability from lymph nodes in the mesentery, indicating incompetent local perinodal adipose tissue, may underlie the wrapping of fat around the bowel which characterises Crohn's disease (Westcott et al. 2006). Similar effects may contribute to lipodystrophy, and its adverse health effects, during treatment for HIV infection (Pond 2003b).

Paracrine interactions highlight the normal regulation of tissue-specific energy requirements at a level below the systemic maintenance of energy balance. Work in this area is demonstrating how individual tissues buffer their local need for both energy and functional biochemical compounds, showing how the body fine-tunes the allocation of resources between a variety of different functions. Further work in this area will doubtless elucidate the human-specific profile of adipose tissue distribution, and its similarity with or difference from that of other mammalian species. To the extent that human adipose tissue biology have responded to unique selective pressures during hominin evolution, this area is likely to prove of particular interest.

Summary

Hormones and other molecules represent the key chemical messengers allocating energy to competing adipose tissue depots and linking these energy stores with other functions, and the proliferation of research into their activities has greatly improved our ability to reconstruct plausible models of adiposity in ancestral populations. In addition to emitting signals of adiposity, adipose tissue is now known to be complex and highly metabolically active (Ahima 2006; Kershaw and Flier 2004), and despite both adipocytes and non-adipocyte components secreting a variety of factors differentially by location, it is beneficial to regard the tissue as a true endocrine organ (Kershaw and Flier 2004). Recent work emphasising the circadian rhythms of some of these hormones (Bray and Young 2006) has helped elucidate the sensitivity of adiposity to changes in diurnal behaviour patterns.

Adipocyte-derived proteins include not only the adiposity signals described above, but also a variety of factors acting on immune function (Tilg and Moschen 2006) and reproductive function (Campos et al. 2008). Furthermore, adipose tissue contains receptors for a wide range of biochemical factors, including leptin, insulin and glucagon, vitamin D, thyroid hormone, glucocorticoid, sex hormones, cytokines such as tumour-necrosis factor α and interleukin 6, and catecholamines (Kershaw and Flier 2004). It is beyond the scope of this book to explore the associations of these factors with adipose tissue in detail; however, the molecular basis of adipose tissue regulation is increasingly researched, shedding light on how adipose tissue regulates many competing energy-demanding biological functions.

3.5   Inflammation

Despite overweight and obese individuals typically lacking any overt symptoms of infection, excess adiposity is associated with a state of low-grade systemic inflammation (Visser et al. 1999; Visser et al. 2001). Adipose tissue, in particular visceral adipose tissue, is now known to secrete a range of inflammatory factors (Wisse 2004). The association between body fat level and inflammatory status is complex, with adipose tissue secreting a variety of cytokines as described above, whilst chronic inflammation appears to predispose to insulin resistance and hence weight gain. This positive feedback cycle may contribute to the notorious difficulty of reversing obesity once it develops.

The inflammatory response to infection is mediated by the cytokine signalling proteins that are often considered 'immune system hormones'. Whilst cytokines play a key role in immune function, another of their effects is to induce fat synthesis in the liver (Grunfeld et al. 1990a; Grunfeld et al. 1990b). Studies of healthy adults have shown that markers of infection are associated with decreased insulin sensitivity, equivalent to a direct association with insulin resistance (Fernandez-Real et al. 2006), and with a direct association between infection burden and fat mass (Fernandez-Real et al. 2007).

It remains uncertain as to whether insulin resistance promotes inflammation or vice versa. Although the above findings might indicate greater susceptibility to infection in those fatter or more insulin resistant, it is more likely that exposure to pathogens triggers inflammatory signals, with the resulting insulin resistance predisposing to fat accumulation. Consistent with that hypothesis, artificial viral infection has been shown in animal studies to increase adiposity (Bernard et al. 1988; Lyons et al. 1982). Insulin resistance has been proposed to contribute to the inflammatory response by influencing the availability of energetic substrates (Fernandez-Real and Ricart 1999). In those obese, surgically induced weight loss is able at least partially to reverse this low-grade inflammation, dramatically increasing insulin sensitivity (Manco et al. 2007) and hence reducing the tendency for weight gain. There may well prove to be a positive feedback association between insulin resistance and inflammation, which would contribute to the difficulty of treating obesity once it has developed.

Evidence therefore suggests that local chronic inflammation may precede systemic insulin resistance and systemic inflammation, thus initiating a positive feedback cycle. An extreme version of this theory considers that exposure to environmental pollution in industrialised societies may trigger cytokine activation and thereby visceral fat accumulation, and hence contribute to the increasing prevalence of obesity (Wlodeck and Gonzalez 2003). For example, one recent study indicated exposure to toxins in utero might contribute to childhood obesity (Smink et al. 2008). This work is of particular importance for exploring aspects of the human obesogenic niche beyond the framework of the energy balance equation, but remains speculative at present.

3.6 Dietary composition

As discussed above, the sum total of energy provided by dietary intake is a problematic variable for consideration in relation to weight gain because of the internal logic of the energy balance equation. A more productive approach is therefore to consider the composition of the diet. The majority of such research has focused on the four major dietary components, namely, protein, fat, carbohydrate and alcohol.

Initial research generally considered protein intake to be unrelated to nutritional status and weight gain. However, a number of studies have now revised this view, and data from both humans and animals show that protein plays a key role in appetite and hence energy intake (Stubbs and Tolkamp 2006). Central to understanding the association between protein intake and appetite is the concept of the p-ratio (the ratio of protein to energy in the diet) in relation to both total energy expenditure and tissue accretion. The p-ratio of the diet influences the rate of nutrient oxidation and storage, and it is also critical in the context of absolute energy and nutrient balance. A low-protein diet may, through effects on appetite, invoke compensatory increased (and hence excess) energy consumption in order to satisfy protein requirements.

An adequate intake of energy has been shown to be an important motive for animal foraging behaviour (Collier and Johnson 2000), but animals also rely on their diet to supply them with amino acids and other essential nutrients. This is particularly important during development, given the need to deposit lean tissue. When animals are confronted with a diet in which the ratio of one or more essential nutrients to energy is lower than that required, energy overconsumption may result. For example, in studies of pigs randomised to diets differing in energy-protein ratio, those on a high-protein diet deposited higher levels of lean mass. As dietary protein content decreased, daily energy intake, lipid retention and the ratio of lipid to protein in weight gain all increased (Ferguson and Gous 1997). However, it is also apparent that animals do not tolerate large excesses in protein intake and instead sacrifice energy intake to avoid the metabolic cost of disposing of large protein intakes by oxidation. Thus, low-protein diets tend to promote overconsumption, while high-protein diets have a larger effect on satiety and so limit excess energy intake. Humans show consistency with such animal studies. For example, low protein intake has been associated with increased waist circumference in a multi-ethnic Canadian population (Merchant et al. 2005).

In addition to such studies in adults, protein intake during early life has also been associated with both growth rate (Kashyap et al. 1988) and subsequent body composition. Dietary protein has been found to influence the level of the hormone Insulin-like growth factor 1 (IGF1) and hence growth rate in infants (Yeung and Smyth 2003), while rapid infant growth rates have been linked to increased IGF1 and IGF2 levels in children aged five years (Ong et al. 2002). Given associations between growth and later body composition (see Chapter 5), these findings indicate that protein intake in early life may induce subsequent adiposity (Rolland-Cachera et al. 1995).

The relative importance of fat and carbohydrate intake for body fat content is notoriously difficult to elucidate. Diets high in one of these macronutrients are often low in the other, making it difficult to determine which is the basis of appetite regulation. Covert dietary manipulations have proven important in addressing this issue (Prentice and Stubbs 1999) but may oversimplify the conditions in which free-living individuals select their dietary intake.

High-fat diets have been linked to greater body mass and fatness (Astrup 2001; Astrup 2001), while low-fat high-carbohydrate intervention diets have consistently demonstrated significant weight loss in both normal weight and overweight subjects (Astrup et al. 2002). High-fat diets have been proposed to promote the over-consumption of energy (Prentice and Stubbs 1999; Prentice and Jebb 2003). Diet-induced thermogenesis is also lower in high-fat diets, whilst fat is more effectively absorbed from the gut than carbohydrate, and hence reduces faecal energy loss (Astrup 2001).

Despite such findings, increased carbohydrate intake has also been associated with weight gain. The form in which carbohydrates are ingested may be particularly important for energy balance. Carbohydrate-containing foods can be categorised in terms of glycaemic index and glycaemic load (Foster-Powell, Holt, and Brand-Miller 2002). These terms refer to the change in blood-glucose levels following ingestion, and the consequent production of insulin. There is some evidence that high glycaemic load induces weight gain by distorting the relationship between food volume and satiety (Bell and Sears 2003), and in some individuals, high-fat diets may paradoxically induce weight loss by impeding this effect. The well-known Atkins diet, for example, appears to promote satiety through high intakes of fat and protein.

Recent work has highlighted sucrose (half glucose, half fructose) as metabolism. Whilst the glucose induces insulin secretion, the fructose is metabolised by the liver and induces triglyceride synthesis. These triglycerides are then readily taken up by adipose tissue under the influence of the insulin. High sucrose diets therefore have a high capacity to induce weight gain (Mayer 1993).

Studies of dietary intake have produced conflicting findings concerning its influence on body fatness, particularly in children (Guillaume, Lapidus, and Lambert 1998; Atkin and Davies 2000; McGloin et al. 2002). It is likely that macronutrient composition is not the only important factor, and that both style of eating and genetic variability in metabolic profile mediate associations between diet and body fat content (Rodriguez and Moreno 2006). However, it is also likely that a more detailed examination of dietary glycemic load will resolve some of these contradictions. In his recent book on the obesity epidemic, Taubes (2008) provides strong evidence that refined carbohydrate is the primary dietary determinant of body fat variability, both within and between individuals. In African populations who practice ritual fattening, for example, carbohydrate-rich foods were central to the excess weight gain, and in view of the role of insulin in lipogenesis, a case can be made that it is not possible to fatten in the absence of carbohydrates (Taubes 2008).

For example, sucrose-containing drinks have been linked to excess weight gain in children (Ludwig, Peterson, and Gortmaker 2001). One argument is that energy from fluids, less satiating than that from solid foods, may increase the risk of over-consumption (DiMeglio and Mattes 2000). However, the high sugar content, and resulting insulin response, is another plausible explanation. Alcohol likewise appears to promote positive energy balance owing to a failure to compensate for the extra energy intake elsewhere in the dietary intake, and it may also induce imbalances in metabolic pathways (Astrup et al. 2002).

The high energy density of the Western diet has also been suggested to be important in mediating associations between macronutrient composition and excessive energy intake. Typical fast foods, associated in many studies with risk of obesity, have an energy density approximately 65% higher than the average British diet, and 145% higher than traditional African diets (Prentice and Jebb 2003). It has been suggested that whilst there are strong homeostatic mechanisms acting to defend the body against energy deficits, equivalent mechanisms to restore energy balance in the face of energy surplus are much weaker (Ulijaszek 2002; Prentice and Jebb 2003). This difference is demonstrated in particular by experimental studies manipulating the macronutrient and energy content of diets. Manipulation of dietary fat content results in substantial over-consumption of energy on high-fat diets, which has been attributed to the tendency of individuals to regulate their intake on the basis of food weight rather than calorie content (Prentice and Jebb 2003). Figure 3.3 presents a schematic diagram illustrating the effects of different dietary fat content on fat balance in such manipulation studies. Nevertheless, the effect of refined carbohydrate within these different energy-density diets may still be important, as it is this component of the diet that is most likely to perturb insulin dynamics and the regulation of appetite, and hence allow chronic weight gain. The interaction of energy density, dietary composition and glycemic load therefore merits greater attention.

Thus, dietary intake is clearly an important determinant of weight gain and fat stores; however, the proportion of energy obtained from protein, fat, carbohydrate and alcohol, whether the diet is consumed as liquid or solid, and the total energy density of specific foods, may all contribute to the regulation of appetite and hence the total number of calories consumed. As with many other factors discussed in this chapter, the biology of dietary intake regulation can be assumed to have evolved in environments of energy stress, and studies of obesity risk may provide an unbalanced perspective on broader regulatory systems. Studies of animal foraging offer a valuable perspective on 'natural'

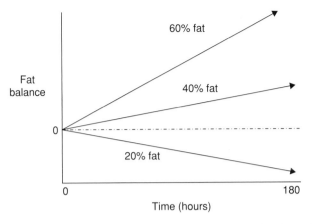

Figure 3.3. Relationship between fat content of the diet and fat balance, demonstrated through studies of covert manipulation of dietary macronutrient content. Increasing fat content promotes positive fat balance and hence weight gain. Redrawn with permission from Prentice and Stubbs (1999).

human appetite regulation (Stubbs and Tolkamp 2006), and there is a need to achieve a greater understanding of how diet composition affects energy balance in the absence of foods high in fat or processed carbohydrate.

3.7 Physical activity level

Although physical activity is often considered merely a proxy for energy expenditure, it has numerous dimensions including frequency, intensity, duration, energy costs, efficiency, work output and locomotory effects. Consequently, physical activity can be measured in a variety of units, and non-energetic indices of activity offer a major advantage over energy-expenditure outputs by potentially suffering less from confounding by body size whilst also providing substantially greater information about an individual's behaviour. Physical activity has traditionally been conceptualised as 'any bodily movement produced by the contraction of skeletal muscle that increases energy expenditure above the basal level' (Caspersen, Powell, and Christenson 1985).

Despite offering a variety of potential approaches to its investigation, the association between physical activity level and body fat has proved remarkably difficult to elucidate. In controlled circumstances, variability in activity level demonstrates a robust association with change in energy stores. Muscles comprise the largest tissue contributing to glucose uptake for storage as glycogen or oxidation, and muscle requirements therefore generate a major impact on energy balance. However, in free-living individuals this association is confounded by variability in energy intake, influenced in turn by appetite. A further important limitation pertaining to research in this area is that objective techniques for the measurement of free-living activity have only recently appeared, and there are few prospective longitudinal studies examining the impact of baseline variability in physical activity on subsequent weight change.

In most developed countries, the obesity epidemic has emerged while energy intakes have been declining (Reilly and McDowell 2003), although the degree of this decline is debatable. The measurement of energy intake is notoriously difficult, as discussed above, and it is plausible that reported declines in energy intake are merely an artefact of increasing underreporting (Rennie et al. 2005). Assuming under-reporting not to be the case, such declines in energy intake must have been matched by broadly similar declines in physical activity level. These are proposed to have been invoked by an increased level of mechanization, along with a number of trends in leisure time behaviour (Prentice and Jebb 1995). Recent research has rapidly improved our understanding of the complexity of such trends, as discussed in greater detail below.

The importance of focusing on physical activity level rather than energy expenditure was initially highlighted by the study of Prentice and colleagues (1986) reporting high levels of total energy expenditure in obese women. These findings were confirmed in children and adolescents (Bandini, Schoeller, and Dietz 1990; DeLany et al. 1995; Treuth et al. 1998), but they are in direct contradiction of other studies suggesting that those overweight are less active than their peers (Dietz, Jr. and Gortmaker 1985; Maffeis, Zaffanello, and Schutz 1997; Dionne et al. 2000). Clearly it is not the high energetic costs of physical activity in those obese that would predispose to weight gain and fat deposition, but rather a reduction in the intensity, duration or frequency of specific behaviours. Body fat is now known to contribute to energy expenditure, both through increasing basal costs and also through increasing the total energy expenditure on account of increased body weight (Garby et al. 1988). Recently, Ekelund and colleagues (2002) measured both physical activity and energy expenditure in obese and nonobese adolescents, and they demonstrated significantly lower activity level but no difference in energy expenditure in those obese (Figure 3.4). These studies therefore demonstrate the importance of assessing physical activity in non-energetic units.

The simplest approach to investigating the association between physical activity and fatness comprises cross-sectional studies. These have been conducted in a variety of age groups, but with particular interest in children, and have generally been consistent in demonstrating an inverse association between physical activity and body fat level. For example, a recent meta-analysis of fifty studies of children identified a significant but moderate inverse association, but with the strength of this association varying markedly according to the methods used to assess physical activity and body fat (Rowlands, Ingledew, and Eston

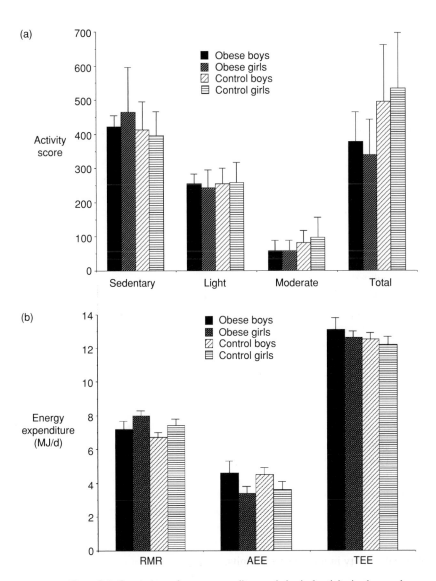

Figure 3.4. Comparison of energy expenditure and physical activity in obese and nonobese adolescents, based on data from Ekelund and colleagues (2002). (a) Daily physical activity level categorised as the number of minutes (and standard deviation) spent sedentary or occupied in light or moderate activity, or if the total number of activity counts (and standard deviation). (b) Resting metabolic rate (RMR), activity energy expenditure (AEE) and total energy expenditure (TEE), or adjusted for fat-free mass and expressed as mean expenditure per day and standard error.

2000). Recently, using objective techniques, activity level and body composition were assessed in 5,500 children aged 12 years (Ness et al. 2007). In both sexes, total physical activity level was directly associated with lean mass and inversely associated with total and trunk fat mass. Nevertheless, interpretation of such cross-sectional data is difficult. Whilst higher activity level might protect against weight gain, greater body weight might conversely inhibit physical activity.

This scenario was elegantly illustrated in a detailed study of physical activity and body composition during infancy (Li et al. 1995). At each of three time points, these authors observed the expected inverse association between body fat level and activity level. However, whilst baseline body fat predicted subsequent activity level, there was no significant association between baseline activity level and subsequent body fatness. These data therefore suggest that high body fat content may constrain activity level in this age group, and it is plausible that such an association may continue through childhood. In a longitudinal study of children's body composition, (Goulding et al. 2003) those fattest at baseline gained the greatest fat mass subsequently. Whilst this finding might merely reflect the expression of genetic predisposition, it is also possible that this scenario is generated by a cumulative constraint of physical activity as fat accumulates. An intriguing hypothesis here is that reduced physical activity is a symptom, not a cause, of greater weight gain owing to the lethargy induced by the high levels of insulin that promote weight gain during diets high in refined carbohydrate (Taubes 2008).

Despite the prediction, based on the logic of the energy balance equation, that physical activity should either reduce body fat content, or constrain weight gain over time, longitudinal studies have produced conflicting evidence concerning this issue. Once again, longitudinal studies vary in the quality of the methods used to assess physical activity, and studies of childhood weight gain are furthermore confounded by the expectation of normal growth. Based on a systematic literature review, Fogelhom and Kukkonen-Harjula (2000) discerned an inconsistent effect of baseline physical activity level on subsequent weight gain, and furthermore they found a stronger association between weight gain and *change* in activity level. A more recent systematic review was able to capitalise on an increased proportion of studies measuring activity with objective methods, but it remained equally cautious in its conclusion, and studies measuring energy expenditure in children and adolescents were particularly inconsistent (Wareham, van Sluijs, and Ekelund 2005). Clinical trials promoting physical activity to prevent weight gain in adults have tended to demonstrate modest success of the intervention, either in preventing weight gain relative to controls, or in achieving modest weight loss. Similar trials in children have been less successful, with only a minority demonstrating differences in follow-up body composition between the intervention and control groups (Wareham, van Sluijs, and Ekelund 2005).

Many specific aspects of behaviour are increasingly associated with the risk of weight gain, but with the underlying mechanism poorly understood. Many studies have associated television viewing with obesity (Dietz, Jr. and Gortmaker 1985), but this may derive not only from a low metabolic rate during the activity itself but also from effects on appetite or exposure to advertisements for particular foods. Short sleep duration, again in contradiction to energy balance logic, has been associated in many studies with increased weight (Patel and Hu 2008), including in prospective studies commencing in early childhood (Al Mamun et al. 2007). Mechanistic studies have demonstrated that short sleep duration is associated with decreased leptin and increased ghrelin concentrations, indicating that manipulation of sleep patterns alters markers of satiety and hunger (Taheri et al. 2004). Increasingly, these hormones are understood to be regulated by circadian clocks, which are sensitive to cues of photoperiodicity (Bray and Young 2006). Both decreased sleep, and evening or night-time television viewing, may therefore induce weight gain through hormonal mechanisms, although it is also possible that metabolic perturbations associated with weight gain disrupt sleep patterns.

Whilst evidence increasingly emerges of the association between sedentary behaviours and weight gain in industrialised populations, studies of non-industrialised populations provide clearer evidence of the way in which high physical activity level constrains the accumulation of fat stores. Low BMI is of course a function both of constraints on energy intake as well as high demand for physical activity. However, in many non-Western societies the demands of activity remain high, particularly in women, who were reported to contribute more than 40% of agricultural labour in 52 developing countries, and more than 50% in 24 of them (Lukmanji 1992). Seasonal demands for physical labour in agricultural populations are associated with profound reductions in body weight, although fluctuations in energy intake also contribute (Ferro-Luzzi 1990; Ferro-Luzzi and Branca 1993; Simondon et al. 2007; Lawrence et al. 1987a; Lukmanji 1992). However, as modernisation takes places, the strength of the impact of physical activity rapidly decreases. In rural South African women, for example, walking is associated with reduced BMI and car travel with increased fatness (Cook, Alberts, and Lambert 2008).

Although activity level is an important factor affecting body energy stores, it also promotes appetite and hence stimulates energy intake. Under conditions of plentiful energy availability, activity levels appear to act primarily to prevent excess weight gain but may be increasingly impeded from doing so as the excess weight accrues, possibly owing to metabolic as well as biomechanical effects. Under a tighter constraint on energy supply, physical activity induces loss of energy stores. In both scenarios, reducing the level of physical activity allows fat deposition, providing that energy intake remains stable.

3.8   Eating style

In addition to the macronutrient composition of the diet consumed, it is also important to consider the manner in which foods are eaten. Food intake is characterised by a variety of physiological behaviours which are extremely sensitive to a range of social cues. For example, whilst at the physiological level there are a number of positive drives for initiating and maintaining feeding (e.g., sight, smell, palatability) operating antagonistically with negative feedback signals (learned associations, gastrointestinal and metabolic signals) (Blundell and Greenough 1994), learned behaviour can impact on these mechanisms by influencing sensory likes and dislikes (Mela and Catt 1996). The palatability of food is therefore a function of conditioned preferences for taste, texture and odour (Mela and Catt 1996) and for energy content. The preference for foods high in sugar or fat content may be considered an inherent human trait, selected in our evolutionary past as discussed in Chapter 8.

Apparent lack of constraints on dietary consumption may account for the tendency for humans to over-consume calories 'passively' (Prentice and Jebb 2003), that is, inadvertently. The physiological regulation of food consumption involves sensations of hunger (the drive to eat), appetite (the desire for specific foods), satiation (fullness after a meal) and satiety (the inhibition of future hunger) (Jequier and Tappy 1999). Each of these factors is sensitive to environmental conditions such as food quality and the physical/social setting.

Hunger is closely associated with circulating insulin levels and plays a key role in promoting feeding during waking hours and satiety during sleep (LeMagne 1971). The anticipation of foods acts on a number of metabolic processes including an initial wave of insulin secretion that occurs before blood-glucose levels actually rise. In this way, even the thought of food can increase appetite (LeMagne 1985), which in turn indicates how social cues may impact on the physiological regulation of appetite.

Studies of twins suggest a strong genetic component in feeding behaviour (DeCastro 1997), but social factors clearly also exert powerful influences. Religious and social conventions often contribute to the range of foodstuffs available for consumption, and commercial companies likewise attempt to influence eating patterns and foodstuffs. Social cues appear to be particularly important in human eating patterns and are likely to derive from our primate heritage (Ulijaszek 2002). For example, the presence of other individuals acts as a powerful influence on the amount of food eaten by an individual during a meal, unless energy availability is constrained (DeCastro 1990). Overall, Ulijaszek has suggested that 'what distinguishes human eating from mammalian feeding is the extent to which personal and psychological constraints may operate in addition to food availability constraints, and the ease with which consumption can exceed physiological requirements when there are few environmental food availability constraints' (Ulijaszek 2002). These social and cultural influences may interact with components of personal temperament, discussed in greater detail below.

3.9   Parenting behaviour

The association between infant behaviour and subsequent body composition is best considered within the theoretical context of 'begging theory'. Traditionally, early life was considered a period of harmonious corporation between mother and offspring. Evolutionary theory conflicts with this assumption, however, and generates the prediction that the two parties will compete against each other over how much of a finite pool of maternal resources should be invested in the offspring (Trivers 1972; Haig 1992). Begging theory was developed in order to understand the role of behaviour in the transfer of resources from mother to offspring.

In broods with multiple offspring, vocalisations might simply represent scramble competition between individuals, with parents responding to those begging the loudest. In broods with only a single offspring, however, such scramble competition does not apply, and vocalisation can more reasonably be considered a signal of demand. Recent developments in begging theory have therefore been addressed to the hypothesis that offspring signal their relative state or need, and that parents respond to this information through their allocation of resources (Godfray 1991; Godfray 1995). Zahavi (1975; 1981) proposed that reliable or honest signals between individuals could evolve only if the signals were costly. Signalling then becomes more costly to cheaters than honest individuals. In the case of offspring soliciting food, the relationship between offspring state and signal intensity is negative, with offspring in the poorest state and most in need of resources predicted to signal at the highest intensity (Wells 2003a).

Many studies testing such begging theory have been conducted on birds, given the primary role of behaviour in such animals' provisioning. Experimental studies confirm that offspring begging may carry a cost in terms of attained size (Rodriguez-Girones, Enquist, and Cotton 2001; Kilner 2001). Food deprivation experiments have likewise demonstrated that hungrier offspring beg more than those recently fed (Mondloch 1995; Price and Ydenberg 1995; Weary and Fraser 1995). Data from single brood species generally support the notion that begging intensity reflects offspring need, whereas further studies indicate that parents respond to signals of hunger and provision appropriately (Wells 2003a).

Several studies have demonstrated that human infant crying is costly in energetic terms (Thureen et al. 1998), and at three months of age, irritability is a significant determinant of total daily energy expenditure in free-living infants (Wells et al. 1996). At six weeks of age, approximately 40% of total energy intake is diverted to growth, with this value declining to around 30% at three months, 10% at six months, and 5% at one year of age (Wells and Davies 1998). Crying is most likely to function as a handicap when growth rate is highest (Kilner 2001), and in humans, the infant crying rate is indeed maximal during the period of highest growth rate (Wells 2003a). Kilner (2001) predicted that offspring solicitation should become more extravagant as growth rate declines. As the human growth rate slows through infancy, however, its regulation switches from nutritional to endocrine mechanisms. Childhood growth is suppressed by hormonal regulation (Sibly, Calow, and Nichols 1985), hence there is only a brief window of time during which postnatal nutrition can increase linear growth rate. When the regulation of growth is not nutritional, expensive begging behaviour is predicted to fail to fulfil the role of handicap as proposed by Zahavi (1975) and may function as blackmail rather than an honest signal of need.

In the breast-fed infant, crying may therefore act as an honest signal of need in the months immediately following birth. Both average crying time and milk volume intake increase steadily during the first three months of life, after which both traits reach a plateau and then decline. Stability of crying behaviour is also highest during this period, which is furthermore the time when catch-up growth can reduce growth deficits incurred during gestation. In later infancy and early childhood, irritability evolves into a range of behaviour including 'fussing' and tantrums. In contemporary populations, the availability of new foods may alter the tension that underlies costly signalling and generate a shift in the ratio of costs to rewards (Wells 2003a). For example, contemporary infants can receive formula milk, as well as high energy-density foods during the weaning period and subsequently. Early infant behaviour may therefore predict not only growth rate, but also subsequent fatness.

Consistent with the general notion of crying as a begging signal, Carey (1985) reported an association between parental perception of infant 'difficultness' and subsequent infant weight gain, suggesting that 'difficult' infants (those that cry or fuss more) might be fed more frequently in order to quiet them. Subsequently, similar relationships were demonstrated between maternally rated infant irritability and childhood body fatness (Wells et al. 1997; Wells et al. 1997; Agras et al. 2004), whereas a covert study of maternal behaviour further found that mothers use foods and drinks to resolve distress even when not attributed to

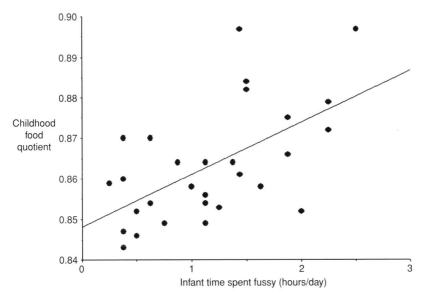

Figure 3.5. Association between maternally rated infant temperament (time spent being 'fussy') at 12 weeks, and childhood food quotient (an index of the relative sugar content of the diet) at three years. $r = 0.58$, $p < 0.001$. Data from Wells and colleagues (1997).

hunger or thirst (Wells 1998a). Figure 3.5 shows that fussier infants tended to consume a diet with higher food quotient (an index of the carbohydrate content) in childhood. Figures 3.6 and 3.7 show that infants rated by their mothers as easily soothable were leaner and more active in childhood (Wells et al. 1997).

These studies, though requiring further confirmation, suggest that increased infant vocal signalling does elicit increased nutritional provisioning by the parent, detectable over time in weight gain and fatness. Maternal temperament itself is an important aspect of such associations, and ratings of temperament are clearly a dynamic construct derived from the interactions between two individuals. Whilst infants with a vigorous feeding style become fatter in childhood (Agras et al. 1987), maternal mood also predicts the perception of infant behaviour. British mothers who are more anxious about their infant's feeding behaviour tend to stop breast-feeding earlier and introduce solids at a younger age (Hellin and Waller 1992). More broadly, this research highlights the role of behavioural signals circulating between individuals, analogous to the biochemical signals represented by hormones that circulate within individuals, in regulating body energy stores.

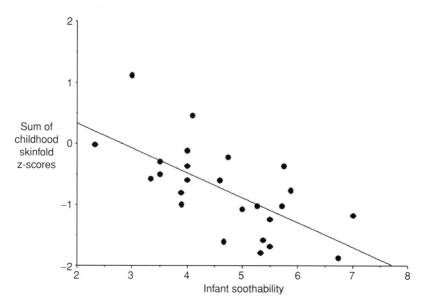

Figure 3.6. Association between maternally rated infant temperament (soothability) at 12 weeks, and childhood fatness (measured by sum of triceps and subscapular skinfold thicknesses) at three years. $r = -0.66$, $p < 0.001$. Data from Wells and colleagues (1997).

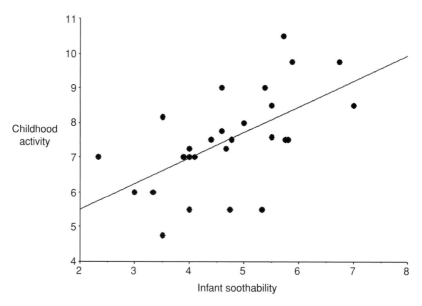

Figure 3.7. Association between maternally rated infant temperament (soothability) at 12 weeks, and childhood activity level at three years. $r = 0.59$, $p < 0.001$. Data from Wells and colleagues (1997).

3.10   Psychological stress

Much interest has been directed to the hypothesis that psychological or psychiatric factors may induce weight gain and hence be implicated in a predisposition to obesity. In general, studies have failed to identify clear differences between those of normal weight and those obese (Wadden and Stunkard 1987). Psychiatric disorders appear no more common in obese individuals and in the nonobese population. Although depression and anxiety may have a higher prevalence, this may arise in part because of a stigmatisation of the condition (Wardle 1999). However, this conceptual framework has important limitations, as it focuses on two categories of individuals rather than the entire spectrum of body weight.

Pioneering work in children by Carey and colleagues (1988) found that indices of 'difficult temperament' were positively correlated with weight for height percentile gains between four to five years and eight to nine years, and a high level of negative emotionality was associated with increased body mass in adolescent boys (Ravaja and Keltikangas-Jarvinen 1995). In a study of 619 Finnish men and women, high levels of negative emotionality predicted increased adult BMI, although no independent effect on waist girth was apparent (Pulkki-Raback et al. 2005). Several studies have further noted a positive association between childhood depression and adult overweight, using both case-control studies and continuous analysis (Pine et al. 1997; Pine et al. 2001).

Similar findings have emerged from studies focusing on exposure to stress, rather than on temperament itself. In a study of 5,867 twin pairs aged 18 to 54 years at baseline, high levels of stress predicted increased weight gain over the following six years (Korkeila et al. 1998). Indices of psychosocial stress and hostility have been correlated with obesity in cross-sectional and longitudinal studies (Ravaja and Keltikangas-Jarvinen 1995; Raikkonen, Matthews, and Salomon 2003; Raikkonen et al. 1996). Internalised racism was correlated with body fat distribution and insulin resistance in Carribean adolescents and adult women (Chambers et al. 2004; Butler et al. 2002), and in a prospective study, indices of anger measured at baseline predicted visceral adipose tissue 13 years later in adult women (Raikkonen et al. 1999). As discussed above, cortisol is now understood to induce central fat distribution, and these findings therefore have a clear endocrinological basis. Animal studies also illustrate how exposure to stress alters appetite, leading to a preference for high energy density foods (Dallman et al. 2003).

Whilst certain types of stress are thus associated with increased central fatness, in other contexts psychosocial or psychological stress can significantly reduce appetite, body weight and energy stores. These effects are not inconsistent with those described above, for central adiposity tends to be preserved during chronic under-nutrition as discussed in Chapters 4, 6 and 7. The most extreme expression of such stress-related effects is the condition of anorexia nervosa, where psychological state contributes to drastic reductions in energy intake, sometimes exacerbated by compulsive exercising. This condition is associated with preferential loss of peripheral adiposity (Zamboni et al. 1997), and hence highlights the prioritization of central fatness. The tendency for stress in industrialised societies to occur in sedentary individuals with access to plentiful food may therefore account for the findings discussed above (Siervo, Wells, and Cizza 2008).

Whilst biomedical research has inevitably focused on psychosocial stress as a risk factor for obesity and the metabolic syndrome, these data illustrate more broadly that adiposity is sensitive to social environmental stimuli, and they demonstrate a link between energy stores and the psychosocial environment.

3.11   Fat deposition in a toxic environment

All the issues referred to above are relevant to behaviour or traits of the individual. At the broadest level, however, it is important to consider the environment itself as a contributing factor to weight change and fat deposition by facilitating a lifestyle at odds with the environment in which our species evolved (Eaton, Konner, and Shostak 1988). According to this approach, the obesity epidemic can be attributed primarily to environmental changes in recent decades, as opposed to changes in composition of the gene pool which are considered to be relatively small. Obesity can be considered the 'normal' response to an 'abnormal' environment (Egger and Swinburn 1997), now popularly conceptualised as the 'obesogenic' environment. However, in the opposite direction, ecological niches often expose the majority of individuals to poor nutrition, often in concert with high physical activity load, for example, in the cases of imperialism, economic transition, or civil war. In Victorian India, imperial economic policies contributed directly to high levels of starvation amonsgt agricultural workers (Davis 2002), and during more recent economic reforms in Siberia, body mass index along with markers of cardiovascular risk declined in adolescents (Denisova et al. 2007).

The strongest evidence in support of the concept of a 'toxic obesogenic environment' derives from so-called natural experiments, where large sections of a population have been exposed to the Western lifestyle. Such natural experiments include, for example, migrants to the United States of America, who have encountered markedly different living conditions in contrast to those who have remained in the traditional environment.

Data on the effects of the toxic environment are available for populations of native Americans, for Pima Indians living either in rural Mexico or Arizona, and Australian aborigines (Poston and Foreyt 1999). In all cases, those exposed to the industrialised lifestyle show substantially greater energy intake, higher body fat content, and increased risk factors for cardiovascular disease (Poston and Foreyt 1999). These data place emphasis on the concept of exposure to specific influences which alter the behaviour of individuals at multiple levels. Changes in total energy intake, dietary composition, the adoption of sedentary behaviour and concomitant reductions in physical labour and exercise, and the uptake of practices such as smoking, are all implicated in this context. An increased contribution of refined carbohydrate to the energy supply appears a key candidate mechanism (Taubes 2008). Where appetite is perturbed, passive overconsumption of energy through exposure to high-carbohydrate and high-fat diets may then be considered to be driven by commercial interests rather than individual intention. An increasing disparity in socioeconomic status further influences exposure to such factors, with those poorest in general least able to avoid their influence.

Central to the Western industrialised lifestyle is the fundamental influence of the capitalist economic model and its connection with a variety of state influences. Capitalist economics utilises a wide range of mechanisms to manipulate the behaviour of individuals so as to maximise profits. Amongst the most important of these mechanisms are those promoting the volume of food consumed, and those promoting high-carbohydrate and high-fat foods which manipulate sensations of satiety. Nutritionists in the United States have noted inconsistency between the economic policies promoted by those responsible for agricultural productivity, and the public health campaigns promoted by those responsible for population health. Fundamental to US agricultural policy is continued expansion, resulting in overproduction and the flooding of the market with inexpensive energy-dense food products (Tillotson 2004).

In addition to the impact of the capitalist economic model, more subtle effects derive from the interactions of individuals. In an innovative analysis, Christakis and Fowler (2007) considered the spread of obesity over three decades in a large social network of Americans, studied between 1971 and 2003 through the Framingham Heart Study. Although the only available outcome was body mass index, the study was able to provide indications of the risk of being categorised as obese according to the proportion of others who are obese in an individual's social network. The study highlighted that although the risk of obesity increased if spouses or siblings were obese, the greatest effect was

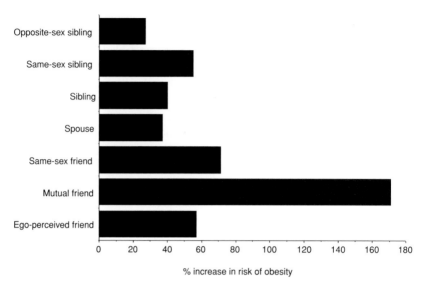

Figure 3.8. Percentage increase in the risk of being categorised obese, according to the obesity status of different members of the individual's social network. Based on data from Christakis and Fowler (2007).

apparent if a mutual friend was obese. The odds ratios for different categories of family and social acquaintance are illustrated in Figure 3.8. Some categories showed no significant risk, including neighbours, or opposite-sex friends. The risk was greater for same-sex than opposite-sex siblings, and greater for mutual friends (i.e., both parties considered each other as friends) than where only the ego or the alter perceived the friendship.

The authors of the study concluded that obesity might be considered to 'spread' through social ties, with the most plausible explanation being that underlying predictive behaviours are transmitted. This finding, supported by the fact that some non-kin relationships exerted stronger effects than kin relationships, may derive from the fact that many of the behaviours associated with obesity are promoted by social interaction, for example, eating and social circumstances, and a tendency either to participate socially in sports or not. The analyses indicated that non-kin effects were not attributable entirely to any tendency of those who are obese to form friendships with others who are likewise obese.

Whilst these studies have focused specifically on obesity, they illustrate the fundamental point that body fatness is sensitive to broader ecological pressures, in particular those which remove individual control over behaviour, and those which impact via social influence, as discussed in Chapter 10.

Summary

This chapter has shown that body fatness is influenced by factors operating at a wide range of biological levels. Looking in the reverse direction to that presented above, fat deposition or oxidation arises through a variety of enforced or proactive behaviours which impact directly on an individual or on those around them, and which are in turn sensitive to predisposing or constraining influences deriving from the broader social and physical environment. Substantial physiological research has elucidated how these factors and behaviours influence disease load, dietary intake and the components of energy expenditure, and hence induce positive or negative energy balance. There is a growing, though still incomplete, understanding of the hormonal signalling systems that represent the mechanisms whereby energy is allocated between different tissues and functions, and furthermore allocated to or withdrawn from specific adipose depots. Our understanding is growing as well in reference to the circuits within the brain on which these signals operate. Recent studies have shown how adipose tissue itself contributes to such metabolic interactions by secreting as well as responding to a diversity of signalling molecules. Finally, there is substantial evidence for genetic variability in the level and metabolic activity of adipose tissue, and also in the epigenetic alteration of gene expression in relation to environmental factors acting through the life-course. However, adipose tissue is also an active endocrine organ that regulates the allocation of incoming and stored energy between different functions. This then generates positive and negative feedback associations between energy stores and the factors that influence them.

As will become clearer in subsequent chapters, this multi-level sensitivity is an indication of the way in which energy stores are interconnected with many biological functions and have evolved to respond to behavioural, physiological and transgenerational stimuli, as well as bearing the legacy of ancestral experience through genotype. Studies of adipose tissue and physiological function are increasing rapidly in number, both in humans and in other animal species, yet for each biological level, much work remains to be done in order to integrate the findings with our understanding of other levels. Nevertheless, this chapter provides a basis from which subsequent chapters aim to review the diverse functions of adipose tissue and to propose likely selective pressures that may have shaped adipose tissue biology in our species.

4 *The ontogenetic development of adiposity*

Human body composition undergoes profound change during the life course. In this pattern our species is unique, indicating that the ontogenetic profile of growth and development is a key feature of human biology. Increases and decreases in body fat content imply changes in the relative value of adipose versus lean tissue at different ages, and between the sexes. In old age in particular, there is substantial variability in fatness between populations, yet this can be interpreted as an interaction with variability in energy availability, mediated by declines in lean mass.

The aim of this chapter is to describe the changes in body composition from fetal life to old age. As was the case for the between-species and within-species comparisons reviewed in Chapter 2, ontological data have been collected with a variety of methods. However, ignoring the varying prevalence of obesity, the ontological pattern of development of body composition shows a relatively high degree of consistency between populations. Although subtle differences between populations are likely to occur, reflecting similar variability in growth rate, it is possible to use data primarily from industrialised populations to illustrate the main changes, provided that analysis is restricted to those within the normal range of weight. Indeed, age-associated changes in the regional adipose tissue distribution characteristic of obesity themselves carry clues about the ontogeny of adiposity (Wells, Cole, and Treleaven 2008). Thus, although further data from non-Western populations remain much needed, the overall life-course pattern of adiposity is reasonably well established.

Recent data from specialised research centres have been obtained using the most sophisticated measurement techniques available and are relatively robust to the variability in the physical and chemical composition of lean mass that confounds simpler body composition methodologies. Whilst the raw data are therefore accurate, their interpretation requires appropriate adjustment for variability in body size. Following the approach described in Chapter 2, the data presented in this chapter make use of the same graphical outputs, whereby lean and fat masses and their regional distribution are adjusted for body size or physique.

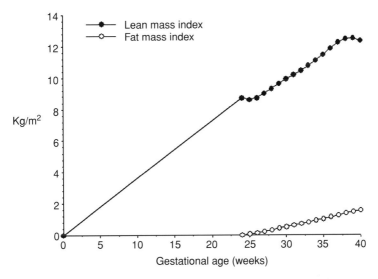

Figure 4.1. Growth of lean mass and fat mass in fetal life, adjusted for length and presented as fat mass index and lean mass index. There are no data prior to 24 weeks, hence the linear trajectory for lean mass index between conception and this age is only an assumption. Based on the data of Ziegler and colleagues, derived from chemical analyses of 22 stillborn infants with no major congenital abnormalities and aligned to conform with standard data for fetal weight gain (Ziegler et al. 1976).

4.1   Fetal life

Measurements using ultrasound images have shown contrasting patterns of accretion of fat versus lean tissue during the second half of pregnancy (Bernstein et al. 1997), supporting prior findings from autopsy studies. Ziegler and colleagues (1976) used data on 22 stillborn infants of 22 weeks gestational age or more to construct a 'reference fetus', providing weekly values for gains in weight, lipid, and other chemical components. These data clearly indicate a lack of any substantial fat deposition prior to the third trimester of pregnancy. Thus, although published data from earlier trimesters are lacking, the approximate pattern of lean and fat deposition must be as shown in Figure 4.1. During the final trimester of pregnancy, the earlier pattern is gradually reversed such that the daily increment in lipid finally exceeds that in protein in the last few weeks of pregnancy (Figure 4.2). This pattern of fat accretion results in the accumulation of around 400 g of fat by birth in an infant of average birth weight (around 3.5 kg) (Figure 4.3).

Measurements of infants born preterm using dual-energy X-ray absorptiometry (DXA) provide support for these autopsy reconstructions, showing, for

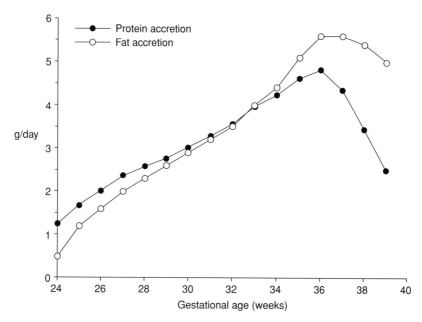

Figure 4.2. The accretion of fat versus protein between 24 weeks of gestational age and term, based on extrapolations from the body composition data of the same 22 stillborn infants described in Figure 4.1. Fat accretion lags behind protein accretion in the late second trimester, but it exceeds protein accretion in the late third trimester. Based on the data of Ziegler and colleagues (1976).

example, that whereas lean mass scales linearly with weight, fat mass scales exponentially (Koo, Walters, and Hockman 2000), in agreement with the ultra-sound data (Bernstein et al. 1997). Further data obtained using DXA indicate a sex difference in these patterns of weight accretion, with males gaining more lean mass than females and less fat mass (Rigo et al. 1998). However, as discussed below, after adjustment for length the sex-difference in lean mass at birth is greater than that in fat mass.

According to data on skinfold thicknesses obtained in 13,609 preterm infants born at varying gestational ages, these increases in total fat mass are accompanied by a relative decline in the level of subcutaneous fatness relative to weight, suggesting either the use of fetal fat stores to fuel growth (Guihard-Costa et al. 2002) or the redistribution of energy between subcutaneous and internal depots. Such declines are furthermore more rapid in males, indicative of their greater accretion of lean mass compared to females (Guihard-Costa et al. 2002). Thus, the profile of adiposity during fetal life appears to involve both absolute accumulation and regional mobilisation. The degree of fetal adiposity has in

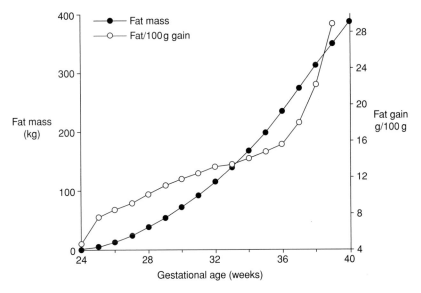

Figure 4.3. The accelerating increase in fat mass, augmented by an accelerating rate of fat deposition per 100 g of tissue gained, through the final 16 sixteen weeks of pregnancy. These data, like those in Figure 4.2, demonstrate the surge of fat deposition (roughly approximate to a doubling in fat mass) that normally occurs in the last month of pregnancy. Based on the data of Ziegler and colleagues (1976).

turn been associated with maternal weight gain and adiposity (Guihard-Costa, Papiernik, and Kolb 2004), as discussed in greater detail below.

4.2   Body composition at birth

Birth represents a key stage in development, not only because it represents the shift from placental to oral nutrition, but also because it provides the first opportunity to apply direct body-composition measurements. Early data from stillborn infants indicated that the percentage fat of male term infants was approximately 12% (Owen et al. 1966). These data, though potentially inaccurate due to loss of water in between the time of death and analysis, were relatively consistent with isotope dilution studies of 51 male newborns, giving an average of 11% fat (Yssing and Friis-Hansen 1966). The subsequent calculations of Fomon and colleagues (1982), which extrapolated from a variety of data sources to provide estimations across the entire infant period, proposed slightly higher values of 13.7% in males and 14.9% in females. Table 4.1 summarises data from a variety of different studies conducted in Western populations.

Table 4.1. *Whole-body composition at or close to birth in Western populations*

Author	Technique	Sex	Birth weight (kg)	Length (cm)	%fat	Lean mass index (kg/m²)	Fat mass index (kg/m²)
(Ziegler et al. 1976)	Modelling	B	3.45	49.8	11.2	12.3	1.6
(Fomon et al. 1982)	Modelling	M	3.54	51.6	13.7	11.5	1.8
		F	3.32	50.5	14.9	11.1	1.9
(Catalano et al. 1995)	TOBEC	B	3.34	49.8	12.0	11.8	1.6
(Harrington et al. 2004)	MRI	B	3.30	50.2	10.3	11.8	1.4
(Butte et al. 2000)*	Multi-component	M	3.79	52.5	11.4	12.1	1.6
		F	3.64	52.0	14.2	11.5	1.9
Average					12.5	11.7	1.7

* 2 weeks post-partum
M = male, F = female, B = both sexes

The notion of a sex difference in early life body composition was supported by the empirical data of Butte and colleagues, who used multi-component models and derived values of 11.4 and 14.2 % fat in males and females, respectively, at two weeks after birth (Butte et al. 2000). However, after adjustment for length (i.e., by calculating the lean mass index and fat mass index), it is the lean component of weight that represents the main difference between the sexes. Catalano and colleagues (1995) likewise reported greater birth weight and lean mass in males, but no difference between the sexes in fat mass. Peripheral measurements of subcutaneous adipose tissue also show only a small sex difference, whereas in fetal life, males have a more central fat distribution than females (Rodriguez et al. 2004). Although data from DXA support the hypothesis of sex differences in both lean mass and fat mass (Rigo et al. 1998), this technique is known to have limitations for soft tissue assessment.

A study based on anthropometric measurements explored the contributions of lean and fat mass variability to birth weight (Catalano et al. 1992). This study suggested that although fat mass in the newborn comprised on average only 14% of birth weight, it explained 46% of the variance. This finding is consistent with studies comparing body composition in different categories of birth size. The greater birth weight of infants born to obese mothers is associated with increased neonatal fat mass, but not lean mass (Sewell et al. 2006). At the other end of the scale of nutritional status, a comparison of infants born within the appropriate range of weight for gestational age versus growth-restricted infants demonstrated significant differences in the distribution of adipose tissue (Harrington et al. 2004). According to magnetic resonance imaging (MRI) measurements, the total amount of adipose tissue was reduced in the

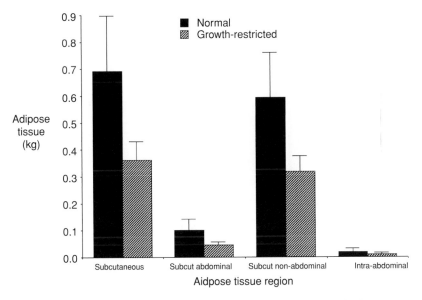

Figure 4.4. Amounts of adipose tissue by regional location in normal and growth-restricted infants. Growth-restricted infants have reduced levels of total, abdominal and non-abdominal subcutaneous fat but similar levels of intra-abdominal fat. Based on data from Harrington and colleagues (2004).

growth-retarded infants, and this difference was detectable in subcutaneous adipose tissue whether in the abdomen or elsewhere (Figure 4.4). However, intra-abdominal adipose tissue did not differ significantly between the two groups, suggesting that the allocation of energy to this adipose depot is maintained during growth restriction (Harrington et al. 2004). Birth composition is also associated with parity, with firstborns having 0.45 and 0.31 SD deficits in adiposity in boys and girls, respectively (Shields et al. 2006).

Birth-weight differs between ethnic groups (Harding, Rosato and Cruickshank 2004) (Shiono et al. 1986), with for example mean deficits relative to white infants of 246 g in black infants, 210 g of Asian infants, and 105 g in Hispanic infants (Shiono et al. 1986). However, little information is currently available on the adiposity implications, and variability in head size appears the main component of population variability (Leary et al. 2006a). A detailed anthropometric study by Yajnik and colleagues (2003) from Pune in India demonstrated that lower birth weight in the Indian neonates, compared to a sample of normal birth-weight infants from the United Kingdom, was associated with substantial deficits in body weight and abdominal circumference, but much smaller deficits in triceps and, in particular, subscapular fatness (Figure 4.5). These data, confirmed by MRI studies (Modi et al. 2009), have

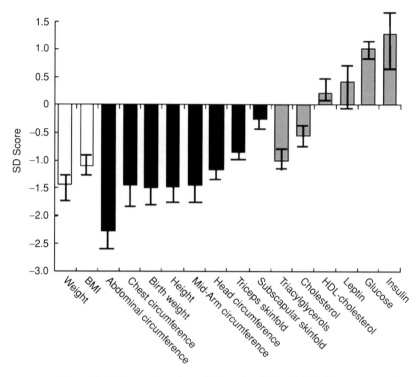

Figure 4.5. Differences in outcome between low birth weight Indian neonates and normal birth weight neonates from the United Kingdom. The Indian neonates have deficits in all anthropometric outcomes, but those for adiposity indices are smaller than those for lean mass indices. These body composition differences are associated with metabolic differences. Reprinted with permission from Yajnik (2004).

been described as the 'thin fat' phenotype (Yajnik et al. 2003), referring to a low level of lean mass in conjunction with a high level of adiposity. Because Asians at older ages have been found to have a greater body fat content for a given BMI value (see on), Yajnik and colleagues have considered whether the thin-fat phenotype might be specific to Asians. However, the MRI data described above suggested it may relate at least in part to low birth weight per se. Furthermore, the findings of Yajnik have been reproduced in some (Krishnaveni et al. 2005) but not all studies of Indian neonates (Muthayya et al. 2006).

Intriguingly, a link between low birth weight and increased fatness has been reported in another context, that of high altitude. Ballew and Haas (1986) found that Bolivian neonates, born at an altitude of around 3,600 m in La Paz, had 340 g lower birth weight and a 1 cm reduction in birth length compared to a sample born at low altitude, but had a sum of five skinfolds almost 5 mm greater. The authors argued that this enhanced level of adiposity makes under-nutrition due to reduced utero-placental perfusion an unlikely explanation and suggested that hypoxia may constrain fetal accretion of lean mass, resulting in the allocation of energy to fat instead. Interpreting this change in allocation is difficult (see Chapter 7), since greater fat stores may be an adaptive strategy rather than a pathological effect. Furthermore, the results were the opposite of those reported from other high-altitude populations, where neonates had reduced fatness (Haas, Baker, and Hunt 1977; Wiley 1994b). Such between-population differences may derive from a differential length of occupation of such harsh environments (influencing the opportunity for genetic adaptation), or a confounding of the effect of altitude by variability in maternal nutritional status (Wiley 1994a). Despite low absolute levels of adiposity in neonates in a high-altitude population in Ladakh, India, the amount of neonatal fat was significantly inversely correlated with the risk of infant mortality (Wiley 1994b).

The thermal environment during gestation may also impact on fetal body composition. A study of 1,750 elderly adults identified significant variability in BMI and the prevalence of obesity according to month of birth, with exposure to cold associated with increased BMI and obesity risk (Phillips and Young 2000). Whilst this study lacked any information on body composition early in life, and might also be demonstrating associations with lean mass rather than adiposity, animal studies do suggest that exposure to lower temperatures before or after birth induces adiposity (Young and Shimano 1998; Symmonds et al. 1992), possibly through changes in maternal dietary intake or the functions of brown adipose tissue. At the other end of the range of temperature, heat stress has been associated with reduced average birth weight (Wells and Cole 2002b), although whether this association extends to fetal fatness is unknown.

During the first few days of postnatal life, the newborn typically loses around 5 to 10% of birth weight (Rodriguez et al. 2000). This weight loss comprises both body water and body solids, indicative of the oxidation of fat stores (Rodriguez et al. 2000). Neonatal glycogen stores are utilised within a few hours of birth (Shelley 1966), requiring the infant to switch to fat metabolism (Pond 1984). The mobilisation of fat stores is critical for supporting metabolism during the first week of life, as the intake of breast-milk is low during this period (Evans et al. 2003) and colostrum has lower energy density than more mature breast-milk (Hosoi et al. 2005).

4.3 Body composition during infancy

As at birth, body composition during infancy has been assessed using a number of different techniques, making it difficult to generalise across studies. In the reference child, Fomon and colleagues (1982) modelled a systematic increase

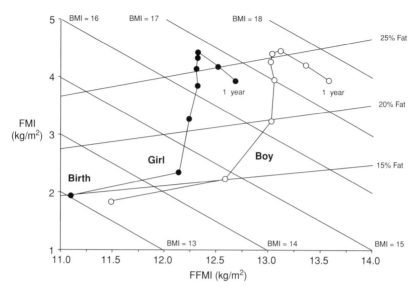

Figure 4.6. A Hattori graph showing changes in body composition during infancy, with sequential data points at birth, 1, 2, 3, 4, 5, 6, 9 and 12 months. At each age, boys and girls have similar levels of body fat relative to their height; however, boys have substantially greater lean mass than girls. Based on data from Fomon and colleagues (1982) and reproduced with permission from Wells (2000).

in lean mass relative to height in both sexes, but with the males having greater lean mass at each age compared to females, along with a similar pattern of fat accumulation in both sexes (Figure 4.6). Empirical data are quite consistent with these findings regarding the pattern of fat deposition, but they provide only limited support for the lean mass model, probably owing to small sample sizes.

Figure 4.7 summarises empirical data from a number of studies in Western populations using different techniques (Fiorotto, Cochran, and Klish 1987; de Bruin et al. 1995b; de Bruin et al. 1995a; Wells and Davies 1998; Butte et al. 1999; Butte et al. 2000; Olhager et al. 2003). Despite this methodological variability, a clear pattern of fat deposition emerges, with a sharp increase in fat-mass index during the first six months of postnatal life, followed by a very modest decline in the next 18 months. It is notable that this second period contrasts with the model of Fomon and colleagues (1982), whose simulations indicated a more substantial decline in body fat after the end of infancy. This difference may well derive from the different historical time periods from which the raw data were obtained, since contemporary infants are exposed to a more obesogenic environment. On the basis of the single study obtaining regional

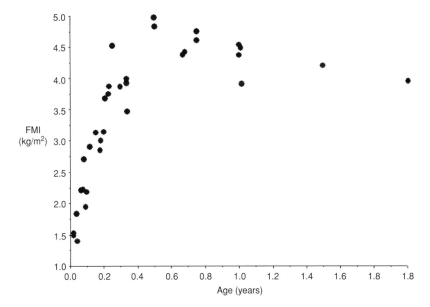

Figure 4.7. The association between fat mass index and age during infancy, using data from a variety of different techniques. Data obtained from de Bruin et al. (1995b); Fiorotto, Cochran, and Klish (1987); Wells and Davies (1998); Butte et al. (1999; 2000); and Olhager et al. (2003).

data using MRI, the majority (averaging around 90%) of the increase in fatness occurs in subcutaneous depots rather than internal fat (Olhager et al. 2003).

These studies generally agree that absolute differences between the sexes in fatness remain negligible, such that the average additional weight of boys can be attributed to maintaining greater lean mass (de Bruin et al. 1995b; Olhager et al. 2003). This means that proportionally, females have a higher percentage fat and fat-lean ratio (Davies 1992).

Numerous studies have addressed the impact of feeding mode on infant body composition. The results have not been wholly consistent between studies, which has been attributed to the fact that breast-fed and formula-fed infants tend to differ in their family backgrounds. Larger studies, which have matched the diet groups for family characteristics, have shown a tendency for formula-fed infants to experience greater fat deposition (Butte et al. 1995; Dewey et al. 1993). This finding has led to interest in whether breast-feeding 'protects' against excess weight gain, perhaps through a biological property such as leptin, or whether higher intakes of formula-milk and earlier introduction of complementary feeding increases weight gain. This debate remains unresolved, but it is of interest that larger studies in different populations tend to find

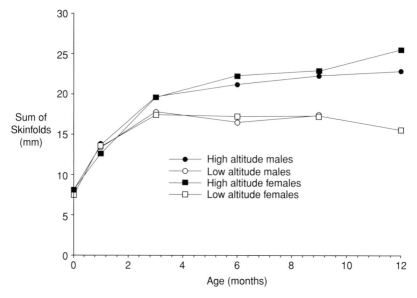

Figure 4.8. The association between age and the sum of skinfolds in male and female infants from high- or low-altitude populations in Bolivia. Based on data from Haas and colleagues (1982).

negligible systematic effects of breast-feeding on later body fatness (Toschke et al. 2007; Victora et al. 2003).

Despite having lower body weight and reduced length compared to those at low altitude, Bolivian infants living at high altitude showed significantly increased levels of triceps and subscapular skinfolds through the first year of life (Figure 4.8) (Haas et al. 1982). As described above for neonatal body composition, however, these findings are inconsistent with those from Peru (Haas 1976), and it is not clear whether low birth weight or altitude is the key factor.

Given the strong association between thermal environment and birth weight (Wells and Cole 2002b), we can be confident that absolute levels of adiposity are substantially decreased in hotter environments. Whether this effect reflects the preferential accumulation of fat stores by the infant in colder environments, or the maternal constraint of offspring weight gain in hotter environments (Wells 2002), remains unclear. The high birth weight typical of populations such as Iceland may simply reflect increased lean mass (Gunnarsdottir et al. 2004). Similarly, any impact on regional fat distribution is also not known. The impact of the thermal environment on infant body composition thus represents an intriguing area for further research.

Body composition is also altered following catch-up growth. However, the differences in body fatness appear to manifest primarily after, rather than during, infancy (Ibanez et al. 2006), as is discussed in greater detail in Chapter 5.

4.4   Body composition during childhood and adolescence

The general pattern of tissue accretion during childhood and adolescence was described in the reference child of Fomon and colleagues (1982) and the reference adolescent of Haschke (1989). These datasets were generated by collating information from a number of different sources, simulating body composition values, and smoothing all data onto the 50th percentile of the United States growth reference. Actual measurements were restricted to infancy and later childhood, hence most values were predicted on the basis of extrapolation from these time points. Furthermore, the data on body fatness derived mainly from skinfold measurements and hence did not address internal fat stores. Despite these limitations, these datasets provided the first attempt to model the ontogenetic development of body composition during childhood and adolescence. More recent datasets indicate that the general pattern identified by these pioneering simulations is valid, but that a number of factors influence the magnitude of adiposity at any one time point.

From the end of infancy, absolute lean mass shows a relatively consistent increase with age, up until puberty when the sexes diverge. Absolute fat mass likewise increases; however, when these two tissue masses are adjusted for height, the relative allocation of energy between the two compartments, and sex differences therein, becomes clearer. Thus in both sexes, relative fatness declines from infancy towards around six years of age, and then increases again but substantially more in girls than boys (Figure 4.9). From six years onwards, the majority of gains in BMI comprise lean mass in boys, but fat in girls. Thus these idealised datasets imply that the pattern of tissue accretion during adolescence is very different, with females achieving final lean mass relatively early, and boys continuing to accrete it up until around 20 years of age (Figure 4.10).

Unpublished data from my research group on 249 individuals measured with the criterion-four component model confirms these broad patterns, even though the new data were collected up to four decades after the data on which the modelling of Fomon and Haschke was based, and hence incorporate exposure to the obesogenic environment. Mean fat mass index in boys shows relatively little change between the age of 5 and 20 years, whereas in girls there is a systematic increase during the same period (Figure 4.11). Relative lean mass in boys shows a marked upward shift from around 12 years of age, whereas in

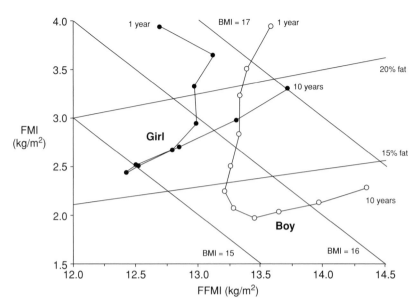

Figure 4.9. A Hattori graph showing changes in body composition during childhood, with sequential annual data points from 1 to 10 years. Relative fatness declines in both sexes until around six years of age, but less so in girls than boys. Both sexes start to gain in BMI from around six years, but boys gain more lean mass and less fat mass than girls. Based on data from Fomon and colleagues (1982), and reproduced with permission from Wells (2000).

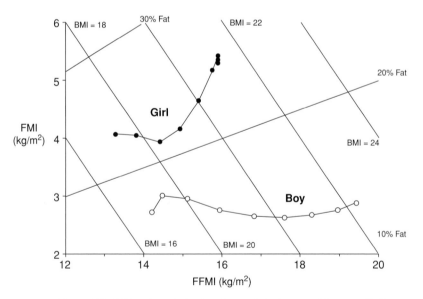

Figure 4.10. A Hattori graph showing changes in body composition annually from 10.5 to 18.5 years during adolescence, with boys gaining primarily in relative lean mass and girls gaining primarily in relative fat mass. Based on data from Haschke (1989), and reproduced with permission from Wells (2006).

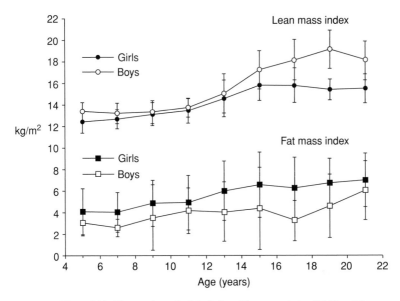

Figure 4.11. Mean and standard deviation of lean mass index (LMI) and fat mass index (FMI) in 252 boys and 267 girls aged 4 to 21 years, measured using the four-component model. Boys have greater LMI than girls from early adolescence onwards. Girls have greater FMI throughout childhood, especially so during adolescence. These data broadly confirm earlier simulations by Fomon (1982) and Haschke (1989), though the differences in both body components are less extreme. Based on unpublished data from Williams, Fewtrell and Wells.

girls there is minimal increase after around 13 years (Figure 4.11). The data also confirm that whilst sex differences are apparent earlier in life, they are greatly amplified during pubertal development (Wells 2007c).

Also evident in these graphs is the wide range of variability in both relative lean mass and relative fatness, reflecting the fact that both components account for variability in BMI. Studies have demonstrated that childhood obesity is associated with greater lean mass as well as fat mass (Wells et al. 2006), while eating disorders likewise deplete both components of weight (Nicholls et al. 2002). These changes are not distributed equally across the whole of the body; rather, the greater lean mass associated with overweight is found disproportionately in the leg, whereas greater fat is found disproportionately in the trunk region (Wells et al. 2006). Variability in BMI therefore impacts not only on absolute tissue masses, but also on their regional distribution (Figure 4.12).

As discussed in Chapter 2, many of the commonly used anthropometric ratios for assessing fat distribution are problematic from a conceptual and statistical perspective (Wells and Victora 2005). Nevertheless, when comparing the sexes

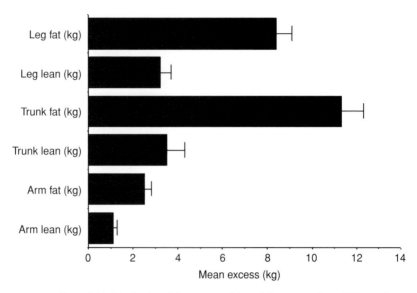

Figure 4.12. Distribution of the excess weight, relative to non-obese children, of obese children aged years obtained using dual-energy X-ray absorptiometry. Whilst both lean and fat masses are significantly increased in each of the arms, trunk and legs, the greatest increases in adiposity are in the trunk and legs. Based on data from Wells and colleagues (Wells et al. 2006).

such approaches are likely to be capable of discerning the direction of differences, although they may fail to capture the magnitude accurately. Figure 4.13 illustrates, using the data of Rolland-Cachera and colleagues (1990), relative consistency between boys and girls in the ratio of limb to trunk skinfold thicknesses up until around 14 years of age, followed by a rapid divergence such that boys develop a more central fat distribution towards adulthood. Figure 4.14 also illustrates the divergence in subcutaneous fat that occurs around 11 years of age, with boys transiently increasing in fat prior to their pubertal growth spurt in lean mass, in contrast to girls who accrete subcutaneous fat earlier and more consistently throughout childhood and adolescence (Rolland-Cachera et al. 1990; Malina and Bouchard 1991). In addition to gender-variability in regional subcutaneous fat distribution, the sexes also differ in their relative accretion of fat in subcutaneous versus deep-lying adipose tissue depots. These changes appear to occur primarily during puberty, as such sex differences appear relatively modest in childhood, and internal fat deposition is relatively low in both sexes (Arfai et al. 2002). By adulthood, the differences are more evident, as discussed in the next section.

The extent to which the general pattern of body-composition development is consistent across populations has been inadequately studied. Broadly, data from industrialised populations indicate that the major ethnic groups within the

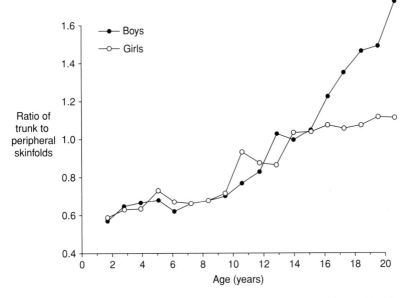

Figure 4.13. Associations between age and the relative ratio of trunk to peripheral skinfold thicknesses in French children from 2 to 19 years. The two sexes have very similar values until around 14 years of age, when boys demonstrate a substantially more central distribution owing to reduced levels of peripheral fatness. Based on data from Rolland-Cachera and colleagues (1987).

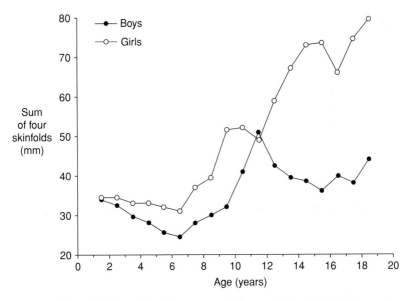

Figure 4.14. Associations between age and the sum of four skinfold thicknesses in French children from 2 to 19 years. Girls have moderately greater skinfold thicknesses until 10 years of age, and then substantially greater skinfold thicknesses from 12 years. Boys experience a brief increase in skinfold thicknesses prior to puberty. Based on data from Rolland-Cachera and colleagues (1987).

US population all illustrate the same fundamental pattern, showing both the sex differences described above and the changes in body fatness (Malina 2008), although there is also variability therein (Kimm et al. 2001). As reviewed in Chapter 2, all studied human populations show a significant gender dimorphism in fat mass, and with the exception of a few African populations[1], males also show systematically greater lean mass. Thus, given that these differences must materialise during adolescence, a common human pattern of tissue accretion during childhood and adolescence may be broadly assumed. However, subtle ecological variability in relation to the tempo of tissue accretion has yet to be addressed, and there remains a dearth of information on body composition variability during development in non-industrialised populations.

Differences in the tempo of fat accumulation are likely to be greatest in girls and to relate to the schedule of pubertal maturation. The timing of puberty appears to be regulated by a number of complementary mechanisms, including genotype, intrauterine conditions and nutrition (Parent et al. 2003). Environmental stresses including social factors can also exert effects; for example, loss of the father in early life has been shown to accelerate pubertal maturation (Belsky, Steinberg, and Draper 1991). The mean age at menarche has changed dramatically in recent decades (Parent et al. 2003), and contemporary variability between populations reflects an underlying variability in various environmental and genetic factors.

During puberty, female fat accumulation occurs disproportionately in the gluteofemoreal region, with most of the 10 to 20 kg of fat deposition in Western populations directed to this depot (Lassek and Gaulin 2007a). A high proportion of fat in this depot furthermore accelerates the onset of menarche, whereas a more central fat distribution delays menarche (Lassek and Gaulin 2007a). The impact of pubertal status on menarche is found across populations, though the pattern of fat accretion varies (Bhadra, Mukhopadhyay, and Bose 2005; Sampei et al. 2003; Kimm et al. 2001). Such differential strategies of fat accumulation in relation to maturation are integrated more generally with growth variability, as reviewed in Chapter 5. Early menarche is associated not only with increased body fatness well into adulthood (Pierce and Leon 2005) but also with reduced final height (Onland-Moret et al. 2005).

4.5   Adulthood

As discussed in Chapter 2, after adjustment for size, gender dimorphism is apparent for both tissue masses, whilst further variability is also evident in

---

[1] Possibly an artefact of using equations developed in European populations in African populations.

regional fat distribution. As a proportion of weight, adult males average around 14% fat but can range from 7% to 27%, while females average 26% fat but can range from 14% to 41% (Norgan 1994b). If the data reviewed in Chapter 2 are expressed relative to height, the average values for fat mass index are 3.2 (range of 1.1 to 7.4) and 5.8 (range of 2.6 to 12.1) kg/m^2 for males and females, respectively, whereas those for lean mass index are 18.4 (range of 14.0 to 22.5) and 16.2 (range of 13.7 to 19.2) kg/m^2, respectively. During prolonged starvation, fat content can fall to around 4 to 6% of weight in men, (Friedl et al. 1994) whereas at the other extreme, fat can exceed 60 or 70% of body mass in the obese, with some estimating that 80% fat may be attainable in those of extreme weight (Shell 2002). Fat can be differentiated into central and storage fat, as reviewed by Norgan (1997). Essential fat, located in the bone marrow, the heart, lungs, liver, kidneys, intestines, muscles and central nervous system, comprises around 3% of body mass in men and 9% in women. It comprises both triglycerides and other compounds such as phospholipids, and it is considered higher in women owing to fat located in the breast and pelvic region. Storage fat comprises around 12% and 15% of body mass in men and women, respectively (Norgan 1997).

Males distribute fat predominantly on the trunk and abdomen, whereas in women it is deposited primarily on the buttocks and thighs. This difference in distribution is regulated by the sex hormones testosterone and estrogen, partly acting through the enzyme lipoprotein lipase (Norgan 1997). Adipose tissue contains receptors for estrogen, androgens and progesterone; however, the expression of these receptors differs between internal and subcutaneous depots (Rosenbaum and Leibel 1999). Androgen receptors are more dense in internal adipose tissue in both males and females, whereas estrogen receptors are reduced in internal adipose tissue in males but not females. Estrogen is strongly implicated in the increased fatness and gynoid fat distribution of females, and the cessation of gonadal estrogen production at menopause is associated with the emergence of a more android fat distribution (Rosenbaum and Leibel 1999). This converging of female phenotype on that of males in old age is demonstrated by data on body shape (Wells, Treleaven, and Cole 2007; Wells, Cole, and Treleaven 2008).

Detailed gender differences in regional fat distribution are revealed by imaging studies. Studies using DXA illustrate reduced lean mass in the arms of women compared to men, but similar amounts of lean in the trunk and legs (Nindl et al. 2002). Conversely, females have similar fat in the trunk, but significantly more in the arms and legs (Figure 4.15). Several studies have assessed internal adiposity versus subcutaneous adiposity in the abdomen using CT or MRI scanning. These studies collectively indicate the emergence of increased visceral adiposity in males during adolescence, with this difference increasing

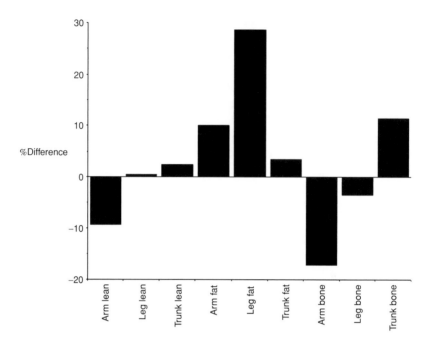

Figure 4.15. Sex differences in regional body composition using data obtained by dual energy x-ray absorptiometry. Women have relatively less lean mass in the arms, but similar levels in the trunk and legs, compared to men. Conversely, women have relatively greater fat in the arms and legs, but similar levels in the trunk. Based on data from Nindl and colleagues (2002).

through adulthood (de Ridder et al. 1992a; Seidell et al. 1988; Weits et al. 1988), but the magnitude of these differences is unclear without adjustment for body size. Using MRI scanning, Kuk and colleagues found that, for a given waist circumference, there were significant sex differences in total adipose tissue in the abdomen, and in the subcutaneous versus internal distribution (Kuk et al. 2005). Whereas women had greater subcutaneous fat, men had significantly greater visceral fat, with this difference increasing at larger waist circumference. In general, men show greater accumulation of visceral fat with age than women; however, this difference decreases when older men are compared with post-menopausal women (Kotani et al. 1994).

The impact of variability in relative weight status on body composition is shown in Figure 4.16. Across the range of BMI, all adipose tissue depots increase with increasing weight (Thomas et al. 1998). In absolute terms, excess fat is disproportionately gained as subcutaneous fat (the difference between fattest and leanest groups is 48 litres). However, on a relative basis, visceral fat mass was around five times greater in those fattest compared to those

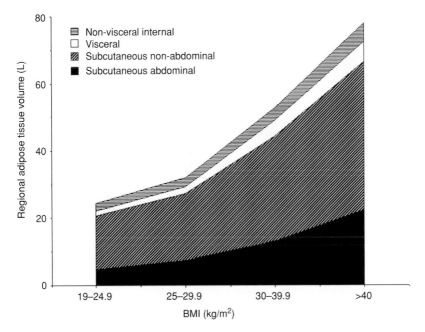

Figure 4.16. Relationship between body mass index and regional volumes of adipose tissue measured by magnetic resonance imaging in 47 adults divided into four categories of BMI. Although in absolute terms, excess fat is disproportionately gained as subcutaneous fat, visceral fat is over three times greater in those fattest. Lean mass also increases with BMI, estimated at 40, 44, 46 and 50 kg in the four BMI groups. Based on data from Thomas and colleagues (1998).

leanest, whereas subcutaneous fat was only three times greater. As in children, lean mass also increases with BMI, thus supporting the hypothesis of Webster and colleagues (1984) concerning the composition of weight gain comprising around 70% fat.

Data from a large sample of Swiss men and women show a minor increase in relative lean mass during adulthood until around the seventh decade, when a clear decline occurs (Figure 4.17). In both sexes, body cell mass tends to decline, owing in part to declining activity levels. Such declines in lean mass might be assumed to predict concomitant decreases in fatness given the tight association between lean mass and fatness observed between species as discussed in Chapter 2. Inconsistent with that assumption, relative fat mass in the Swiss *increases* steadily in both sexes throughout adulthood (Figure 4.17) (Schutz, Kyle, and Pichard 2002). In the Fels Longitudinal study in the United States, fat mass increased by 0.37 and 0.41 kg per year in men and women, respectively (Guo et al. 1999). Similar increases have been reported elsewhere (Hughes

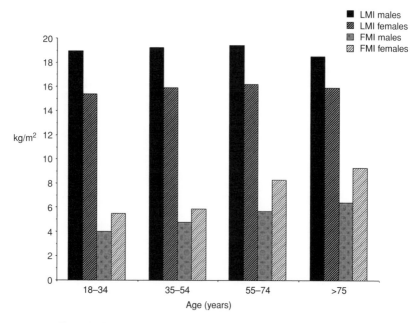

Figure 4.17. Fat mass index and lean mass index in male and female adults across the adult age range, using data from Switzerland obtained using bioelectric impedance analysis. Lean mass index begins to decline after 70 years of age, whereas fat mass index accumulates steadily across the adult lifespan, especially in women. Based on data from Schutz and colleagues (2002).

et al. 2002; Cohn 1987); however, in less-affluent conditions elderly men were found to show substantial declines in the sum of ten skinfold thicknesses over a sixteen-year period (Parizkova and Eiselt 1980). Similarly, the elderly in non-industrialised populations are often relatively malnourished (Strickland and Ulijaszek 1994; Ahmed et al. 1998). These data suggest that outside of the Western economic niche, both lean mass and absolute adiposity tend to decline in old age, probably owing in part to reduced productivity of the individual himself or herself. However, where food is plentiful and not dependent of physical effort, adiposity need not decline.

Increases in adiposity in Western women tend to be even greater than those in men, as revealed by studies of body shape. Although in both sexes there is a tendency in Western populations for BMI to increase with age, whereas associations of male shape with age are accounted for by such BMI changes, female shape alters profoundly with age *within* narrow categories of BMI. Thus in normal weight, overweight and obese women, age is associated with significant increases in central adiposity, as revealed by waist and bust girths, while thigh girth decreases (Wells, Cole, and Treleaven 2008). Such changes in body shape are associated not only with age, but also with the menopause in women which is independently associated with increasing intra-abdominal fat (Poehlman 2002). These changes imply that in women, shifts in the regional allocation of adipose tissue are more significant than changes in the sum total of stored energy.

4.6   Pregnancy

The energetics of pregnancy and lactation, and the accompanying body composition changes, are highly variable between populations, as reviewed previously (Durnin 1987b; Lassek and Gaulin 2006). During the first months of pregnancy, women in Western populations tend to gain 3 to 4 kg of weight (Hytten and Leitch 1971), primarily as fat and deposited particularly in the hip and thigh regions (Forsum, Sadurskis, and Wager 1989; Sidebottom, Brown, and Jacobs, Jr. 2001; Rebuffe-Scrive et al. 1985). A similar increase in weight and lower body fatness is also seen in women from other settings, provided that energy intake is not constrained (Piperata et al. 2002; Piers et al. 1995). However, in poorer circumstances pregnancy may induce little or no weight gain, as demonstrated by data from several Asian or Pacific populations (Alam et al. 2003; Guillermo-Tuazon et al. 1992; Kardjati et al. 1990; Thongprasert et al. 1987). In the more severe hungry season in the Gambia, when energy intake is severely constrained and the demand for physical activity is high, a loss of 4.7 kg fat during pregnancy was observed (Lawrence et al. 1987a).

The total energy cost of pregnancy (comprising energy contained in the fetus, maternal fat deposition and maintenance energy costs) thus appears to vary substantially between populations. Such variability has been interpreted as functional plasticity offering survival value to fetuses under varying ecological conditions (Prentice and Goldberg 2000). In view of such plasticity, it is extremely difficult to describe 'normal' fat accumulation during pregnancy. One approach is to estimate the energy requirements compatible with the level of maternal weight gain associated with minimal levels of fetal morbidity and mortality. Data from the WHO have proposed this to be 12.5 kg. Hytten and colleagues (Hytten and Leitch 1971; Hytten 1991) have then estimated the details of such a pregnancy as comprising the fetus (3.40 kg), the placenta (0.65 kg), the uterus (0.97 kg), breast tissue (0.40 kg), blood volume expansion (1.45 kg), increased extracellular and extravascular water (1.48 kilograms) and maternal fat accumulation (3.35 kg). Importantly, the last two of this list are the non-obligatory ones, such that although most women accumulate fat during pregnancy, this is not inevitable as demonstrated by the data from the Gambian farmers (Lawrence et al. 1987a). Towards the end of pregnancy, some of this

Table 4.2 *Energetics of pregnancy in the 5-country study*

	Scotland	Netherlands	Gambia	Thailand	Philippines
Age (y)	27.7	28.6	25.9	23.0	23.4
Height (m)	1.62	1.69	1.58	1.52	1.51
BMI (kg/m^2)	21.8	21.9	20.6	20.6	19.5
Fat mass (kg)	15.1	17.7	10.3	11.3	11.2
% fat	26	28	20	24	25
FMI (kg/m^2)	5.8	6.2	4.1	4.9	4.9
Birth weight (kg)	3.37	3.46	2.98	2.98	2.88
Weight gain (kg)	11.7	10.5	7.3	8.9	8.5
Fat gain (kg)	2.3	2.0	0.6	1.4	1.3
Energy costs					
Fetus (MJ)	34.0	34.4	29.9	29.9	28.9
Placenta (MJ)	3.0	3.1	2.3	2.5	2.5
Expanded tissues (MJ)	12.1	12.3	10.4	10.4	10.1
Maternal fat (MJ)	106.0	92.0	27.6	64.4	59.8
BMR (MJ)	126	144	8	100	79
Total (MJ)	281	286	78	208	181

Data from Durnin (1987b)

accumulated fat may be redirected to fund the growth of the fetus (Hytten and Leitch 1971), reflected in declines in some skinfold thicknesses (Forsum, Sadurskis, and Wager 1989).

Notwithstanding such recommendations for healthy weight gain, the five-countries study, comparing women from the Gambia, the Philippines, Thailand, Scotland and the Netherlands, illustrates the extreme population-variability of fat accumulation during pregnancy (Durnin 1987b). Baseline body composition and subsequent changes were estimated on the basis of weight and skinfold thickness measurements, with adjustment for height aiding comparability between populations. Table 4.2 summarises the energetic components in the different populations. Absolute weight gain was greater in the industrialised populations, but similar (14 to 20%) as a proportion of baseline weight (Durnin 1987b). The total energy cost of pregnancy in the Gambia was less than 30% that in Scotland, owing primarily to incorporating only 6.3% of the additional basal metabolic costs and 26% of the fat deposition costs. Thus, substantial fat accumulation is clearly not necessary for viable pregnancy; however, this lack of post-conception weight gain stands in contrast to the high levels of body fat at the time of conception. In all five populations, baseline body fatness was 20% or more, suggesting that the key issue is a 'metabolic guarantee' for subsequent costs, with further 'income' boosting energy stores if available but not actually prerequisite. In the Gambian women, this metabolic guarantee is so successful that they actually experienced a net gain of 46 MJ through pregnancy (Durnin 1987b). That fat gains are not necessary for viable pregnancy is also indicated by the lack of effect of high gestational weight gain in African-Americans on birth weight (Schieve, Cogswell, and Scanlon 1998), including adolescents (Nielsen et al. 2006), who might be predicted to benefit most from additional energy accumulation.

Whilst the energy costs of pregnancy are clearly directed to growing and supporting a viable fetus, there are external ecological forces which may act in opposition. Heat stress may constrain both maternal weight gain and fetal growth, since increased adiposity increases vulnerability to heat stress through several physiological mechanisms (Wells 2002). Consistent with that hypothesis, there is an inverse association between thermal load and birth weight between populations, after adjusting for economic circumstances, maternal size and disease load (Wells and Cole 2002b). Thus, the balance between dietary energy intake and demand for physical activity on subsistence is not the only factor determining weight accumulation.

Where energy intake is unconstrained, the weight gain accompanying pregnancy may persist over the longer term. In a prospective cohort study of 2,788 women, aged 18 to 30 years, women who remained nulliparous were compared with women who had experienced a single pregnancy. Those experiencing pregnancy gained 2 to 3 kg more weight over five years and had greater increases in waist-hip ratio independent of that weight gain (Smith et al. 1994). Similar findings have been reported from Brazil (Rodrigues and Da Costa 2001), and successive pregnancies tend to induce cumulative weight gain (Keppel and Taffel 1993; Harris et al. 1997). However, over and above any change in absolute weight, there are further changes in fat distribution. Lassek and Gaulin (2006) suggested that each cycle of pregnancy and lactation mobilises fat from the gluteofemoral store (see also below) but redeposits it in the abdomen. This redistribution accounts for the increasing waist-hip ratio seen with increasing parity in industrialised populations. However, unpublished 3D photonic data from the United States Sizing Survey show that changes in abdominal shape occur in equal magnitude both in women of child-bearing age, and in middle-aged and older women. Hence, the importance of parity itself in these changes remains to be confirmed.

4.7   Lactation

During lactation, the gluteofemoral fat stores accumulated during adolescence and through pregnancy tend to contribute to the energy burden of lactation. Once again, however, their relative role in this regard appears to vary in relation to dietary energy intake, and the Gambian farmers showed a capacity to gain weight during lactation during the energy-plentiful harvest season whilst losing weight during the hungry season (Prentice et al. 1981).

Where energy intake is constrained, studies from diverse populations consistently show that lactation induces weight loss (Alam et al. 2003; Butte and Calloway 1981; Barbosa et al. 1997; Guillermo-Tuazon et al. 1992; Schutz, Lechtig, and Bradfield 1980), though the degree may be relatively modest (Piers et al. 1995). The fat stores mobilised to meet these energy demands are those of the lower body (Rebuffe-Scrive et al. 1985), such that subcutaneous fat on the hip and thigh decreases (Motil et al. 1998; Barbosa et al. 1997). The use of adipose tissue in this regard protects lean mass, which has been found to be stable over the period of lactation (Motil et al. 1998).

Lactation is substantially more costly in terms of energy requirements than pregnancy, with the typical breast-milk production of 800 ml per day imposing an energy demand of 2.5 MJ (WHO 1985). These demands, considered to be broadly similar regardless of the nutritional status of the mother (Brown et al. 1986), may be partially or largely met through increased dietary energy intake. Mothers of low BMI have an extraordinary capacity to maintain breast-milk production (Prentice, Goldberg, and Prentice 1994), although the volume is reduced in those of very low weight (Bailey 1965). However, maternal nutritional status may deteriorate across successive pregnancies if the energy expended on lactation is not recouped during the inter-birth interval, and 'maternal depletion' has been observed in numerous populations (Alam et al. 2003; Merchant, Martorell, and Haas 1990; Adair 1992; Little, Leslie, and Campbell 1992; Adams 1995).

Summary

Overall, body fat is as remarkable for its consistent age-associated fluctuations across populations (with the exception of old age) as it is for its inter-individual variability at any time point. Humans gain and lose fat at different periods of the life-course in a pattern that has clearly been incorporated into the human genome. Infants are born with substantial fat, and they accrete further adipose tissue into early childhood but then tend to lose it. Subtle sex differences, indicative of genetic effects, are apparent from fetal life onwards but become substantially stronger from puberty. Males deposit little fat and allocate it primarily to the abdomen. Females accumulate almost twice as much but allocate the majority to the lower body and breasts. Sexual dimorphism in fat content and distribution is maximal in early adulthood and decreases steadily with age so that the elderly are relatively similar in fat distribution. However, the absolute level of adiposity in old age appears strongly dependent on the nutritional niche, such that those in the seventh and subsequent decades may range across a wide spectrum of nutritional status.

These regional shape differences imply that fat has contrasting primary functions according to age and gender, indicative of shifting strategies for optimising the level of, and utility of, energy stores. Within this broad age- and sex-associated pattern, there is substantial between-individual variability. Individuals of any age and of either sex can be substantially below or above the average level of fatness and can themselves alter markedly and rapidly in relation to ecological factors. For example, despite its fundamental role in reproduction women appear able to gestate and lactate whilst losing weight. This can be attributed to the tendency even of women with low BMI to comprise around 20% of their weight as fat (Kulin et al. 1982; Lawrence et al. 1987b).

These characteristics illustrate that adiposity is both a fundamental human trait under genetic influence, and yet a highly plastic trait sensitive to the environment. These traits are not contradictory, for energy stores are by their nature a form of phenotypic flexibility. An evolutionary perspective on the age- and sex-specific strategies for regulating energy stores is presented in Chapter 7.

5   *The life-course induction of adiposity*

The previous chapter discussed the ontogenetic development of body composition, highlighting how body fat content and distribution varies substantially across the life-course and between the genders. Sexual dimorphism is apparent from fetal life onwards, but it increases significantly from puberty and then declines again in old age. This pattern of development is unique to humans and appears broadly to be found in all populations. However, over and above this ontogenetic pattern, it is important to consider the different within-lifetime growth trajectories of individuals and the way in which early environmental exposures influence subsequent adiposity.

Understanding of the life-course induction of lean mass and adipose tissue will clarify the integrative role that it performs in relation to a variety of biological functions, whilst also highlighting the trans-generational effects whereby the adiposity of one generation responds to the experience of previous ones. Because adiposity is a relative concept, expressed relative to size and physique, this chapter addresses the developmental trajectories of these different aspects of body composition. Indeed, energy stores in early life make up a critical component to the trajectory of these other traits, either by providing the energy for the accretion of lean tissue, or by matching variability in their energy demand with appropriate energy insurance. The life-course trajectory of development also links body composition with reproductive function, particularly in females. Whilst this area has become of particular interest to those researching obesity, because of the long-term effects of early experience, biomedical researchers tend not to appreciate the importance of trade-offs between survival and reproduction in accounting for phenotypic variability. The combination of early-life phenotypic plasticity and later life stability described in this chapter is fundamental to the discussion of strategies for risk management presented in Chapter 7. The contribution of adiposity to the unusually slow human rate of development is also discussed in Chapter 8.

5.1   Phenotypic induction and tracking

Through their pioneering work in the 1960s, the two British nutritionists McCance and Widdowson demonstrated that the effect of variability in the nutritional intake of rats on growth was markedly different according to the developmental stage in which the nutritional variability occurred. Rats malnourished during early infancy remained small for the rest of their life, whereas those malnourished later in the life-course suffered only a temporary loss of body weight which was readily recovered when food supplies were resumed (Widdowson and McCance 1960; McCance 1962). Together with analogous work on the brain (Davison and Dobbing 1968), this work gave rise to the concept of sensitive periods during development, in which environmental factors could generate long-term effects on the organism's phenotype. Such sensitive periods are now known to apply to many aspects of phenotype.

McCance and Widdowson's work has subsequently inspired extensive research into the long-term consequences of early-life variability in nutritional intake. Amongst the outcomes now known to be affected are size, maturation rate, body composition and metabolism, along with the risk of a range of diseases such as stroke, hypertension, type-2 diabetes and cardiovascular disease (Barker 1998). Medical researchers were initially surprised to discover that many of these common western diseases, traditionally considered adult-onset and lifestyle diseases, might derive in part from experience relatively early in the life-course (Hales & Barker 1992), but the validity of the 'early-life origins of adult disease' concept is now well established.

The concept of 'nutritional programming' (Lucas 1991) is now widely used by medical researchers to interpret studies linking early growth and nutrition with subsequent health status, though other terms such as 'metabolic imprinting' (Waterland and Garza 1999) are also common. This latter concept refers to the tendency for environmental stimuli to generate permanent effects on the subsequent structure or function of the organism. The term 'programming' has been criticised by Bateson (2001) on the grounds that it incorrectly suggests that early environmental factors themselves contain 'instructions' for later diseases. Bateson has argued that it would be more appropriate to refer to the induction of phenotype by environmental factors, since the concept of phenotypic induction fits more closely with other aspects of developmental biology. The terminology of programming has now entered medical research, and it appears popular amongst those who research the early life aetiology of specific diseases. However, for those focusing on evolutionary and broader aspects of the developmental process, the concept of phenotypic induction is more appropriate and will be used here to describe how environmental factors impact on the ontogenetic development of body composition.

Despite widespread interest and considerable research investment, the exact nature of the link between early experience and later phenotype remains controversial owing to a number of factors. First, studies vary in whether they are prospective or retrospective, in whether they are epidemiological or involve experimental intervention and in the nature of outcomes. Second, work on animals has shown both some consistency between species but also significant differences, and it remains difficult to interpret the significance of research on rats, for example, for humans. Third, and perhaps most important, alternative statistical approaches have been used which complicate the interpretation of longitudinal studies (Wells 2009b). These issues will emerge frequently in the following chapter.

Initial epidemiological studies emphasised strong associations between low birth weight and the risk of later disease (Barker 1998). Importantly, however, these associations were not limited to a categorical effect of low birth weight but rather comprised inverse associations between birth weight and health across the entire spectrum of birth size. Thus these studies indicated that in general, larger birth size was associated with improved subsequent health, with the worst health being associated with those of the lower extreme of birth weight. However, such epidemiological studies are not easy to interpret, for they may be confounded by other variables associated with birth weight variability. Furthermore, it became apparent that the associations between low birth weight and later ill health emerged most strongly after adjustment for current size (Lucas, Fewtrell, and Cole 1999). The most appropriate interpretation of this scenario is not that low birth weight itself is the key determinant of later ill health, but rather that change in size between birth and follow-up may be most important. Some studies, for example, link fast rather than slow post-natal growth with later ill health (Singhal, Cole, and Lucas 2001; Singhal et al. 2003a), leading to confusion as to how early experience contributes to later disease.

These differing perspectives have yet to be fully resolved, and there remains a vigorous debate on the relative importance of fetal versus postnatal growth (and nutrition) in the causation of adult diseases. As with many such debates, apparent controversy derives in part from the unwillingness of the protagonists to converge on a common set of terminology and its interpretation. Much confusion derives from a lack of clarity regarding physiological traits (for example, nephron number), as opposed to function (for example, blood pressure) as opposed to the clinical diagnosis of diseases (for example, hypertension). Recently, I have attempted to clarify this controversy by differentiating more clearly between the metabolic consequences of physiological variability that emerges during one or other periods of development. Organ phenotype (e.g., nephron number, beta cell mass) is strongly influenced by fetal development.

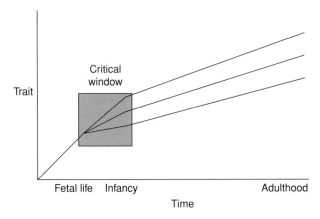

Figure 5.1. Schematic diagram illustrating the environmental introduction of phenotype. During early development, the offspring passes through sensitive periods or 'critical windows', during which ecological factors induce variability in many components of phenotype including lean mass. Towards the end of infancy, such plasticity is lost and existing variability is preserved subsequently, tracking into adulthood. Reproduced with permission from Wells (2003b).

I have suggested that such physiological traits, closely associated with organogenesis and sensitive to fetal experience, be conceptualised as 'metabolic capacity'. Subsequent growth is directed primarily to increases in size and tissue mass, which I suggest be conceptualised as metabolic load (Wells 2009b). Disease risk appears greatest when metabolic load exceeds metabolic capacity, as noted in the classic paper by Hales and Barker (1992) and demonstrated by many studies since (Leon et al. 1996; Bavdekar et al. 1999; Adair and Cole 2003; Byrne and Phillips 2000). The controversy regarding fast or slow early-life growth can then be resolved by noting that the epidemiological studies are emphasising how low birth weight reduces metabolic capacity, whereas studies of catch-up or childhood growth highlight how these processes exacerbate metabolic load (Wells 2009). This model is equally applicable to body composition as discussed below.

The concept of phenotypic induction involves two discrete components – first, the variability in phenotype that emerges during initial sensitive periods, and second, the tracking of phenotype once sensitive periods have closed. This is displayed in a schematic diagram in Figure 5.1. In their classic experiments on the timing of nutritional insults, McCance and Widdowson clearly demonstrated sensitive periods for body size in the rat, after which growth becomes canalised, a concept developed by Waddington (1966). Once a trait is canalised, it is resistant to the influence of environmental factors and has a 'self righting' ability such that environmental insults generate only transient effects, and the canalised trajectory is retained once the environmental stress is removed. Humans show both such early life plasticity in weight and length gain as well as the canalisation or tracking of growth after infancy (Smith et al. 1976). Integrating these models, one can argue that many aspects of metabolic capacity become canalised after a brief period of flexibility, and thus track on into adulthood. Because of this, increases in metabolic load occurring afterwards require normalising in order to maintain homeostasis. Those with least metabolic capacity have a limited capacity to achieve this normalisation, resulting in the appearance of disease symptoms such as hypertension or glucose intolerance.

Whilst much 'early origins' research has focused on such disease outcomes, body composition has increasingly been the focus of attention. Body composition may be involved in the induction of disease through several different mechanisms. First, adult body composition may be induced through early nutritional experience or growth patterns, for example, through epigenetic changes or effects on the hormonal axes that regulate childhood growth (Wells, Chomtho, and Fewtrell 2007). Second, body composition may be a central component of early life growth variability and track from fetal life or infancy onwards (Wells, Chomtho, and Fewtrell 2007). Such effects may plausibly apply to both lean mass and adiposity; however, the data require careful consideration. Because BMI is highly correlated with both lean mass and adiposity, the fact that associations between birth weight and adult disease risk rely on adjustment for BMI does not reveal which body-composition component is more strongly associated with that risk (Wells, Chomtho, and Fewtrell 2007).

Shifting attention away from the contribution of body-composition development to the aetiology of disease, the terminology of phenotypic induction, tracking and metabolic capacity and load remain very valuable for life history perspectives. Lean mass, which includes the sum of organ masses such as the heart, kidney, liver and pancreas, is clearly integral to metabolic capacity as defined above. However, it can also contribute to metabolic load, particularly with the increases in muscle mass that develop during childhood and adolescence. Larger body size places greater strain on the organs that maintain metabolic homeostasis. Adiposity is more readily considered as metabolic load, though even here it may be worth considering certain functions of adipose tissue as contributing to metabolic capacity. Studies of unusual patients, in whom minimal levels of fatness are associated with inability to regulate blood-glucose content (Coelho et al. 2007), suggest that there is indeed an element of metabolic capacity, sensitive to early-life experience, in this tissue.

Thus, although much of the evidence concerning the phenotypic induction of body composition derives from biomedical studies investigating the causation of adult diseases, the phenomenon is equally interesting from a broader biological perspective. As this chapter will show, early life experience exerts strong influences on subsequent adiposity, and it does so by more than one different mechanism. These associations illustrate the sensitivity of adiposity to a variety of influences acting within and between generations.

5.2   The limitation of outcomes

Before reviewing the relevant literature, it is important to consider the limitations of the existing data. Despite widespread interest in human body composition, the practical difficulties of making measurements in large samples of individuals at different ages has generally required the adoption of simple techniques. Often such techniques are satisfactory for basic clinical issues, but they may be particularly unsuitable for investigations of the phenotypic induction of body composition.

Body composition involves not only tissue masses (for example, lean mass, fat mass or central fat mass) but also elements of body size and shape. On average, a taller individual will have greater total tissue mass, and comparison of specific tissue masses of individuals therefore requires variability in body size to be taken into account, as discussed in Chapter 2. Body composition is also closely associated with body shape, given the fact that fat depots are primarily distributed outside the central muscular or skeletal structures. Again, therefore, physique may need to be taken into account when comparing individuals. These issues are important regardless of the technique by which body composition is measured, but they become particularly important when body composition is not measured directly but is predicted from simpler indices which themselves incorporate elements of size, physique and shape (Wells, Chomtho, and Fewtrell 2007).

Investigations of the phenotypic induction of body composition have until recently largely been limited to such predictive methods. Thus, body mass index has been widely used as an index of body fatness, while the waist-hip ratio and ratios of trunk-to-peripheral-skinfold thicknesses have been used to assess central adiposity. These approaches suffer from a number of limitations which will briefly be reviewed here.

The limitations of body mass index as an index of body fat were discussed in detail in Chapter 2. Figure 2.12 illustrated the twofold range of adiposity apparent for a given BMI value in children of the same age and sex, a scenario equally applicable to adults. BMI also fails to reflect body shape and hence fat distribution, as shown in Figure 5.2 which illustrates age-associated variability in waist girth adjusted for hip girth in women of different age stratified by categories of BMI. The oldest age group of women with low BMI have

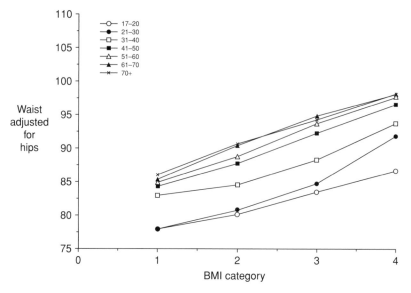

Figure 5.2. Waist girth adjusted for hip girth in four categories of BMI in women from the UK National Sizing Survey, stratified according to age. BMI categories less than 20, 20 to 24.99, 25 to 29.99 and greater than 30 kg/m². Regardless of BMI, waist girth adjusted for hip girth increases in each age group. Reproduced with permission from Wells, Cole, and Treleaven (2008).

approximately the same waist-hip ratio as the youngest age group of obese women (Wells, Cole, and Treleaven 2008), indicating the inability of BMI to reflect central abdominal adiposity. Thus, the use of BMI as an outcome in life-course research precludes the identification of which tissue mass is influenced by any given factor.

Central adiposity has often been evaluated using the waist-hip ratio, or trunk-to-peripheral-skinfold thickness ratios. These outcomes are likewise problematic in epidemiological analyses. Differences between individuals in waist-hip ratio may reflect physique (hip girth) as much as abdominal adiposity (waist girth). Figure 5.3 plots waist circumference z-score versus hip circumference z-score in approximately 2,000 young adult women from the UK National Sizing Survey. A high waist-hip ratio is present in all those individuals with values lying above the regression line; however, many of those with such high ratios nevertheless have a low waist girth, along with low hip girth, and hence the values reflect physique as much as abdominal adiposity. Skinfold thickness ratios have likewise been shown to have poor statistical validity. The relationship between limb and torso skinfolds is not linear (Figure 5.4), and dividing one skinfold by another is hence a problematic way of assessing relative fat

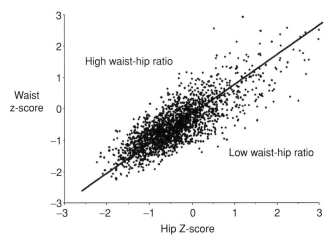

Figure 5.3. Waist girth z-score plotted against hip girth z-score in 2,000 young women from the UK National Sizing Survey. All those individuals with values above the regression line have high waist girth relative to hip girth (i.e., a high waist-hip ratio); however, those individuals with values in the lower left-hand corner of the plot may have a higher waist-hip ratio only because hip girth is small. Reproduced with permission from Wells, Chomtho, and Fewtrell (2007).

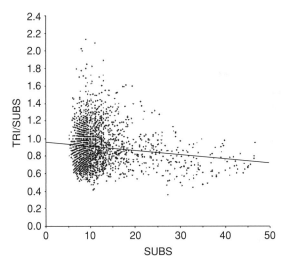

Figure 5.4. Relationship between the ratio of triceps to subscapular skinfold thickness and subscapular skinfold in adult men from Brazil. The scatter of the data demonstrates non-linearity of the ratio plotted against its denominator, highlighting the pitfalls of such ratios as indices of regional fat distribution. Reproduced with permission from Wells and Victora (2005).

distribution (Wells and Victora 2005). Furthermore, as with waist-hip ratio, a high ratio of triceps to subscapular skinfold may reflect a low triceps value, or high subscapular value; hence, such a ratio represents an unreliable independent index of central abdominal fat.

5.3   Induction of body size

The best starting point for examining the phenotypic induction of body composition is size, reflected by outcomes such as height and body mass index. Height in particular is a useful outcome given that individuals can vary in the rate at which height is attained but cannot lose height prior to attaining adulthood. A number of studies have explored associations between growth during different periods of the life course and final height, whereas recent research has also considered associations between early growth patterns and the rate of maturation.

Twin studies offer a useful perspective on the association between early growth patterns and later height, since they avoid confounding by genetic factors. In a study of 4,020 twin pairs, both monozygotic and dizygotic, birth weight was strongly associated with adult height and weight (Allison et al. 1995). Intra-pair differences in birth weight in monozygous twins were also significantly correlated with intra-pair differences in adult height, demonstrating that such associations could not be attributed to genetic influences or maternal phenotype. This large study demonstrates that intrauterine experience has a long-term effect on adult height, but a much weaker one on adult weight (Allison et al. 1995). A number of other studies have supported the notion that birth weight predicts later height in diverse populations and ethnic groups. Such findings have been reported both in children in the United Kingdom (Singhal et al. 2003b; Rogers et al. 2006) and Brazil (Wells et al. 2005), and in adults in the United Kingdom (Kensara et al. 2005; Sayer et al. 2004), Holland (Euser et al. 2005) and Guatemala (Li et al. 2003).

Detailed studies have identified the different time periods during which early experience impacts on linear growth rate. Using data from a British cohort of 2,547 girls born in 1946, birth weight was found to be associated with height at two years, but not to be associated with the rate of change in height between two and seven years (dos Santo Silva et al. 2002). Girls who were heavy at birth also reached menarche earlier than lighter girls who grew at comparable rates during infancy (discussed further in Section 5.9). Further studies have also demonstrated associations between the rate of infant growth and later height. For example, in a study of Brazilian boys, both fetal weight gain and infant weight gain were positively associated with height at nine years of age (Wells et al. 2005).

A large number of studies have demonstrated associations between birth weight and later body mass index. In their comprehensive systematic review, Parsons and colleagues (1999) found that each kilogram increase in birth weight was typically associated with approximately 0.5 to 0.7 kg/m^2 of subsequent BMI. As with the data on height, these studies indicate a significant association between fetal growth and later size, but they do not reveal which component of body composition is influenced. The simplest interpretation of these data might be to assume that those heavier at birth are also fatter and tend to preserve that fatness into later life. For example, the macrosomic infants of mothers with gestational diabetes do tend to remain obese in later life (Whitaker et al. 1998). However, the scenario for diabetic mothers should not be taken to imply a linear association between birth weight and later fatness across the entire range of birth size. Other studies have suggested J-shaped or U-shaped associations between birth weight and subsequent obesity categorised by BMI, implying a high prevalence of obesity in those of low or high birth weight (Rogers 2003).

Again, however, apparent associations between early-life experience and later obesity, categorised by BMI, should not be assumed to hold for body fatness itself. Much of the evidence from BMI shows simply that faster growth in early life results in bigger size subsequently, without clarifying how total and regional adiposity has been affected.

5.4 Induction of neonatal body composition during fetal life

One source of evidence for the fetal induction of body composition derives from investigation of the effect of gestational age at birth. It is well established that preterm infants have low levels of body fat at birth (Rigo et al. 1998), a condition that can be attributed to the fact that fat deposition occurs largely during the final trimester of pregnancy. Infants born preterm and fed *ex utero* in the last trimester of pregnancy struggle to gain adequate energy to achieve the fat deposition that would occur in utero. By the time term age is reached, preterm infants often continue to show low levels of body fat (Uthaya et al. 2005) (although this outcome depends on early postnatal diet), and this tendency for reduced adiposity is preserved into mid-childhood (Fewtrell et al. 2004). Despite their reduced total adipose tissue mass, MRI studies have suggested that by term age preterm infants have a more central adipose tissue distribution (Uthaya et al. 2005), with some indication that this trait likewise persists into childhood (Fewtrell, Lucas, Cole and Wells, unpublished data).

The hypothesis that experience during fetal life affects body composition in term neonates is supported by analyses of phenotype at birth. The most well-known examinations of this issue comprise investigations of anthropometric

Table 5.1. *Effect of maternal malnutrition during different trimesters of pregnancy on placental and fetal growth*

	Reference	First trimester	Second trimester	Third trimester
Placental weight (g)[1]	605	599	570	511
Birth weight (g)[2]	3461	3495	3329	3148
Placental index[3]	17.5	17.1	17.1	16.2
Birth length (cm)[2]	50.6	50.4	50.6	49.9
Head circumference (cm)[2]	35.5	35.5	35.1	34.5

Reference population not exposed to famine in utero
[1] Data for Rotterdam from Lumey (1998) with 163, 299, 275 and 173 individuals per group
[2] Data for Rotterdam from Stein et al. (2004) with 109, 105, 43 and 107 individuals per group
[3] Calculated as (placental weight divided by birth weight), 100%, as proposed by Lumey (1998)

measurements at birth in survivors of the Dutch hunger winter at the end of the Second World War. Stein and colleagues (2004) were able not only to identify effects of maternal malnutrition on size at birth, but also to stratify these effects according to the particular trimester of pregnancy during which maternal under-nutrition occurred (Table 5.1). Other data allow the relative effects on the fetus versus the placenta to be examined (Lumey 1998). These studies demonstrated that the effects of maternal under-nutrition were strongest if occurring in the third trimester of pregnancy. The findings from the Dutch hunger winter are similar to those observed in other populations that also experienced maternal famine during pregnancy. Infants born during the siege of Leningrad, also during the Second World War, showed a mean deficit in birth weight of around 0.5 kg (Stanner and Yudkin 2001), even greater than the 0.3 kg seen in the Dutch population.

Recent research using ultrasound measurements of fetal growth have supported the hypothesis that the influence of intrauterine growth retardation on size at birth depends on the trimester during which the growth retardation occurred. Similar to the findings from the Dutch famine, the constraining effect of intrauterine growth retardation on birth phenotype was strongest if it occurred in the final trimester of pregnancy (Hemachandra and Klebanoff 2006). Paradoxically, fetuses below the 10th percentile at the end of the first trimester of pregnancy showed higher than average birth weight, length and skinfold thicknesses (Hemachandra and Klebanoff 2006), suggesting some kind of compensatory catch-up occurring within the period of fetal growth (Figure 5.5).

More recent studies have also described in detail the size and body composition of small neonates for gestational age infants at birth. Neonates small

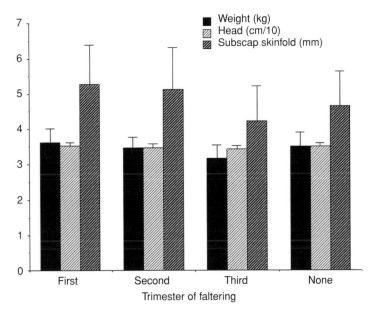

Figure 5.5. Weights, head girth and subscapular skinfold thickness according to the trimester during which fetal growth faltering occurred. Whereas growth faltering in the first trimester significantly reduces all outcomes, faltering in the first trimester is not associated with reduced size at birth, and adiposity is greater than those in whom no faltering occurred. Head girth divided by 10 to aid in the presentation of data. Based on data from Hemachandra and Klebanoff (2006).

for gestational age have a reduced ponderal index (weight adjusted for height), a lower percentage fat and reduced concentrations of leptin (Verkauskiene et al. 2007; Martinez-Cordero et al. 2006). Studies using MRI imaging have further shown a preservation of intra-abdominal fat (Figure 4.4) (Harrington et al. 2004). Low birth weight Indian infants likewise appear to have reduced peripheral but preserved central fat (Yajnik et al. 2003). Nevertheless, interpretation of these data regarding the induction of *subsequent* body composition is controversial, as discussed in Section 5.5.

The influence of maternal diet during pregnancy on fetal body composition remains poorly understood. Supplementation studies conducted on women considered to be malnourished have generally demonstrated only relatively modest improvement in birth weight, and the magnitude of any increment is notable only in those most malnourished at baseline. Observational studies in industrialised populations show that pregnancy weight gain is positively associated with birth weight only in the offspring of mothers of low baseline weight (Brown et al. 1981; Nielsen et al. 2006). In developed countries, supplementation studies have in general resulted in very small increases in birth weight of about 40 g (Rush 1981; Viegas et al. 1982a). However, when supplementation was restricted to undernourished East Asian mothers in the United Kingdom, birth weight increased by more than 300 g (Viegas et al. 1982b). Supplementation studies from developing country populations have shown slightly larger mean birth weight increments, but again they found these effects to be limited to mothers with low weight for their height at baseline (Lechtig et al. 1976). In the Gambia, maternal supplementation substantially increased birth weight (by approximately 200 g) only if applied during the 'hungry season' (Prentice et al. 1983; Ceesay et al. 1997). Such studies indicate significant but relatively modest effects of gross maternal energy intake on the birth size of the offspring.

Maternal diet itself, and circulating maternal nutrient concentrations, also show modest or undetectable associations with birth weight (Godfrey et al. 1996; Ceesay et al. 1997; Mathews, Yudkin, and Neil 1999; Mathews, Youngman, and Neil 2004). However, the glycaemic index of the maternal diet showed a strong association with offspring birth weight and ponderal index. Women consuming a higher glycaemic-index diet produced offspring who were heavier and had a higher ponderal index compared to those consuming a lower glycaemic-index diet (Moses et al. 2006). Other studies have further linked maternal preconceptional BMI, and gestational weight gain, with the magnitude of fetal growth and fetal body composition (Villar et al. 1992; Brown et al. 1996; Brown et al. 2002; Frisancho, Klayman, and Matos 1977; Jovanovic-Peterson et al. 1993). For example, the size and adiposity of offspring born to Peruvian mothers varied in relation to both maternal fatness and maternal lean mass (Frisancho, Klayman, and Matos 1977). Significantly, however, indices of baseline maternal nutritional status correlate more strongly with birth weight than does gestational weight gain (Hypponen, Power, and Smith 2004; Thame et al. 2004).

In contrast with the modest effects of maternal diet, maternal metabolism therefore shows much stronger associations with birth weight. This is further demonstrated by the effects of abnormal maternal glucose control, or blood pressure (Wells 2007f). Compared to women with normal glucose metabolism, mothers with gestational or type-1 diabetes produce significantly fatter offspring (Parretti et al. 2003). Collectively, these data indicate that maternal phenotype is an important factor in the induction of fetal body composition, but with longer-term characteristics more important than dietary intake during pregnancy. When mothers supply adequate energy to the fetus, body composition at birth exhibits a high level of lean mass and a peripheral distribution of adipose tissue. When maternal energy supply is constrained, absolute masses of both fat and lean mass are reduced in the offspring, whereas there is some indication of a relative preservation of central fat at the expense of peripheral fat.

5.5   Induction of later body composition by fetal experience

Over the last decade, there has been a substantial rise in the number of studies exploring in greater detail the relationship between birth weight and later body composition. In this context, birth weight may be considered to act as an imperfect proxy for fetal experience, since although those with low birth weight can be assumed to have grown poorly in the final trimester of pregnancy, those with average or higher birth weight may have faltered in earlier trimesters as discussed above.

The studies have differed widely in the age ranges that they have considered, the methods used to assess body composition and in the statistical approaches for analysing the data. Such variability complicates interpretation of the available evidence, and inconsistencies in the approaches adopted have led to a number of controversies which are surprisingly difficult to resolve. Of particular importance is identifying what exactly might have been induced during early life as opposed to during later periods of growth.

In a highly cited paper describing the follow-up of the Dutch-hunger-winter cohort, Ravelli and colleagues (1976) reported associations between the trimester of pregnancy during which maternal malnutrition occurred and the risk of obesity, defined using BMI, in the offspring. Those experiencing maternal famine during the first trimester had an increased risk of adult obesity compared to those unexposed, whereas those experiencing maternal famine during the final trimester had a reduced risk of adult obesity. However, a further follow-up reported similar findings in older women but did not reproduce the original findings in the older men (Ravelli et al. 1999). More detailed studies support this second study, suggesting that undernourished female offspring have a more central weight distribution, as indexed by sagittal-diameter-to-thigh-girth ratio (Stein et al. 2007). The data regarding the third trimester are consistent with the findings described above, highlighting this trimester as a critical period for fat deposition. The data regarding the first trimester are more difficult to interpret. First, higher adult BMI values may reflect lean mass rather than adiposity, although in women, waist girth was also increased (Ravelli et al. 1999). The finding that growth retardation in the first trimester of pregnancy is associated with increased size at birth (Hemachandra and Klebanoff 2006) might be consistent with either hypothesis. Second, it is plausible that these findings reflect maternal or offspring genotype rather than the life-course induction of adiposity. Fatter mothers may have more readily conceived during famine conditions, whereas thrifty offspring may have had higher survival rates (Wells, Chomtho, and Fewtrell 2007). Thus, whether maternal under-nutrition during early pregnancy genuinely induces adiposity of the offspring remains uncertain. Unlike in the Dutch population, maternal famine in the Leningrad siege did not predict later obesity, which may be due to the absence of growth recovery during infancy in the Russian population (Stanner and Yudkin 2001).

A number of studies have explored associations between birth weight or other indices of size at birth and later indices of lean mass, as shown in Table 5.2. The studies are largely consistent in demonstrating positive associations between birth weight and later lean mass, whether assessing whole body lean mass or regional muscle mass. In many cases, these associations remain apparent after adjusting for height, suggesting that greater size at birth induces lean mass not only in proportion to stature but also in relatively greater amounts as well. Table 5.2 illustrates that these associations are apparent across the entire life-course, in diverse populations and regardless of the technique by which lean mass is measured. The one study that did not demonstrate such an association was an examination of preterm infants whose growth during the last trimester of pregnancy is constrained by an abnormal artificial diet (Fewtrell et al. 2004). It is reasonable to conclude, therefore, that the induction of adult lean mass by fetal growth is a common component of human biology, providing that the normal duration of pregnancy is achieved.

Very few studies have adequate data for examining the association between body composition in early infancy and in later life. A small study of 41 infants measured at 12 weeks and in adolescence using isotope dilution showed that neither lean mass nor fat mass in infancy were associated with later body composition (Chomtho, Wells and Fewtrell, upublished data). This may reflect an inadequate sample size; however, it is also possible that associations between early and later body composition might be attributable to long-term hormonal programming rather than the consistent tracking of tissue masses throughout the life-course. Equally relevant, recent studies indicate that neonatal fat stores may be important in providing the energy for infant lean mass deposition (Chomtho, Wells and Fewtrell, upublished data).

Unlike the findings for lean mass, the available evidence for the association between birth weight and later indices of adiposity is notably inconsistent. Some studies have again reported positive associations between birth weight and later adiposity, whereas many have failed to find any significant association at all. Some studies have even reported negative associations, particularly when an adjustment is made for current size. These findings are again listed in Table 5.2. Most of these studies have focused on the entire spectrum of birth weight, and despite considerable interest in the role of low birth weight as a predictor of ill health in later life, few studies have examined in detail the effects of low birth weight on later body composition.

Those that have done so have confirmed the positive association between birth weight and later lean mass, but they have shown weaker or non-significant associations with later fatness. A study of elderly men born either normal or low birth weight identified an increased percentage of fat in those born with low birth weight after adjusting for their adult body mass index (Kensara et al. 2005). This finding may appear consistent with those other studies reporting a general inverse association between birth weight and later adiposity. Nevertheless, there is some concern as to whether such a statistical approach is appropriate. By adjusting for current BMI, this analysis inadvertently incorporates the effect of change in size between birth and follow-up. A more appropriate interpretation might therefore be that, given the association of low birth weight with reduced adult lean mass, those who have gained more BMI since birth have a higher proportion of fat in their adult weight. Thus, despite this study's suggestion that there is an association between low birth weight and an increased percentage of fat in later life, it is inappropriate to consider that fetal experience directly induced adult adiposity. Rather, the contrary is the case – high body fatness in old age in this study is best explained by postnatal weight gain, and this study provides no information as to when during post-natal life that weight gain occurred.

This study ably illustrates the difficulties of interpreting different statistical approaches. For those many studies which have reported a negative association between size at birth and later adiposity, that is, *dependent* on a statistical adjustment for current size, the best interpretation is that post-natal rather than prenatal growth patterns account for the variability in later adiposity.

This scenario is again apparent when regional rather than total indices of adiposity are considered. A number of studies have associated low birth weight with an increased waist-hip ratio or subscapular-triceps skinfold ratio, but with the association often emerging only after adjustment for current weight or BMI (Table 5.2). As discussed above, such findings cannot resolve the issue of whether physique (hip girth) or adiposity (waist girth) was the primary target, the same issue applying to ratios of peripheral to central skinfolds. Other studies have failed to find any significant association between birth weight and later body shape at all. The ALSPAC study, using DXA measurements of trunk fat mass, demonstrated a direct rather than inverse association between birth weight and subsequent trunk adiposity, which disappeared after adjustment for total body fat (Rogers et al. 2006).

As with lean mass, associations of birth weight with later adiposity direct attention to the issue of whether variability in size at birth is itself associated with variability in adiposity at birth. Some studies have suggested an increased central adiposity in small Indian neonates (Yajnik et al. 2003), with recent MRI data supporting this hypothesis (Modi et al. 2009). Yajnik and colleagues (2003) have referred to this as a 'thin-fat' phenotype that comprises reduced lean mass but disproportionately high fat mass. At later ages, Indians and other Asians likewise appear to have a disproportionately high fat content for any

Table 5.2. *Associations between birth weight and indices of lean mass, fat mass and fat distribution across the life course*

Reference	Population	n	Age	Outcomes	Design	Lean	Fat	Central fat
Childhood								
Hediger et al. 1998	US mf	4431	2 to 47m	AA, SKF	R	+	0	
Duran-Tauleria, Rona, and Chinn 1995	UK mf	8374	5 to 11y	W/H, SKF	R		+	–
Okosun et al. 2000	US mf	2488	5 to 11y	SKF	R		+	
Mulligan, Betts, and Elia 2005	UK mf	85	6 to 9y	DXA, BP	R		–	
Garnett et al. 2001	Australia mf	255	7 to 8y	BMI, DXA	A, R, PC		–[1]	–[1]
Bavdekar et al. 1999	India mf	477	8y	BMI, WHR, SKF	R		+	–[1]
Walker et al. 2002	Jamaica	306	7, 11y	BMI, SKF	R			–[1]
Malina, Katzmarzyk, and Beunen 1996	US mf	237	7 to 12y	BMI, SKF	PC			–[1]
Fewtrell et al. 2004	UK mf P	497	8 to 12y	DXA	R, TT	0	0	
Wells et al. 2005	Brazil m	172	9 to 10y	BMI, BIA	A, R	+	0	
Rogers et al. 2006	UK mf	6086	9 to 10y	DXA	R	+	+f	0
Singhal et al. 2003b	UK mf	164	7 to 16y	BIA, DXA, SKF	R	+	0	0
Chomtho et al. 2008	UK mf	391	4 to 20	4C, DXA, WC	R	+	0	0
Adolescence								
Labayen et al. 2006	Spain mf	234	13 to 18y	DXA, SKF	R	+	+	–b
Barker et al. 1997	UK f	216	14 to 16y	BMI, WHR, SKF	R			–[1]
Matthes et al. 1996	UK mf	165	15.7y	BMI, SKF	CC		0	0
Frisancho 2000	US mf	1993	15 to 17y	BMI, SKF	R		0	0
Kahn et al. 2000	US m	192	17 to 22y	BMI, WC, TA	R		+	+
Euser et al. 2005	Holland mf	403	19y	W/H, BMI, SKF	R	+	0	0

		n		Outcome	Design			
Young adulthood								
Sachdev et al. 2005	India m	1526	26 to 32y	BMI, SKF, WHR	PC	+	+f	–
Weyer et al. 2000	US (Pima)	272	25y	DXA, UWW	R	+	0	
Loos et al. 2001	Belgium m	229 tp	18 to 34y	BIA, skinfolds	R	+	–¹	–¹
Loos et al. 2002	Belgium f	238 tp	18 to 34y	Skinfolds, WHR	A,R	+	–¹	–¹
Middle age								
McNeely et al. 2007	US mf	91	40y	CT	R			0
Gunnarsdottir et al. 2004	Iceland mf	3707	50y	SKF	R		–f	–f
Law et al. 1992	UK m	1084	51 to 60y	WHR	R			–¹
Sayer et al. 2004	UK m	737	64y	BMI, SKF, WHR	R	+	0	0
Kensara et al. 2005	UK m	32	64 to 72y	DXA, BP	A	+	–¹	–¹
Gale et al. 2001	UK mf	143	70 to 75y	DXA	R	+	0	0

Population: m = male; f = female; P = preterm

n: tp = twin pairs

Outcome: AA = arm anthropometry; BIA = bioelectrcial impedance analysis; BMI = body mass index; BP = Bodpod; DXA = dual-energy x-ray absorptiometry; SKF = skinfold thicknesses; TA = thigh anthropometry; W/H = weight for height; WC = waist circumference; WHR = waist-hip ratio; UWW = underwater weighing; CT = computed tomography; 4C = 4 component model

Design: A = ANOVA; CC = case-control study; PC = partial correlations; R = regression; TT = t-test

Results: 0 = no association; + = positive association; – = negative association

¹ Results significant only after adjustment for current weight or BMI

Reproduced with additional data with the authors' permission from Wells, Chomtho, and Fewtrell (2007)

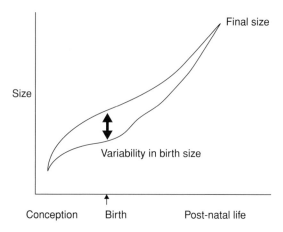

Figure 5.6. Alternative growth trajectories leading to a common final size. Low birth weight is associated not only with reduced fetal growth, but also with faster post-natal growth. Birth weight therefore acts as a marker of both prenatal and post-natal growth patterns and does not exclusively index fetal experience. Reproduced with permission from Wells (2007f).

given BMI value (Deurenberg, Deurenberg-Yap, and Guricci 2002; Park et al. 2001). However, it remains unclear whether such a 'thin-fat' baby represents a thrifty genotype effect, possibly characteristic of Asian populations, or a thrifty phenotype effect, characteristic of low birth-weight infants in general (Harrington et al. 2004).

Overall, there is substantial evidence in favour of the hypothesis that fetal experience induces later body composition, but with this effect being markedly stronger for indices of lean mass than for indices of adiposity. There are inadequate data based on sophisticated body-composition methodologies to address the induction of adiposity in detail, and it remains possible that fetal nutrition does contribute to the induction of later fatness and its distribution. Current experience, however, suggests that post-natal weight gain, which is in turn related to fetal growth, is of considerable importance for the induction of the adipose phenotype. This inverse association between fetal and post-natal growth patterns reflects both regression to the mean (a statistical phenomenon) and catch-up growth (a biological phenomenon) (Cameron, Preece, and Cole 2005). Thus, birth weight may be predictive of later body composition without neonatal body composition itself representing the causal pathway. The difficulty of interpreting birth weight in such longitudinal associations is shown schematically in Figure 5.6, which shows that low birth weight is associated with specific patterns of both prenatal and post-natal growth rates.

5.6   Induction of body composition by post-natal growth

Post-natal weight gain is now understood to make an important contribution to the induction of adult diseases. For many outcome components of the metabolic syndrome, risk is greatest in those born small who subsequently gained the most weight in post-natal life (Adair and Cole 2003; Bavdekar et al. 1999). In general, this emphasises the importance of disparity in growth rate between different periods of the life-course, and, more specifically, recent studies have begun to elucidate the contributions of different periods of post-natal weight gain to later phenotype and disease risk (Barker et al. 2005). However, the findings of this research appear to vary according to the population being researched (Victora et al. 2008), a scenario which may also apply to the life-course induction of body composition.

As with birth weight, the majority of studies on infant growth rate have used body mass index or skinfold thicknesses as the outcome. Studies are generally consistent in demonstrating a positive association between infant weight gain and later body mass index or skinfold thicknesses. For example, recent systematic reviews found that both large and rapidly growing infants had a significantly increased risk of subsequent obesity categorised by BMI (Baird et al. 2005; Ong and Loos 2006). However, the extent to which these studies demonstrate a clear link between early growth and later fatness, as opposed to later size, is less clear. Fewer studies have measured body composition directly, and even fewer studies have adjusted childhood body fat for differences in height, even though infant growth is positively associated with a subsequent greater height.

In the large ALSPAC cohort, faster infant growth was associated with greater central adiposity as indicated by skinfold thicknesses. Rapid growth in this study was designated as an upwards crossing of a centile band within the first two years of life and was observed in approximately one-third of the entire sample (Ong et al. 2000). In the same study, rapid infant growth was associated with indications of growth faltering in utero, which was more likely in the offspring of mothers who smoked or in offspring who had other clinical signs of fetal-growth retardation. The study therefore confirmed that associations between birth weight and later fat distribution are generated at least in part by the rate of post-natal growth but are also associated with prenatal growth experience.

A smaller set of studies have examined body composition in greater detail, using two component methods capable of differentiating more accurately between fatness and lean mass, and allowing adjustment for body size. These studies at present suggest that the effect of infant weight gain on later body composition appears to differ systematically between industrialised and developing

Table 5.3 *Associations between infant weight gain and indices of lean mass, fat mass and fat distribution across the life course*

Reference	Population	n	Age (years)	Growth (years)	Outcomes	Design	Lean	Fat	Central fat
Childhood									
Ong et al. 2000	UK	848	5	0 to 2	SKF	ANOVA		+	+
Karaolis-Danckert et al. 2006	Germany	206	7	0 to 2	SKF	MR	+	+	
Botton et al. 2008	France	468	8 to 17	0 to 0.25	BIA	PC	+**	+	+
Chomtho et al. 2008	UK	234	4 to 20	0 to 1	4C, DXA, WC	MR	+	+	+
Cameron et al. 2003	South Africa	193	9	0 to 2	DXA, SKF, WC	T		+	+
Wells et al. 2005	Brazil**	172	9	0 to 0.5	BIA	M	+	0	
Adolescence									
Eriksson, Tynelius, and Rasmussen 2008	Sweden	2453	15	0 to 1	BIA	R	+	+	+
Ekelund et al. 2006	Sweden	248	17	0 to 0.5	ADP, WC	R	+	+	+
Adulthood									
Victora et al. 2007	Brazil	2250	18	0 to 1	BIA	R	+	+	
Euser et al. 2005	Holland	403	19*	0 to 1	SKF, WC	MR	+	+	+
Li et al. 2003	Guatemala	267	21 to 22	0 to 2	SKF	MR	+	+$	0
McCarthy et al. 2007	UK	679	23 to 27	0 to 0.5	WC, SAD	MR			0
Schroeder, Martorell, and Flores 1999	Guatemala	533	c17 to 32	0 to 3	SKF, WC	MR, ANCOVA			0
Sachdev et al. 2005	India	1526	26 to 32	0 to 0.5	SKF, WHR	R, PC	+	+	0
Corvalan et al. 2007	Guatemala	710	26 to 41	0 to 1	WT, HT, WC	MR	+	+	+
Demerath et al. 2007	USA	232	18 to 76	0 to 2	DXA, WC	ANCOVA	0	+	0
Yliharsila et al. 2008	Finland	1917	56 to 70	0 to 1	BIA	MR	+	+	0

Outcome: WT = weight; HT = height; SKF = skinfolds; WC = waist circumference; SAD = sagittal diameter; BIA = bioelectrical impedance analysis; ADP = air displacement plethysmography; DXA = dual-energy X-ray absorptiometry; 4C = 4-component model;

Design: R = regression; MR = multiple regression; T = t-test; PC = partial correlation

Results: 0 = no association; + = positive association

* cohort born preterm, may influence findings; ** males only; $females only

countries. In studies of European or other Western populations, greater infant weight gain is associated with later height, weight, lean mass, fat mass and waist circumference in children and adolescents, and weight at one year likewise predicted weight, lean mass and fat mass in adults (Ekelund et al. 2006; Euser et al. 2005; Chomtho et al. 2008). These findings contrast with three studies from non-Western populations (Wells et al. 2005; Sachdev et al. 2005; Li et al. 2003) in which infant weight gain is associated with later weight, height and lean mass but weakly or not at all with later fat mass (Table 5.3). In general, infact growth is much more strongly associated with later lean mass than adiposits in developing country population.

Recent studies suggest that an important factor mediating the target of infant growth is the duration of catch-up. Catch-up growth in small-for-gestational-age infants was associated with later fatness and the risk of being overweight only if the catch-up persisted beyond the first year of life (Ezzahir et al. 2005). Although in the ALSPAC cohort catch-up growth was associated with indices of growth retardation and with central adiposity at five years, in this study rapid growth was quantified over the first two years of life (Ong et al. 2000). Thus the ALSPAC findings may simply reflect the persistence of fast growth beyond the optimum window, resulting in associations between total early weight gain and later fatness.

This interpretation would be consistent with more detailed studies of post-natal tissue accretion. Low birth weight babies appear to be insulin sensitive at birth (Soto et al. 2003), which appears to promote catch-up in length during infancy. Where this catch-up continues beyond infancy into early childhood, insulin resistance develops and is then associated with central fat accumulation (Mericq et al. 2005; Ibanez et al. 2006; Ibanez et al. 2008a; Ibanez et al. 2008b). Thus, recent studies emphasise that the excess fat accumulation takes place *after* one year of age and appears not to manifest during infancy itself. The most recent studies further show a tendency for increased visceral adiposity in children following catch-up growth even in the absence of overweight developing (Ibanez et al. 2008a). The associations between birth weight versus catch-up growth and later body composition are shown in a schematic diagram in Figure 5.7.

More recently, several studies have focused specifically on the immediate post-natal period. Weight gain in the first eight days of life was significantly associated with the risk of being categorised obese in early adulthood (Stettler et al. 2005). Consistent with this data, weight gain in the first two weeks of post-natal life in preterm infants was significantly associated with insulin resistance during adolescence (Singhal et al. 2003a). In this randomised controlled trial, those given a lower-nutrient diet had reduced insulin resistance in adolescence,

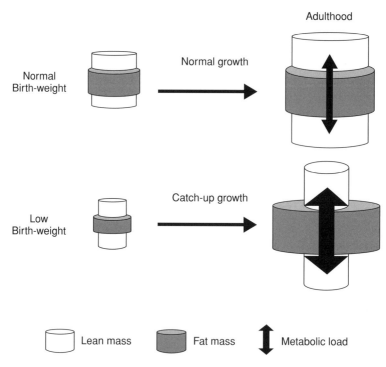

Figure 5.7. Schematic diagram illustrating the two complementary processes whereby early growth is associated with later body composition and metabolic profile. First, normal fetal and infant growth promote the accretion of lean mass, whereas poor fetal and infant weight gain appear permanently to constrain it. Second, catch-up growth, especially when it persists into childhood, promotes excess fat accumulation, especially in the abdomen. The relative ratio of central fat to lean mass is then represented as 'metabolic load'. The low-birth-weight infant is at risk of high metabolic load through both routes. Further work is required to elucidate differences between populations from industrialised versus developing countries regarding this scenario. Reproduced with permission from Wells (2007d).

an effect attributed to slower growth. It remains unclear whether such associations reflect an altering of hormonal axes by diet, or if they generate effects on later body composition directly through impacts on growth and infant body composition. The sensitivity of phenotype during this period is likely to reflect the transition from placental to oral nutrition and the low energy intake normally encountered by breast-fed infants during this period (Evans et al. 2003).

Seemingly contrary to the association between rapid growth and increased subsequent fatness, early-life stunting also appears to induce greater fatness. Stunting has been associated with an increased risk of obesity in several developing country populations (Popkin, Richards, and Montiero 1996; Schroeder, Martorell, and Flores 1999; Grillol et al. 2005; Hoffman et al. 2000b), although some reports from similar settings fail to support the hypothesis (Gigante et al. 2007; Jinabhai, Taylor, and Sullivan 2003). In the UK National Sizing Survey, height was positively associated with all body girths except waist girth, which had a negative association (particularly in men), implying a similar association between short stature and abdominal adiposity in a Western population (Wells, Treleaven, and Cole 2007). Detailed studies in Brazil suggest that stunting may impair the capacity for fat oxidation (Hoffman et al. 2000b) or predispose to increased energy intake (Hoffman et al. 2000a), or that metabolic rate may be reduced (Grillol et al. 2005), in each case favouring fat accumulation. Whether these mechanisms apply more generally requires confirmation.

As with fetal life, infant nutrition is assumed to be a primary mechanism underlying variability in growth. The mode of infant feeding has been associated in many studies, such as the comprehensive study of Dewey and colleagues (1993), with differences in growth rate or in later body composition during infancy; however, identifying clear effects is notoriously difficult given that mothers who breast-feed differ systematically from those who choose not to. Many studies have reported that breast-feeding is associated with a decreased risk of later obesity as categorised by body mass index. For example, two meta-analyses have supported this hypothesis and have suggested both categorical and dose-response protective effects of breast-feeding (Owen et al. 2005; Arenz et al. 2004). However, as discussed above body mass index is a poor outcome for investigating the induction of body composition. Studies which have focused on body composition itself as the outcome have in general failed to support this hypothesis (Victora et al. 2003; Toschke et al. 2007). It also remains unclear whether biological components of breast-milk, such as leptin, might constrain growth (Locke 2002), or conversely whether the ease with which formula-feeding can maximise the volume of intake might promote growth (Stettler et al. 2002). Differences between the diet groups in the age at which complementary foods are introduced may also be important.

There is an urgent need for further studies to address the early-life induction of adiposity in greater detail, and the disparity between Western and developing countries is potentially of considerable importance in relation to public health policies regarding early infant care. At the present time, current evidence suggests that whether infant weight gain is directed to subsequent lean mass fatness is mediated by factors such as size at birth, appetite, genetic potential and the duration of early catch-up. Individuals from industrialised populations, typically near their genetic potential for growth (and hence metabolic capacity) at birth, may be unable to translate increased energy intake into greater lean mass and may be obliged to store the excess energy as fat (metabolic load), whereas individuals from modernising countries, on average small at birth, may have a greater capacity to direct any additional energy to reducing deficits in lean mass (Wells, Chomtho, and Fewtrell 2007). This scenario, illustrated in

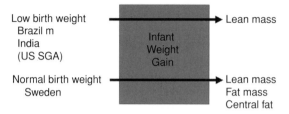

Figure 5.8. Schematic diagram illustrating the different targets of growth in infants according to birth weight. In populations with low birth weight (for example, Brazil, India, or small-for-gestational-age babies from the United States), moderate catch-up growth appears to benefit lean mass subsequently, whereas in populations with average birth weight (for example, Sweden), increased income weight gain is associated with greater fat mass in central fat subsequently.

Figure 5.8, would be consistent with other data from developing countries, suggesting that increased linear growth in infancy has beneficial effects on later blood pressure and cardiovascular risk profile (Victora et al. 2008). However, it is also possible that the differing scenarios also relate to population variability in when the period of maximal growth rate can occur.

5.7   Induction of body composition during childhood

The impact of post-natal growth on later body composition is not restricted to the infant period. Weight gain during childhood also appears to exert effects on later body composition. Initial studies suggested that 'adiposity rebound', the age at which childhood BMI reaches a natural nadir before increasing again, was a significant predictor of later obesity as categorised by BMI (Rolland-Cachera et al. 1987). More recent studies have suggested that such rebound is both a misnomer, in that it refers to BMI rather than adiposity (Wells 2000), and also a statistical artefact since the time of rebound is inherently a function of initial BMI magnitude (Cole 2004). A more appropriate interpretation of this data is simply that those gaining weight rapidly in childhood maintain this extra weight subsequently, and the data may express little other than that weight once gained, especially lean mass, is difficult to lose. More generally, it is not clear whether childhood weight gain represents phenotypic induction, given that linear growth is by this time canalised and any effect on fatness is theoretically reversible.

A variety of studies have investigated the tracking of BMI across different periods of the life-course. These studies are able to capitalise on large sample sizes characterised by this outcome; however, much of the consistency of BMI may be due to the tracking of physique rather than adiposity. The strength of tracking has been proposed to be categorised as low for correlations less than 0.3, moderate for correlations between 0.3 and 0.60, and high for correlations greater than 0.6 (Malina 1996).

In a study of 164 French subjects studied from the age of one month to adulthood, there was substantial within-individual variability over time in BMI category. The majority of infants with high BMI values did not have high BMI in adulthood, although 41% of the lower weight infants at one year remained lean in adulthood (Rolland-Cachera et al. 1987). In a similar study from the Czech Republic, most of the infants characterised as lean or fat developed into average-sized adults (Prokopec and Bellisle 1993). In 100 Finnish children, BMI at six months was associated with BMI at 7 years but not at 15 years, whereas there was a highly significant association between BMI at the last two time points (Fuentes et al. 2003). In the United States, fewer than half of 3-year-old subjects, but the majority of 7- and 11-year-old subjects, remained within a given relative weight group at 13 years (Kelly et al. 1992). In a study of 213 Australian adolescents followed since infancy, tracking of BMI was stronger in those initially of normal weight compared to those initially overweight or underweight (Tienboon and Wahlqvist 2002).

Studies commencing in childhood show a greater tendency of BMI to track. The correlation between childhood BMI at 9 to 11 years and adult BMI at 19 to 35 years was 0.66 in 841 individuals from Louisiana (Deshmukh-Taskar et al. 2006). In a cohort of 975 Chinese children aged 6 to 13 years, categorised into quartiles, BMI 6 years later was similar in 40% of the subjects, whereas 30% had moved into a higher quartile and 30% into a lower quartile, suggesting the increasing influence of genotype. Unlike in younger age groups, tracking of BMI was strongest in those thinnest or fattest (Wang, Ge, and Popkin 2000). Several studies show that as childhood proceeds, the tracking of BMI becomes stronger (Casey et al. 1992; Guo and Chumlea 1999). From a mean age of 13.5 years to a mean follow-up of 25 years, the correlation was around 0.6 for BMI in both sexes, with similar tracking for fat mass but weaker tracking for central adiposity (Campbell et al. 2001). Guo and Chumlea (1999) observed that the prediction of adult overweight was excellent for BMI at 18 years, good for BMI at 13 years, but only moderate at ages below 13 years. Table 5.4 shows correlation matrices for BMI over various time periods between 5 and 40 years of age. In males, the correlation for the longest tracking period was 0.41, whereas in females it was 0.05, and the correlation became significant only from mid-adolescence onwards (Casey et al. 1992).

Given that relative muscle mass and physique or frame size are relatively stable from early childhood onwards, and are also profoundly influenced by the pubertal growth spurt, these data are clearly strongly influenced by non-adipose components of body build. Childhood BMI, measured at 9 years,

Table 5.4. *Correlation coefficients for the association between BMI at 6 time periods and BMI at 50 years*

	males		females	
	n	r	n	r
Childhood	40	0.41	44	0.05
Early adolescence	39	0.47	44	0.25
Late adolescence	38	0.55	43	0.26
18 years	32	0.51	35	0.44
30 years	36	0.74	43	0.80
40 years	40	0.77	44	0.87

Data from Casey et al. (1992)

was correlated with BMI at age 50, but not significantly so with percent fat at the same time point, in 412 members of a UK cohort study (Wright et al. 2001). Studies of subcutaneous skinfold thickness or waist-hip ratio show good tracking over short time periods (Mueller, Dai, and Labarthe 2001), but with the effect declining over time. In large samples of Canadian men and women monitored over seven years, tracking of subcutaneous fatness or fat distribution was poorer than that of BMI, again implicating consistency instead in physique (Katzmarzyk et al. 1999). Data from 105 Belgian twin pairs showed that tracking in skinfold ratios can be predominantly attributed to additive genetic sources of variance, in other words genetic factors that continue to impact on phenotype through the life-course (Peeters et al. 2007).

Very few data are available for early life. Infant fat mass was shown to track into childhood in a small cohort of UK children, with infant skinfold explaining half the variance in childhood skinfolds (Wells, Cole, and Davies 1996); however, over a longer time period, no such tracking of fatness was apparent (Figure 5.9). Intriguingly, increases in skinfold thicknesses between 3 and 6 weeks were associated with childhood fatness (Figure 5.10), whereas increases in skinfold thicknesses between 12 weeks and 6 months were not (Figure 5.11). These data may indicate particular sensitive periods during infancy, perhaps simply because growth is faster earlier on, but this requires further confirmation. Others have also shown short-term tracking of fatness between the end of infancy and mid-childhood, (Weststrate, Van, and Deurenberg 1986), with Goulding and collagues (2003) showing that increases in fat mass during early childhood were positively associated with adiposity at baseline (Figure 5.12). However, from 6 to 7.5 years, tracking coefficients for skinfold thicknesses appear to decline (r = 0.3 – 0.6) (Oja and Jürimäe 2002). Of particular interest are unpublished data (Chomtho, Wells and Fewtrell) showing that infant adiposity predicts later lean mass, indicating a function of infant adiposity in fuelling growth trajectory.

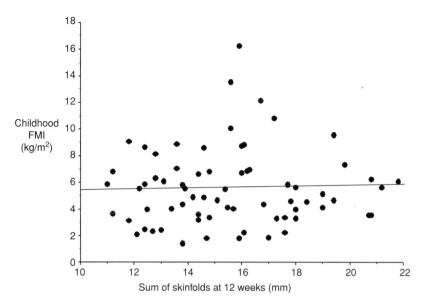

Figure 5.9. Association between sum of skinfold thicknesses at 12 weeks of age and fat mass index in late adolescence, in UK children. Adiposity does not appear to track between these time points. Based on unpublished data of Chomtho, Wells and Fewtrell.

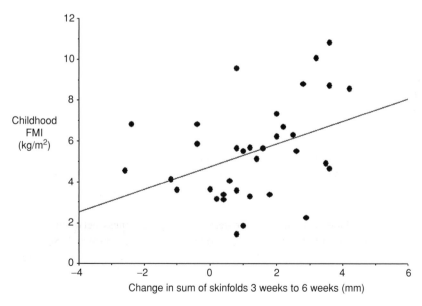

Figure 5.10. Positive association between change in sum of skinfold thicknesses between three and six weeks of age, and fat mass index in childhood. Thus, greater fat accumulation during early infancy is associated with increased fatness subsequently. Based on unpublished data of Chomtho, Wells and Fewtrell.

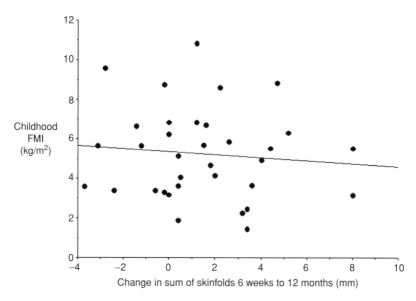

Figure 5.11. Association between change in sum of skinfold thicknesses between six weeks and 12 months and fat mass index in late adolescence. Contrary to the positive association shown in Figure 5.10 for earlier infancy, no association is apparent. Based on unpublished data of Chomtho, Wells and Fewtrell.

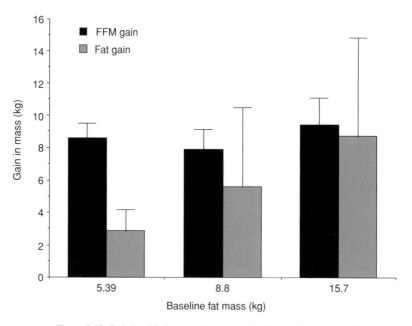

Figure 5.12. Relationship between fat mass at baseline and subsequent five-year changes in both fat mass and lean mass, in children initially four years of age. Whereas changes in lean mass are similar between the groups, those with highest baseline fatness gain three times the mass of fat compared to those with lowest baseline fatness. Adapted from data from Goulding et al. (2003).

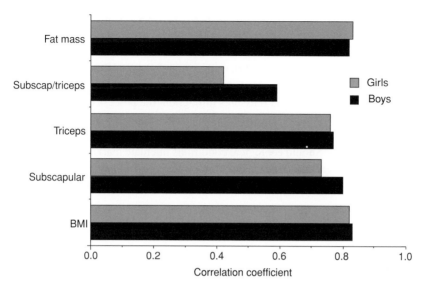

Figure 5.13. Correlation coefficients for different indices of adiposity in each sex, between the two periods 7 to 8 years and 11 to 12 years in 306 children from Kingston, Jamaica. Most indices of adiposity appear to track within this time, although the relative distribution as indexed by the subscapular-triceps ratio is less stable. Based on data from Gaskin and Walker (2003).

Very few data are available for non-Western populations. Figure 5.13 shows correlation coefficients for the tracking of adiposity outcomes between 7 and 8 and 11 and 12 years in 306 children from Kingston, Jamaica (Gaskin and Walker 2003). Tracking was relatively high for BMI, fat mass or individual skinfold thicknesses, but not for the ratio of subscapular to triceps skinfold. However, in the Amsterdam Growth and Health Study, following 155 individuals from 13 to 29 years of age, tracking coefficients were approximately 0.4 for single skinfolds, but around 0.5 to 0.6 for skinfold ratios (van Lenthe et al. 1996). In this population, the strength of the correlations for individual skinfolds approximately halved between 16 and 29 years; however, for skinfold ratios the tracking was more consistent (van Lenthe et al. 1996). These contrasting results might suggest that exposure to the obesogenic niche, reflected in abdominal adiposity, shows greater consistency in Western populations, whereas physique and absolute size tracked more strongly in the Jamaican children. Clearly this issue requires greater attention in further studies in different ecological environments.

In summary, the available data indicate that there is poor tracking of BMI from infancy, but that this improves substantially as childhood progresses. Such tracking may apply more to physique than adiposity, and although fatness tracks well over short time periods, consistency appears to wash out over longer periods. There is some evidence of greater consistency over time in fat distribution, attributable to genetic or epigenetic influence, but this consistency also varies by population. Most of the available data derive from well-nourished populations in which living conditions may be relatively stable across the life-course. The evidence collected in Gambian farmers shows the high flexibility of fat in response to ecological pressures throughout the process of reproduction. Instead, the data strongly suggest that height, physique and lean mass are the components of phenotype that track most strongly from early life within any given population. Should ecological conditions fluctuate markedly, and impact variably on different individuals, within-population ranking in lean mass is likely to be far more stable than within-population ranking in fat mass.

5.8   Mechanisms of body composition induction

The induction of body composition can be attributed to a number of different mechanisms operating at different biological levels, including the induction of appetite (Martin-Gronert and Ozanne 2005), maturation rate and hormonal axes, along with possible epigenetic modifications of DNA expression. That epigenetic mechanisms operate is elegantly illustrated by a study revealing an impact of paternal experience on adiposity of the offspring. Fathers exposed to famine during adolescence produced offspring with an increased risk of obesity (Pembrey et al. 2006). Paternal inheritance implies an epigenetic modification of paternal DNA; however, the same mechanism clearly has substantially greater opportunity to operate in the mother. Although the underlying mechanisms remain under investigation, maternal phenotype appears to induce not only body composition in the offspring, but also the schedule of maturation.

5.9   Induction of the rate of maturation

Few biologists can be unaware of the general trend towards earlier menarche that has taken place over the last century. Although precocious puberty may in some cases be due to specific pathological factors, the broader trend can be traced to secular trends in diet and growth (Parent et al. 2003). There is some evidence of genetic influence on the timing of menarche, with, for example, some populations in similar environments systematically different from others (Parent et al. 2003). Nevertheless, it is abundantly clear that environmental factors exert a strong influence on the initiation of menarche. Nutritional factors appear to exert contrasting effects according to the time during the life-course when they act.

A number of studies have associated small size at birth with earlier menarche; however, the effect is modest (Gluckman and Hanson 2006; Dunger, Ahmed, and Ong 2006). Conversely, there is an inverse association between childhood weight gain and the initiation of menarche, with rapid childhood weight gain a strong predictor of earlier puberty (Dunger, Ahmed, and Ong 2006). Data from the Harvard Growth Study indicated that early maturation, categorised according to peak height velocity, was associated with increased weight relative to height (Tanner 1955). This observation might merely indicate the effects of earlier maturation, but more recent data clearly indicate that the rate of weight gain during the *prior* childhood period influences the timing of puberty in both sexes (Mills et al. 1986; Cooper et al. 1996). Whilst the Frisch hypothesis proposing the regulation of menarche by a specific threshold of adiposity has been criticised (Ellison 2001), Dunger and colleagues (2006) noted that the discovery of the hormone leptin provided a plausible underlying mechanism whereby body fatness might contribute to the regulation of puberty progression. Animal studies have demonstrated a marked role for leptin instigating the onset of puberty; however, human studies have failed to identify a sharp threshold effect and have instead indicated a more permissive role for this hormone (Dunger, Ahmed, and Ong 2006; Clayton et al. 1997; Cheung et al. 1997).

These environmental effects may be considered additive, with earlier menarche most notable in those of small birth size migrating to improved childhood environments (Parent et al. 2003). The main effect of earlier puberty is to advance the attainment of increased levels of body fat that accompany pubertal maturation in females (Ong et al. 2007). However, it has long been recognised that variability in the timing of puberty also generates more subtle effects on final body size and composition (Lassek and Gaulin 2007a).

Longitudinal studies have suggested that the age at menarche is heritable. Data from the Fels Longitudinal Study suggested that approximately half the phenotypic variation in the timing of menarche could be attributed to genetic factors (Towne et al. 2005). However, heritability and genetic causation are not equivalent, and biologists are now increasingly considering how non-genetic pathways contribute to heritability in the timing of menarche.

Data from the ALSPAC cohort elegantly illustrate the heritability of both body composition and age at menarche in females (Figure 5.14), with this mechanism also exerting some influence on male development. In this cohort, shorter and fatter mothers had offspring who grew rapidly during the first two years of life when contrasted with the slow-growing infants of taller, leaner mothers (Ong et al. 2007). Between two and nine years of age, the offspring of both maternal groups grew at approximately similar rates; however, those that had grown fast in the first two years of life remained significantly heavier and taller at nine years and tended to enter puberty earlier. Despite being taller at nine years of age, however, these earlier maturing girls appear destined to complete their growth earlier and hence achieve reduced final height. For example, data on a large cohort of 286,205 individuals from nine European

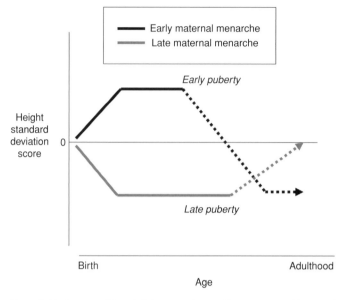

Figure 5.14. Patterns of female infant growth according to upper and lower quintiles of maternal age at menarche. The offspring of early-menarche mothers grow faster during infancy and reach puberty earlier. They have greater adiposity during puberty but are likely to have a reduced period of total growth and end up with reduced final height. The offspring of late-menarche mothers grow slowly during infancy and reach puberty later. They have lower adiposity during puberty but are likely to grow for longer and therefore attain greater final height. Through these growth patterns, both groups of female offspring reproduce the phenotype of their mothers. Reproduced with permission from Wells and Stock (2007), based on the data of Ong et al. (2007).

countries demonstrated that those with earlier menarche reached a shorter final height compared to those maturing later (Onland-Moret et al. 2005).

Thus, shorter and fatter mothers appear to reproduce their phenotype in their daughters through faster infant growth, earlier puberty and a reduced total growing period. Although this transmission of phenotype might have a genetic basis, there are strong indications that the mechanism is in fact one of phenotypic induction. In particular, the fact that the fast growth associated with earlier puberty occurred during infancy (the period of growth under nutritional regulation) strongly implicates a non-genetic regulatory mechanism. Lactation is the most expensive period of maternal care, and it is likely that earlier menarche mothers somehow signal their high energy stores to their offspring *in utero*, setting up a faster post-natal growth trajectory (Ong et al. 2007). This perspective is supported by the finding that the effects of maternal phenotype on offspring phenotype is apparent in boys as well as girls (Ong et al. 2007).

The shorter height of the early-menarche mothers was associated with lower birth weight in female offspring, presumably owing to reduced uterine size. The faster post-natal growth rate may therefore represent a strategy for recovering this fetal growth deficit. Consistent with that hypothesis, other factors associated with poor fetal growth were associated with faster post-natal growth and earlier puberty in the same sample (Ong et al., unpublished data).

This association between maternal phenotype and offspring body composition highlights the induction of body by trans-generational influences. Few data are available for examining whether such effects persist across the life-course. Because of the cross-sectional association between childhood BMI and age at menarche, the fact that age at menarche remains associated with BMI in adulthood is not itself strong evidence for long-term independent effects of age at menarche on later body composition (Pierce and Leon 2005). However, follow-up of a cohort of 3,743 Scottish women born between 1950 and 1955 demonstrated that earlier menarche remained strongly associated with BMI and the risk of obesity in middle age, independently of the influence of childhood BMI (Pierce and Leon 2005).

5.10   Transgenerational effects

In each generation, the early-life induction of body composition manifests as a parental effect. It is particularly valuable to consider this as a multi-generational process, whereby body size and physique track across generations (Emanuel et al. 1992; Ramakrishnan et al. 1999; Hypponen, Power, and Smith 2004), subject to perturbations which exert their greatest impact during the plastic periods of fetal life and infancy. The induction of adiposity in each generation is therefore part of this larger-scale process, linking the life-course strategy of storing energy with complementary strategies of tailoring growth rate and maturation rate to the interaction between energy availability and maternal phenotype (Wells 2010).

Summary

The induction and tracking of body composition refer to both lean mass and adiposity, and good quality measurements are required to elucidate these different phenomena. High quality maternal phenotype, reflected in large size and plentiful energy stores, appears to be associated with a larger neonate with greater lean mass, a phenotype which tends to track on into adulthood. Poor quality maternal phenotype constrains such investment in offspring size and lean mass, with similar effects being generated through malnutrition of the offspring during post-natal life. Under these circumstances, the ratio of lean mass to fat may be altered, with further potential influences on fat distribution and insulin metabolism, especially if catch-up growth occurs. From childhood onwards, there is less evidence for the strong tracking of adiposity, perhaps because the underlying predisposition for a given level of fatness may be located in part at the level of behaviour, and hence may be moderately responsive to changes in circumstances and lifestyle. There is ample evidence, for example, of catastrophic events generating profound alterations in individuals' adiposity, whereas lean mass and physique resist such changes and can revert to a baseline phenotype if conditions allow. Collectively, the evidence suggests that adiposity phenotype is most sensitive to the interaction between growth rates occurring during the fetal and early post-natal periods. These in turn implicate exposure to the maternal phenotype as the primary determinant of phenotypic induction.

The U-shaped association between birth weight and later obesity status (Rogers 2003) suggests that we have yet to achieve a comprehensive understanding of how maternal phenotype induces that of the offspring. One possibility is that low-birth-weight infants induce an excessive metabolic load through their catch-up growth, whereas high-birth-weight infants may already have begun this process in utero. Support for this hypothesis of alternative growth trajectories to a common end point comes from the increasing recognition of the high adiposity of many high-birth-weight infants, and studies linking higher birth weight with growth faltering in the first trimester are also consistent. Obesity itself is furthermore a highly variable phenotype, with substantial variability in lean mass as well as adiposity. Longitudinal studies are required to examine the trajectories towards obesity in greater detail, and they will doubtless reveal much about the maternal induction of body composition more generally. More generally, obesity and undernutrition appear intricately connected, both within and between generations.

From an evolutionary perspective, such data imply variation in the transgenerational transfer of maternal 'capital'. High quality mothers invest in larger offspring and use their adipose tissue depots to accelerate the rate of infant growth in order to allow the offspring to breed earlier. Since the energetics of lactation improve at larger body size (Oftedal 2000), the investment of mothers in larger daughters is clearly a fitness-enhancing strategy. Conversely, mothers with poor energy resources produce small offspring, who may need to extend their total growth period in order to reach a viable size for reproduction. Smaller offspring may also alter their own 'investment strategies' during growth, favouring higher levels of adipose tissue. The hypothesis that variability in the ontogenetic development of body composition constitutes an adaptive strategy played out across generations is reconsidered in Chapter 7 as part of a broader 'game theory' model.

6   *The fitness value of fat*

The value of fat deposition and oxidation may be interpreted in terms of its effects rather than its causes (Tinbergen 1963). By convention, it is common for biomedical researchers to focus on adipose tissue as a physical substance. Strictly speaking, however, natural selection acts most strongly on life cycles (Bonner 1965) and strategies (Houston and McNamara 1999), and in this case the relevant strategy is the capacity both to deposit energy in adipose tissue and to release it as required. This point was explicitly made by Pond (1998), who distinguished between the functions of fattening and the functions of fat.

In Tinbergen's original approach (1963), the focus was on survival value. Since his pioneering article was published, biologists have incorporated a broader approach to assessing the value of a given trait or strategy. Traits are best assessed in terms of their total contribution to genetic fitness rather than to the mere survival of the organism (Williams 1966). Human fatness plays important roles in reproductive fitness and sexual selection, including trans-generational transfers of energy, and these components of evolutionary biology must therefore be incorporated into assessments of function. Furthermore, adipose tissue is increasingly recognized to play a sophisticated role in the regulation of competing functions, as well as providing the energy required for them.

6.1   Buffering famine and malnutrition

The fat content of adipose tissue represents an energy store, and its most basic function is to buffer against fluctuations in dietary energy supply. In this respect humans are no different to mammals in general, which illustrate a wide variety of strategies in relation to the storage and use of fat (see Chapter 7). Lipid mobilisation is slow in relation to the immediate rate of energy utilisation, hence fat stores are not appropriate for rapid bursts of activity (Pond 1998). The energy demands of physical exercise are met instead primarily by glycogen stores located in muscle tissue, whereas lipid stores are used for longer term imbalances between energy demand and availability. In metabolic terms,

153

starvation is similar to very slow-rate exercise, except that lipolysis is stimulated by a continuously low level of insulin rather than noradrenaline (Pond 1998).

Although famine is often considered a major selective pressure in humans (see Chapter 8), the issue as to whether human adipose tissue biology evolved in response to famine remains controversial. Rarely does the historical record offer precise estimates of mortality in past famines. Whilst those dying may be recorded, the size of the surviving population may not (Speakman 2006). Furthermore, in recent centuries where more information is available, it is not clear that death from starvation is the primary cause of mortality during famine conditions. For example, in the Irish potato famine during the middle of the nineteenth century, almost one million individuals are estimated to have died out of a population of approximately eight million. Of those one million deaths, a minority have been attributed directly to starvation, for example, only 6,000 of the 250,000 recorded deaths during 1847 (Speakman 2006). Instead, data from several populations demonstrate that the majority of famine deaths tend to occur in those under 5 or over 60 years old, and to derive from infectious diseases due to reduced immunocompetence (Watkins and Menken 1985; Speakman 2006). This scenario is consistent with that demonstrated by animal research, with Widdowson (1976) reporting that the principal cause of death following extreme under-nutrition in pigs was infection due to organisms in the lungs and gastrointestinal tract. Undernourished humans are also vulnerable to infections and parasites (Barac-Nieto et al. 1978). Figure 6.1 illustrates the percentage of increase above the background mortality rate according to age during the 1974 famine in Bangladesh, showing a negligible impact in older children and young adults (Menken and Cambpell 1992).

Nevertheless, the hypothesis that famine is not the primary selective pressure favouring fat stores in humans should be considered separate from the hypothesis that during famine, those not susceptible to infectious diseases can survive for long periods through drawing on the energy reserves provided by adipose tissue. A number of datasets illustrate this point, demonstrating long-term survival of people during chronic negative energy balance through a combination of continuous weight loss and reduced levels of physical activity. Figure 6.2 illustrates the rations recorded in prisoner of war camps from the First and Second World Wars, or from refugee camps in Somalia. For obvious reasons, severe famines typically occur in conditions precluding the collection of detailed data; however, recent monitoring of refugee camps has provided important information about the magnitude of long-term weight loss, and the lower levels of nutritional status, compatible with life.

Collins (1995) investigated the association between BMI and mortality during the Somalian famine of 1992 to 1993. This famine followed civil war at the beginning of the decade and caused extremely high levels of mortality in the

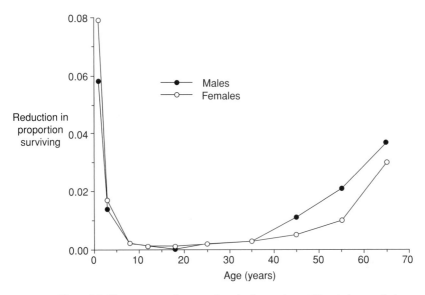

Figure 6.1. The percentage increase above background mortality rate by age, during the 1974 famine in Bangladesh. The data indicate negligible impact of the famine on older children and young adults, with mortality largely affecting the very young and older adults (Menken and Cambpell 1992).

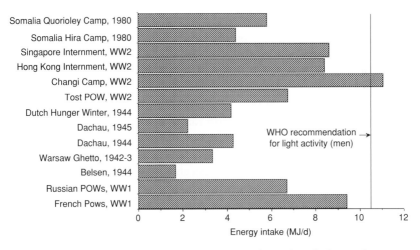

Figure 6.2. Data on average daily energy supply in a variety of prisoner-of-war or internment camps during the twentieth century, as well as the Dutch hunger winter. In all but one case, the rations were substantially below the World Health Organisation recommendation for adults exhibiting light activity levels. The lowest levels, recorded in Belsen concentration camp in World War II, represented less than 1/5 of total energy requirements. Based on data from Rivers (1988).

civilian population. Of 573 adult inpatients treated at a therapeutic centre in the town of Baidoa, 413 survived, 122 died and 38 were lost to follow-up. The association between BMI and mortality was strongly influenced by whether severe famine oedema was present. Famine oedema comprises increases in the interstitial fluid of tissues owing to low levels of plasma proteins which upset the osmotic pressure of blood plasma. As well as worsening the prognosis for survival, famine oedema also confounds the use of BMI as an index of nutritional status, as the excess fluid inflates the BMI value. Considering only patients with absence of severe famine oedema, the mean BMI of survivors at admission was 12.9 and 12.8 kg/m^2 in males and females, respectively. However, 22 % of survivors aged 25 years and older declined to a BMI of below 12 kg/m^2, as did 49% of survivors aged 15 to 24 years. One individual young adult survivor declined to a BMI of 8.7 kg/m^2. The mean BMI of survivors with severe oedema was significantly higher, at 15.4 and 13.5 kg/m^2 in men and women, respectively, and the case rate of mortality was also substantially higher (Collins 1995).

Generalising from these findings is difficult. First, Somalians, like many East African populations, have a linear physique and have relatively long leg length which is known to contribute to variability in the association between BMI and relative tissue masses (Norgan 1994c). However, as Collins (1995) pointed out, in the absence of famine conditions Somalians tend to display mean BMI values of around 19 to 21 kg/m^2, typical of values recorded in other African countries. Second, famine survival is undoubtedly improved in warmer conditions, and higher levels of mortality are typically recorded in colder climates due to the inability of malnourished individuals to regulate body temperature (Leyton 1946). Nevertheless, these data are important in demonstrating the capacity for humans to survive at levels of body weight substantially below the cut-off of 18.5 kg/m^2 conventionally used by the World Health Organisation to categorise chronic energy deficiency (James, Ferro-Luzzi, and Waterlow 1988).

Similar work by Henry (1990) elucidates the role of disease in mediating the influence of low BMI on mortality risk. Henry described the minimal BMI values recorded in a variety of categories of patients who either did or did not survive, with the categories including subjects surviving or dying from starvation, famine victims and women with anorexia nervosa. The mean (SD) BMI of those dying from starvation was 13.1 (1.1) kg/m^2 in males, and 11.0 (2.0) in females, whereas the values for those surviving total starvation were 15.9 (0.7) and 17.3 (0.7) kg/m^2 in men and women, respectively. In 16 men exposed to the Dutch famine during the Second World War, the mean BMI was 17.4 (1.8) kg/m^2, whereas in 30 women with anorexia nervosa, the mean BMI was 13.5 (2.2) kg/m^2. Collectively, these data illustrate a threshold, particularly in men, below which the risk of mortality is greatly increased (see

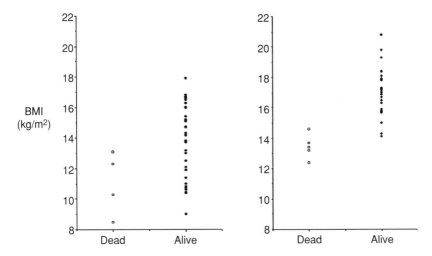

Figure 6.3. BMI values recorded in a variety of categories of patients, who either did or did not survive. Left panel – females; right panel – males. The categories included subjects surviving or dying from starvation, famine victims and women with anorexia nervosa. Data from Henry (1990).

Figure 6.3). However, unlike in the Somalian data, there is clear indication of a sex difference, with the critical threshold around 13 kg/m^2 in men but around 11 kg/m^2 in women (Henry 1990).

Such extreme values of BMI clearly indicate a loss of the majority of adipose tissue; however, more detailed data are required to elucidate the magnitude of the depletion of fat stores. Although such data are lacking, studies of extreme weight loss offer important insights into the selective depletion of lean and fat mass, and of specific adipose tissue depots.

Friedl and colleagues investigated the composition of weight loss in 55 young adult men participating in an Army Ranger course (Friedl et al. 1994). Over 8 weeks, the participants lost an average of 15.9% of baseline body weight. This weight loss was associated with a 65.5% loss of fat mass, and a 7.2% loss of lean mass. Skinfold thicknesses at four depots all declined, with the greatest loss at the suprailiac site and the lowest loss at the subscapular site (see Figure 6.4). This differential depletion of different skinfold depots resulted in a relative increase in the ratio of subscapular-to-triceps skinfold thickness, from 1.19 to 1.55. As discussed in Chapter 2, the use of skinfold thickness ratios to assess central fat deposition is problematic because of allometric associations and non-linearity. In this study, for example, the waist-hip ratio declined, indicating loss of central adipose tissue. Nevertheless, the data are sufficient to indicate a selective preservation of trunk fat relative to limb fat, and similar data are

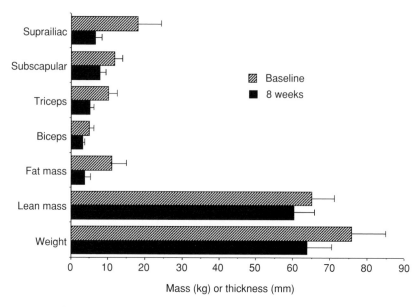

Figure 6.4. Changes in skinfold thickness and tissue masses in adult men during an eight-week Army Ranger course. Decreases in weight were attributable to declines in both lean mass and adiposity, with the greatest reduction in the suprailiac skinfold depot. Based on data from Friedl et al. (1994).

indicated from studies of women with anorexia nervosa (see below). Expressed as a percentage of body weight, fat mass declined from 14.3% at baseline to 5.8% after 8 weeks, with the lowest value in any individual being 3.8%. These values show a high consistency with that of 5.3% fat recorded after a 25% weight loss in the 1950 Minnesota starvation study (Keys et al. 1950), and they indicate that in males, around 2.5 kg of fat, or approximately 4% of weight, may represent a physiological lower limit in healthy active men (Friedl et al. 1994). These levels are also similar to those observed in many wild animals (Pond 1998). Clearly, however, a greater loss of fat is plausible at the cost of normal healthy function.

Data from women with anorexia nervosa indicate a similar selective depletion of subcutaneous fat stores during weight loss, with a preservation of central fat stores and a reversal of this difference on refeeding (Mayo-Smith et al. 1989; Zamboni et al. 1997). Table 6.1 presents data for patients with moderately severe anorexia nervosa (mean BMI 15.8 kg/m^2) and control women (mean BMI 22.5 kg/m^2). The reduction in body weight is primarily fat rather than lean mass, and within the loss of fat, subcutaneous rather than intra-abdominal fat. Growth-retarded neonates likewise show depleted subcutaneous fat stores

Table 6.1. *Body composition differences between patients with anorexia nervosa and control women*

	Controls (n = 39)	Patients (n = 15)	Difference
Age (y)	26	24	
BMI (kgm²)*	22.5	15.8	−30 %
Lean mass (kg)*	42.4	37.1	−12 %
Fat mass (kg)*	17.3	5.5	−68 %
Total fat area (cm²)*	191	42	−78 %
Subcutaneous fat area (cm²)*	166	30	−82 %
Intra-abdominal fat area (cm²)*	25	12	−53 %
Ratio subcutaneous: total fat**	0.86	0.62	−0.24
Ratio intra-abdominal: total fat**	0.14	0.40	+0.26

* Difference calculated as ((patient value − control value)/control value) × 100
** Difference calculated directly as difference between ratios
Data from Mayo-Smith et al. (1989)

but similar intra-abdominal fat relative to normal weight neonates, as was illustrated in Figure 4.4 (Harrington et al. 2004). These studies indicate that across the life-course, peripheral fat depots are more sensitive to conditions of energy imbalance, and that central fat is prioritised by the body as essential fat.

Few data are available regarding changes in lean mass or the weight of specific organs during starvation. Undernutrition in Colombian males, with a mean BMI of 17.7 kg/m², was associated with a 40% loss of muscle mass and a 30% loss of cell mass (Barac-Nieto et al. 1978). A comparison between anorexic and control women suggested that alongside a 30% reduction in muscle mass, the weight of the liver, spleen and heart also declined (Heymsfield and McManus 1985). Figure 6.5 shows the percentage loss of weight for different organs following a 40% weight loss (Rivers 1988). Clearly, such organ changes are life threatening, and the low levels of BMI described above indicate the capacity of less essential tissues such as adipose tissue to decrease more markedly in order to protect the vital organs.

An appreciation of the survival benefits of fat derives not only from studies of exposure to famine or malnutrition, but also to broader cross-sectional associations between nutritional status and morbidity and mortality (Norgan 1997). The association between BMI and health is problematic owing to to inherent associations between weight loss and disease, or between weight loss and disease-inducing behaviours such as smoking. Nevertheless, a meta-analysis of 19 large cohort studies suggested an increase in the risk of mortality in white men at moderately low BMI after taking these confounding factors into account

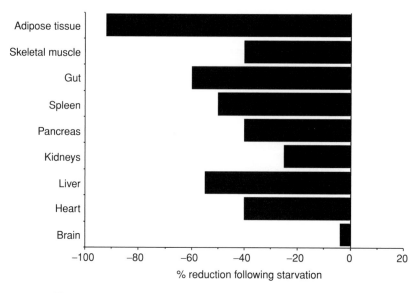

Figure 6.5. Percentage reduction in the mass of various organs or tissues during starvation. Although almost all organs other than the brain show some ability to decrease in weight, the most extreme depletion occurs in adipose tissue, demonstrating its value in buffering other tissues. Based on data from Rivers (1988)

(Troiano et al. 1996), with the magnitude of this risk similar to that observed in extremely overweight individuals. The evidence is substantially weaker for women, with little indication of a greater risk of mortality in lean women. Thus, whilst thinness in the absence of weight loss may be considered a 'hazard' in men, the scenario is less clear for women (Norgan 1997).

One kilogram of fat contains 37 MJ, equivalent to approximately 6 days supply for an adult individual expending approximately 6 MJ per day (Norgan 1997). Typical Western adults, as encapsulated in the concept of the reference man and woman of Behnke (McArdle, Katch, and Katch 1991), have a percentage body fat content of 15 and 27%, respectively. As reviewed in Chapter 2, men and women from other populations vary substantially around these values, but all datasets display a mean fat content greater in women than men (see Figures 2.23 and 2.24). Norgan has differentiated total adipose tissue into essential and storage fat, comprising 3 and 12%, respectively, of weight in men, and 9 and 15%, respectively, in women. The essential fat is located 'in bone marrow, heart, lungs, liver, kidneys, intestines, muscles and lipid-rich tissue of the central nervous system with roles other than energy storage' (Norgan 1997). In women, essential fat also extends to depots associated with the reproductive system, in the pelvic region and thighs (Norgan 1997).

The differences in mean body-fat content between men and women predict a differential ability to survive famine. The levels of body fat typical of Western young men and women are equivalent to energy stores of approximately 370 and 555 MJ, respectively, suggesting the potential to survive around 60 and 90 days, respectively. This prediction of sex differences in survival capacity is broadly supported by data from studies of Europe during the Second World War (Keys et al. 1950; Widdowson 1976; Henry 1990). Such sex differences are by no means unique to humans and were evident in Widdowson's classic studies of animal under-nutrition. Following extreme undernourishment during infancy, 87% of female pigs but only 22% of males were alive at one year (Widdowson 1976). The composition of weight loss has likewise been found to differ between the sexes in rats, with a substantially greater catabolism of protein in males. The capacity of fat stores to relieve protein catabolism is also observed in undernourished human infants, who derive only 4% of their energy requirements from this source, in contrast to 20% in adult males (Widdowson 1976).

Summary

It is therefore clear that fat represents a key resource for enduring a prolonged negative energy balance; however, I suggest, along with others (Speakman 2006), that this function has been over-emphasised to the detriment of our understanding of a wide variety of other functions drawing on energy stores.

6.2 Accommodating fluctuations in energy supply

Despite frequent reference to supposed cycles of feast and famine during human evolution (Neel 1962; Chakravarthy and Booth 2004), famine is likely to be a scenario associated in particular with agriculture (Dando 1980; Wells 2006). Prior to the emergence of sedentary agricultural populations, energy stress is likely to have derived from a variety of factors, including seasonality, longer term climate change, local ecological fluctuations, predator-prey cycles, disease load and population boom-bust dynamics (see Chapters 8 and 9). Similar conditions are encountered by a variety of mammal species (Pond 1998). Non-sedentary populations are able to use a number of strategies to address such energy perturbations, and energy stores in adipose tissue represent only one of a broader range of options. Contemporary foraging populations use mobility as a key strategy for relieving energy stress and migrate from energy scarcity towards improved resource distribution (Fagan 1999). Some such populations also maintain mobile extra-somatic energy stores in the form of domesticated stock animals (Clutton-Brock 1989).

The period during which fat stores can buffer lean mass when food intake is merely reduced, rather than eliminated, is clearly much longer than the period of starvation that can be survived. Body fat stores are therefore most important from an evolutionary perspective for their capacity to allow the organism to accommodate periods of time when energy supply does not match energy needs (Pond 1998).

The stresses imposed by seasonality vary in relation to latitude and other geographical features. Close to the equator, the earth's surface receives consistently high levels of solar radiation, such that the tropics can be broadly defined as a region that has no winter (Gill 1991). At higher latitudes, the sun's rays strike the earth more obliquely such that the amount of radiation is spread over a wider area. These regions also experience greater variability owing to the tilt of the Earth's axis, and hence greater seasonality in temperature. However, the equatorial regions are not in fact the hottest, as cloud or dust particles in the atmosphere either filter out or reflect back a proportion of the solar radiation (Gill 1991). From a temperature perspective, equatorial regions are less variable and temperate regions substantially more variable, with the cloud-free zone on either side of the tropics experiencing the greatest temperatures. Associated with these temperature differences are variability in day length, which impacts on plant growth by constraining the opportunity for photosynthesis. However, the regional pattern of rainfall variation is the opposite, with the most seasonal distribution occurring in the tropics (Gill 1991). Such variability occurs in tropical regions regardless of whether mean annual rainfall is high or low. In general, it is the duration of the dry season that represents the key ecological pressure on human subsistence in the tropics, whereas in temperate latitudes day length and its influence on the growing season and hence food resources is most important.

Populations practising farming are, on account of their inability to relocate during times of energy stress, most vulnerable to seasonal variability in energy supply. Typically, energy stress is greatest in the period prior to the harvest, which often coincides with high demands for physical effort (Ferro-Luzzi and Branca 1993). Cycles of 'hungry' and 'harvest' seasons therefore impose energy stress, which may be further compounded by seasonal epidemics in disease. These associations generate important links between the biology of energy balance and the biology of the immune system. This issue is explored in greater detail in Chapters 7, 8 and 9.

Data on nutritional status are available for a number of populations inhabiting seasonal environments in developing countries (Table 6.2). Annual fluctuations in weight tend to average around 2 kg in both sexes, but maybe as great as 5 kg,

Table 6.2. *Annual weight changes in adult men and women exposed to seasonality*

Population	Reference	Weight change (kg) Male	Female
Africa			
Benin	Schultink et al. 1990	–	1.8
Cameroon	DeGarine and Koppert 1988	3.4–5.2	2.1–4.7
Ethiopia	Ferro-Luzzi et al. 1990	–	1.7
Gambia	Singh et al. 1989	–	3.1
Mali	Adams 1995	2.6	2.0
Niger	Loutan and Lamotte 1984	3.1	2.4
Senegal	Rosetta 1986	2.1	2.1
	Simondon et al. 2007	–	2.5–3.9
Zaire	Pagezy 1984	–	1.4
Asia			
Bangladesh	Abdullah and Wheeler 1985	1.9	1.0
	Chen, Alauddin Chowdhury, and Huffman 1979	–	2.0
Burma	Dugdale and Payne 1987	2.7	–
India	McNeill et al. 1988	1.0	0.3
Nepal	Panter-Brick 1993	–	2.5
Papua New Guinea	Spencer and Heywood 1983	1.4	2.1
South America			
Peru	Leonard and Thomas 1989	1.8	1.2

equivalent to almost 10% of body weight, in women. Year-on-year fluctuations in the weight of Gambian women are shown in Figure 6.6, based on data from Singh and colleagues (1989). Changes in children's nutritional status may be even more extreme, generating seasonality in growth rate as well as nutritional status (Prentice and Cole 1994; Gamboa and Garcia 2007). More detailed metabolic studies have attributed the majority of adult weight changes to body fat mass (Lawrence et al. 1987a), although suppression of basal metabolic rate during pregnancy provides a further means of metabolic flexibility (Poppitt et al. 1994).

Webster and colleagues (1984) suggested that approximately 75% of gain or loss in weight comprises fat, with the remainder lean tissue. However, Forbes (1989) highlighted an association between initial body composition and the composition of subsequent weight loss. The higher the baseline ratio of fat mass to lean mass, the greater the proportion of weight loss attributable to fat (see below). However, seasonal weight loss appears to be inversely related to the magnitude of BMI prior to the seasonal stress. Weight loss was reduced

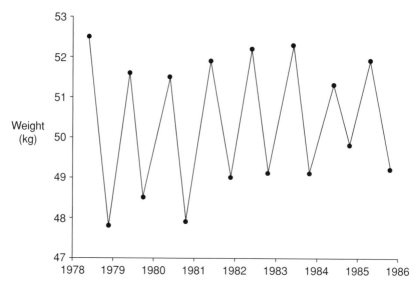

Figure 6.6. Seasonal oscillations in body weight in women from the Gambia, attributable to profound changes in energy balance between hungry and harvest seasons. The typical annual weight fluctuation is 4 to 5 kg. Redrawn based on data from Singh et al. (1989).

in those of low BMI compared to those of higher BMI in Ethiopian women (Ferro-Luzzi et al. 1990). A similar scenario was observed in Benin (Schultink et al. 1990).

To store energy, appetite must increase energy intake beyond that required to match energy expenditure. Studies have demonstrated that where food availability permits, humans can gain weight and fat stores very rapidly, though not as fast as some animals. Close examination of the classic Minnesota starvation experiment shows that when those starved began to regain weight, fat accumulation proceeded at a much faster rate than lean mass accumulation (Keys et al. 1950). Fat mass soon exceeded its initial level owing to massive hyperphagia that continued until lean mass had regained its own initial level (Figure 6.7) (Stubbs and Tolkamp 2006). Other studies are consistent in showing such a 'weight overshoot' during recovery from severe weight depletion (Dulloo 1997). Subsequent physiological studies have attempted to explore the underlying mechanism for this overshoot. Individuals tend to show consistency in their partitioning of energy between protein and fat during both weight loss and recovery (Henry, Rivers, and Payne 1988), implying an influence of baseline body composition. Compared with lean individuals, fatter individuals mobilise more energy from fat than from protein during weight loss, and subsequently

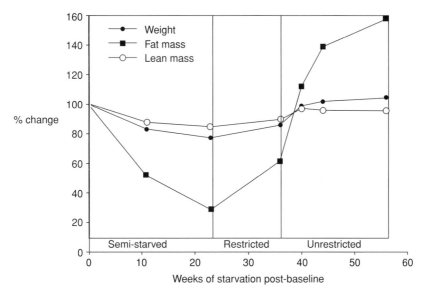

Figure 6.7. The pattern of body-composition change during semi-starvation and recovery in the classic Minnesota starvation experiment. The percentage deficit in lean mass was less than that in weight during the 24-week period of semi-starvation owing to the much larger decrease in fat mass. During the 12-week period of recovery on a restricted diet, the recovery in fat mass was substantially greater than that in lean mass. During the further recovery period during which dietary intake was unrestricted, fat mass increased well beyond its baseline level, leading to an 'overshoot' in weight. Data from Keys and colleagues (1950).

deposit more energy as lipid during weight regain (Henry, Rivers, and Payne 1988). Whilst some have suggested a role for thermogenesis in such differences (Dulloo 1997), variability in physical activity is an alternative possible explanation.

Further insight into the effect of rapid weight gain on body composition is provided by the 'natural experiment' of the Guru Walla ceremony, practised by the Massas people of Cameroon (Pasquet et al. 1992). This traditional fattening session, lasting around two months, involves each participant being isolated with a female attendant devoted exclusively to the provision of high-carbohydrate meals day and night, at approximately 3 hour intervals. Data on nine individuals demonstrated an average increase of approximately 25% in body mass, of which around 70% was fat (Pasquet et al. 1992). As shown in Figure 6.8, extreme positive energy balance was achieved by a doubling of energy intake with no significant change in energy expenditure. Figure 6.9 also shows a significant correlation between the magnitude of positive energy balance and the magnitude of weight gain. The increase in fat mass is equivalent to

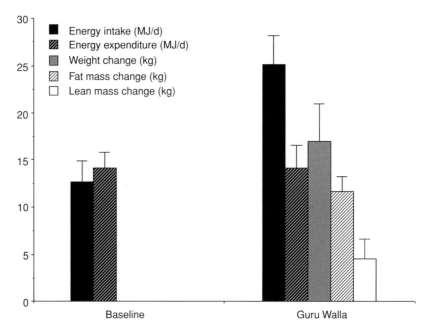

Figure 6.8. Changes in energy intake and expenditure, and in weights, fat mass and lean mass during the Guru Walla traditional feeding period in the Massa of Cameroon. No significant change in energy expenditure occurs; however, energy intake more than doubles, resulting in major increases in body weight, of which the majority of the gain is in fat mass. Based on data from Pasquet et al. (1992).

approximately 400 MJ, which would provide approximately two months supply of energy during famine conditions. The ritual fattening session is clearly associated with long-term experience of seasonal energy stress. In most years, a moderate period of food shortage is experienced which has little biological impact, but severe nutritional stress has been a regular experience, and starvation-induced death still occasionally occurs during particularly challenging seasons (De Garine 1993). The Guru Walla tradition may be considered a symbolic expression of control over such seasonal hardship, through allowing some to indulge in excessive food consumption during the season of reduced energy availability (De Garine 1993).

Detailed studies of weight loss in the obese show that in proportional terms, the greatest loss of adipose tissue occurs in the visceral depot (Figure 6.10). However, in absolute terms this depot is relatively small, and the main site of adipose tissue depletion is in abdominal subcutaneous fat (Kamel, McNeill, and Van Wijk 2000). At the other end of the scale of nutritional status, the findings that emerge from the refeeding of patients with anorexia nervosa

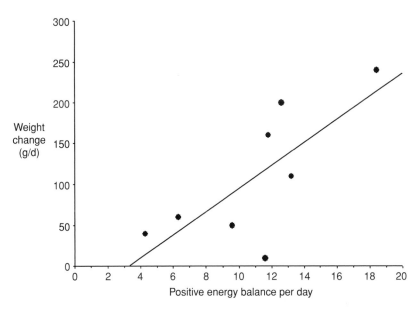

Figure 6.9. Association between the magnitude of positive energy balance per day and the increase in body weight during the Guru Walla traditional feeding period in the Massa of Cameroon. Based on data from Pasquet et al. (1992).

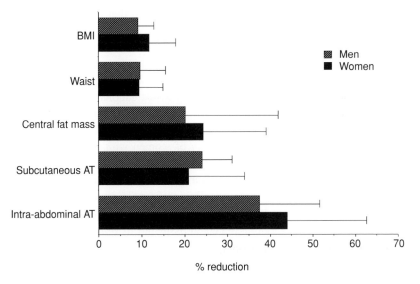

Figure 6.10. Percentage reduction in BMI, waist girth, fat mass and regional adipose tissue depots during six months of weight loss in 36 obese adults, measured by magnetic resonance imaging. The weight loss was dominated by loss of central fat, with visceral fat showing the greatest relative reduction. Adapted from data of Kamel, McNeill, and Van Wijk (2000).

Table 6.3. *Effect of refeeding on body composition in 29 women with anorexia nervosa*

	Baseline	Refeeding	Difference (kg)	% change
Age (y)	23			
Weight (kg)	42.0	54.1	12.1	29
BMI (kgm^2)	15.9	20.6	4.7	30
Skeletal muscle mass (kg)	14.0	17.0	3.0	21
Total adipose tissue (kg)	6.6	14.8	8.2	124
Subcutaneous adipose tissue (kg)	5.9	13.0	7.1	120
Visceral adipose tissue (kg)	0.38	1.04	0.66	174
Intramuscular adipose tissue (kg)	0.37	0.81	0.44	119

Data from Mayer et al. (2005)

imply the same mechanism. In 26 patients with mean baseline BMI of 16.5 kg/m^2 followed over six months, an increase of 6.7 kg in weight (2.5 kg/m^2 BMI) was associated with a 4% increase in lean mass but a 64% increase in fat mass (Orphanidou et al. 1997). Regional analyses showed that subcutaneous skinfold thicknesses increased more in the abdomen and thigh than in the chest or limbs, and DXA measurements likewise indicated that fat mass increased more in the torso than in the thigh (Orphanidou et al. 1997). However, other studies using CT have shown that whilst the accumulation of adipose tissue during refeeding is central rather than peripheral, it is also subcutaneous rather than visceral (Mayo-Smith et al. 1989; Zamboni et al. 1997) (Table 6.3).

Collectively, the studies of seasonal weight fluctuations and refeeding of patients demonstrate the capacity of gains and losses in fat mass, rather than lean mass, to accommodate perturbations in energy availability. The example of the Gambia demonstrates the capacity of women with BMI at the lower end of the normal range, but on average above the cut-off for chronic energy deficiency, to conceive and gestate offspring within this scenario (Lawrence et al. 1987a). Although there is statistically significant seasonality in birth rates (Billewicz and McGregor 1981), the magnitude is modest, and these effects might further be due to variability in coital frequency as well as any metabolic constraints (Ulijaszek 1993).

Summary

Buffering mismatches between energy intake and expenditure, rather than outright famine, is the ecological scenario common to most other animal species, as discussed in detail by Pond (1998). It is perhaps curious that human nutritionists have placed so much emphasis on the notion that the function of human energy stores is to relieve famine. The most likely explanation for this emphasis is that we appear to have become more prone to famines in our recent history, which offers a poor model of the longer-term past.

6.3   Mechanical Functions

Whilst most attention has been directed to the energetics or signalling of adipose tissue, it also contributes to mechanical functions. Pond (1998) has referred to 'structural' adipose tissue, comprising collagen and adipocytes in different proportions located in a variety of anatomical locations. The adipocytes in such depots are substantially less metabolically active, and respond minimally to positive or negative energy balance.

Such structural depots are found in the limbs, for example at the tips of fingers and toes and on the base of the heel, around the eyeball, and in the mouth, particularly in neonates. Internally, fat may also offer a protective cushion around vital organs such as the kidney and heart, although allometric analyses provide no specific support for this hypothesis, and in most cases the presence of shared blood supply between the organs and adjacent fat depots implies a metabolic connection (Pond 1998). As with the hypothesised role of fat as insulation, possible benefits of adipose tissue in this context may be merely a side effect deriving from other functions, and structural fat has minimal bearing on the evolutionary perspective that is the main topic of this book.

6.4   Adaptation to cold

The notion that adiposity represents an adaptation to cold is widely held in the literature. Adipose tissue may contribute in two ways to thermoregulation, first in comprising an organ of heat production in the form of brown adipose tissue, and second in providing a store of energy from white adipose tissue for more general metabolic functions including thermoregulation.

Cannon and Nedergaard (2004) suggest two generic functions of brown adipose tissue. First, at low environmental temperatures, it can produce heat and hence contribute to homeostasis. This appears particularly important in small-sized mammals, when surface area (the primary site of heat loss) is large relative to body mass (the primary determinant of heat production). Around 5% of human neonatal adipose tissue is brown, and its contribution to thermoregulation is indicated by the poorer thermoregulatory capacities of malnourished infants (Brooke, Harris, and Salvosa 1973). In some species, brown adipose tissue remains important in adult life, for example, periodically raising body temperature to interrupt torpor during hibernation (Dark 2005). Though widely assumed to lose function in older humans, recent work has suggested it remains metabolically active in some adults (Nedergaard, Bengtsson, and Cannon 2007). The second function of this tissue is that by decreasing the efficiency of metabolism, it may aid the processing of larger volumes of food, thereby aiding the extraction of essential nutrients such as protein. This second function has been little explored in humans.

Although the role of brown adipose tissue in cold adaptation merits greater research, especially in populations which have inhabited polar environments for many generations, at the present time the evidence for human fatness as an adaptation to cold primarily concerns white adipose tissue, though even here, there is some controversy as to the exact function performed.

In marine mammals, a thick layer of blubber is found beneath the skin, but whether this distribution has been selected for the function of insulation as often proposed requires careful scrutiny. Pond (1998) has suggested that while blubber does show a thermal gradient across its thickness, demonstrating insulation capacity, this function is achieved only in very large animals. In smaller-sized species of cetacean, such as porpoises and dolphins, the thickness of the blubber layer is reduced compared to that of larger whales, and whereas the latter can access polar oceans, the former remain restricted to temperate or tropical regions (Pond 1998).

To address this issue in non-marine species, Pond and colleagues investigated body fat distribution across a range of carnivore species (Pond 1998; Pond and Ramsay 1992; Ramsay, Mattacks, and Pond 1992). They found that after taking into account allometric relationships between lean body mass and adipose tissue mass, polar bears showed no additional trend for allocating fat to subcutaneous rather than internal depots and instead had a fat distribution similar to that predicted for a warm-climate carnivore. This analysis indicates that the disproportionate allocation of fat to subcutaneous depots arises for anatomical rather than functional reasons. As animals increase in size, their surface area relative to volume or mass decreases. Consequently, even if relative fatness itself does not increase, larger size generates a thicker subcutaneous layer of fat, and this effect is enhanced if relative fatness increases (Pond 1998). Other organisms such as penguins also periodically acquire an enhanced subcutaneous fat layer, accumulated to fund the lengthy fast experienced during the breeding season. Once again, however, Pond (1998) has attributed this tissue not to insulation, but to the need to distribute energy stores across the body surface in order not to impede mobility during swimming. Others have furthermore demonstrated that the primary role of these energy stores is to meet energy requirements during the incubation of the egg, such that experimental intervention to increase cold stress causes too rapid of a depletion of the energy store and the abandonment of the egg (Ancel et al. 1997).

These animal data provide an important perspective when interpreting findings from humans. A study of Korean women who regularly dived in cold water showed that they had less subcutaneous fat than other Korean women (Rennie et al. 1962), suggesting no specific function of fat as insulation.

A detailed study of pastoral nomads inhabiting Mongolia, where the mean annual temperature is $-1.7°$ C, described high levels of abdominal adiposity in women and children but not men (Beall and Goldstein 1992). Such central adiposity was indicated both by a high waist-hip ratio and a high ratio of subscapular-to-triceps skinfold thicknesses. Arm fat indices were significantly higher than expected in adults of both sexes, but not in children. These authors suggested several ways in which this pattern of fat deposition could be considered an adaptation to cold conditions, but insulation was not amongst the proposed mechanisms. First, a more central fat deposition decreases surface area relative to volume, consistent with ecological 'laws' relating this ratio to climatic conditions (Bergmann 1847). Second, abdominal fat deposition increases resting metabolic rate, previously shown to be a characteristic of Siberian populations (Snodgrass et al. 2005), and hence increases heat production. Third, abdominal fat can further respond to cold stress via the action of catecholamines by generating heat (Shephard 1985). Finally, Beall and Goldstein (1992) suggest that these traits may be particularly beneficial in children and women because of their smaller body size compared to men, with children furthermore having reduced body fat content relative to adults. Thus, adipose tissue distribution appears to represent an important adaptation to cold environments, but with central rather than subcutaneous deposition the most notable characteristic.

Any benefit of adipose tissue in buffering cold stress must also be offset against any need to dissipate excess thermal energy. For example, marine animals may be exposed to high as well as low temperatures, and there may be an upper limit on blubber thickness to prevent overheating (Pond 1998). In walruses, expansion of blood flow through superficial blood vessels in the layer of blubber allows heat loss in hot conditions, but also the minimisation of such loss through vasoconstriction during cold conditions. Pond (1998) makes the important point that adipose tissue is able to play this role because it is not unduly affected by periodic reductions in blood supply, unlike other tissues. Heat stress is likewise an important ecological stress in many human populations, and even those inhabiting cold environments may need to lose heat rapidly during physical exertion. The findings of Beall and Goldstein

(1992) are again relevant in this context, since activation of the *metabolism* of central fat stores in response to cold stress represents a more flexible mechanism than whole-body insulation, even given variable blood flow as discussed above.

Summary

Adipose tissue undoubtedly provides energy for maintaining body temperature in cold environments, and recent research suggests that the metabolic contribution of central abdominal may be sensitive to signals of cold stress such as catecholamines. Further work is required to elucidate this metabolic role and to determine whether brown adipose tissue contributes to this function in older age groups.

6.5   Regulation of reproduction

Energy is fundamental to reproduction in all species (Bronson 1989). It has been said that time and energy are the primary scarce resources, and that natural selection favours those individuals converting energy successfully into offspring during the time available (Ellison 2003). Humans are no different to this general mammalian pattern; however, the details of the way in which energy constrains reproductive effort have emerged only relatively recently. There is rapidly improving understanding of the influence of energy supply on the likelihood of conception, on the physiology and outcome of pregnancy and on the quantity and quality of milk produced during lactation.

Conception

The notion that adipose tissue contributes to the regulation of female reproduction in humans dates back to pioneering work by Frisch and colleagues in the 1970s. In the original hypothesis, a critical threshold of fatness was proposed, below which menarche is prevented (Frisch and McArthur 1974). Subsequent versions extended this hypothesis to constraints on ovulation (Frisch 1990). A large volume of work has probed this hypothesis from a number of angles, and though it has intuitive appeal, the evidence fails to support it directly (Ellison 2001). Nevertheless, as our understanding of the regulation of mammalian reproduction improves, it can be seen that body fat content and reproductive function may be strongly correlated even though the former does not specifically *constrain* the latter.

Frisch observed a decline in the mean age at menarche co-occurring with secular trends in growth, and suggested that a minimum level of body fat was required for onset of menarche (Frisch and McArthur 1974; Frisch 1985). Apparently consistent with the Frisch hypothesis is evidence that women with eating disorders and other types of malnutrition experience difficulty conceiving. Malnourished mothers further have an increased risk of miscarriage early in pregnancy (Wynn 1987), or stillbirth (Stein et al. 1975), both of which may be considered adaptive strategies (Wells 2003b). However, maternal malnutrition typically involves more than low energy stores alone, and it usually presents in combination with either very low energy intake, or very high activity levels. A series of studies by Ellison and colleagues (Ellison 2001) has demonstrated that energy flux has a closer association with reproductive function than energy stores, and these findings are supported by research on mammalian reproductive function.

From a mechanistic perspective, increasing oestrogen levels are associated with both menarche and fat deposition, generating an apparent association between them (Ellison 2001). Thus, hormonal changes that occur during pregnancy may be considered to underpin the association, but these changes are most closely associated with growth rather than body composition *per se*. Ellison (1981; 1982; 1990), for example, has suggested that growth of the pelvis is most strongly associated with age at menarche.

A second key issue is the inherent connection between energy stores, energy balance and energy flux. Those with low levels of fat tend also to be characterised by extremes of energy balance or energy flux. For example, athletes (who often lack menstrual function) tend to operate at high levels of energy expenditure, while those with eating disorders tend to have low energy intake (Ellison 2001). At either extreme, metabolic flexibility is reduced. Unless weight change is drastic, energy expenditure and intake are very closely associated. Those with high energy expenditure tend to have high energy intake, and likewise at the other end of the scale. Positive energy balance is therefore difficult to achieve at these extremes, as those with high energy expenditure may struggle to increase energy intake, whilst those with low energy intake may struggle to decrease energy expenditure.

The emphasis by Ellison on energy flux and balance as opposed to energy stores is strongly supported by data from animal studies, in particular the work by Wade and Schneider (Wade and Schneider 1992; Wade, Schneider, and Li 1996; Schneider 2004) focusing on the availability of metabolic fuels. These authors, like Pond (1998), emphasise the difficulty in any species of simultaneously and continuously maintaining all physiological processes at an optimal level. Rather, inconstancy in the form and availability of energy must be accommodated with a set of physiological priorities, of which reproduction must be traded off against survival. Reproductive function is generically deferred or interrupted when dietary energy supply is constrained or when competing physiological functions increase their own demand (Wade and Schneider 1992).

As discussed in more detail in Chapter 7, energy is inherently a constraint on reproduction, and there is a strong association between the availability of food and reproductive fitness (Schneider 2004). The key question concerns the nature of the physiological link between energy availability and reproductive function. Wade and Schneider (1992) have elegantly elucidated how a variety of ecological factors act on the availability of oxidisable metabolic fuels, which in turn influence reproductive function. Ecological factors such as thermal environment and exercise load alter the partitioning of metabolic fuels and impact on the probability of conception. These effects can be reversed through manipulations of dietary energy supply, as demonstrated in studies of human athletes (Kopp-Woodroffe et al. 1999). Furthermore, when conditions favour reproductive investment, the same molecular signals that promote reproductive function act to attenuate other functions prioritising survival or feeding (Schneider 2004).

This perspective emphasises the limitations of the concept of fat itself as a constraint on female reproduction. Rather, 'survival during the most extreme energetic challenges requires that mobilisation and oxidation of free fatty acids from adipose tissue take precedence over defence of a particular level of body fat content' (Wade and Schneider 1992). However, this does not refute an important role of body fat within this broader metabolic model. A number of studies have generated a sophisticated model of physiological signals controlling energy intake, partitioning and expenditure, and identifying the molecules and their receptors. Mechanisms that regulate energy balance are sensitive to signals deriving from alterations in metabolic fuel oxidation, and they in turn are sensitive to leptin, the hormonal signal of body fat content.

Schneider has differentiated between (a) primary sensory stimuli that act on sensory detectors, (b) hormonal mediators and modulators of the effects of such stimuli, and (c) central effector systems. Primary metabolic stimuli derive from changes in the oxidation of metabolic fuels and can occur substantially more rapidly than changes in body fat content. Ultimately, these changes impact on effector systems in the brain stem and hypothalamus, which control the hypothalamic-pituitary-gonadal system and estrous cyclicity (Schneider 2004). This fundamental association is then sensitive to a number of mediating and modulating factors. Mediating hormones contribute to this association when their concentrations and activities reflect the magnitude of energy stores or the availability of oxidisable metabolic fuels. They include sex hormones, pancreatic and adrenal hormones, and leptin (Schneider 2004). Leptin is a key mediating hormone, which acts to decrease food intake and increase energy expenditure, fuel availability and oxidation. Experiments have shown that exogenous provision of the hormone to leptin-deficient mice restores reproductive function, and a similar mechanism is predicted to be found in humans (Prentice et al. 2002). Leptin, for example, predicts age at puberty (Ong, Ahmed, and Dunger 1999; Chehab et al. 2002). However, this implicates the capacity of leptin to influence the availability of oxidisable fuels, but it does not indicate that either leptin or fat are themselves essential for reproductive function. Hormones may also modulate the association between oxidisable fuels and effector systems by acting on intracellular availability and oxidation of fuel supplies. Both leptin and insulin have been proposed to act in this way, indicating a more fundamental role for them in reproductive function (Schneider 2004).

Whilst further work is necessary to clarify the contribution of leptin, and other signals associated with adipose tissue, to reproductive function in our species, current understanding suggests that fat is not in itself physiologically necessary for reproductive function but acts as an important mediating/modulating factor such that the likelihood of conception is associated with the magnitude of fat. The Frisch hypothesis is not supported, in the sense that a critical level (and, in relation to other species, a very high level) of fat is not necessary, but it is now easier to understand why epidemiological associations between body composition and reproductive function are often observed.

Pregnancy

Mammals vary in their energetic strategy in relation to pregnancy. Ecologists differentiate between 'income breeders', which capture the energy required for reproductive effort from the environments on a daily basis, versus 'capital breeders' which accumulate energy stores prior to breeding (Stearns 1992; Jönsson 1997). The key difference is that capital breeders can breed in a range of ecological circumstances (Pond 1984; Stearns 1992). Whilst rats accumulate adipose tissue at the start of pregnancy for utilisation during late pregnancy and lactation, other species mobilise stored fat throughout. Primates are characterised by relatively moderate energetic stress during pregnancy (Prentice and Goldberg 2000). Fat stores may therefore offer only limited direct contribution to the energy costs of pregnancy, although during the final weeks maternal skinfold thicknesses may reduce slightly, indicating the funding of fetal growth from maternal capital (Forsum, Sadurskis, and Wager 1989) rather than dietary intake.

In affluent ecological conditions, mothers continue to acquire energy stores during pregnancy in order to meet the future costs of lactation, but the evidence from Gambian farmers shows that such fat accumulation is not obligatory, and that pregnancy can proceed during a net loss of fat (Lawrence et al. 1987a). Ellison (2001) has suggested that the offspring itself initiates birth when its metabolic requirements exceed the maternal capacity to meet them, inducing fetal starvation.

Lactation

The accumulation of fetal fat commences only in the last trimester, and Ellison has proposed that fat deposition is constrained during fetal life because of the inability of fatty acids to cross the placenta (Ellison 2001). Conversely, breast-milk contains higher levels of lipids and can fund more rapid fat accumulation. In turn, the energy costs of lactation are substantially higher than those of pregnancy (Clutton-Brock, Albon, and Guinness 1989), and though they may be met in part through increased energy intake, they may also be funded through the oxidation of fat stores, with this option clearly of greater importance during constraints on energy intake. Biopsy measurements indicate that when lactation is funded by adipose tissue, the costs are met disproportionately from peripheral fat depots such as the thigh (Rebuffe-Scrive et al. 1985). This is consistent with the tendency of adolescent females to store fat disproportionately in the same depots prior to reproduction (Lassek and Gaulin 2006; Wells 2006). The particular value of lower-body adipose depots in this context derives from their high content of long-chain polyunsaturated fatty acids (Phinney et al. 1994) which are critical for neural development in the offspring. Hence, adipose tissue quality as well as energy content is important in lactation.

During lactation, fatty acids are the main means of energy transferred to the offspring (Pond 1998). The milk of most mammal species is high in fat and low in carbohydrate, but as in other primates with relatively slow infant growth rates, human breast-milk is rich in lactose and low in triglycerides (Pond 1998). Adipose tissue makes no direct contribution to milk synthesis and instead accommodates the more general relationship between energy intake and output. Nevertheless, many studies have illustrated how peripheral maternal fat stores are depleted during lactation in subsistence communities, as recently reviewed (Lassek and Gaulin 2006) (see also Chapter 4).

The contribution of maternal fat stores to lactation enables the protection of milk supply during moderate maternal malnutrition. Infants of malnourished mothers can attain the same milk volumes as those of well-nourished women by suckling with greater intensity and more often (Delgado, Martorell, and Klein 1982). Milk production is surprisingly robust to maternal nutritional status, even in chronically energy-deficient mothers (Prentice, Goldberg,

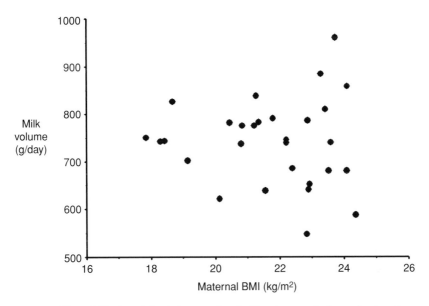

Figure 6.11. Association between maternal milk volume production and maternal BMI in a variety of populations worldwide, demonstrating no significant relationship between the variables. Based on data from Prentice, Goldberg, and Prentice (1994).

and Prentice 1994). Figure 6.11 shows the lack of a systematic association between maternal BMI and breast-milk intake of the baby, using data from a variety of populations ranging in maternal BMI from 17.9 to 23.7 kg/m^2, as reviewed by Prentice and colleagues (1994). Figure 6.12 shows a similar lack of association between maternal BMI and breast-milk energy content, using the same data. Compensatory 'energy sparing' reductions in basal metabolism may be one explanation for such apparent robusticity, while in baboons, compensations in physical activity have also been observed (Roberts, Cole, and Coward 1985).

However, during more severe malnutrition maternal milk yield may decrease (Bailey 1965), as also reported in baboons (Roberts, Cole, and Coward 1985), and *within* some of the populations reviewed (Prentice, Goldberg, and Prentice 1994), maternal BMI was associated with both breast-milk volume intake and energy content. For example, a number of studies have reported positive associations between maternal fatness and breast-milk fat content (Prentice, Prentice, and Whitehead 1981; Nommsen et al. 1991; Villalpando et al. 1991; Brown et al. 1986; Ettyang et al. 2005), although others have reported either no association or an inverse association (Marin Spring et al. 1985; van Steenbergen et al. 1983).

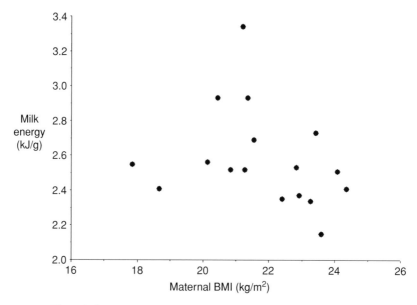

Figure 6.12. Association between breast-milk energy content and maternal BMI in a variety of populations worldwide, demonstrating no significant relationship between the variables. Based on data from Prentice, Goldberg, and Prentice (1994).

Breast-milk provides not only energy to the offspring but also leptin, such that breast-fed infants have higher circulating levels of the hormone compared to those not breast-fed (Locke 2002). These higher leptin contributions have in turn been associated with increased levels of lean mass during infant growth (Savino et al. 2002), implying that by inflating signals of body fatness, increased accretion of lean tissue may be achieved. Given reported associations between maternal BMI and offspring leptin concentration, the implication is that maternal fatness itself drives lean accumulation in the infant (Savino et al. 2006).

Summary

Maternal energy reserves contribute to reproductive function in two key ways. Most importantly, energy flux and energy stores influence the rate of maturation and the likelihood of conception, and therefore provide a store of energy-capital for funding the subsequent reproductive costs. In doing so, they also contribute some of the biochemical compounds important for specific aspects of offspring phenotype. Second, these energy costs are greatest during lactation rather than pregnancy, and the transfer of energy to the offspring is therefore a function of maternal nutritional status interacting with constraints on dietary energy intake.

6.6   Regulation of offspring growth

Compared to other species, humans exhibit a relatively slow rate of childhood growth. Humans also appear unique in their lengthy period of juvenile dependency, such that in the majority of populations offspring do not become net calorie produces until reaching adulthood (Kaplan et al. 2000) (though this does not mean that they do not forage or contribute anything to the parental energy budget). Although their energy needs may be met in part by a variety of family members, it is usual for the mother to play the critical role during infancy and childhood. This central maternal role places a high stress on the maternal energy budget, as successive offspring are 'stacked' (Robson, vanSchaik, and Hawkes 2006) such that the mother may simultaneously be provisioning an adolescent, a child and an infant, with another pregnancy due once the infant has been weaned.

The accumulation of body fat during infancy has, as discussed below, been attributed in part to the need to buffer the high energy demands of the brain during infancy and the weaning period (Kuzawa 1998). However, another need met by the same fat stores may be early childhood growth, which likewise is highly sensitive to the burden of infection during early childhood (Prentice and Darboe 2008). The ontogenetic pattern of fat deposition suggests that energy stores may be mobilised during infancy and the toddler period in order to fund deposition of lean mass. Unpublished data from a UK infant-growth study (Chomtho, Wells and Fewtrell) show that skinfold-thickness measurements during infancy are positively associated with the relative amounts of childhood lean mass, indicating that infant energy stores are used to meet the costs of growth. Accretion of lean tissue is a slow and steady process, with it requiring energy both for its construction and its subsequent maintenance. Thus, though protein availability is also a limiting factor, the baseline supply of energy appears important in permitting the deposition process to occur.

The sensitivity of infant and childhood growth to malnutrition and infection is notorious, such that measurements of weight and height are widely used to assess population growth status by international organisations. Comparisons between populations routinely demonstrate lower levels of subcutaneous fat mass in children from developing countries, as well as shorter height (Olivieri et al. 2008; Semproli and Gualdi-Russo 2007). Growth rates are strongly sensitive to ecological conditions (Walker et al. 2006), and slowed childhood growth is considered an adaptation specifically to accommodate the high maternal energy burden where multiple offspring are being provisioned (Gurven and Walker 2006).

Recent research has clarified trans-generational components of the association between body fatness and growth rate. More generally, of course, many aspects of parental phenotype are transmitted to the offspring through non-genetic mechanisms, the best-known example comprising secular trends in height (Cole 2000). Maternal phenotype can impact on offspring height through both fetal growth and influences on infant weight gain as discussed in Chapter 5. There is now growing evidence that maternal adiposity impacts on offspring growth rate. Although of modest magnitude, a number of cohorts have associated increased maternal fatness with greater birth-weight (Wells 2007f). For example, in an analysis of 51,199 non-malformed live singletons home births in a Canadian hospital between 1978 and 1996, mean birth-weight for gestational age was found to increase by 0.22 z-scores (Kramer et al. 2002). This mean change was accompanied by a decrease in the number of infants categorised small-for-gestational-age, and an increase in those categorised large-for-gestational-age (Kramer et al. 2002). After adjustment for confounders, this trend was no longer significant, indicating that the confounding factors explain the trend in birth-weight. The significant factors were secular increases in pre-pregnancy maternal BMI, gestational weight gain, the incidence of gestational diabetes and a secular decline in maternal smoking.

The trajectory of lean mass is particularly sensitive to maternal influence during fetal life and infancy, during which the accretion of fat and lean tissue may be considered to optimise the trade-off between somatic growth (lean tissue) and energy stores for funding future growth. The presence of leptin in breast-milk (Savino et al. 2006), acting a as signal of the availability of maternal energy supplies, may be assumed to promote increased lean tissue growth, as the infant need not store so much fat itself.

6.7   Buffering of the offspring brain

Whilst growth represents a plastic trait, mediating the balance between energy intake and requirements, the brain has an obligatory energy demand but has a minimal capacity to shrink during starvation, unlike other organs (Kuzawa 1998). The fact that brain metabolism is unable to compensate its demands during starvation means that energy is necessarily diverted from other sources to this end during a negative energy balance. In a comprehensive review of the literature, Kuzawa (1998) described in detail how energy stores in the infant buffer the brain's demands against perturbations in energy supply.

Table 6.4. *Metabolic rate by age for different organs and tissues*

Organ/tissue	Age (y)	Weight (kg)	VO^2 (ml/100g)	MR (kcal/d)	MR/BMR (%)
Brain	20	1.40	4.2	414	23.3
Liver	20	1.60	4.1	464	26.1
Heart	20	0.30	8.2	182	10.2
Kidney	20	0.30	5.5	116	7.1
Total 4 organs	20	3.6		1177	66.7
Skeletal muscle	20	28.3	0.3	500	28.1
Brain	0	0.47	4.2	140	87
	0.3	0.65	4.2	192	64
	1	1.04	4.2	311	53
	5	1.23	4.2	367	44

Adult weight assumed to be 70 kg
VO$_2$ = organ-specific oxygen consumption
MR = organ-specific metabolic rate, BMR = total basal metabolic rate
Collated from Holliday (1978)

Organ tissues are metabolically more costly than muscle tissue, which in turn has greater needs than adipose tissue (Holliday 1971; Holliday 1978), and the metabolic cost of brain tissue is amongst the highest, as shown in Table 6.4. The human brain is large compared to that of other species at any age, such that whereas cerebral oxygen uptake is approximately 10% of the total in non-human animal species, it is around 20% in human adults (Kuzawa 1998). However, this difference is substantially greater during early life. Figure 6.13 shows the classic drawing of Stratz (1909), illustrating changes in body proportions from birth to adulthood. The high proportion of weight in the brain at birth (though still <15% (Holliday 1978)) means that around 60% of total oxygen uptake is diverted to this organ in comparison with less than 10% in the newborns of other species (Kuzawa 1998). Figure 6.14 plots brain metabolic rate and glucose requirements per kilogram of body weight against age, using the data of Holliday (1978). The close agreement between these age-associated changes highlights the extraordinary influence of the brain on energy requirements in early life.

These high and obligatory energy costs in human neonates are generally met through glucose metabolism, but during starvation the brain preferentially metabolises ketones, unlike in most other species (Kuzawa 1998). Malnourished infants have been shown to switch rapidly from carbohydrates to fat metabolism during fasting, with over 90% of energy expenditure derived from fat metabolism during malnutrition (Kerr, Stevens, and Robinson 1978). Fat

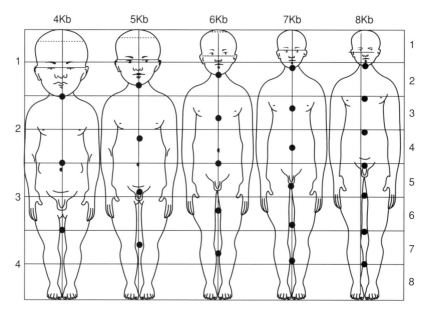

Figure 6.13. The classic illustration of Stratz (1909), showing the changes in body proportions between birth and adulthood. The head is roughly one quarter of height at birth but declines to around one eighth of height at adulthood.

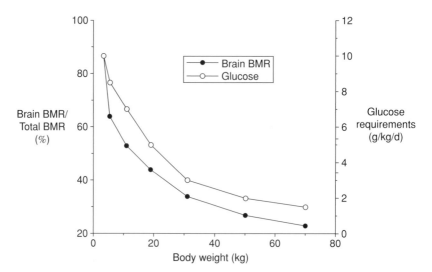

Figure 6.14. Associations of brain metabolic rate as a proportion of total basal metabolic rate, and daily glucose requirements, with age. At birth, almost 90% of basal metabolism is directed to the brain, reflected in glucose requirements of around 10 grams per kilogram per day. By adulthood, these values have declined to around 20% and less than 2 grams per kilogram per day. Based on the data of Holliday (1978).

stores therefore represents a fundamental limiting factor for surviving energy deprivation during early life (Kuzawa 1998).

The presence of fat stores at birth can be attributed in part to the fact that breast-feeding provides a very low energy intake during the first days postpartum (Evans et al. 2003). It is completely normal for breast-fed infants to lose weight following parturition and only to recover birth-weight by around the end of the first week of life (Wright and Parkinson 2004). During these first days, energy requirements rapidly increase, in particular owing to the greater thermoregulatory stress resulting from exposure of the large skin surface area to the air (Fleming, Azaz, and Wigfield 1992). The further accumulation of fat stores during infancy has been attributed to their benefit in buffering uncertainty in energy supply and the anticipated costs of infection during the weaning period (Kuzawa 1998), with infectious disease a particularly strong stress in early life as pathogens are encountered for the first time. These energy stores are of course not obtained directly from the external environment but from the mother during placental nutrition and lactation.

6.8   Immune function

Research increasingly supports the hypothesis that the immune system requires substantial energy to maintain optimal functioning and to respond to specific infections, although there appear to be differences in how these costs manifest in relation to specific diseases and different host species. Adipose tissue biology is implicated in more than one generic way in this context.

It might be assumed that immune function would be most closely associated with the survival component of evolutionary fitness given the obvious risk of death if this function is compromised. Increasingly, however, it is becoming clear that mechanisms regulating survival and reproduction are not exclusive, with immunity impacting on a variety of other life history traits such as mate selection, reproductive success and growth (Lochmiller and Deerenberg 2000). As should be evident from other sections of this chapter, adipose tissue likewise contributes to these other functions, and hence it is a highly plausible candidate trait for underpinning these interconnections. Further work has also elucidated the role of leptin and insulin as key signals.

The immune system can be divided into two components: innate defence, which responds to novel pathogens, and the adaptive part which mounts responses highly specific for pathogens, and which confers immunological memory for previously encountered pathogens (Raberg et al. 2002). The adaptive component is considered to have evolved more recently and to be exclusive to vertebrates (DuPasquier 1993). It is considered a more appropriate strategy for long-lived species, which are more likely to reencounter local pathogens during the life-course.

In most species, infection results in a reduction in appetite and food intake, which paradoxically occurs exactly at the time when the immune response increases metabolic demand (Lochmiller and Deerenberg 2000). Energetic stresses deriving from infection include catabolic processes for meeting the fuel requirements of immune cells and protein synthesis, increases in metabolic rate due to fever, and the possibility of malabsorption following certain infections, while the combination of immunological and behavioural stress increases the total metabolic impact (Laugero and Moberg 2000).

A variety of studies have demonstrated increases in metabolic rate following infection, with data from species as diverse as insects (Freitak et al. 2003), birds (Martin II, Scheuerlein, and Wikelski 2002), rodents (Demas et al. 1997) and humans (Kreymann et al. 1993). In an elegant study, artificial activation of the immune system in bumblebees under a state of starvation (to prevent compensatory energy intake) greatly reduced the odds of survival by 50 to 70% (Moret and Schmid-Hempel 2000). Subsequent work identified a 7.5% increase in energy consumption in response to immune stimulation, quantifying the cost of the immune response in the absence of energy constraint (Tyler, Adams, and Mallon 2006). However, more detailed studies of mice suggested that the energy budget can adapt in different ways to meet these additional costs. In some circumstances, they are met through decreased thermoregulatory function (Schwanz 2006), or compensations in the function of internal organs (Ksiazek et al. 2003). In birds, in which provisioning of the offspring occurs behaviourally rather than placentally, immune stimulation decreased reproductive success most in females with large broods (Bonneaud et al. 2003). Collectively, these animal studies indicate generic costs of the immune system but some flexibility regarding the functions obliged to compensate in order to meet these costs.

Specific costs of the immune response derive from a number of components, including the immune defence of tissues, the repair of damaged issues, the metabolic cost of fever, and the production and maintenance of lymphocytes, antibodies and other immune agents (Romanyukha, Rudnev, and Sidorov 2006). Ironically, these costs also include the growth and metabolism of the pathogens themselves. The relative contribution of these different costs varies according to the particular disease invoking them. Although typically regarded as a clinical problem, fever may be considered a beneficial adaptation at the cost of an approximately 15% increase in metabolic rate for each degree-Celsius rise in temperature (Long 1996; Benhariz et al. 1997). Other important energy costs include elevated protein synthesis (acute phase inflammatory proteins, antibodies), which may account for approximately 50% of the elevation in metabolic rate (Lochmiller and Deerenberg 2000), and high needs for glucose and glutamine. Insulin resistance is commonly induced in animals in order to maintain sufficient glucose concentrations to meet the requirements of insulin-independent immune cells (Chiolero, Revelly, and Tappy 1997).

Studies of rodents have elegantly illustrated the role of adipose tissue and the hormone leptin in meeting these energy requirements. Leptin-deficient mice have suppressed immune function (Lord 2002), which can be restored through an exogenous leptin administration that provides a false signal of energy and availability (Drazen, Demas, and Nelson 2001). Equally, experimental removal of body fat decreases immune function in rodents (Demas, Drazen, and Nelson 2003). These findings are replicated in humans, with congenital leptin deficiency associated with increased vulnerability to infections (Lord 2002). In Gambian children with low body-fat levels, leptin level was not associated with markers of immune function (Moore et al. 2002), hence its exact role remains to be determined. In contrast, body fatness of neonates has been shown to predict survival in high-altitude populations (Wiley 1994b), and it is possible that leptin's effects are most evident at extremes of malnutrition and during early life when pathogens are encountered for the first time. This issue therefore requires further research.

On the one hand, it is therefore clear that adipose tissue plays an important role in providing energy for the immune function. The importance of this role is emphasised by the tendency for infection to decrease energy intake, resulting in the activation of catabolic processes (Lochmiller and Deerenberg 2000). However, a second major role of adipose tissue concerns its secretion of the cytokines which promote the immune response. Numerous studies have now demonstrated that adipose tissue, especially the visceral and other deep-lying depots, is the source of a range of cytokines which contribute to inflammation (Ritchie and Connell 2007; Berg and Scherer 2005). A selection of these are listed in Table 6.5. The importance of deep-lying adipose depots is emphasised by studies reporting greater expression of complement genes in such depots than in subcutaneous fat (Gabrielsson et al. 2003). While many addressing obesity have viewed these cytokines as a toxic product of high fat levels, the adaptive nature of the immune response requires emphasis. Importantly, the increased metabolic rate of fever is not induced directly by external pathogens but rather by the cytokines that are produced in response to the pathogen's appearance (Long 1996). The combination of insulin resistance maintaining fuel availability to immune cells, and cytokines promoting inflammation, therefore constitutes a comprehensive adaptive package conferring immune function, with adipose tissue underpinning both components. Furthermore, a proportion of cytokines are anti-inflammatory, whilst adipose tissue also secretes a variety of growth factors. Collectively, these products promote the recovery of tissue

Table 6.5. *Selected cytokines and growth
factors secreted by human adipose tissue*

Pro-inflammatory cytokines
Interleukins 1, 6, 18
Tumor necrosis factor α
Eotaxin
Resistin
Leptin

Anti-inflammatory cytokines
Adiponectin
Interleukin 10
Interleukin-1 receptor antagonist
Prohibitin

Growth factors
Angiopoietin-1
Fibroblast growth factors
Epidermal growth factor-like GF
Hepatocyte growth factor
Insulin-like growth factor
Nerve growth factor
Platelet-derived growth factor

Collated from Atanassova et al. (2007), Permana and
Reardon (2007) and Badman and Flier (2007)

from damage and illustrate how adipose tissue is intricately involved with both the destruction of pathogens and the repair of damaged tissue.

Work on paracrine interactions between adipose tissue and neighbouring elements of the lymphatic system (Pond 2003a; Mattacks, Sadler, and Pond 2004) further illustrates how precursors for immune function are distributed unequally between different body regions, allowing tailoring of immune response to different sites of entry sought by different pathogens. This issue is discussed further in subsequent chapters in relation to ethnicity.

The importance of adipose tissue in immune function has been emphasised by recent work analysing the cause of death during famine. As discussed above, the analysis of data from the Irish famine of the nineteenth century suggests that death from starvation was rare, and that the majority of deaths could be attributed to infectious disease or other challenges to the immune system (Mokyr and O Grada 2002). The authors suggest that this pattern applied to the majority of famines, but that in certain circumstances starvation can contribute more directly to the death toll, examples including El Niño-induced famines during the late Victorian period (Davis 2002), and the siege of cities or ghettos during World War II (Mokyr and O Grada 2002).

The role of adipose tissue in immune function may also be relevant to the association between social stress and fat deposition. Subordinate animals tend to have poorer access to resources, which impairs their nutritional status and hence increases their vulnerability to infectious disease. Under these conditions, increased allocation of energy to the visceral fat depot is predicted to be favoured. Several studies have associated childhood risk of infectious diseases with social status (Victora et al. 1992; Cohen et al. 2004), but since poverty is often associated with reduced total adiposity, whether visceral fat is indeed increased in these populations remains to be confirmed. Increasing pathogen load is associated with increased adiposity in both animals (Bernard et al. 1988; Lyons et al. 1982) and humans (Fernandez-Real et al. 2007), with this effect apparently mediated by alterations in insulin metabolism (Fernandez-Real et al. 2006).

Summary

Whilst the full details of the role of adipose tissue in immune function remain to be established, it is already clear that it contributes both energy and molecular signals, that such molecular signals regulate both pathogen destruction and tissue repair, and that fat distribution is an important mediating factor in these activities.

6.9   Sexual selection

Although natural selection has been the primary force shaping the evolution of fat stores, sexual selection may also have contributed (Norgan 1997). In both sexes, body shape has been proposed to be associated with the likelihood of mating, a key determinant of reproductive fitness. The preference of one sex for the shape of another is therefore hypothesised to be an important selective pressure.

Based on the available evidence, adiposity plays a substantially more important role in signalling reproductive fitness in females than in males. The primary secondary sexual traits in males comprise non-adipose components of body size and shape, such as height, physique and upper-body muscle mass. Although the paunch fat depot in male primates may signal status (Pond 1998), males appear to signal their fitness primarily by investing in components of lean mass rather than adiposity, reflected in female appreciation of such traits (Lynch and Zellner 1999; Maisey et al. 1999). This is consistent with likely female appreciation of specific behaviours (e.g. hunting) capitalising on muscle mass and considered to represent mating effort (Hawkes and Bliege Bird 2002), though empirical evidence for this connection remains sparse. Male investment in muscle mass rather than adipose tissue is also consistent with our understanding of the hormone testosterone, which is implicated in the differential allocation of energy to lean versus adipose tissue.

The vast majority of work on sexual selection in relation to adiposity has therefore focused on female shape. However, there is more than one possible underlying mechanism whereby female shape may correlate with reproductive success, and the area remains controversial. Two broadly differing approaches have characterised research on this issue – investigations of the shape associated with high female fertility, and investigation of male preferences for different shape representations. A variety of studies have demonstrated associations between female shape and fertility status. A low waist-hip ratio (WHR) has been associated with a hormonal profile conducive to reproduction (de Ridder et al. 1992b; Wass et al. 1997; Jasienska et al. 2004), and with an increased probability of conception (Wass et al. 1997; Zaadstra et al. 1993). Women with low WHR ovulate more frequently (Moran et al. 1999) and exhibit a vaginal milieu more conducive to sperm penetration (Jenkins et al. 1995). Collectively, these studies indicate the potential utility of males evaluating female shape as a marker of reproductive fitness, but how such a mechanism might operate remains unclear.

One plausible mechanism whereby shape might index fertility comprises their common link with relative youthfulness. For example, Buss and colleagues carried out cross-cultural research in 37 populations and proposed that whereas females were attracted to males on the basis of cues of status, males preferred females according to physical signals of attractiveness, in which youthfulness was often important (Buss 1989). Much attention has subsequently focused on indices of fat distribution, such as the waist-hip ratio (WHR), on the grounds that such traits are unique to our species and should reliably signal reproductive quality (Symons 1979), otherwise their persistence over time would not occur. It might appear logical that male preference for low WHR should derive directly from the association of low WHR with high fertility, but such male preferences appear more variable than this hypothesis would predict.

Given the multiple functions of fat in female reproductive biology discussed above, at the simplest level those displaying very low levels of fatness may be considered generically to signal poor reproductive function. Females with anorexia nervosa, for example, provide multiple signals of their condition – low body weight and failure to emphasise any of the key characteristics of female shape, including greater circumferences of the thighs, buttocks, hips and breasts relative to the waist. Beyond such basic signals, however, it is necessary to consider whether more subtle information is conveyed about reproductive function across the normal range of body composition.

Singh (Singh 1993; Singh and Young 1995) initiated a series of studies using silhouettes of female shape to gauge male preferences. These studies, conducted in Western populations, showed that females with slender bodies, low waist-hip ratio (close to 0.7), and large breasts were considered more attractive, feminine, healthy and desirable as both short-term and long-term partners (Singh and Young 1995). Furthermore, other studies have demonstrated that a high waist-hip ratio is associated with unattractive traits such as hirsutism, as well as indices of ill-health such as menstrual irregularity and the components of the metabolic syndrome (Singh 1993). Singh has therefore argued that WHR functions as a 'wide first-pass filter, which would automatically exclude as mates women who are unhealthy or have low reproductive capacity' from male preferences.

Support for Singh's results seemed to have emerged from several cross-cultural studies (Furnham, McClelland, and Omer 2003; Henss 2000). In cross-cultural analyses, Brown and Konner (1987) found that fatter legs and hips in females were valued in 90% of 58 different societies. Nevertheless, a universal preference for a WHR of 0.7 is not consistent with other findings. In their study of the Matsigenka people of Peru, who have experienced minimal exposure to Western culture, Yu and Shepherd (1998) found first that overweight females were considered most attractive and healthy, and second that for any given category of weight, a high WHR was preferred. Others have likewise failed to demonstrate male preference for low WHR (Wetsman and Marlowe 1999).

Leaving aside for the moment inconsistencies in the evidence, apparent widespread preference for low WHR is generally attributed to the 'good genes' hypothesis, proposing that specific genes underlie both the secondary sexual signal and aspects of reproductive function. The value of such signals in humans has been attributed in part to the lack of direct information concerning female ovulation or fertility in our species. In many primates, female fertility is signalled overtly through sexual swellings or changes in skin colouration. However, such signals may also relate to longer term components of fertility and reproductive fitness, independent of short-term variability of the likelihood of conception, including the capacity to lactate. Studies have demonstrated associations between WHR and female reproductive hormones (de Ridder et al. 1992b; Jasienska et al. 2004), and the likelihood of conception (Wass et al. 1997; Zaadstra et al. 1993). WHR is also associated with the timing of menarche, which is slowed by higher levels of abdominal fat and accelerated by a greater level of gluteofemoral fat (Lassek and Gaulin 2007a). Given the association between age at menarche and early life growth rates, associations between female shape and biological profile may derive from phenotypic plasticity (i.e., developmental experience) as well as genetic factors.

A recent study proposed an association between maternal shape and the IQ of both mother and offspring (Lassek and Gaulin 2007b). Gluteofemoral triglycerides contain more essential long-chain polyunsaturated fatty acids than abdominal or visceral fat (Phinney et al. 1994), and stable isotope studies of Western populations indicate that the majority of breast-milk long-chain polyunsaturated fatty acids come from maternal fat stores rather than dietary intake (Fidler et al. 2000; DelPrado et al. 2000). Maternal fat distribution thus appears to have important implications for the provision of these compounds for the offspring brain. Lassek and Gaulin (2007b) reported in an American study that maternal WHR is inversely associated both with maternal and offspring IQ, and that in adolescent mothers (who have yet to accumulate substantial gluteofemoral fat stores) the impact of a high WHR is more adverse on offspring IQ. These authors argued that despite high levels of overweight in American women, poor dietary quality results in their being more deficient than most populations in docosahexaenoic acid, the polyunsaturated fatty acid considered especially important for offspring brain development. Whether this scenario applies to other populations warrants further investigation, but the capacity for maternal fat stores to contribute specific nutrients for brain growth in the absence of dietary supply may be important in accounting for male preferences for female shape.

Given clear associations of female fat distribution with indices of fitness, how can the controversy regarding inconsistency between populations in male preferences be explained? Tovee and colleagues criticised the use of silhouettes on the grounds that manipulations of WHR inadvertently alter apparent BMI at the same time, thus reducing the confidence with which preferences can be attributed to WHR (Tovee and Cornelissen 1999; Tovee et al. 1999). Such covariance of WHR and BMI is common to the vast majority of research and extends also to studies using edited photographs of women (Henss 2000). Findings from studies based on actual photographs (Tovee et al. 1998; Tovee et al. 2002) or three-dimensional images (Fan et al. 2004) have been proposed to implicate BMI as the most important criteria for attractiveness.

Further cross-cultural studies have demonstrated variable male preferences according to ecological conditions. Several studies have demonstrated that men from resource-poor environments, or those who experience hunger, are likely to prefer heavier women (Nelson and Morrison 2005; Swami and Tovee 2006). An elegant study by Tovee and colleagues (2006) demonstrated that the preferences of Zulu males altered if they moved from South Africa to the United Kingdom, thus experiencing changes in ecological conditions and in cultural exposure. In contrast, in populations characterised by greater energy availability, males tend to prefer slimmer women; hence, the evidence collectively suggests an unexpected degree of flexibility in male shape preferences.

However, in all these studies no information about age was provided. Given the strong tendency for individual women to gain weight with age in Western populations, and to lose weight in many other populations, male preference for women with high or low BMI may simply index a preference for younger women. Thus, whilst WHR is strongly associated with hormonal profile, in turn associated with female reproductive function, both traits are strongly associated with age. Human female fertility peaks in the mid-20s, declines through the 30s and tends to be terminated during the fifth decade of life. Most studies of WHR have not taken into account this dual impact of age on both shape and fertility, and it is also worth considering whether WHR is indeed the appropriate body region for studies on sexual attractiveness.

Data from the UK National Sizing Survey show that WHR increases steadily with age, whereas the thigh-hip ratio decreases (Wells, Treleaven, and Cole 2007). More detailed analyses on the US Sizing Survey showed that, within each category of BMI, age is associated with significant increase in WHR (Wells, Cole, and Treleaven 2008), such that the oldest category of thin women were found to have a WHR similar to the youngest category of obese women. Conversely, obese women were able to maintain a mean WHR of 0.84 prior to their 20s. These findings suggest that regardless of whether males prefer plump or slim women, in different societies, WHR conveys significant information about age. Given the strong association between age and fertility, it is plausible that WHR offers more reliable signals of the age-component of fertility. Previously, Singh (1993) argued that WHR allows differentiation of pre-menarchal, menstruating, pregnant and postmenopausal women, and the sizing survey results are consistent with that model.

However, even more notable in these data is the strong inverse association of age with thigh girth, expressed, for example, relative to hip girth. Data on this ratio, using data from the US National Sizing Survey, are shown in Figure 6.15 and illustrate declines both during early adulthood (when reproductive events might occur) and from middle-age onwards. The figure presents data for white women only; however, similar declines were apparent in African and Hispanic Americans. If men are responding to signals of age in order to identify those most fertile, as proposed, then thigh-hip rather than waist-hip ratio is a more appropriate body region to assess. It is also an important body region for signalling fitness value given the proposed role of this adipose tissue depot in providing nutrients for the offspring brain, as discussed above. It is possible therefore that reported inconsistencies in male preferences between populations are due in part to not addressing the appropriate body region. The cross-cultural analyses of Brown and Konner (1987), for example, emphasised widespread male preferences for large thigh and hip size.

The notion that female shape is assessed in part as a marker of age, which in turn is highly correlated with fertility, appears able to account in part for the variable male preferences between populations. This hypothesis requires

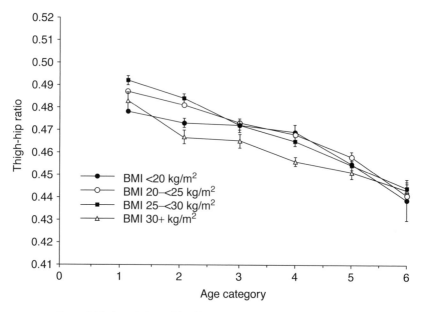

Figure 6.15. Associations of the thigh-hip ratio with age in 3,330 white women stratified by BMI. Age is broadly associated with a reduced thigh-hip ratio, throughout adult life and in each BMI category, though in the lowest BMI group little change occurs till middle-age. These changes indicate the loss of fat from the thigh adipose tissue depot, as in absolute terms the hip also declines slightly. The relatively linear nature of this decline suggests that it is not specifically related to reproduction but rather implies a steady shift in energy allocation. Based on unpublished data from the US National Sizing Survey (Wells, Bruner and Treleaven 2008a).

further attention and will benefit if thigh-hip ratio is given as much attention as has so far been accorded waist-hip ratio.

Regardless of what female shape signals, it is important to remember that signalling systems are not necessarily entirely honest (Johnstone and Grafen 1993), and the signalling of female attractiveness need not be entirely consistent with fertility. One sex may value a trait in the other simply because, once gene-based preferences have become established in a population, alternative preferences become handicapped by reducing mating opportunities (the bandwagon effect) (Ridley 1993). In this context, breast tissue may appear to give the impression of predicting breast-milk supply; however, data show first that breast tissue is typically only around 4% of total adipose tissue (Katch et al. 1980), and therefore constitutes a poor signal of total energy stores, and second that breast-milk output appears relatively independent of body fat content until fat stores are substantially depleted (Prentice, Goldberg, and Prentice 1994). Thus, the notion that breast volume signals lactation capacity is not supported.

Furthermore, breast development precedes maturation of the birth canal, which does not reach adult dimensions until about five years after menarche. Thus, breast tissue generates an appearance of fertility before full physiological function has been obtained (Pond 1998).

Summary

The available data therefore suggest that both functional and bandwagon models are implicated in the sexual selection of human adipose tissue. Males appear to have been selected for relatively low fat stores, particularly in the upper torso where secondary sexual signals in the form of muscle mass are prioritised. Females appear to have been selected for a dynamic fat distribution, whereby a less central fat distribution is correlated with greater fertility and overall reproductive fitness. Male preferences for female shape appear complex, and previous research has struggled to ascertain which body components are rated, what they might signal, and how such signals are generated (genes versus plasticity). It is suggested that insufficient attention has been directed to the changing of female shape with age, in particular regarding the thigh region.

Summary

This chapter has reviewed evidence for the contribution of adipose tissue to a variety of biological functions. Though fat is clearly beneficial in accommodating negative energy balance, its amount and distribution are related to a number of other functions. The age- and sex- variability described in Chapter 4 correlates with varying needs for energy stores and further variability in the optimal anatomical location for them.

It is becoming increasingly clear that adipose tissue has a dual role, in both providing the energy required for different activities, along with biochemical compounds for immune function and nutrition of the offspring; and regulating the allocation of energy between competing functions and tissues. Studies in both humans and other species have illustrated how leptin and other messenger molecules, acting as signals of relative and regional energy availability, allow adipose tissue to integrate trade-offs between competing functions. This is demonstrated, for example, by strategic shifts towards the inhibition of reproduction in women when other functions, more necessary for survival, are required. Conversely, the energy costs of reproduction are met both through energy reserves and increases in dietary energy intake when ecological conditions permit.

How important leptin itself is in orchestrating these trade-offs remains to be established. Despite it attracting widespread interest as a signal of energy availability, especially in relation to reproductive function in females, data from several populations show a poor correlation between indices of body fatness and leptin concentrations in males (Bribiescas 2001; Kuzawa, Quinn, and Adair 2007; Sharrock et al. 2008). Whether such poor correlations are genuine, or whether, deriving from field studies with limited methodologies, they reflect the failure to measure the particular adipose depots most strongly associated with leptin, remains to be determined. It is likely that other adiposity signals are also important, and this is a major area of research interest at the current time. Insulin signalling is increasingly considered important in coordinating life history trade-offs (Harshman and Zera 2007) and is already known to be involved in growth, longevity, reproduction, immunity and brain phenotype in humans, as well as energy homeostasis (Watve and Yajnik 2007). However, human insulin metabolism remains most commonly studied in the context of disease, and its broader regulatory role requires elucidation.

What should have become clear from this chapter, however, is that the notion of adipose tissue as an inert store of calories functioning primarily to buffer weight loss during chronic dietary energy insufficiency is grossly simplistic. Adipose tissue provides stored energy for a range of competing functions whilst also contributing substantially to the signalling mechanisms, at different biological levels, that coordinate the integrating trade-offs. The work of Pond and colleagues, emphasising the local paracrine nature of such regulatory activity (Pond 2003a; Mattacks, Sadler, and Pond 2004), demonstrates an unexpected sophistication of this regulatory role. Our increasing understanding of adipose-tissue signalling looks set to transform life-history approaches to human biology, which until now have focused on growth rates and gross energy allocations, without exploring the hypothesis that those energy stores might themselves regulate competing functions. Although substantial work in this area remains to be done, it is now possible to begin teasing out the selective pressures that may have acted on adipose tissue biology during human evolution.

7 The evolutionary biology of adipose tissue

This book is primarily about the adipose tissue biology of humans in the context of their recent evolutionary history and contemporary ecological variability. Humans, however, are just one amongst a multitude of vertebrate species, in particular mammals, which benefit from adipose tissue as an adaptive trait and use it to mediate the match between energy capture from the environment and energy demand. To understand how adipose tissue has responded to specifically hominin selective pressures, it is helpful first to consider the longer-term evolution of the adipocyte, both as a type of cell, and in its larger form within adipose tissue, and how adipose tissue was shaped during early mammalian evolution.

The first part of this chapter draws extensively on the work of Caroline Pond, described in her 1998 monograph (Pond 1998) and further extended in subsequent papers (Pond 2003a; Mattacks, Sadler, and Pond 2004; Pond 2007). This work highlights the properties of adipocytes and indicates the likely selective pressures which favoured the emergence of this specific cell and its aggregation in discrete adipose tissue depots. The second part elucidates a number of concepts regarding the adaptive nature of energy stores, including a discussion of modelling the costs and benefits of adipose tissue and of the differential allocation of energy between storage and other functions. Such an approach is essential for generating clear hypotheses for empirical investigations in extant humans. These approaches are then exploited in the following two chapters, reconstructing possible hominin and early human profiles of adiposity.

7.1 Evolution of the adipocyte and adipose tissue

The adipocyte differs from other cells in its capacity to store triglyceride for export to other tissues as required. Most cells require a store of energy, most commonly in the form of glycogen (polymerised glucose), but some also include lipid droplets. The adipocyte represents a more specialised store of triglyceride, which is likely to improve its ability to allocate energy between competing target tissues (Pond 1998). In contrast to other cells, adipocytes are able to expand substantially, conferring high flexibility on this form of

195

energy store. Adipose tissue is composed not only of these storage cells, but also of protein, water and a perfusion of blood vessels enabling the transport of biochemical compounds to and from the tissue. Rather than being supplied by single arteries, adipose tissue depots are maintained through many smaller blood vessels from adjacent tissues, which generates close connections with these tissues. A variety of receptors for the molecular signals that control uptake and discharge of triglyceride, located on the cell membrane, and in the internal cytoplasm, provide integration with regulatory systems (Pond 1998).

The differential energy requirements of other tissues are mediated through variable sensitivity to the hormone insulin. Though some organs can respond to circumstances by changes in size, such as reductions of muscle mass during starvation or lack of use (Pond 1998), or increases in gut mass in response to demand for digestion, others such as the brain have minimal flexibility and hence impose a constant energy demand with respect to glucose uptake. Organs with obligatory energy demand are insulin insensitive, whereas insulin-sensitive organs receive greater or lesser amounts of fuel depending on its availability and the impact of regulatory mechanisms. Both low circulating levels of insulin, and insulin resistance, divert proportionally more fuel to insulin-independent tissues at the expense of those that are insulin dependent (Swinburn 1996). These varying energy needs must always be met by a supply of fuel, obtained either from dietary intake, the utilisation of glycogen stores from muscle tissues or the liver, or the breakdown of triglycerides from adipose tissue depots.

Adipose tissue is thus integrally related to insulin metabolism, the two traits collectively regulating the accretion or depletion of energy stores, and allocating circulating glucose and other fuels between competing tissues. Mammalian adipose tissue tends to be distributed between a number of discrete depots (subcutaneous, intra-abdominal and intra-muscular), reflecting both selective tissue functions but also anatomical and morphological constraints. According to Pond (1998), no other tissue is so variable between species as adipose tissue, and on top of that there is further variability within any organism, as energy stores fluctuate within the life-course. Indeed, the variability is so great as to have daunted investigation of adipose tissue as an anatomical trait (Pond 2007).

The need to improve control over such fuel supplies is the likely explanation for the emergence of discrete adipose tissue depots, rather than relying on a looser distribution of lipid droplets in muscle and liver tissue (Pond 1998). The aggregation of fuel within adipose tissue allows a substantially greater sophistication of the regulation of energy balance. On the one hand, adipose tissue can be targeted by molecular signals from the brain, improving the specificity and efficiency with which energy stores respond more reliably to ecological stresses. On the other hand, adipose tissue as an aggregation of lipid can itself emerge as a regulatory organ, transmitting information about the level of fuel stores to the brain and hence favouring or constraining energy-using functions (Kershaw and Flier 2004). This reciprocal association between central regulation and peripheral fuel depots allows the integration of energy stores with a wide range of other biological functions.

Recent work by Pond and colleagues (Pond 2003a; Pond 2003b; Mattacks, Sadler, and Pond 2004; Iacobellis, Pond, and Sharma 2006) has emphasised the local specialisation of adipose tissue, such that perinodal adipocytes effectively function collectively as a 'lipid management' system, 'taking up fatty acids from the blood and holding them until they are required, thus emancipating the cellular immune system from the vagaries of diet' (Pond 2003a). Other intermuscular, intra-muscular and cardiac adipose tissue depots may likewise function to buffer the fuel requirements of local tissues from dietary variability. Collectively, this generates a connection between the immune system and other energy-requiring functions, such that reproduction can be facilitated when the organism is healthy but suppressed when immediate survival is paramount (Klein and Fasshauer 2007).

A key characteristic of triglyceride stores in humans is that they are unsuitable for accommodating rapid short-term fluctuations in energy demand. The release of triglyceride from adipose tissue is too slow to fund short-term muscular activity, and such energy requirements are met through circulating glucose or its release from glycogen stores. Adipose tissue therefore accommodates longer-term fluctuations in energy demand, and this slow-response scenario allows it to exert influence on counterbalancing factors such as appetite. However, many other species are better able to exploit lipid stores directly for physical activity, most notably migratory species of bird and fish, as well as some insects (Pond 1998).

As discussed in Chapter 2, cross-species comparisons reveal two key patterns: first, substantial variability within and between different orders, but also generic associations between adiposity and body size. This variability is related directly to the accommodation of a variety of ecological stresses: put simply, adipose tissue vastly increases the range on niches in which mammals can live (Pond 1984; Pond 1998). Many mammals do not require energy stores; they can survive and reproduce successfully with body fat content around 1 to 2% (Pond 1998). For such species, increases in energy availability may be translated directly into increased reproductive output. However, many other species occupy ecological niches where seasonal activities prevent a contin-uous close match between energy intake and energy expenditure. Behaviours such as long-distance migration, courting and mating, investing in the care of offspring, or hibernation may generate profound imbalances between energy supply and energy utilisation (Pond 1998). Many species also occupy seasonal environments, where periods of energy plenty are separated by periods when food is inaccessible or absent.

Adipose tissue provides a common, though not the only, solution to these diverse ecological problems, but its value must be offset against its potential costs. Adipose tissue contributes both to body mass, with implications for the total energy requirement for physical activity, and also to body volume, which may impact on locomotion traits such as speed and agility. For these reasons, the highest levels of fatness are encountered in marine species, where large size and volume are less of an impediment to movement. Adipose tissue also imposes small energy-maintenance costs; however, these increase at higher levels of activity due to the work required to move large body weight (Garby et al. 1988). Finally, maintaining large adipose tissue depots in some species, including human, elevates cardiovascular load. It is therefore valuable to consider how adipose tissue might initially have been favoured in mammalian evolution, before becoming co-opted for a wider variety of functions.

7.2   Fat stores as adaptive strategy

In general, our understanding of the benefits of body fat is based on short-term studies, associating energy stores with beneficial outcome, or reviews of the historical literature, or models (either logical reasoning, or mathematical simulations). Remarkably few opportunities exist to test prospectively the hypothesis that storing energy is an adaptive response to ecological conditions, and that the optimal strategy may change according to circumstances.

One of the few studies to address this experimentally comprised investigation of the moth, *Plutella xylostella*, where animals were restricted over a number of generations to high-energy or low-energy diets (Warbrick-Smith et al. 2006). In this experiment, multigenerational exposure to a high carbohydrate diet cumulatively improved the ability to consume the diet without accumulating fat depots, which the authors considered strong evidence that high levels of fat storage have a fitness cost. At the other extreme, caterpillars reared on a low carbohydrate diet improved their capacity to deposit fat. Of particular interest was the finding that animals reared on the low carbohydrate diet preferred to lay their eggs in the same conditions, whereas no such preference was observed in those exposed to the high carbohydrate diet (Warbrick-Smith et al. 2006). This study illustrates how long-term exposure to particular ecological conditions favours an adaptive response regarding energy allocation to storage, and it indicates that the costs of storing energy are only worthwhile during conditions of long-term dietary scarcity.

7.3 Adipose tissue in mammalian evolution

Many strategies targeted by natural selection are subject to counterbalancing forces, offering a limited capacity for variability. Consequently, some traits may appear relatively fixed, unable to vary within or between individuals. Adipose tissue lies at the other end of this continuum, representing a trait which offers significant flexibility in strategy. Nevertheless, counterbalancing forces are still relevant, particularly in smaller species owing to the effects of allometric scaling.

Because of such scaling, there is a substantial difference in the potential functions of fat between large and small animals. Per unit body size, metabolic rate is substantially greater in small animals; hence, even large amounts of fat relative to body weight may be capable of accommodating energy require-ments only for short time periods (Oftedal 2000). Thus at one extreme, large mammals such as orang-utans are able to survive several months during which energy requirements exceed dietary energy intake (Knott 1998). At the other extreme, total body fat stores in a shrew may provide energy for only a few hours. As discussed by Oftedal (2000), in terms of mass (M), energy stores are proportional to $M^{1.0}$, whereas energy demand scales with $M^{0.75}$. The ratio of energy stores to demand is therefore proportional to $M^{0.25}$, such that one species 10 times larger than another should have 1.78 times the reserves of energy in terms of meeting daily requirements.

The earliest mammals were all small (Crompton, Taylor, and Jagger 1978) and faced a set of common ecological stresses that are considered by Pond (1984) to have been critical in shaping mammalian adipose tissue. Brown adipose tissue, for example, is found in the adults of small mammals such as rodents, where it contributes to thermoregulation and the maintenance of core body temperature. It is widely encountered in neonatal mammals, especially in precocial species, indicating selective preservation of this thermogenic capacity during the life-course period when cold stress acts most strongly. Indeed some have suggested that brown adipose tissue may be as fundamental to, and as much a distinguishing feature of, mammalian biology as lactation (Cannon and Nedergaard 2004). Most mammals from groups considered to have evolved early on hibernate and/or undergo daily torpor (e.g., insectivorous bats (Dark 2005)), whereby body temperature drops to conserve energy (Pond 2003a). Hibernation, which has been proposed to reduce energy requirement by around 85% (Dark 2005), is associated either with extra-somatic food stores or with adipose tissue depots that are maximised during the autumn and almost depleted during hibernation. During hibernation, measurements of respiratory quotient in species using their fat stores indicate almost 100% fat oxidation (Dark 2005). Although commonly considered a store of energy for buffering lean tissue, the reverse scenario occurs in some species. For example, adipose tissue is prioritised prior to hibernation in ground squirrels, such that restriction of food during this period causes loss of lean mass (Dark 2005).

All warm-blooded organisms have less flexible energy demands than cold-blooded organisms, which is assumed to account for the greater complexity of adipose tissue in mammals and birds compared to reptiles (Vernon and Pond 1997). However, the relative simplicity of adipose tissue in birds highlights not only constraints on flying capacity but also ecological stresses that must have been specific to mammals. Ecologists conventionally consider animals to use two different strategies in breeding: 'income' breeders fund the costs of parental care by gathering more resources, whereas 'capital' breeders acquire the resources required for parental care prior to breeding (Stearns 1992). In practice, species are distributed across a continuum between these two extremes, but the model is of great value for differentiating broad reproductive strategies.

Species such as birds tend to be income breeders, necessarily increasing their rate of energy capture from the environment during the breeding season. Income breeders must obtain all the energy required for provisioning their offspring within their daily range. For most species, such energy capture must also further occur within the hours of daylight. Lacking the opportunity to transduce raw food supplies through maternal metabolism, birds must obtain foods appropriate for consumption by their offspring. Although a few species of bird produce quasi-milk secretions, such as 'pigeon-milk', most parent birds must therefore make countless foraging trips through the day whilst also meeting their own energy requirements. The majority of birds are capable of breeding only once per season and must often migrate between habitats to cope with seasonal changes in energy availability, breeding only when the availability of energy and other nutrients is highest (Pond 1984).

Mammals have two complementary adaptations that negate these stresses, namely, lactation and the role of fat stores in meeting the energy requirements of this mode of nutrition. Several authors have recently converged on the hypothesis that lactation may have evolved initially as a component of the innate immune system, aiding the transfer of immune agents from mother to offspring. Goldman (2002), for example, has argued that this increased the flexibility in the nature of immune agents transferred, tailoring immune system priming to the likely disease load. Increased nutrient and energy content is considered to have developed subsequently, giving rise to the nutritious maternal milks (also varying profoundly in composition) now observed in diverse species (Vorbach, Capecchi, and Penninger 2006). Thus, lactation and adiposity are likely to have evolved in tandem during early mammalian evolution, though this issue requires further attention.

Many mammals are, like birds, primarily income breeders, particularly those of small size where the daily energy cost of lactation are too expensive to be met by adipose tissue stores alone (Wade and Schneider 1992; Oftedal 2000). However, whereas small-sized species such as hamsters must therefore increase their dietary intake to fund lactation, they may still do so pre-emptively by accumulating extra-somatic energy stores in the form of food hoards (Wade and Schneider 1992), and hence at least improve control over dietary energy supply.

In the smallest mammals, the relative energy burden of lactation is so high that typical energy reserves could not even meet the energy costs for a single day. Oftedal (2000), for example, calculated that for a 4-gram shrew, of 25% fat, the energy contained in a single gram of fat could provide 15 kJ of energy, barely a quarter of the 52 kJ daily energy burden generated by a litter of six young. Pond (1984) suggested that for such small species, the initial value of adipose tissue may have been to mediate the diurnal disparity between energy capture (during the night) and energy costs of lactation (during the day). The distribution of the energy required for lactation within maternal adipose tissue depots also increases maternal control over their depletion, through paracrine regulatory systems (Pond 2003a).

Through lactation, small mammals achieve substantially greater independence from external ecological conditions compared to birds, which in turn allows them to breed more often. Mothers can consume a variety of foods according to season and yet convert the energy into a more homogenous milk appropriate for offspring consumption. Maternal fat stores also buffer the offspring from short-term fluctuations in energy availability. This scenario has been supported using mathematical simulations, highlighting the value of maternal energy reserves for both mother and offspring when food supplies are unpredictable (Dall and Boyd 2004). These characteristics enhance the capacity of mammals to colonise new environments and to breed in poorer-quality environments. By displacing the offspring from direct contact with food supplies, mammals are typically able to breed in any conditions where the adult can survive (Pond 1984). Small mammals also mature substantially more rapidly than birds, further improving colonising capacity. The allometric associations between body size and energetics contribute to greater efficiency of lactation in larger species (Oftedal 2000) and further enhance these capacities.

As body size increases, and maternal fat stores become capable of funding a larger proportion of the total period of lactation, maternal adipose tissue helps resolve the challenges of poor dietary quality. Thus 'species with indigestible, highly specialised or irregularly available diets, such as koalas, anteaters, and polar bears usually rely more heavily upon adipose tissue stores to fuel lactation than generalists such as rats, pigs, and man' (Vernon and Pond 1997). Larger mammals are able to accumulate fat prior to and during pregnancy, and they are able to meet the energy requirements for lactation from these somatic stores. The most extreme examples of this strategy are provided by bears, seals and whales, in which lactation often occurs while the mother is fasting. Hibernating black bears, for example, with a litter of three cubs can transfer around 34 kg of milk, high in fat and low in carbohydrate, over a three-month period (Oftedal 2000). Lactation is supported by a maternal fat content of 40% at parturition and is all the more impressive given the fact that the mother consumes no water except for the excreta of the cubs.

Once adipose tissue depots had evolved under these selective pressures, they could adapt to meet a wider range of functions, all having in common the challenge of meeting energy requirements in the face of uncertainty in food supply. For example, high levels of body fat are found in many species occupying higher latitudes, where adipose tissue, often in combination with hibernation, reduces the risk imposed by uncertainty in energy supply in a cold environment. All warm-blooded species have essential energy requirements for maintaining homeostasis unless torpor is induced, and these requirements are clearly increased in cold conditions. Higher latitudes are also characterised by marked seasonality, further increasing the value of energy stores for accommodating the season of scarcity. Although mammals inhabiting cold environments are often assumed to have fat for insulation, the primary stress of such environments is the need to maintain homeostasis and reproductive function (Pond 1998). Species such as the polar bear and arctic fox maintain relatively high fat stores in order to buffer food supply unpredictability and to enable seasonal migrations between foraging areas. Grazing animals may suffer less unpredictability than carnivores, but they are still exposed to seasonality (for example, in day length); hence, reindeer likewise have significant fat depots. A similar scenario is apparent in young penguins, which are fed on average approximately every 40 days but which may endure up to five months between feedings (Pond 1998).

These functions of fat are typically notable in more specialised species, enabling specific ecological niches to be tolerated. In each case, fat may be considered to contribute two complementary benefits: a store of energy to meet the needs of homeostasis and reproduction despite ecological uncertainty, and a regulatory role such that reproductive effort is matched to the availability of energy. Substantial work on hamsters, for example, has shown how adipose tissue biology is regulated by photoperiodicity in order to match reproductive schedule to the season of maximal food availability (Wade and Schneider 1992; Schneider 2004). Given this broader mammalian perspective, it is now possible to consider humans as merely one type of thrifty mammal and to elucidate what specific ecological stresses shaped the hominin and human profiles of adiposity. The next stage is to describe two complementary models of thrift, which refer to different time scales over which the 'adaptive logic' of acquiring energy stores is incorporated into phenotype.

7.4　　The thrifty-genotype hypothesis

Almost five decades ago, a highly influential paper was published proposing that some populations are characterised by a 'thrifty genotype' (Neel 1962). According to this perspective, selection favoured metabolic thrift in ancestral populations exposed to regular 'cycles of feast and famine'. The genetic factors underlying such thrift would then predispose to diseases such as obesity and type-2 diabetes, when exposed to the abundant food supplies and sedentism characteristic of the modern Western lifestyle.

Neel initially directed his hypothesis at the concept of a 'quick insulin trigger', which he suggested would favour the storage of energy during times of surplus and hence aid survival during periods of energy scarcity. The value of this rapid insulin response would be to avoid urinary glucose loss, which would be particularly detrimental during famine. Little evidence has been obtained in support of this specific hypothesis, and Reaven (1998) subsequently argued that insulin resistance in muscle tissue is a more plausible candidate, based on the assumption that the primary target of selection was the maintenance of muscle mass during negative energy balance, when muscle protein might be oxidised to provide glucose. Muscle insulin resistance would act to divert glucose to adipose tissue during positive energy balance, and it would similarly conserve glucose for the central nervous system during negative energy balance.

Whilst the mechanisms underlying genetic thrift continue to be debated, the significant element here is the notion of selective pressures having generated population genetic variability in adipose phenotype. Consistent with the idea of local selective pressures acting on metabolic traits, Kagawa and colleagues (2002) have identified a wide variety of single nucleotide polymorphisms relevanct to energy metabolism that differ between ecological regions and between populations. Some of the genes identified, such as PPARγ2 and UCP3-p, have been implicated in the risk of obesity, but it is probably more appropriate to consider these genetic factors as relating to energy metabolism than to adiposity itself. Kagawa and colleagues argue that differences in energy metabolism are likely to have developed in response to different agricultural systems, the frequency of famines and broader climatic stresses. To this list could be added migrations through hostile environments, which might have acted on small gene pools through bottleneck and founder effects and variable disease loads.

Bouchard has similarly described five broad types of genes associated with metabolic variability (Bouchard 2007), categorising them according to variability in metabolic rate or thermogenesis, predisposition for physical activity, the efficacy of fat oxidation, appetite and adipocyte lipid storage capacity. In both these models, much of the genetic variability must have emerged since the evolution of *Homo sapiens*, although admixture amongst archaic and modern human population within Africa would have allowed genetic variability within *Homo erectus* to pass into early modern humans (Garrigan & Hammer 2006). Of further significance is the broad agreement between Kagawa and Bouchard and colleagues that genetic variability relevant to adiposity may often comprise components of metabolism and behaviour, indicating that metabolic strategies rather than energy stores were the key targets of selection.

Although the existence of genetic variability in metabolism is now established, the details of its origins remain more controversial. Evidence for Neel's 'cycles of feast and famine' is proving remarkably difficult to obtain, and there is increasing dissatisfaction with the hypothesis that famine-induced weight loss was the primary selective pressure acting on metabolic traits. The stress of 'feast and famine' remains more an interesting idea than a well-supported hypothesis, and other hypotheses are discussed later in Chapter 9. Furthermore, the next section addresses a contrasting hypothesis, namely, that variability in phenotype derives from the organism's own life-course experience, which can be attributed in part to the experience of its immediate recent ancestors.

7.5   The thrifty-phenotype hypothesis

Population variability in metabolism could derive from cumulative environmental experience, potentially incorporating a component of inheritance without deriving directly from differences in genotype. Evidence for the within-lifetime induction of body composition was reviewed in detail in Chapter 5. Here, I focus on a broader model of phenotypic plasticity in relation to metabolism.

Disentangling within-lifetime effects from genetic factors is notoriously difficult, since trans-generational effects may plausibly operate via both pathways. Generally, biologists increasingly appreciate the role of phenotypic plasticity in biology (West-Eberhard 2003; Schlichting and Pigliucci 1998; Bateson et al. 2004), and much that is heritable is now known not to be genetic. Epigenetic modification of DNA expression, hormonal programming and behaviour are all mechanisms whereby one generation may influence phenotype of the next without directly involving genetic transmission. The point of emphasising trans-generational influences is that it is unrealistic to consider early-life plasticity of an individual without acknowledging that such plasticity is moulded by the phenotype of the parental generation (Wells 2007f). Furthermore, fathers (Pembrey et al. 2006) as well as mothers (Wells 2007f) can influence adiposity in the offspring through epigenetic effects.

Phenotypic plasticity in the biology of adiposity and metabolism is well illustrated by the study of type-2 diabetes. An elegant series of studies conducted on the Pima Indians of Arizona, who have a notoriously high risk of this disease, has proven critical in differentiating genetic and non-genetic transmission between generations. Generalisation from this population requires caution, as they may be influenced by specific genetic factors not relevant to other populations, but there is now comprehensive evidence that maternal phenotype, independent of genotype, has strong effects on the offspring. Unlike type-1 diabetes, it is maternal rather than paternal disease that increases the risk of impaired glucose tolerance, obesity and type-2 diabetes in the offspring (Pettitt et al. 1983; Pettitt et al. 1988; Silverman et al. 1991). Exposure to the intrauterine environment is the strongest risk factor for the offspring developing the condition (Dabelea and Pettitt 2001), and offspring born to women who subsequently developed type-2 diabetes have a substantially lower risk of developing obesity than offspring born once the mother is already diabetic (Pettitt et al. 1983; Dabelea, Knowler, and Pettitt 2000). Although maternal diet may contribute to these associations, maternal pregnancy physiology and metabolic control represent the niche to which the developing offspring is exposed.

It should be noted that an association between in utero development and later risk of type-2 diabetes need not operate only through the maternal phenotype. Paternal diabetes has been associated with both low birth weight and later disease risk, suggesting that there may be a genetic link between the two factors (Lindsay et al. 2000) and implicating the thrifty-genotype hypothesis described above. McCance and colleagues (1994) likewise proposed the selective survival of low-birth-weight infants genetically characterised by insulin resistance. Thus, low birth weight could represent a marker either of genetic factors, or of later outcome, rather than causal evidence for effects of exposure to adverse maternal factors in utero. Twin studies showing an association between low birth weight and the risk of developing type-2 diabetes in adulthood are unable to resolve this dilemma (Iliadou, Cnattingius, and Lichtenstein 2004), and the finding that the offspring of diabetic mothers have a greater risk of developing obesity than the offspring of pre-diabetic mothers might plausibly be attributed to genetic factors likewise.

However, this issue can be investigated by following the outcome of successive offspring within mothers who at some stage developed type-2 diabetes. Such studies show that within a given family, the risk of developing type-2 diabetes is much greater in those offspring born after the maternal diagnosis of diabetes than in those before the diagnosis (Dabelea et al. 2000). The under-lying mechanism for this raised risk of diabetes remains uncertain, although fetal hyperinsulinaemia, with complementary insulin resistance, and impaired insulin secretion have been proposed to contribute (Hultquist and Olding 1975; Heding, Persson, and Stangenberg 1980). These data thus show that metabolic phenotype of the offspring tracks that of the mother through plasticity, with long-term effects.

Nevertheless, it is worth considering which traits actually respond to such trans-generational influence. As discussed in Chapter 5, environmental factors acting during fetal life primarily induce variability in lean mass rather than adi-posity, whereas appetite and metabolism are also induced by early-life experi-ence. I have suggested that growth during fetal life in infancy targets 'metabolic capacity', whereas growth from infancy into childhood and adolescent impacts metabolic load (Wells 2009b). The character of lean mass certainly influences the sensitivity of the organism to the various ecological factors that promote fat accumulation, but it is metabolic sensitivity (appetite, insulin metabolism, leptin metabolism) rather than total fat mass that is induced. However, fat dis-tribution may be considered more directly induced by early-life developmental trajectory, although the details of this process remain incomplete, and post-natal rather than prenatal induction may be more important.

Because lean mass is a major determinant of energy requirements, variability in lean size is an important means of adapting the organism to ecological conditions. Some have argued that the small neonate has proactively reduced its size in anticipation of poor conditions in adulthood (Gluckman, Hanson, and Spencer 2005). I have argued strongly against this view, considering that such long-term prediction on the basis of a brief experience during pregnancy is implausible (Wells 2007f; Wells 2007a). Rather, I have suggested that the small baby is obliged to adopt such a developmental trajectory in view of energetic constraints acting on the mother (Wells 2003b), since the small baby will be less expensive for the mother to feed during childhood. Figure 7.1 illustrates the effect of differing offspring sizes on the maternal energy budget for a mother producing five offspring at 4-year intervals (Wells 2007f). This scenario illustrates two important points: first, that thrift may be encapsulated in lean mass as well as adiposity, with body size a more permanent adaptation than metabolic profile; and second, that such thrift is induced by maternal phenotype owing to the period of offspring plasticity occurring *within* the window of maternal physiological care.

Kuzawa (2005) has referred to such trans-generational effects as 'phenotypic inertia' that allow the tracking of ecological conditions on a timescale inter-mediate between genetic and physiological adaptation. Epigenetic alterations to gene expression are not permanent but rather can wash out after several

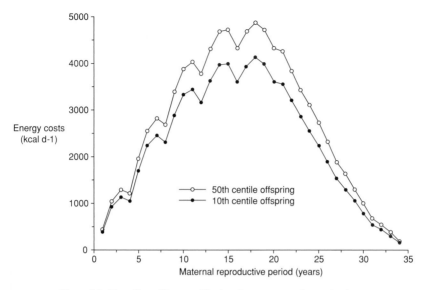

Figure 7.1. The effect of human offspring size on maternal reproductive energy
load. The model assumes that the mother produces five offspring at a rate of one every
four years, and that she supplies 100% of offspring energy requirements from birth to
three years, and then a linearly declining proportion of offspring requirements, from
100% at three years to zero at 18 years. Producing offspring of 10th centile weight, as
opposed to 50th centile weight, reduces maternal energy load by almost 20% by the
midpoint of the maternal reproductive schedule, which occurs some 15 years after the
first offspring is produced. This figure illustrates that the energy-benefit to the mother
of producing a small baby is greatest when the cost of other offspring are taken into
account. Reproduced with permission from Wells (2007f).

generations. This means that parents can transmit characteristics to their offspring through altering DNA expression in the short-term, but they do not
inflict these characteristics on descendants in the long-term future. However,
there are subtle differences between the logic of phenotypic inertia and that
of tracking maternal phenotype (Wells 2007a), and it is likely that both processes are relevant to the trans-generational impact of maternal phenotype. On
the one hand, phenotypic inertia might allow coherent adaptation to relatively
stable climatic conditions, tracking long-term trends. However, even within
a common physical environment, mothers may differ in phenotype owing to
variation in social rank. Offspring may then benefit from tracking maternal
phenotype simply because this indicates their likely supply of energy during
development (Wells 2007a). The benefits of this overall approach become clear
if we consider the different strategies of high- and low-quality phenotype parents. High-quality parents can invest materially in their offspring, whilst also
modifying the offspring's DNA expression to continue that strategy in the near

future. Low-quality parents can reduce that investment and induce a different developmental strategy in their offspring, but because this strategy is encoded in DNA expression rather than content, both strategies can change if ecological conditions alter in the future.

7.6   Integrating two models of thrift

In both the thrifty-genotype and phenotype models, the profile of adiposity in one generation is considered to be influenced by the experience of previous generations. The key difference comprises the timescale over which the ancestral legacy has accumulated – trans-generational phenotypic plasticity operates over a substantially shorter timescale than genetic selection, and it may respond to quite transient pressures. Both models are likely to be relevant in explaining variability in adiposity, and they indicate complementary components of the strategy of optimal energy use.

Although the thrifty-genotype hypothesis is often invoked to explain population variability in risk of diabetes, I would argue that the concept is of most use when applied to our species in its entirety, thus attributing certain selective pressures to the period prior to the evolution of *Homo sapiens*. The genetic basis of thrift is perhaps most clearly demonstrated by gender differences in adiposity in all human populations, and by broadly similar age changes between infancy and maturation (see Chapter 4). These traits represent the location of life-course strategy in the genome, resulting in their emergence, to some degree, in all individuals. However, body size and adiposity as components of physiological flexibility also benefit from tailoring to more recent ecological conditions, and the evidence for epigenetic effects and early-life induction demonstrates that a proportion of metabolic strategy is not contained directly in the genome but is rather transmitted through parental experience, in particular that of the matriline (Wells 2007f). Secular trends in growth highlight the fact that body size is not especially strongly genetically determined, even though in any given environment, variability in height has a genetic component.

These two levels of adaptation can also be considered as alternative forms of risk management. Genetic adaptation is a relatively inflexible form of risk management, best considered as bet-hedging (Philipi and Seger 1989). Genetically variant offspring of a given parent are essentially different investment strategies, increasing the likelihood that at least some offspring are well-suited to the conditions that are encountered over the life-course. For example, the majority of small babies tend to undergo catch-up growth during infancy; however, clinicians are well aware that some neonates fail to do so and remain small throughout infancy and childhood. The reasons why infants vary in their capacity for catch-up remains poorly understood, but it is likely to reflect genetic variability, and although that genetic variability may concern growth *per se*, it may also pertain to sensitivity to the maternal resources that enable catch-up (Pigliucci 2007). That is, some infants despite having access to energy resources may not utilise them. This scenario would increase variance in offspring phenotype within a population and might prove beneficial during harsh conditions

However, whilst bet-hedging is an ideal strategy for reducing penalties during challenging conditions, it is less successful at capitalising on good conditions. Shorter-term trans-generational plasticity allows mothers to guide the developmental trajectory of their offspring, transferring their energy-capital to the next generation and maximising their reproductive success in good conditions while capping offspring investment in poor conditions. In Chapter 5, reference was made to shorter, fatter mothers who necessarily constrain the fetal growth of their offspring owing to reduced uterine size, but who appear to mitigate this effect by inducing catch-up growth during infancy through their enhanced fat stores (Ong et al. 2007). Both bet-hedging and capital-transfer strategies are advantageous to a colonising organism such as humans, as discussed in greater detail in the next two chapters.

These biological models of thrift are therefore complementary, and both assume that storing energy is a beneficial means of adapting to ecological conditions. However, it is useful both to present a more detailed model of such benefits and to consider counter-balancing costs. The final section of this chapter presents a game-theory model of adiposity, suggesting that adipose tissue as a store of energy can be modelled as an economic resource. Economic game theory was developed to identify the optimum strategy for any one individual when the returns of that person's strategy depend in part on what others are doing. This approach may prove particularly beneficial given that the life-course investment of energy is complex. In early life, energy is a resource subject to competing strategies between mother and offspring, yet as the offspring matures, it may itself adopt the maternal role and contest the struggle from the opposite perspective.

7.7   A game-theory model of fat stores

Game-theory approaches are now popular in many areas of biology, and energy is a particularly useful phenomenon to consider from this perspective because it is so readily expressed as a currency. Economic terminology such as income and expenditure, investment and returns, capital and balance are easily applied, enabling the consideration of related concepts such as risk management and profit maximisation, as described above. Often the use of such language merely facilitates understanding of how energy utilisation represents a strategy rather than a component of nutrition, although specific models can of course be developed. The advantage of pursuing game-theoretical approaches is that they may reveal non-intuitive scenarios, while also enabling competing strategies to be evaluated through simulation models. There is insufficient space here, as well as insufficient expertise of the author, to present a formalised dynamic model of energetics and adiposity, and this discussion will therefore remain at the conceptual level. It is hoped that this summary will stimulate further work on the issue.

Before describing the game-theory model, it is critical to distinguish between the *strategy of allocating energy to storage* and the *strategy of accumulating large fat depots*. The first strategy results in the second only during sustained positive energy balance. Prior to the emergence of agriculture, the energy expenditure on subsistence efforts (hunting or gathering) would have been displaced in time from the energy intake deriving from ingestion. Individuals would regularly have experienced transient fluctuations between positive and negative energy balance, and fat and glycogen stores would have fluctuated concomitantly without substantial weight gain occurring. Since the emergence of agriculture, some individuals have been able to access plentiful food with minimal activity levels, accumulating substantial fat stores, and high levels of weight are now rapidly increasing in prevalence in many populations.

According to the game-theory model, an organism must decide whether to use or store incoming energy. If the decision is taken to store the energy in tissue, the organism must further allocate it between competing targets: protein in organs or muscles, or lipid in adipose tissue depots. The various alternatives for using or storing energy are illustrated in Figure 7.2. Factors influencing the optimum allocation strategy may include age, gender, body size, growth rate, current energy stores and reproductive status. Information about human body fatness, described in detail in Chapters 4 to 6, provides the opportunity to illustrate such allocation trade-offs and how they vary across the human lifespan. This particular profile is of course the *product* of selection during hominin evolution; hence, the aim of the following description is to emphasise the generic trade-offs between growth, immunity, reproduction and survival which are clearly important to all organisms.

First, differences in energy allocation are clearly illustrated in the growth process, with energy allocated only to lean tissue during the first two trimesters of pregnancy but subsequently divided between lean and adipose tissue during the last trimester and infancy. Second, the sexes pursue different allocation strategies, and these are evident from fetal life onwards. Compared to girls, boys

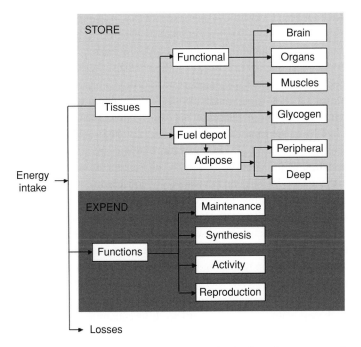

Figure 7.2. Competing targets for dietary energy intake. Incoming energy may be expended, stored or lost in waste products. Storage energy may be allocated to the growth of functioning tissues (organs, muscles or the brain), or to fuel depots meeting short-term (glycogen) or long-term (adipose tissue) energy demands. The relative prioritisation of these different ends varies as a function of numerous factors such as age, gender, pubertal maturation, reproductive status and health. The optimal allocation strategy between these competing ends maximises the combined benefits for survival and reproduction over the combined costs. Reproduced with permission from Wells (2009a).

have similar average fat mass but greater average lean mass at birth (Rodriguez et al. 2004). Such differences become substantially stronger during puberty, when boys accrete primarily lean mass, and girls primarily fat mass (Haschke 1989). The sexes also contrast in their allocation between competing adipose tissue depots. Females, especially during puberty, allocate substantially more fat to subcutaneous adipose tissue depots, whereas the smaller male allocation of fat is disproportionately targeted at the intra-abdominal depot.

   In later life, female strategy alters and energy shifts from peripheral to central depots (Wells, Treleaven, and Cole 2007). Both sexes reduce their muscle mass (limiting their work capacity), whilst prioritising survival (favoured by the central adiposity) over reproduction (peripheral fat distribution in younger females). Although central fat increases the risk of cardiovascular disease, the effects are delayed by a lengthy 'incubation period' (Rose 1982), such that the benefits of greater immune function precede the risks.

Allocation strategies are further influenced by nutritional status. Growth-retarded neonates show depleted subcutaneous fat stores but similar intra-abdominal fat to normal weight neonates (Harrington et al. 2004). Likewise, women suffering from anorexia nervosa deplete their subcutaneous stores substantially more than their visceral fat, but they reduce this difference on refeeding (Zamboni et al. 1997). These findings are strongly indicative of a prioritisation of the deep-lying adipose depots during malnutrition. Thus, the game-theory model may be developed by considering the different functions funded by energy stores, as listed above, and ranking them in terms of their survival importance. There is also increasing awareness of the role of specific hormones as the endocrine messengers regulating such trade-offs – for example, leptin signalling the absolute level of energy stores to the brain, and cortisol providing information regarding the current level of stress.

During chronic negative energy balance, some functions are 'put on hold', whilst other more fundamental functions are prioritised. Evidence from studies of chronic weight loss allows us to differentiate these different priorities. Anorexia nervosa results in the loss of peripheral fat stores, resulting in the conversion of 'hourglass' shape to a tubular form which essentially ceases to signal female shape. Therefore, a prolonged negative energy balance negates the function of fat in sexual selection. At the same time, negative energy balance interacts with the regulatory mechanism controlling female reproductive biology, reducing the likelihood of conception (Schneider 2004). Biopsy measurements indicate that the energy costs of lactation are met disproportionately from peripheral fat depots such as the thigh (Rebuffe-Scrive et al. 1985); hence, prolonged weight loss reduces breast-milk output as well (Bailey 1965). Sustained negative energy balance therefore curtails female reproductive function. Childhood growth is also temporarily slowed or halted when energy intake is reduced (Frongillo, Jr., de Onis, and Hanson 1997), until sufficient supply is restored. In contrast, perinodal adipose tissue depots, closely associated with local immune function, appear insensitive to nutritional status (Pond 2007).

Closing down these functions reduces the more fundamental priorities of adipose tissue to two functions: meeting obligatory energy needs, and funding the immune system. Support for these functions being prioritised also derives from the fact that both sexes are vulnerable to starvation and disease, whereas the contribution of adipose tissue to reproduction is primarily a female trait. There is substantial evidence demonstrating that the immune system itself loses efficacy when energy supply is reduced (Schaible and Kaufmann 2007).

Conversely, there is also increasing evidence that immune function tends to be of greater importance for survival during famine than energy stores per se, and that adipose tissue is directed to protecting this function during malnutrition (Mokyr and Ó Gráda 2002). Likewise, increased levels of a marker of immune activation were associated with reduced subsequent height increment in Bolivian children, particularly if they had low levels of adiposity (McDade et al. 2008). Nevertheless, the enhanced cardiovascular risk characteristic of those obese, especially those centrally obese, indicates that whilst fat is beneficial for immune function in the short term, its role in doing so carries long term metabolic consequences, manifesting as the metabolic syndrome.

This generic game-theory perspective is based on the notion of multiple trade-offs between competing biological functions. The optimum allocation trade-off is assumed to vary according to age, sex and current ecological conditions, and also in relation to prior experience during the life-course, including trans-generational influences of the parents. The approach may be made more sophisticated by differentiating different adipose tissue depots for specific biological functions – for example, deep-lying and perinodal adipose depots for immune function versus peripheral depots for reproduction and longer-term maintenance of energy balance. Ideally, the game-theory model should be formalised in order to simulate how the trade-offs respond to ecological variability and change. A similar approach has been developed for the immune system (Romanyukha, Rudnev, and Sidorov 2006). However, the aim here is merely to describe such a model and to highlight fat as a key resource and regulating influence acting on competing functions. This model is used in the next two chapters as an aid to understanding how selective pressures generated change in adipose phenotype during hominin and human evolution.

7.8   Summary

This chapter has considered how mammals in general store energy in adipose tissue for use as a source of 'capital' in order to accommodate temporary disparities between capturing energy (income) from the environment, and expending it on competing biology functions. The distribution of fat stores across a variety of localised adipose tissue depots makes the properties of such capital much more sophisticated. The optimum strategy for storing and using energy depends on a variety of factors, which vary between individuals, across the life-course and between populations inhabiting different ecosystems. Mammalian adipose tissue emerged under a particular set of selective pressures, relating to small mammals with high energy needs relative to body size. With the evolution of greater body size, the costs and benefits of adipose tissue shifted and energy stores allowed a new set of ecological challenges, such as marked seasonality or extreme cold stress, to be met. This evolutionary background endowed hominins with a sophisticated adipose tissue biology, capable of responding adaptively to further novel selective pressures.

As in other species, evolution has favoured a proportion of energy storage strategy, reflecting relatively consistent ancestral experience, to be located at the level of the human genome. This results in the strategy being relatively reliable in each generation, but with a limited degree of flexibility. Genetic variability also favours bet-hedging, of particular value to organisms occupying a variety of niches, or niches that are unstable over time. However, adiposity is also sensitive to more immediate influences acting within the life-course, and hence it also reflects both external ecological conditions and recent parental experience. Both genes and 'energy capital' pass between generations, with genotypes favoured by selection according to their different strategies for using capital, and capital in turn reducing the strength of selective pressures acting back on the genome. The life-course induction of adiposity represents one component of a trans generational strategy for risk management, linking energy stores with the transmission of body size and physique across generations.

What is rapidly emerging, and merits particular interest from those addressing human life history, is that this store of energy capital, though highly variable in its magnitude between and within individuals, has developed a regulatory role regarding other traits and functions. Capital can be used to buffer ecological uncertainty, to transfer phenotypic quality to the next generation and to hedge bets in both these contexts. Maintaining capital may also impose short-term and long-term costs, and many species make little use of it, translating their income directly into reproductive fitness. Humans in contrast clearly make great use of capital, indicating that strategies for optimal energy allocation have been subjected to intense selective pressures during hominin evolution. It is hoped that further economic modelling will be used to investigate human adiposity in the future, but the simplified approach presented here already allows preliminary attempts at reconstructing the hominin experience.

8   *Adiposity in hominin evolution*

The profile of adipose tissue through hominin evolution cannot be reconstructed with surety because of the paucity of direct fossil evidence relating to soft tissue. Nevertheless, a variety of approaches are available for proposing likely scenarios, and traits common to all contemporary humans can be broadly assumed to have evolved along with, or prior to, the speciation of *Homo sapiens* and hence may have had relevance at least to the biology of *Homo erectus*.[1] The approximate dates of widely recognised members of the hominin family tree are shown in Table 8.1, based on Lewin and Foley (2004). Owing to the lack of available evidence on body size for some of these species, along with a confusion as to how various fossils should be allocated to the proposed species, this chapter will concern itself with a smaller variety of hominis – extant chimpanzees, four *Australopithecus* species (*A. afarensis, A. africanus, A. boisei* and *A. robustus*), and three *Homo* species (*H. habilis, H. erectus* and *H. sapiens*).

The close associations between adipose tissue and various functions described in Chapter 6 favour the hypothesis that hominin energy stores coevolved alongside other hominin features. Differences in adipose tissue biology between contemporary humans and extant apes similarly imply that many traits emerged only since the time of the shared common ancestor and therefore can be attributed either to australopithecine or *Homo* evolution. A further source of useful information comprises patterns of environmental change, for example, in climate and in the distribution of flora and fauna (Foley 1987). Collectively, these sources of evidence can be used to start teasing out different selective pressures and the likely time periods during which they may have been most important.

This chapter therefore reviews a variety of specific ecological factors, each proposed to have played an important role in favouring the emergence of adipose tissue characteristics in hominins. As in previous chapters, it is important to bear in mind that adipose tissue should be considered as a set of strategies,

---

[1] Although some distinguish two populations of early *Homo*, namely *Homo ergaster* from Africa and *Homo erectus* from east Asia, for simplicity the term *Homo erectus (sensu lato)* is used here for both variants.

215

Table 8.1. *Dates and distributions of commonly recognised hominin species*

	Date (mya)*	Geographical distribution
Earliest hominins		
Sahelanthropus tchadensis	7.5	Central Africa: Chad
Orrorin tugenensis	6	East Africa: Kenya
Ardipithecus ramidus	4.5	East Africa: Ethiopia
Gracile Australopithecines		
Australopithecus anamensis	4.5	East Africa: Kenya
Australopithecus afarensis	4–3	East Africa: Ethiopia, Kenya, Tanzania
Australopithecus africanus	3.5–2	South Africa: South Africa
Australopithecus bahrelghazali	3.6	Central Africa: Chad
Robust Australopithecines		
Australopithecus aethiopicus	2.5–1	East Africa: Ethiopia, Kenya
Australopithecus boisei	2–1	East Africa: Tanzania
Australopithecus robustus	2–1	South Africa: South Africa
Transitional Homo species		
Homo rudolfensis	2.5–1.8	South Africa: Malawi
Homo habilis	1.8–1	East Africa: Kenya, Tanzania; South Africa: South Africa
Homo		
Homo erectus	1.8–1	East Africa: Ethiopia, Kenya, Tanzania; South Africa: South Africa; North Africa: Morocco, Europe: Italy; Asia: Indonesia, China
Homo heidelbergensis	0.5–0.2	Europe, Africa, Asia
Homo neanderthalensis	0.2–0.1	Europe
Homo sapiens	0.2–present	Global

* Mya – millions of years before present
Table based on Lewin and Foley (2004)

including the maintenance of energy stores across potentially lengthy time periods, the capacity to acquire them rapidly, the capacity to utilise them at an appropriate rate when beneficial, and the capacity to regulate the allocation of energy between competing functions.

8.1   Trends in seasonality

Seasonality is now considered to have been a major source of selective pressure in hominin evolution, particularly in the radiation that occurred during the mid- and late Miocene (Foley 1993). Seasonality may impact on a number of biological parameters, including heat stress, water availability and disease load, but fluctuations in energy supply are likely to have been of considerable importance. As discussed by Pond (1998), seasonality in energy supply accounts for much of the variability in average fatness between species. Broader climatic trends which appear to have shaped the distribution of Miocene apes (Folinsbee and Brooks 2007) continued to exert effects during hominin evolution.

During the middle Miocene, evidence suggests the existence of extensive evergreen tropical forests. During the later Miocene, a decline in global temperatures induced the fragmentation of this forest, creating in its place a mosaic pattern of varied habitats including woodlands, bushland and grassland (Foley 1993). These new habitats were in turn substantially more seasonal, in terms both of rainfall patterns and resource availability (Foley 1987). Whereas rainfall was likely to have been relatively consistent throughout the year in the mid-Miocene, substantial dry seasons lasting from four to eight months are thought to have become typical in the late Miocene and Pliocene (Foley 1993). This impact of climate change on habitat distribution and seasonality is the context within which early hominin evolution occurred.

The common ancestor to contemporary chimpanzees, bonobos, gorillas and humans is considered to have occupied a warm, wet, fruit-rich forest niche in central Africa. As the different ape lineages emerged, they appear to have distributed themselves across a series of niches varying in relation to the degree of seasonal stress. Indeed, the effects of climate change on habitat distribution is likely to have represented a 'pull factor', favouring speciation (Foley 1993).

Foley (1993) has highlighted the relationship between the distribution of contemporary African hominoids and the duration of the dry season. Gorillas occupy habitats with a relatively short dry season, typically no more than four months per year. Chimpanzees occupy habitats with slightly longer dry seasons, typically five months per year. Early fossil hominins such as *Australopithecus afarensis* have been recovered from areas currently characterised by dry seasons exceeding five months per year, and this degree of seasonality is likely to have applied five million years ago. Foley therefore suggested that the capacity to tolerate the dry season was a trait subject to major selection, with more versatile hominins acquiring a larger geographical distribution than chimpanzees and gorillas. Foley also noted that the more eastern area of the broad hominoid radiation was not only characterised by more extreme conditions but also subject to profound evolutionary change.

Studies of chimpanzees illustrate a number of ways in which the dry season is tolerated; these include alterations in foraging strategy, feeding party size and dietary intake (Foley 1993). Early hominins are likewise predicted to have utilised a variety of means for tolerating seasonality. Foley (1987; 1993) has suggested that several aspects of the australopithecine radiation are intricately connected with adaptation to increasing seasonality, which would have impacted on both plant and animal resources. The greater abundance of plant foods in the wet season influences the distribution and population density of herbivores, critical if meat (from either hunting or scavenging) were an important component of the early hominin diet. Possible strategies to accommodate these effects include migration along with herbivore herds, or switching between meat and vegetable diets by season. Foley has proposed that the first of these options was pursued by the forebears of the *Homo* lineage, whereas the robust australopithecines displayed adaptations to a coarse vegetable diet (Foley 1993). Whilst the role of meat in the australopithecine diet remains uncertain, the key issue here is Foley's emphasis that there was no single hominin strategy, and that the different species must all have developed viable adaptations to seasonal uncertainty in energy supply.

Recent studies of contemporary apes suggest that body fat stores are a plausible adaptation in this context. In general, the diet of great apes is dominated by fruit, which tends to have a seasonal pattern of availability in their contemporary habitats. Seasonal scarcity in the availability of fruit obliges apes to incorporate 'fallback foods' into their diet (Knott 2005). These fall-back foods include leaves, pith, terrestrial herbaceous vegetation, bark, invertebrates and less favoured fruits. Such foods, typically of lower nutritional quality and more fibrous, are also exploited by other non-ape primates such as baboons. The extent of variability in dietary quality between good and fallback foods accounts for the level of seasonal dietary stress. For example, contemporary orang-utans appear to experience greater seasonal dietary stress than chimpanzees, which is reflected in greater variability in body fat content (Knott 2005).

An elegant study of orang-utans has demonstrated evidence both of marked seasonal variability in energy intake and of the use of fat stores to buffer these fluctuations. During the season of high fruit availability, orang-utans consume substantially more energy than their daily requirements, and thus they gain weight. During the season of poor fruit availability, ketones (products of fat metabolism) are detected in their urine samples, with the highest levels evident in pregnant or lactating females (Knott 1998). This indicates significant oscillations in adiposity in response to seasonality in energy supply. In contrast to this strategy, crab-eating monkeys (*Macaca fascicularis*) in the same general region exploit more reliable local habitats and have little need to accumulate fat stores (Wheatley 1982). Thus, adipose tissue represents a clear adaptation by orang-utans for accommodating seasonal variability in energy availability and is of particular benefit in mitigating the high energy burden of reproduction in females.

Seasonal fluctuations in body weight have also been observed in chimpanzees (Wrangham 1977; Uehara and Nishida 1987), and captive gorillas have been shown to attain body fat contents of greater than 40% (Zihlman and McFarland 2000). However, the extent to which weight fluctuations in wild populations of African apes can be attributed to fluctuations in body fat is unknown and represents a deserving research topic. To date, systematic ketone production has never been detected in chimpanzee urine (Knott 2005), suggesting any oscillations in adiposity are modest.

The use of body fat stores to accommodate seasonal fluctuations in energy supply is therefore found in at least some apes, and of course in many mammals more generally. As noted by Pond (1998), seasonality is exactly the kind of stress predicted to have favoured adiposity, since lipid stores are most effective in buffering long-term energy imbalances. The benefits must however be set against possible costs, the main one comprising limitations on escape from predators. Given that none of the apes rely primarily on speed for predator avoidance, and that even large apes are able to climb trees for security, this constraint is unlikely to have been of major significance in hominins (though see Speakman (2007)). It is likely therefore that increased body fat stores were favoured during the australopithecine radiation, contributing to a variety of adaptive strategies to resolving the high level of seasonal stress they encountered.

Seasonality remained a stress throughout later hominin evolution, though increasingly it involved exposure to variability in rainfall, cold and day length as the geographical range expanded (Foley 1993). Furthermore, as hominins migrated into new habitats, a positive-feedback cycle is likely to have developed, relating an improved tolerance of seasonal variability to an improved capacity to invade more volatile ecological niches. Thus, seasonality and habitat expansion are closely associated, reflected in the increasing colonising behaviour of hominins (Foley 1987; Wells and Stock 2007).

In summary, seasonality is likely to have been a key factor favouring energy stores in the hominin lineage. This selective pressure is further likely to have interacted with others described below, such that for any given scenario, seasonality would have exacerbated energy stress and hence favoured a more dynamic adipose tissue biology. The stress of seasonality is also important because, by increasing metabolic flexibility in australopithecines, it may have contributed to the increasing capacity of hominins to probe novel ecological niches, and hence eventually colonise new territory.

8.2   Trends in body size

Energetics and body size are related in terms of both causes and consequences. On the one hand, increasing body size offers benefits to organisms in terms of

Table 8.2. *Body size and proportions of chimpanzees (Pan), hominins (Australopithecus, Homo) and humans*

Species	Age	Male			Female			Dimorphism		
		Wt	Ht	BMI	Wt	Ht	BMI	Wt	Ht	EQ
P. troglodytes		54			40			26%		2.0
A. afarensis	4.0–2.9	45	151	19.7	29	105	26.3	−36%	−30%	2.4
A. africanus	3.0–2.4	41	138	21.5	30	115	22.7	−27%	−17%	2.6
A. robustus	1.8–1.6	40	132	23.0	32	110	26.4	−20%	−17%	3.1
A. boisei	2.0–1.3	49	137	26.1	34	124	22.1	−31%	−9%	2.7
H. habilis	2.4–1.6	52	157	21.1	32	125	20.5	−38%	−20%	3.1
H. erectus	1.7–0.7	63	180	19.4	52	160	20.3	−17%	−11%	3.3
H. sapiens		65	175	21.2	54	161	20.8	−21%	− 8%	5.8

Age = geological age in millions of years; Wt = weight in kg; Ht = height in cm; BMI = body mass index in kg/m²

Dimorphism = female value minus male value, expressed as percent of the male value

EQ = encephalisation quotient, derived from actual versus predicted brain volume for body weight

Data on age, weight, height and EQ from McHenry (1992a; 1992b) except weight for *Homo erectus* (Aiello and Wells 2002)

enabling access to particular niches. On the other, increasing size is associated with a variety of life-history traits, which have implications for the rate at which energy is converted into reproduction (Foley 1987).

Ancestral gorillas and chimpanzees appear morphologically similar to contemporary species (McBrearty and Jablonski 2005; Suwa et al. 2007), indicating that they occupied similar niches to those of their contemporary representatives. During hominin evolution, body size initially showed a degree of stability, followed by a marked increase with the emergence of the genus *Homo*. Table 8.2 provides estimated values for body size, using the data of McHenry (1992b; 1992a), with further calculations to provide BMI. McHenry used a variety of different approaches for the prediction of weight, based on different components of the skeleton, but favoured equations based on hindlimb joint size derived from human rather than hominoid data (McHenry 1992a). Although the reconstructed weights vary according to whether physique is considered more similar to that of humans or chimpanzees, the data are sufficiently robust to reveal several broad trends.

First, there is no systematic increase in body size over the last five million years. Rather, the australopithecines remained similar in size to non-hominin apes, and some evidence indicates a sudden step up in size with the evolution of the genus *Homo*. This interpretation of a sudden increase relies heavily on the skeletal evidence of a single individual dating from 1.66 mya, the 'Nariokotome boy', whose likely adult height has been estimated. Little

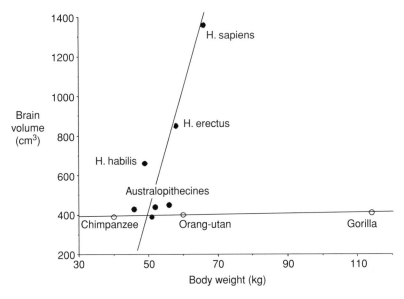

Figure 8.1. Increases in encephalisation during hominin evolution. Relative to the brain volumes encountered in extant apes, over a wide range of body size, australopithecines do not appear encephalised. However, successive members of the *Homo* lineage show increasingly large brain volume relative to size, with the largest increase occurring with the evolution of our own species. Redrawn with permission from Lewin (1998).

information is available for earlier *Homo*, but some examples of *erectus* (e.g., from Dmanisi, Georgia) are similar in size to australopithecines, as are other early *Homo* species such as *H. habilis*. Nevertheless, regardless of how rapidly *erectus* increased in height, this shift appears to have post-dated the australopithecine era.

In early australopithecines, sexual dimorphism in weight and height was profound (McHenry 1992a); however, when expressed in relative terms, the BMI of females appears greater than that of males (Table 8.2). With the evolution of the genus *Homo*, females appear to have become more gracile, but this is due in part to sexual dimorphism in height decreasing, with increases in female height greater than those in males. Encephalisation appears to have proceeded in a not dissimilar fashion. Figure 8.1 plots brain volume against body size in three non-hominin apes and in the same hominin species as described in Table 8.2. The australopithecine data fall within the same range as that for apes, whereas there is a steady upwards trend evident in the *Homo* data (Lewin 1998).

What would the significance of these trends in body size have been for adiposity itself? As discussed in Chapter 2, there is a relatively tight association

Table 8.3. *Estimated lean and fat mass of hominin species, based on predictions from human data*

Species	Age (mya)	Male					Female				
		Lean	Fat	LMI	FMI	%fat	Lean	Fat	LMI	FMI	%fat
A. afarensis	4.0–2.9	39.9	5.1	17.5	2.3	11.4	24.6	4.4	22.4	3.9	15.0
A. africanus	3.0–2.4	36.0	5.0	18.9	2.6	12.2	26.0	4.0	19.6	3.0	13.4
A. robustus	1.8–1.6	34.8	5.2	20.0	3.0	13.1	26.4	5.6	21.8	4.6	17.5
A. boisei	2.0–1.3	40.9	8.1	21.8	4.3	16.5	28.5	5.5	18.5	3.6	16.1
H. habilis	2.4–1.6	45.0	7.0	18.2	2.9	13.6	27.7	4.3	17.7	2.7	13.3
H. erectus	1.7–0.7	54.4	8.6	16.8	2.6	13.6	39.1	12.9	15.3	5.1	24.9
H. sapiens		55.1	9.9	18.0	3.2	15.2	39.9	14.1	15.4	5.4	26.1

Age (mya) = geological age in millions of years
Equations used to predict Lnlean from the data reviewed in Chapter 2, as described below
Fat then calculated as difference of lean and weight
Weight (WT), lean and fat masses in kg, height (HT) in cm, lean mass index (LMI) and fat mass index (FMI) in kg/m^2

between body size (as represented by lean mass) and fat mass. Figure 2.3 illustrated the association between log lean mass and log fat mass in a variety of mammalian species. In the human body composition data compiled for diverse populations reviewed in Chapter 2, both height and weight are positively associated with lean mass and fat mass. These data are now used to derive sex-specific equations for the prediction of log lean mass from the raw data on log weight (in kg) and log height (in cm), using average values specific to each population. These equations may be considered broadly representative of humans, incorporating a wide range of populations occupying different ecosystems. The fit as given by the r^2 values is poorer for females than males, indicating a greater contribution of adiposity rather than lean mass to variance in weight in females.

$$\text{Males (n = 76): Log lean} = -0.9794 + 0.7308 \text{ log weight}$$
$$+ 0.3752 \text{ log height } r^2 = 0.91$$
$$\text{Females (n = 66): Log lean} = -0.3156 + 0.5074 \text{ log weight}$$
$$+ 0.3893 \text{ log height } r^2 = 0.75$$

These equations are then applied to the data on hominin weight and height given in Table 8.2 to estimate lean mass. These lean mass values are subtracted from weight, to give fat mass, and adjusted for height as described in Chapter 2, allowing calculation of lean mass index, fat mass index and percentage fat.

Table 8.3 shows estimated body composition of the hominins. Clearly these estimations assume a humanlike association between weight, height and lean mass, which may not be valid in other species. The robust australopithecines, for example, may well have had greater muscle mass for a given weight and height than humans. The early taxa (australopithecines and *Homo habilis*) are considered to have had basic body proportions significantly different from those of later species. Upper limbs were larger relative to lower limbs, and body breadth was large in relation to height (Ruff 2002), differences which may relate both to retained arboreal capabilities in the earlier species and allometric effects of their smaller size. Thus, early australopithecines may similarly have had greater lean mass for a given weight than later species.

Nevertheless, such errors are partially addressed through predicting lean mass from both weight and height, since heavier humans also have greater lean mass as well as fat mass. The data in Table 8.2 suggest that male hominins may have been relatively consistent in having a fat mass index of around 2 to 3 kg/m^2 (or 11 to 15% of weight as fat) across the entire period of hominin evolution, except in *A. boisei*, when a higher value of 4.3 kg/m^2 (16.5% fat) is suggested. In females, the predictions suggest that relative to height fatness was greater than in males (3–4.6 kg/m^2) but similar as a proportion of weight (13–15% of weight in gracile species, and 16–17% in robust species), until the evolution of *H. erectus*, when a sudden drastic increase to 5 kg/m^2 (or 25% of weight) is predicted, similar to the value typical of contemporary human populations. However, female gracile australopithecines also have higher predicted LMI and FMI than males, suggesting that their shorter height may have been associated with altered body proportions and shape. In the *Homo* genus, females have lower predicted LMI than males. Rather than implying that greater muscle mass may have been selected in males (the male values remain relatively stable), reduced muscle mass appears to have been selected in females.

These data must be treated with caution, especially for non-*Homo* species, and future work should address variability within *Homo erectus*. Nonetheless, they indicate several interesting possibilities. First, estimated levels of greater than 2 kg/m^2, or more than 10% fat, in both sexes of australopithecines suggest that energy stores may already have been favoured by the stress of seasonality, as discussed above. Any interpretation of this proposition is complicated, as mentioned previously, by the lack of equivalent data from chimpanzees and gorillas; however, 10% fat is substantially higher than the 2% recorded in another savannah primate, the baboon (Altmann et al. 1993). This conclusion is the most tenuous, since as discussed above stockier body build might explain the BMI of these species, which would then suggest lower body-fat content. Second, significant sexual dimorphism in adiposity may have emerged only with *H. erectus*, an issue discussed further below. Intriguingly, the increase in female fatness emerges even as BMI decreases, implying a much stronger decline in female LMI than in males over the entirety of hominin evolution. The lower levels of lean mass in humans compared to other primates imply reduced energy needs (Leonard et al. 2003), hence 'under-musculation' of females may be another correlate of the increased reproductive load. Third, little change in male adiposity is suggested over the entire five million year period, indicating again that seasonality may have been a key factor favouring hominin adiposity. Again, this conclusion depends on the relationship between physique and lean mass being interpreted appropriately.

In general, increasing body size tends to be associated with a variety of other traits (Foley 1987; Stearns 1992). Larger organisms can achieve a greater size only by growing for longer, or growing more rapidly. Typically, larger size is associated with later maturation, which in turn can be attributed to reduced mortality rates. These factors then generate associations of large size with smaller litter size, larger individual offspring, and hence longer gestation periods and inter-birth intervals (Stearns 1992). Body size has a number of implications specifically for energetics, reflected, for example, in the well-established allometric relationship between body size and basal metabolic rate (Kleiber 1961). This equation is increasingly considered to be somewhat simplistic for failing to take into account differences between phyla (White, Phillips, and Seymour 2006), but the notion that greater body size is associated with relatively lower metabolic rate per unit of mass is not contested. Larger organisms therefore have greater relative energetic efficiency, aiding the conversion of energy intake into offspring (Oftedal 2000). There are also constraints on size, with heat stress acknowledged to have been an important example in human evolution (Wheeler 1992; 1993; Aiello and Wells 2002).

Of particular importance is the effect of increasing body size on the relative energy costs of lactation. Given that small animals expend energy at a substantially higher mass-specific rate than larger animals, body size has implications for the proportion of energy needs that can be stored in the form of adipose tissue (Oftedal 2000). An animal of large mass such as the human need only mobilise a relatively small fraction of total fat stores to meet a single day's energy requirements for lactation. Such scaling relationships mean that increasing body size represents a highly successful strategy for accommodating increased energy costs of lactation. Aiello and Key (2002) have previously proposed that the increase in female adult size in *H. erectus* was favoured for this reason, owing to the marked increase in infant energy requirements attributable to the larger *Homo* brain, as discussed below.

The marked sex difference in body composition evident in our species, suggested here to have emerged in *Homo erectus*, implies that the energetics of reproduction represented a stronger selective pressure than seasonality, though the two stresses must also be assumed to have compounded one another.

This scenario suggests that the large *Homo* brain may ultimately be the most important factor in the evolution of human adiposity. Maternal fat represents only one strategy for accommodating these costs, with slowed childhood growth also important (Walker et al. 2006; Gurven and Walker 2006; Bogin and Varela-Silva 2006). This slowed pattern of growth is assumed to have evolved in stages, with the 'childhood' period of the life-cycle proposed to have characterised *Homo erectus* but the lengthy total developmental period emerging only our own species (Bogin 2001). Increased infant fat stores may have been an important component of the slowed childhood growth pattern, possibly contributing through positive feedback to the strategy of encephalisation. Thus, size must be separated from growth rate, with each representing an adaptation with further implications for the evolution of adiposity.

In summary, trends in predicted weight and height suggest underlying trends in both lean mass and adiposity. The simulations conducted here indicate sexual dimorphism in size rather than body composition in the australopithecines, with the 17 to 30% shorter height of females compensated by relatively greater tissue masses. This pattern appears to have shifted to a reduced dimorphism in size in the genus *Homo* but a more drastic dimorphism in body composition, with females showing both reduced lean mass and greater fatness. Though in need of further work, this indicates an increased female energetic burden of reproduction of *Homo*, which in turn implies the impact of encephalisation and perhaps the Homo pattern of growth.

8.3   Trends in encephalisation

Arguably the first major trait to emerge during early hominin evolution that distinguished the australopithecines from ancestral apes was bipedalism, although in fact a form of bipedalism may predate these hominins (Thorpe, Holder, and Crompton 2007). In previous decades, bipedalism was assumed to be closely associated with increases in brain size (Washburn 1960). The substantially improved fossil record now discredits this notion. It provides strong evidence that increases in brain size were negligible until late australopithecine evolution and were primarily a feature of the *Homo* genus.

As shown in Figure 8.1, the first species departing significantly from the ape baseline for encephalisation is *Homo habilis*, which increasingly is not considered a true member of the genus (Wood and Collard 1999), in which case it represents the final stages of the australopithecine adaptive radiation. Encephalisation underwent further systematic increases throughout the evolution of the *Homo* genus, the most marked transition occurring with the emergence of *Homo sapiens*. The selective pressures driving encephalisation remain poorly understood, but increasingly complex diet (Jones 2007), more complex sociality (Humphrey 1986) along with the colonising of new territories, considered below (Wells and Stock 2007), may have been particularly important. In that context, I suggest that positive feedback cycles relating cognitive capacity and diet are likely to have been very important. First, Jones (2007) has argued that physiological trade-offs implicated in increased brain size (Aiello and Wheeler 1995) suggest a variety of behavioural strategies for increasing dietary energy capture. Second, the challenges of feeding big-brained infants are proposed to have favoured cooperative breeding, itself favouring greater cognitive capacities.

A substantial body of work supports the notion that this increase in brain size had a profound influence on hominin energy requirements. As discussed in Chapter 6, brain tissue is well established to be amongst the most costly within the body, sharing with other vital organs a relatively high metabolic rate per unit mass (Holliday 1971). Larger brain volume therefore significantly increases basal metabolism, which translates directly into increased total energy requirements. Although contemporary humans have been suggested to have a basal metabolic rate as expected for an average mammal of our size (Armstrong 1983), closer examination suggests this is not the case. Relatively high energy requirements per unit of weight are partially concealed behind the low metabolic rate of large adipose tissue depots (Aiello and Wells 2002); hence, energy expenditure per unit lean mass is higher than generally assumed.

The increased energy requirements imposed by the large *Homo* brain have been proposed to have been met via a number of specific adaptations. First, Aiello and Wheeler (1995) have proposed a reduction in expensive tissue in order to divert energy to the increased brain. This hypothesis is supported by comparisons of brain and gut size across primates. Second, Foley and Elton (1998) have proposed an increase in the energetic efficiency of locomotion. Third, Leonard and Robertson (1997) have suggested increased energy capture through greater foraging territory. Fourth, the same authors (Leonard and Robertson 1994) have suggested changes in dietary composition through shifts to higher return foods. Jones (2007) has suggested technological developments such as 'extra-corporeal digestion' (rotting, fermentation) may also have been important in this context. Fifth, Aiello and Key (2002) have proposed shifts in the energetics of reproduction, most notably a shortening of the lactation period (see below). Similarly, others (Bogin 2001) have identified slower childhood growth as a further relaxation of pressure on the maternal energy budget. Sixth, technological developments have increased the efficiency of a wide variety of subsistence activities, reducing the energy costs of foraging (Torrence 1983).

Increases in adipose tissue stores should therefore be considered merely one amongst a wide variety of adaptive strategies in hominin energetics, and they relate primarily to *buffering* the brain's energy requirements rather than funding them on a continuous basis. Adipose tissue may, however, be considered a particularly significant adaptation, not least because adaptations in physiology cannot be jettisoned as and when required in the way that technological or behavioural strategies can. The expensive metabolic requirements of the *Homo* brain, particularly in infancy (see below), can be assumed to have been critical to the emergence of the human profile of fatness with its oscillations across the life-span.

The impact of high brain costs is felt most severely during early life. Figure 6.13 illustrated the changing association between head volume and other body proportions with age in our species. Primates in general have large neonatal as well as adult brain volume, thus inflating neonatal energy requirements across the entire family, but humans continue this trend to a particular extreme, as shown by a significantly increased ratio of brain mass to non-brain lean mass in human neonates compared to other extant ape neonates (Wells and Stock 2007).

As reviewed previously by Kuzawa (1998), the domination of body weight by brain weight in early life has a profound impact on energetics. Foley and Lee (1991a) calculated that the size of the human infant brain increases total energy requirements by 9% above that of similar sized apes. This increased requirement for energy can be subdivided into two related needs: first, a high rate of glucose utilisation, and second, a store of adipose tissue capable of meeting these requirements should dietary intake fail to do so. These energetic associations must be further set within several particular challenges facing the infant – the difficulty of transferring fat to the offspring via placental nutrition, the low intake of breast-milk in the immediate period after birth, the increased risk of infection during weaning (Kuzawa 1998), and the need to fund childhood growth after the end of lactation.

On the basis of limited available data, the human infant is strikingly fat at birth (Kuzawa 1998; Pawlowski 1998). Figure 8.2 plots log fat mass against log lean mass for the data collated by Kuzawa (1998), which highlight the guinea pig, harp seal and human as unusually adipose neonates. The majority of species are 3% fat or less at birth, including baboons, the only other primate species with data. Humans, guinea pigs and harp seals all have in common the inability of maternal milk to meet energy needs immediately after birth (Kuzawa 1998). This raises the question of why lactation should take so long to establish given that human infants typically take one week to recover their birth weight and oxidise fat stores in the meantime. Hrdy (2000) has suggested that mothers

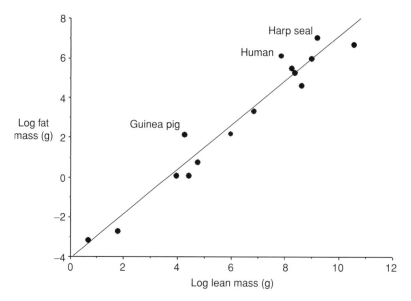

Figure 8.2. Log fat mass plotted against log lean mass for a selection of species for whom natal body composition data are available. Three species stand out for their high fat content at birth – the guinea pig, harp seal and human. Based on data from Kuzawa (1998).

may evaluate the 'worth' of their neonate before deciding whether to continue investment[2]. It is plausible that 'chubby' babies may first signal their 'viability' visually, before indicating their hunger and vitality vocally (Wells 2003a). Thus, the immediate neonatal period may represent an important bottleneck, through which only robust offspring with adequate energy stores may pass.

Once lactation is established, the human infant rapidly gains further fat, such that typically by six months 25% of weight is fat. Kuzawa (1998) has proposed such energy stores to provide the fuel supply for the immune system, predicted to be activated as complementary foods begin to be introduced. Related to this need is the unusually short duration of lactation typical of modern human populations, resulting in the older infant having to fund immune function from its own energy reserves rather than energy intake. However, infections also reduce the energy available for growth (Prentice and Darboe 2008); hence, infant fat may also be targeted at funding the period of childhood growth when the mother may be investing more of her own resources in a new pregnancy.

[2] A well-known though controversial example of 'maternal evaluation' was reported by Shostak in her description of the !Kung bushwoman Nisa, who recalled her mother temporarily abandoning Nisa's newborn brother whilst the two of them considered whether Nisa should start breast-feeding again.

Table 8.4. *Composition of the maternal milk of different species*

Species	% protein	% fat	% carbohydrate	Energy density (kJ/d)
Non-primates				
Dog	7.5	9.5	3.8	6.11
Pig	5.6	8.3	5.0	5.19
Deer	7.1	8.5	4.5	5.73
Reindeer	9.5	10.9	3.4	6.95
Sheep	4.1	7.3	5.0	4.64
Rat	8.1	8.8	3.8	5.98
Rabbit	10.3	15.2	1.8	8.54
Average	7.5	9.8	3.9	6.16
Primates				
Monkey*	2.1	3.0	7.2	2.80
Marmoset	2.7	3.6	7.4	3.22
Tamarin	2.6	5.2	7.2	3.77
Baboon	1.5	4.6	7.7	3.31
Human	0.8	4.1	6.8	2.89
Average	1.9	4.1	7.3	3.20

* genus Cercopithecus
Data from Sellen (2006)

The high maternal energy burden, generated by encephalised offspring, appears to have been reduced by a number of strategies, including slowing the rate of offspring growth, which is in turn associated with a reduction in the energy and protein content of maternal milk (Oftedal and Iverson 1995). For example, gorillas grow at 1/12th the rate of reindeer, despite maternal body size being very similar (Lee, Majluf, and Gordon 1991). Likewise, primate milk solids comprise approximately 12 to 14% of milk volume by mass, in comparison with a minimum of 30% in other terrestrial mammals and 30 to 60% in cetaceans (Oftedal 1984). Table 8.4 displays the composition of milks of different species. Primates in general have low protein and fat content, but greater carbohydrate (lactose) content, relative to non-primates (Sellen 2006). Within the general primate pattern, humans have similar fat and carbohydrate content, but a protein content less than half that of the other species (Sellen 2006). The high carbohydrate content may be attributed to the continued brain demand, whereas the very low protein can be attributed to the markedly slowed growth rate in our species. In these circumstances the fat, although low in concentration relative to other species, is readily available for deposition in adipose tissue. The growth of the brain itself is relatively modest, although fatty acids play an important role in this process, too.

Modelling suggests that if *Homo erectus* were to have continued to lactate for the same proportional time period attributed to australopithecine females, the impact of the encephalised brain would have been to increase the maternal energy burden by 40% (Aiello and Key 2002). A reduction in the duration of lactation is therefore considered to represent an important shift in female reproductive strategy in *Homo erectus* (Aiello and Key 2002), as indicated by a shorter inter-birth interval in humans compared to other apes (Galdikas and Wood 1990). However, not only has the total duration of lactation apparently decreased, but humans also start using complementary foods to displace breast-milk within the first months of life. Although the WHO recommends exclusive breast-feeding for the first six months, few societies do so (Dettwyler and Fishman 1992), and it is generally considered that complementary foods are expected around the sixth month. Complementary foods are typically much lower in energy content than breast-milk, particularly in terms of lipid content (Gibson, Ferguson, and Lehrfeld 1998). The rapid accumulation of adipose tissue in the first few months of life may therefore represent the strategy of depositing lipid in a very brief window, so that immune function is viable by the time the first complementary foods are introduced.

Complementary feeding has been associated with another unusual trait in humans, the provisioning of infants by non-maternal kin, especially grandmothers (Hrdy 2000). Humans appear unusual in the loss of female reproductive capacity well before typical age at death. Grandmothering has been proposed to play a key role in more general cooperative breeding (Hrdy 2000). Whilst this activity reduces the energy burden acting directly on the mother, it also has intriguing implications for body composition in old age. Zafon (2007) has proposed that senescence may be an adaptive process whereby post-reproductive individuals are transformed into more economical organisms, requiring less energy because of their reduced lean mass and lower activity levels. This shift in energy demand would then reduce competition within the extended kin group (Zafon 2007), whilst still enabling high quality offspring care through grandparenting. The accumulation of fat through middle-age would buffer such elderly individuals against deficits in food supply without detracting from their ability to perform grandparenting activities.

In summary, the evolution of increased adiposity in human neonates thus appears to be closely associated with the large brain, implying that the evolution of early life fatness may have followed the pattern of encephalisation evident in the fossil record. Positive feedback cycles may have driven this encephalisation in relation to both dietary and parenting strategies. Alongside reductions in the duration of lactation, selection can also be assumed to have favoured increased energy stores in females in order to guarantee funding of that lactation period, which in turn provides the main source of energy for the infant's energy stores. Increased fatness with age may represent a further adaptation in the context of grandmothering. These changes can be broadly attributed to the *Homo* genus, though it is also likely that increased adiposity developed cumulatively, in combination with increasing brain size.

8.4   Trends in growth patterns

Complementary to such trends in reproductive energetics, the pattern of hominin growth also altered. Reconstructing such changes is extremely difficult, and has been undertaken on the basis of fragmentary information regarding brain development, maturational age and dental development (Bogin and Smith, 1996). Relative to chimpanzees, it is clear that modern humans have a shorter period of infancy, as indicated by shorter inter-birth intervals, but an extended period of growth prior to puberty (Bogin and Smith, 1996). Although the details remain unclear, hominin evolution must have been characterized by shift towards a more complex process regulating growth and maturation, with the emergence of a greater number of distinct developmental phases. Bogin and Smith (1996) suggest that childhood and adolescence both emerged during the evolution of *Homo*, either side of the more general juvenile period that they attribute to other species. Their suggested pattern of evolution is illustrated in Figure 8.3.

Patterns of growth are essentially strategies for the investment of energy in adult size and phenotype. The more complex pattern of human growth implies that control of these strategies has become linked with ecological conditions via the mediating influence of maternal phenotype. The evidence reviewed in Chapter 5 showed that human growth demonstrates two key axes of variability. The first is an axis of 'more or less', and involves an association between the magnitude of nutritional supply during fetal life and infancy, and stature and lean mass in adulthood. The second is an axis of 'faster or slower', and involves an association between the magnitude of nutritional supply during childhood, and the time taken to reach puberty and hence final size.

Such plasticity in human growth rates show that selection has favoured sensitivity both to prevailing ecological conditions, and also to maternal experience. In good conditions, the offspring can mature faster and start to breed earlier, as observed in many other species. However, the size of the offspring is also profoundly influenced by maternal investment during early life, such that the growth costs of the offspring are constrained by the maternal capacity to supply them.

This plasticity in growth and physique has integral knock-on effects on adiposity, for several reasons. First, the absolute requirement for energy stores varies in relation to lean mass. Second, energy stores may be accumulated in one developmental period in order to fund growth in the next period. Finally,

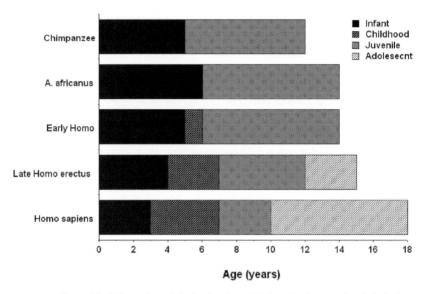

Figure 8.3. Estimated trends in the duration of distinct developmental periods during hominin evolution, as suggested by Bogin and Smith (1996). Chimpanzees and early Australopithecines may have passed through only infant and juvenile stages. During the evolution of Homo, two further stages, childhood and adolescence, emerged on either side of the juvenile stage, conferring greater complexity in the regulation of growth and development, and its sensitivity to nutritional supply. Based on data from Bogin and Smith (1996).

indications of poor energy availability may shift energy allocation strategy from lean to fat, so as to maintain higher reserves during stochastic conditions.

Thus, the emergence of the modern human pattern of growth is strongly sassociated with the life-course development of adiposity, as discussed in Chapters 2 and 5. The powerful influence of maternal phenotype on offspring development indicates a link between maternal reproductive strategy and offspring growth strategy. This issue is discussed later in this chapter in the context of the human colonising reproductive strategy.

8.5   Trends in diet, metabolism and appetite

Closely related to the proposed evolution of large brains and greater body fat stores are complementary changes in hominin diet (Leonard and Robertson 1994; Leonard and Robertson 1997). In general, primates may be considered frugivores on the basis of the characteristics of their gut physiology (Ulijaszek 2002). However, frugivory still permits considerable flexibility, with small species supplementing their diet with animal matter, larger species incorporating folivory, and seasonal variability within species further possible (Ulijaszek 2002). Contemporary humans remain broadly within this general pattern, being omnivorous though also consuming a relatively high-energy density diet (Ulijaszek 2002). In general, larger animals have reduced energy requirements per unit of body weight, which in turn opens up a wider variety of potential food sources. Large-brained humans conflict with this pattern by maintaining a highly variable diet also characterised by high diet quality. These atypical dietary requirements co-evolved alongside appetite and metabolism, each of which is relevant to adiposity.

The energy content of fruit, along with its ripeness, is positively correlated with sweetness. An appetite for sweet foods may have been favoured through this component of diet, with some suggesting a similar scenario for alcohol, which is often present owing to fermentation in over-ripe fruit. The preference for a sweet taste is also present in infants and may likewise have been favoured as a strategy for promoting the energy density of food intake. In general, however, taste sensitivity for sucrose declines with increasing body size in primates, suggesting that larger animals with lower metabolic rate are less discerning and hence able to exploit less energy-dense foods (Simmen and Hladik 1998). Humans are consistent with that pattern, supporting the notion of humans as omnivores rather than fruit specialists (Ulijaszek 2002). A broader hypothesis, given the value of carbohydrates for fattening, is that a sweet preference simply helps achieve a positive energy balance and is important in a species that benefits substantially from adiposity. Since most fruit contains negligible fat content, a different selective pressure must have driven the human preference for fat, most likely in the context of meat consumption.

Although meat may have contributed to the diet of late australopithecines, and chimpanzees are known to hunt regularly, large-scale meat consumption appears to have emerged along with the evolution of *Homo*, probably initially through scavenging (*Homo erectus*) and then subsequently through hunting (*Homo heidelbergensis, Homo sapiens*) (Stanford and Bunn 2001; Bunn 1994). Exploiting the increase in herbivore numbers that accompanied the emergence of the *Homo* genus would have provided a key opportunity for meeting increased energy requirements (Anton, Leonard, and Robertson 2002). Since the composition of meat varies less than that of plant matter, hunting has been proposed to allow convergence on a common ecological niche (Foley 2001), thereby favouring adaptation to diverse habitats.

However, it is not widely appreciated that diets high in animal protein may be relatively marginal in terms of energy, especially during seasons when non-meat sources of food become scarce. A high meat diet imposes its own metabolic load because of elevated metabolic rates which in turn increase energy requirements (Speth and Spielmann 1983). Based on carcass analyses, the meat of wild ungulates at the low point in the annual cycle tends to have extremely low fat content, typically 1.5 to 2.0% (Speth and Spielmann 1983; Speth 1987). Given a diet of lean meat only, a human male would have to eat approximately 1.8 kg, and a female 1.6 kg, per day simply to satisfy basal needs, with this intake rising to over 3 kg per day to take into account physical activity (Speth and Spielmann 1983). A high meat diet may also induce essential fatty acid deficiencies. To address these challenges, contemporary foraging populations actively seek animals with high fat content, and they also store or exchange foods that are high in fat or carbohydrate content. Hayden (1981) observed that Australian aborigines abandoned kangaroos that were found, on butchering, to have low fat content. Equally, high levels of body fat provide protection against the wastage of body proteins during severe dietary restriction (Speth and Spielmann 1983). Thus, meat-eating may have favoured the accumulation of fat stores to buffer seasonal variability in energy and fat intake.

Extraction of the fat from within animal bones represents a further strategy for increasing dietary lipid content. Much of the archaeological evidence for early meat-eating comprises split bones from which the marrow has been extracted (Speth 1987). According to this perspective, an enhanced preference of humans for fat may derive from the period of evolutionary history during which our ancestors consumed a meat-rich diet. Preference for fat may be adaptive in providing a source of essential fatty acids, whilst also relieving the monotony of a meat-rich diet. Fats and oils remain important sources of flavour in all human diets, most of which derive the majority of calories from staple carbohydrates (Mintz 1985).

The changing nature of the hominin diet can be assumed to have driven alterations in insulin metabolism. Assuming our more distant hominin ancestors to have been frugivores consuming a high-carbohydrate diet, then the switch to a high-protein low-carbohydrate diet, such as is assumed to have characterised the genus *Homo* when hunting large herbivores, would favour peripheral insulin resistance without any need for compensatory hyperinsulinaemia (Colagiuri and Brand 2002). A return to a diet with a high glycaemic load, following the emergence of agriculture, may then challenge this metabolic balance, as discussed in Chapter 10. Whether humans as a species have 'thrifty genes' (Neel 1962) in relation to their metabolism, or whether thriftiness is more a trait comprising variability *within* contemporary human populations, is likewise discussed in Chapter 9.

Increased dietary energy requirements must inevitably impact on foraging behaviour, for example, increasing the daily range. The rate at which energy is captured from a given area of territory also influences what size of hominin group can be maintained, and for how long before poor foraging returns oblige relocation elsewhere (Kelly 1995). Estimations of the physical activity level (PAL, expressed as total energy expenditure divided by basal metabolism) of pre-agricultural populations of *Homo* converge on values of around 2 in males and 1.6 in females, very similar to those of contemporary foragers and agriculturalists in non-industrial environments (Malina and Little 2008). Thus, in order to provide the high-quality diet for the larger brain, *Homo* would also have needed to fund the energetic costs of the underlying foraging activity, ensuring a close fit between energy intake and energy expenditure that could only have become relaxed once food began to be stored (see Chapter 10). Such broader foraging activities would also have contributed to the capacity to probe novel environmental niches.

In addition to the evolution of dietary preferences, there must also have been neurobiological changes in the manner of eating. Hominins appear to continue broader primate trends whereby social cues are an important component of eating behaviour. Social cues appear especially important in the regulation of human appetite and indicate that as individual foraging gave way to pooled energy budgets, with both males and females contributing hunted or gathered foodstuffs to communal meals, eating and appetite became fundamentally social entities. Little work has been conducted as yet on the neurobiological basis of these changes, but Allman and colleagues (2002) have argued that the *Homo* brain demonstrates two types of neurobehavioral specialization that enable adaptive responses to changing conditions, and they suggest that these may have been particularly important for the intergenerational transfer of food and information characteristic of human extended families. In this content, it would have benefited appetite to respond to social cues as well as physical properties of the diet. Once again, therefore, it is intriguing to consider how social eating and brain evolution may have driven each other by positive feedback cycles. Like adipose tissue, food sharing and meals may be considered another form of risk management in relation to energetics.

8.6   The evolution of a colonising reproductive strategy

Whilst increased adiposity in infants and females can be attributed to the energetic challenges posed by encephalisation, any changes in the schedule of reproduction would generate further impacts. As discussed above, a reduced duration of lactation reduces the reproductive energy burden on the mother, achieved in part by slowed childhood growth and in part by the substitution of breast-milk with complementary foods. This reduction in investment in each reproductive event can also, however, be traded off against a faster rate of breeding. Hill and Hurtado (1996) referred to humans as a 'colonising ape' following their ethnographic work amongst the Ache of Paraguay, and this perspective is supported by comparison with other ape species.

By convention, reproductive strategy is evaluated along a continuum between two extremes – 'r-strategist' opportunist species with high reproductive rates

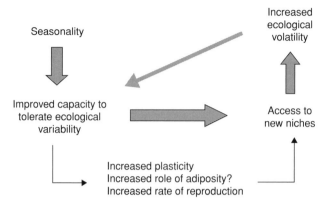

Figure 8.4. Schematic diagram illustrating the positive feedback cycle whereby initial exposure to seasonal variability in ecological conditions induces greater tolerance of ecological variability, and thus aids the penetration of increasingly volatile niches.

but short life-spans, and low levels of parental investment per offspring, or 'K-strategist' species that grow and reproduce more slowly, but invest highly in a small number of offspring (May and Rubenstein 1984). The opportunist r-strategy is attributed to unstable environments, where the risk of local extinctions is high, but where high reproductive rates allow rapid population recovery. The K-strategy is attributed to more stable environments, predicting high levels of genetic specialisation. In the absence of population crashes, K-reproductive rate would be more sensitive to population density (May and Rubenstein 1984).

The r-K concept has been criticized on both theoretical and empirical grounds, but the existence of fast-slow life-cycle variation is not disputed. Although humans are often considered K-strategists *par excellence* because of their large size and long developmental period, life-span and duration of parental care, their biology shows a significant degree of r-selection (Hill and Hurtado 1996) and is consistent with the profile of a colonizing organism (Wells and Stock 2007). High levels of plasticity, in physiology and behaviour, and a lack of local genetic specialization are complemented by a reproductive strategy capable of rapid population growth when juvenile mortality is low (Wells and Stock 2007). Colonization is also strongly evident in the archaeological record, most notably in widespread dispersals of *Homo erectus* and *Homo sapiens* from Africa over the last two million years (Wells and Stock 2007).

The capacity to colonise is likely to have emerged from the improved capacities of australopithecines to tolerate ecological volatility. The same characteristics that buffer stochasticity allow the opportunistic probing of new habitats and niches, as illustrated in Figure 8.4. The fossil record suggests that the migratory behaviour of *Homo erectus* was of an order of magnitude greater than that of the australopithecines, even though the rate of territorial expansion may have been relatively modest.

Growth is a key component of life-history strategy and thereby generates an intrinsic link between the growth rates of individuals and populations (Bogin 2001). Greater body size can be attained only by either extending the growth period or increasing the rate of growth. These life-history traits reflect not only energy availability but also age-specific mortality risk (Hawkes 2006), such that the long human life-span can be attributed to low adult mortality, increasing the reproductive fitness of those who achieve maturity. This combination of short inter-birth intervals with long offspring growth periods means that population growth rate is very sensitive to juvenile, rather than adult, mortality risk (Hawkes 2006). When juvenile mortality is low, the population can increase in size rapidly, which favours the colonisation of new territory. The data presented in Chapter 5 illustrate how maternal capital, in the form of energy stores, allows the funding of offspring growth even in volatile habitats. This capacity is further enhanced by the stacking of several offspring simultaneously (Robson, vanSchaik, and Hawkes 2006), leading to faster reproductive output compared to other apes (Galdikas and Wood 1990; Walker et al., 2008).

Thus, maternal adiposity plays a key role in funding the rapid production of offspring, and this role is predicted to become more valuable if compounded by the stress of migration. Because physiological plasticity is largely restricted to early life, adaptations of the offspring are targeted not at ecological conditions themselves, but at the 'niche' of maternal metabolism (Wells 2007f) which acts to buffer the offspring from short-term perturbations in energy availability. In turn, fat stores in combination with lactation represent a key strategy allowing mammals to breed in any conditions where the *adult* can survive, regardless of the specific nutritional requirements of the offspring (Pond 1984). Migrating hominins may therefore have benefited greatly from maternal fat stores in enabling reproduction during migration or when probing new ecological niches.

However, rapid rates of reproduction in good conditions may lead to over-exploitation of resources and hence induce population crashes. Population boom-busts are well known in many mammal species, often in the context of predator-prey cycles. Most female primates, unless severely malnourished, spend the majority of their adult life pregnant, lactating or both. Until industrialization, humans are assumed broadly to have conformed to this pattern, with minimal capacity for contraception and exogenous mortality or infanticide comprising the main determinants of population growth. Following the origins of sedentism and agriculture, spectacular growth has been observed during favourable conditions, for example, the doubling of the Kenyan population within a generation (Livi-Bacci 1992). Such high fertility has often been constrained by high mortality, but rapid recovery from population crashes is now well known (Hill and Hurtado 1996), indicating the capacity of humans for rapid population growth.

Regular over-exploitation of resources and natural predator-prey cycles would induce boom-bust population cycles, which in turn would select for the predisposing traits by positive feedback mechanisms. Data from contemporary populations illustrate that foraging returns are highly sensitive to group size such that even modest population growth may result in local over-exploitation of resources (Kelly 1995). Boom-bust population dynamics, inflicted by *Homo* groups on themselves through regular over-exploitation of resources, are therefore a plausible contributing factor favouring continued selection for an aggressive colonizing reproductive strategy despite relatively stable population size, and global territorial saturation, over the long-term. Adipose tissue could have played a double role in such colonising strategy. Whilst maternal energy stores can be used to fuel faster rates of reproduction, fat also improves the capacity to tolerate the consequences of population crashes and reductions in the availability of energy.

Colonisation may have been a particularly *Homo*-specific selective pressure, given the tendency for most colonising species to be of small body size and dietary generalists. Further work is required to simulate the costs and benefits of fat stores in this context and to establish in greater detail the evolutionary history of the human reproductive schedule. This hypothesis nevertheless merits attention, as there is no doubt that population variability in adiposity in extant humans is associated with their life history and reproductive traits.

8.7   Trends in disease load

As discussed in Chapter 6, human adiposity is closely associated with immune function, with adipose tissue providing both the energy required to mount an immune response, and secreting cytokines which play a key role in activating cells that destroy pathogens. The fossil record contains minimal direct evidence on possible trends in disease load, given that the majority are micro-organisms and few leave markers of their impact in skeletal material, but cross-species comparisons and consideration of the impact of migrations allow broader trends to be inferred.

From a more indirect perspective, humans share many parasites and infections with other contemporary primates, indicating a probable lengthy history of these diseases in hominins. Examples include a variety of parasitic helminths, lice, malaria parasites and viruses such as herpes and hepatitis (Cockburn 1971). Arboreal animals are exposed to different disease vectors compared to terrestrial animals, in terms both of biting insects and the faeces of other organisms

(Cockburn 1971); hence, early hominins may have encountered a new range of diseases by becoming more terrestrial (Foley 1987).

Most primates spend their entire life within a relatively small geographical area and therefore develop a closer association with local parasites (Cockburn 1971). By increasing their habitat range, first in the australopithecine radiation and then in the dispersal of *Homo* from the African continent, hominins would have encountered a much wider range of pathogens and diseases. For example, zoonoses are diseases which have a local distribution and tend to infect organisms opportunistically, as and when they come in contact (Cohen 1989). Many of the diseases exerting powerful effects in modern humans are associated with much larger and sedentary populations than those assumed to have characterised australopithecines and early *Homo*, implying that the infectious disease load prior to agricultural populations would have been weaker (Cohen 1989). Nevertheless, small populations of non-human primates suffer from many types of viral infections (Cockburn 1971), some of which are known to exert effects on energy metabolism.

Understanding the probable impact of disease in hominin populations is difficult given that the link between adiposity and immunity has been researched for only a relatively short time. Recent work has highlighted the cost of parasite infections on childhood growth (Prentice and Darboe 2008), and diseases such as malaria are known to alter energy expenditure (Binh et al. 1997), and by inference impact on energy stores (Wells 2009a). The metabolic load of infection may then have impacted on adipose tissue biology, given that the immune response is closely associated with various aspects of metabolism. For example, proteolytic enzyme differences between humans and chimpanzees have been reported (Puente et al. 2005), indicative of immune system variation; however, further work is required to clarify differences between humans and other apes in their immune biology. Given the lack of direct evidence, it may be beneficial here to invoke the game theory model described in Chapter 7. The cessation of growth and reproductive function during chronic negative energy balance allows basal metabolism and the immune system to be prioritised. This generates the hypothesis that providing energy for survival and immune function are the primary targets of selective pressures during famine.

Understanding the effects of famine on human biology is complex. Accurate interpretation requires detailed information about the proportion of individuals dying, and the cause of death. Even where records have been compiled, they often suffer from methodological problems (Mokyr and Ó Gráda 2002). However, recent re-evaluation of the Irish famine during the nineteenth century has highlighted the contribution of disease, as opposed to starvation, as the principal cause of death (Mokyr and Ó Gráda 2002). Famines increase the risk of disease through several mechanisms, including reducing the quality as well as quantity of nutritional intake, decreasing the energy available for immune function, increasing exposure to novel pathogens, reducing the facilities available for hygiene, and creating favourable conditions for the spread of infectious diseases such as cholera and influenza (Mokyr and Ó Gráda 2002). Clearly, each famine is different, and starvation has sometimes been a more important primary cause of death; however, there is no doubt that the immune system represents a priority function of adipose tissue during malnutrition.

In addition to providing the energy required to mount an immune response, adipose tissue, especially the visceral depot, is increasingly recognised as the source of cytokines which contribute to inflammation (Ritchie and Connell 2007; Berg and Scherer 2005). There may therefore be an innate link between allocating energy to the visceral depot and activating immune function to increase protection against infectious diseases. Likewise, at the molecular level it is now recognised that nutrient-sensing and pathogen-sensing pathways have much in common, such that the connection between metabolic and inflammatory responses is fundamental to the 'mechanistic core of chronic and common metabolic diseases' (Hotamisligil 2006).

Such a strategy of preferential allocation to abdominal adiposity would be beneficial during chronic negative energy balance, allocating energy to maintain the adipose tissue depots primarily responsible for supporting immune function and increasing resistance to infection. This perspective is consistent with findings of greater expression of complement genes in the visceral adipose depot than in subcutaneous fat (Gabrielsson et al. 2003), and animal studies also demonstrate that artificial viral infection increases adiposity (Bernard et al. 1988; Lyons et al. 1982). This issue may be of particular importance for understanding the selective pressures which acted on human fat distribution, as opposed to adiposity in general.

Although our understanding of this component of hominin evolution remains limited, the common role of adipose tissue in human immunity, as discussed in Chapter 6, signifies powerful selective pressures having acted on *Homo erectus* and its forbears. An increasing pathogen burden may have favoured increased adiposity, but whether or not that was the case, it is likely also to have favoured an increased sensitivity of adipose tissue to immune system biology. The greater expression of genetic factors in deep-lying adipose tissue indicates such increased sensitivity. As discussed in Chapter 9, contemporary variability in adipose tissue biology may then derive in part from differing local disease loads.

8.8   Trends in social stress

In general, mammalian sociality has been characterised by a shift from aggressive behaviour to more nurturant interactions – for example, nurturing parental care only evolved in post-reptile evolution (Eibl-Eibesfelt 1997). In primates, nurturant relationships tend to occur between kin, whereas more dominant-repressive relations tend to occur between unrelated individuals (Eibl-Eibesfelt 1997). Non-human apes display a variety of complex social organisations, characterised by variability in social rank according to age and gender. Chimpanzees, for example, form coalitions of related males, which compete with those of other groups, whereas gorillas show a harem social structure. Access to food amongst chimpanzees is strongly dependent on social ranking and on coalition membership. Sharing of food is used to generate and maintain social relations (McGrew 1997); hence, there is a very close association between access to food and social status, and indeed to health status (McGrew 1997).

Hominins would undoubtedly have had similarly complex social groupings, characterised again by social rank variability. The extent of such ranking is difficult to reconstruct – in general, contemporary human forager societies are much more egalitarian than farmer societies. However, anthropologists have observed a universal tendency for children to vary amongst themselves in their ability to form alliances, whereby status differences emerge (Hold-Cavell 1997), implying that such characteristics either appeared with the evolution of *Homo sapiens* or occurred in *Homo erectus*. More generally, social rank has been suggested to represent a key resource in allowing parents to improve the fitness of their offspring, and thereby of themselves (Grammer 1997). Analogous to the notion of energy as somatic capital, as discussed in Chapter 7, rank represents social capital whereby a high phenotypic quality of the parent can be passed to the offspring. In baboons, maternal rank passes to daughters, resulting in stable matrilineal status across generations (McGrew 1997).

Those of higher rank gain improved feeding opportunities and convert this advantage into reproductive fitness by breeding more often, producing more offspring per reproductive event, and producing higher-quality offspring. This benefit of maternal status, which is closely associated with maternal size, has been reported in several species of primate (Mori 1979; McGrew 1997; Packer et al. 1995; Johnson 2003). Assuming a similar scenario to have applied to hominins, those of lower rank are likely to have exhibited poorer nutritional status, in turn increasing vulnerability to infectious diseases. Flinn and England (1997), for example, have shown social stress to be associated with immuno-supression in Caribbean children.

It is likely that the association between response to stress, driven by cortisol, and the tendency to accumulate visceral fat emerged or at least strengthened during hominin evolution (Siervo, Wells, and Cizza 2008). Those of lower status may be more vulnerable to disease, further favouring the association between stress and the abdominal fat depot as discussed in Chapter 9. Our understanding of these associations will improve as increasing research is conducted into both the social factors predicting stress, and the metabolic consequences.

An increased tendency to prioritise visceral fat is not the only proposed response to social stress. In an intriguing paper, Watve and Yajnik suggested that insulin metabolism might respond to population density and orchestrate trade-offs between different phenotypes (Watve and Yajnik 2007). They suggest that under conditions of higher population density, it may benefit to switch from producing larger offspring ('soldiers') to smarter offspring ('diplomats') who would benefit from cognitive rather than somatic investment. In support of their hypothesis, they note that gestational insulin resistance not only reduces the birth rate by reducing ovulation, but also shifts the target of energy allocation from muscles to brain tissue in the offspring (Watve and Yajnik 2007). Such a hypothesis requires examination in small-scale communities likely to have been the norm during the majority of hominin evolution. That insulin metabolism contributes to the regulation of reproduction is not contested, but whether the brain might have responded to such cues when the majority of foraging is likely to have involved individual effort is less clear.

Summary

This chapter has reviewed a number of universal features of human biology which are associated with increased levels of adiposity, implicating their emergence at or prior to the speciation of *Homo sapiens*. The chapter has further attempted to identify the approximate time periods during which certain selective pressures acted on these traits. Seasonality, encephalisation, changes in life history and the rate of reproduction, and exposure to new diseases are all implicated as selective pressures favouring greater adiposity in hominins compared to non-human ape species.

Some of these selective pressures are suggested to have acted across the entirety of hominin evolution. In particular, high levels of seasonality in food supply appear to have acted on the australopithecines more strongly than on other ancestral apes, and may have favoured greater adiposity in both sexes. Other factors may be more specific to the genus *Homo*. The steady increase in encephalisation demonstrated in the fossil evidence for *Homo erectus* suggests an increased demand on the maternal energy budget. Simulations of body composition, though limited by the quality of the data on weight and height predicted from bone proportions, suggest sexual dimorphism may have occurred in both lean mass and fat mass during this period, leading to the significant sex-differences in body composition encountered in all extant human populations.

An increased tendency to colonise by the genus *Homo* may have linked some of these selective pressures through positive feedback cycles, whereby the roles of fat and behavioural flexibility in buffering stochasticity in ecological conditions favoured the penetration of increasingly volatile niches, in turn increasing the premium on fat stores. In such circumstances, fat may in particular have represented a form of 'capital' acquired by higher-status members of social groups, aiding the generation of beneficial maternal effects on the next generation. However, with the emergence of large-scale hunting or the exploitation of specific high-quality resources, *Homo* may have inflicted boom-bust population dynamics on itself in the process of colonising new territory. In this case, capital would have increased the capacity to survive the busts, again presumably more so in high-status individuals. Fat stores may also have become increasingly important in funding an immune system under greater stress owing to encountering a broader range of pathogens.

Whether such feedback systems operated during the period of *Homo erectus*, or characterised the evolution of *Homo sapiens* and fuelled the more systematic colonising of this species, remains to be answered. Our understanding of hominin life history grows steadily, and it is likely that future work will attribute some of these selective pressures to specific time periods with greater confidence. Our growing understanding of the trans-generational transfer of phenotype is likewise shedding more light on the concept of energy stores as maternal capital. The perspective presented here is necessarily preliminary, but it will hopefully stimulate further research on the issue.

9 *Adiposity in human evolution*

The final period of evolutionary history considered here is that of anatomically modern humans. The aim of reconstructing this part of evolutionary history is therefore to address within-species variability, and also to explore the extent to which contemporary variability in adiposity may be attributed to genetic or non-genetic mechanisms.

A combination of fossil, genetic and archaeological evidence indicates a relatively recent origin of modern humans in Africa (Lahr and Foley 1994; Lahr and Foley 1998). However, caution is required when interpreting this speciation in relation to the source of modern human genetic variability.

Reconstructions based on mitochondrial DNA suggested a common ancestor of contemporary humans from between 200–150,000 years ago (Cann et al. 1987; Harpending and Rogers 2000), while the earliest known fossils similarly date from 200–120,000 years ago (White et al. 2003; McDougall et al. 2005). However, this relatively simple model is not supported by polymorphism data from the X chromosome and autosomes (Garrigan and Hammer 2006). Modelling the evolutionary history of the human genome remains a challenging task, with the theoretical assumptions utilised (e.g. relative stability in population size) contributing to the inferences, and in the future, more sophisticated models are likely to improve clarity (Garrigan and Hammer 2006). At present, the most plausible genetic model indicates a degree of admixture between archaic and modern human populations within Africa, allowing genetic variability within Homo erectus to pass into early modern humans (Garrigan and Hammer 2006). The same model suggests a relatively tight bottleneck at the time of the exodus from Africa, indicating that the majority of the genetic variability in non-African populations arose *de novo* in non-African environments (Garrigan and Hammer 2006). Mitochondrial DNA analysis likewise suggests that a variety of discrete lineages had already appeared prior to any migration outside of the African continent (Behar et al. 2008).

Such genetic variability as passed from Homo erectus to Homo sapiens would be predicted to reflect very different selective pressures, arising from different environments, to that emerging within the last 200,000 years. Some genetic variability might reflect relatively ancient stresses acting on dry season tolerance, the emergence of the large brain along with putative compensatory adaptations

244

in gut physiology, and the distinctive human growth pattern, whereas other variability might reflect more recent and local adaptations to specific dietary niches or disease loads following the exodus from Africa. Current evidence suggests that the first dispersal out of Africa occurred around 100,000 years ago, yet it was only within the last 60,000 years that humans began to occupy the majority of global regions, reaching Europe, Asia and Australia around 40–50,000 years ago (Mellars 2006a; Barker et al. 2002; Bowler et al. 2003) and the American continents rather more recently. These dispersals are associated with ancestral bottlenecks arising from local extinctions. For example, genetic analyses indicate an early bottleneck between 200 and 130,000 years ago, with population size as low as approximately 10,000 individuals (Rogers and Jorde 1995; Takahata et al. 1995). This bottleneck was then followed by significant expansion of population size between 80 and 60,000 years ago (Mellars 2006b), resulting in a degree of population subdivision prior to subsequent dispersals from Africa.

The pattern of dispersal of humans has clearly contributed to contemporary human diversity owing to regional selective pressures, the geographical routes taken and subsequent local isolations (Lahr 1996; Lahr and Foley 1998). These patterns, involving at least two primary dispersals out of Africa (Jobling, Hurles, and Tyler-Smith 2008), have acted to increase inter-group differences and genetic diversification (Watson et al. 1997). However, the human species is also characterised by a high level of genetic unity, associated in turn with high levels of phenotypic plasticity. These characteristics collectively support the concept of humans as a colonising organism (Wells and Stock 2007).

9.1   Genetic diversification and physical environments

The dispersal of anatomically modern humans from Africa exposed populations to a wide variety of ecological niches. There is substantial evidence that this process involved two complementary and counterbalancing pressures. On the one hand, exposure to different climatic stresses, diet bases, levels of seasonality and dynamic interactions with a wide variety of other species would have favoured local genetic adaptation. On the other hand, there is abundant evidence for a range of levels of plasticity, which acted to buffer such local ecological pressures and preserve a more homogenous human gene pool. Between-population gene flow would further have reduced the potential for local genetic specialisation and increased selective pressures on plasticity.

Given our tropical African origins, dispersals into higher latitudes would have exposed migrating populations to novel cold stress (Hancock et al. 2008). Genetic response to this stress may have involved adaptations in both physique and metabolism. For example, a number of anthropologists have collated evidence for adaptation in body size and physique to local climatic stresses (Roberts 1953; Katzmarzyk and Leonard 1998). In general, heat stress is associated with a more linear physique, increasing the ratio of surface area to mass. Such adaptation is strongly evident in skeletal dimensions, whereas data on secular trends in BMI suggest that associations with thermal load are weakening, as populations are increasingly exposed to the obesogenic niche (Katzmarzyk and Leonard 1998).

Given this scenario, it might be assumed that thermal load would have less significance for variability in adiposity. However, modelling suggests that thermal load must influence body fat and its distribution, with this effect likely to be stronger in populations required to invest considerable physical effort in their subsistence. Body fat has implications for accommodating heat stress because adipose issue has a lower specific heat than lean tissue, such that fat individuals heat up more readily than leaner individuals in response to a given thermal load (Wells 2002). More generally, through their contribution to body mass, fat stores reduce thermoregulatory capacity through reducing the ratio of surface area to mass (Wells 2002). Although fat stores are often considered to be favoured in cold climates owing to fat's insulating properties, it is more likely that hot conditions constrain the accumulation of subcutaneous fat (see Chapter 6). The relationship between adiposity and thermal load may be particularly important during pregnancy, and it may be one factor accounting for variable pregnancy gains in adiposity between populations (Durnin 1987a). Figure 9.1 illustrates the association between thermal load and birth weight in a variety of human populations (Wells and Cole 2002b). Given the association between birth weight and subsequent body composition, the indication is that population variability in size and physique is due in part to fetal growth variability. Reduced birth weight itself represents a degree of thrift, as well as adaptation to thermal conditions.

Other genetic adaptations may have targeted metabolism, such as fat oxidation capacity or basal metabolic rate. Basal metabolism is known to be reduced in tropical compared to high-latitude populations (Henry and Rees 1991), implying an increased metabolic rate in cold environments in order to maintain thermal homeostasis, as has been described (Snodgrass et al. 2005). Such metabolic adaptations are associated with alterations in blood triglyceride and cholesterol content (Snodgrass et al. 2007).

Following adaptation to particular physical environments, there is evidence for further adaptations to dietary niches and disease loads. Genes associated with strong positive selection include those contributing to the immune system, for example, influencing susceptibility to malaria (Barreiro et al. 2008). Kagawa and colleagues (2002) identified a variety of single nucleotide polymorphisms

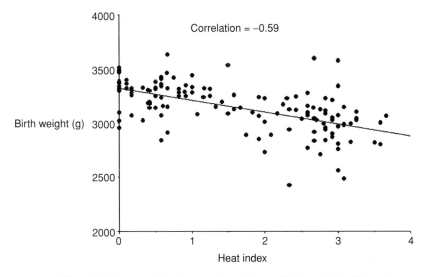

Figure 9.1. The association between thermal load and birth weight in 141 populations worldwide. Increasing thermal load is associated with decreased birth weight, with this association persisting after adjustment for a variety of ecological confounders such as energy intake, disease load and socioeconomic conditions. Reproduced with permission from Wells and Cole (2002b).

which they attributed to local dietary niches, subsequently amplified by varying agricultural systems (see below).

9.2 Genetic diversification through niche construction

There are many references in the literature to proposed genetic adaptations to the process of migration itself. Examples include the stress of lengthy canoe voyages by Micronesians (Dowse et al. 1991) and the colonisation of North America by populations crossing the Bering Strait (Wendorf 1989). Such scenarios may appear to invoke thrifty genes, although the selective pressures may not have been the cycles of feasting and fasting suggested by Neel (1962) and invoked by these authors. Nonetheless, migrations may have acted as bottlenecks generating founder effects in novel environments, and they are likely to have played a role in the emergence of genetic diversification.

As local adaptation consolidated, particularly under the influence of culturally transmitted subsistence modes, humans increasingly contributed to the selective pressures acting on themselves. These contributions may be considered at two distinct levels. At the first level, humans may have contributed directly to ecological stochasticity through their impact on other organisms, and hence on their own food resources. Diamond (1998) has argued that humans were responsible for over-hunting in many habitats between 50,000 and 10,000 years ago, with the effects being sufficiently profound as to influence the distribution of species subsequently available for domestication. There is also evidence for the over-exploitation of marine resources (Mannino and Thomas 2002), and Shennan has likewise argued that much archaeological data can be interpreted in terms of regular overuse of food resources, contributing to population booms and busts (Shennan 2002).

The relative importance of over-exploitation remains debated, with the evidence most convincing for discrete islands such as New Zealand, whereas broader climatic change may have detrimentally influenced the distribution of vegetation in some larger geographical regions. Nevertheless, human population dynamics may plausibly have become linked with those of other species, especially prey animals.

More generally, exposure to a variety of dietary ecosystems would have initiated local selective pressure in relation to the metabolism of varying glycaemic loads. McMichael (2001) has argued that prior to the origins of agriculture, a diet rich in meat would have required insulin insensitivity, in turn requiring insulin resistance to maintain metabolic homeostasis. Populations would subsequently have varied in their exposure to agricultural diets, which tend to impose a higher glycaemic load. Colagiuri and Brand (2002) have suggested that the relative retention of ancestral insulin insensitivity should be proportional to the duration of a population's exposure to agriculture, but genetic evidence for any such associations remains lacking. McMichael (2001) has likewise suggested that exposure to dairy farming may have been an important factor in the emergence of genetic variability in metabolism, as considered in greater detail in the discussion of the thrifty-genotype hypothesis below.

At the second level, therefore, humans contributed to their selective pressures through the development of a variety of agricultural subsistence systems, exploiting a small range of animal and plant species according to geographical region. Kagawa and colleagues (2002) distinguish, for example, between Mediterranean, tropical, savannah and New World agriculture, each variety concentrating on a few species of crop providing the staple diet. These authors suggest that food shortages interacted with dietary ecology and favoured a variety of local polymorphisms, tailoring metabolic adaptations. The best-known example comprises variability in the genetics of lactose tolerance, with pastoralist populations retaining the capacity to digest lactose throughout life (Durham 1991). However, Kagawa and colleagues (2002) listed a variety of other genes that differ between populations, which they attributed to alternative agricultural practices. Varying subsistence systems also influence the physical nature of the environment and have, for example, been implicated in generating ideal breeding conditions for the mosquito in some geographical areas, thereby increasing the risk of malaria (Durham 1991; Cockburn 1971). This might in turn impact on adipose tissue biology (Well 2009a).

The emergence of agriculture may have been particularly important for such genetic diversification. Hunting effectively provides convergence on a common metabolic niche, since tetrapod vertebrate tissue varies substantially less in its nutritional properties compared with plant tissues (Foley 2001). The regional distribution of flora is likely to have been more significant in invoking local physiological or behavioural adaptations than the distribution of fauna (Kagawa et al. 2002). Genetic variability in the gene for salivary amylase, the enzyme responsible for starch hydrolysis, indicates an enhanced capacity to digest high-starch diets in many populations (Perry et al. 2007).

The contribution of humans through their activities to their own selective pressures is now conceptualised as a form of niche construction (Odling-Smee, Laland, and Feldman 2003). Many organisms may be considered ecosystem engineers, altering both the physical environments as well as the niche of other species occupying the same habitats (Jones, Lawton and Shachak 1994). Humans, however, have the capacity to conduct niche construction on a more profound scale because of the combination of their flexible behavioural capacities and their varied technological systems. Relatively modern subsistence modes, such as specific agricultural systems, represent particularly powerful examples of niche construction, but it is clear that human behaviour influenced selective pressures prior to the emergence of agriculture, through practices such as hunting and the inadvertent spread of plant species as modelled by Diamond (1998). More recently, niche construction has derived from increasing population density and the transfer of diseases from domesticated animals (Diamond 1998), along with the accelerating process of urbanisation.

9.3   The origins of farming and famines

Around 12,000 years ago, humans began to shift from foraging to agriculture, and at the present time only a small minority of human populations continue to practise foraging as the predominant subsistence mode. These populations tend to be isolated in marginal habitats, making it difficult to reconstruct the likely nature of foraging in our evolutionary past. Nevertheless, analysis of the archaeological record provides important information about apparent nutritional stresses in these different scenarios. Agriculture clearly increased by an order of magnitude the intensity of niche construction, and it has exerted profound impacts on many aspects of human biology.

Agriculture appears to have emerged independently in several geographical locations, across a broad timescale. The main centres were southwest Asia (the Fertile Crescent), Mesoamerica, China and the Andes, although less-convincing evidence for independent origins is also available for New Guinea, West Africa and Ethiopia (Diamond 1998). The spread of agriculture from such centres is then assumed to have been a function of competition between foraging and farming practices, with either subsistence mode consolidating according to its relative productivity.

What initiated the trends towards agriculture remains debated. Its emergence in the archaeological record is not associated with apparent improvement in health. Compared to late Palaeolithic hunter-gatherers, subsequent populations appear to have suffered similar infant and child mortality, increased rates of certain infectious diseases, and increased nutritional stress, reflected in a downward trend in body size that has only recently been reversed (Cohen and Armelagos 1984). Indeed, the emergence of agriculture appears to have generated a new set of infectious diseases, following the domestication of animals (Diamond 1998) as discussed below. Thus, the idea that farming was initially adopted because of improved returns on subsistence activity is not well supported.

One factor that appears implicated in the development of agriculture is population pressure, as originally argued by Boserup (1965) and subsequently by Cohen (1977). However, recent analyses have suggested that population pressure did not build slowly and consistently but rather developed through cyclical expansions and crashes (Shennan 2002). Population pressure alone is therefore insufficient to explain the relatively rapid spread of farming within a short period of time, and others consider climate change to have been critical.

Richerson and colleagues (2001) argue that during the Pleistocene period, environmental conditions were insufficiently stable to allow the development and diffusion of agricultural techniques. Thus, although population pressure may have built up owing to the over-hunting of large game animals and droughts resulting from global warming, agriculture may have become viable only in the more stable Holocene period, during which it may have out-competed other subsistence modes. This approach is a more plausible explanation for the near-simultaneous emergence of agriculture in several independent locations. Cohen (1989) has additionally argued that hunting large game is the most rewarding subsistence strategy, followed in turn by farming and finally by the combination of hunting small prey and gathering seeds, grains and so forth. Diamond similarly notes that humans cannot digest most organisms or materials, whilst many potentially edible resources are also not energy-efficient to obtain. Thus, over-hunting and the destruction of this dietary niche may have provided a further incentive to farm as game resources dwindled. Farming, by concentrating on particular productive crops, initially restores high-energy yield per unit of land area (Diamond 1998). All the major crops characteristic of modern agriculture have two particularly valuable characteristics, in that they have a high energy content and can be stored after harvest (Cohen 1989).

Thus, as game animal populations declined and climatic conditions improved, a decreasing availability of wild foods may have been countered by improved yields from cultivation. Successful cultivators may also have displaced foragers, not least through their greater numbers resulting from their harvests. Diamond (1998) notes that foragers are not necessarily nomadic, and farmers are not necessarily sedentary. However, sedentism is associated with a reduced inter-birth interval, probably through reductions on the maternal energy burden of reproduction. Cohen (1989), for example, noted decreased inter-birth intervals in fatter compared to leaner !Kung women, as well as improved child survival. The fact that the human population continued to increase after the adoption of farming is not necessarily evidence of its beneficial nature. The sedentism that farming requires may have reduced constraints on female fertility so that population growth could occur even while health and life expectancy declined (Cohen 1998). However, pastoralism, providing dairy products for both adults and infants along with meat, whilst also preserving a degree of population mobility, may have been more advantageous for health than crop agriculture.

The domestication of plants and animals, and the storage of surplus, that characterise the Neolithic revolution transformed the human diet. Compared to that of foragers, the diet of farmers was nutritionally poorer owing to the reduced varieties of food grown and the detrimental effects of long-term storage (Cohen 1989; Cohen 1998), and the burden of infectious disease also increased (Roosevelt 1984). Artificial selection for particular traits in crops, such as high densities, and domesticated animals, such as larger size, has made them more vulnerable to stresses and diseases (Cohen 1989; McNeill 2000). In addition to these direct physical effects, the storing of surplus had more wide-ranging ecological and social implications for human health.

The reliance of farmers on central food stores made them highly vulnerable both to natural disasters such as crop failure, decay of the stores[1] and social stresses in the form of plundering. Increasing population size is likely to have exerted a positive feedback effect, exacerbating competition between neighbouring populations and in turn favouring larger communities to reduce

[1] A particularly extreme ecological stress occurs in the northeastern region of the Indian subcontinent, where the 48-year flowering cycle of a local bamboo species induces an explosion in the numbers of rodents, which subsequently decimate crops and food stores. Despite the extraordinary regularity of this '*mautam*' event, allowing accurate predictions to be made (Pathak and Kumar 2000), significant malnutrition still occurs (Times 29/03/2008).

vulnerability. These sociological changes, along with climatic pressures rather than any genuine subsistence advantages of agriculture, may have encouraged its rapid spread (Cohen 1998).

Thus, although 'feast and famine' have conventionally been considered the lot of our more distant ancestors, the archaeological record suggests that farming may have worsened rather than ameliorated the situation. Nomadic populations invariably use their mobility to relieve the stress of local food shortages, migrating to more productive areas. Famine therefore has an inherent connection with sedentary agriculture, and in particular that associated with large-scale civilisations which often have the least flexibility for accommodating difficult conditions (Dando 1980). Comparisons of farmers and foragers from the ethnographic record have consistently failed to find evidence that foragers are more vulnerable to food shortages (Dirks 1993; Benyshek and Watson 2006), and Keys and colleagues (1950) found that over 400 famines have been documented in the historical literature worldwide. Although the most comprehensive records date from European populations, there is ample evidence of famines throughout all global regions. Archaeologists have also noted how many 'great civilisations' were brought to an end by famines induced by climate change, which destroyed the underlying agricultural production systems (Fagan 1999). The severest impacts could be attributed in part to the inflexibility of the political regime dominating the agricultural system concerned (Fagan 1999).

The extent to which agriculture and famine are intrinsically related is difficult to confirm because the historical record itself is a product of the agricultural mood of subsistence. Writing emerged specifically in order to provide documentation of food resources in early civilisations (Diamond 1998). Much recent scientific research has emphasised the contribution of climatic variability to ecological stochasticity, which might imply a link to a history of severe food shortages. For example, regular famines in the Indian subcontinent and other global regions have been attributed to El Niño oscillations (Fagan 1999). However, the significance of such climatic variability in earlier time periods is debatable. Davis (2002) has argued that the impact of El Niño was radically worsened by Imperial economic policies (see below), such that more famines were recorded in the Victorian era than the entire previous two millennia. Nevertheless, population cycles are certainly evident in the archaeological record from the pre-agricultural era (Shennan 2002) and imply over-consumption of resources interacting with climate change, but with mobility likely to have reduced the severity of the energy stress.

What is clear is that famine has been a regular and almost unrelenting stress during recent human history. Prentice (2001) has discussed how famines continued to affect large proportions of the human population throughout the twentieth century, and many populations also continue to practise agriculture in seasonal environments. Although, as discussed in Chapters 6 and 7, seasonality is considered a long-term and important stress in hominin evolution, the magnitude of its impact may have increased following the emergence of agriculture. Sedentary food-producing populations are necessarily dependent on the previous year's harvest during the season during which food cannot be grown. A large volume of research on Gambian farmers (Prentice 2001), inhabiting a highly seasonal environment, has made clear the role of adiposity in accommodating major fluctuations in the balance of energy intake and energy requirements.

The extent to which famines shaped the human genome remains controversial. Speakman (Speakman, 2008) has suggested that famines have been too rare, and to have imposed insufficient increases in mortality, to have generated much genetic adaptation. Prentice and colleagues (Prentice et al. 2008) have responded by arguing that even within the last few thousand years, differential fertility during famines could have contributed to adaptation. Disease may also have been an important selective pressure during food shortages as well as famines. High levels of mortality reported in recent Indian famines could certainly have generated strong selective pressures. Nevertheless, as discussed later in this chapter, much contemporary human variability in adiposity need not be attributed to genetic differentiation. The importance of phenotypic plasticity in buffering genomic change is likely to have been a hallmark of the genus *Homo*, and the main impact of agriculture may have been to favour such plasticity in response to increased stochasticity in energy supply.

9.4 The emergence of social stratification

The trends in the subsistence mode that characterised the emergence of agriculture were accompanied by significant changes in social structure, and these have their own independent implications for the evolution of human adiposity. The simplest model of social structure distinguishes between (a) an 'egalitarian' society, (b) ranked societies which date predominantly from 15,000 to 10,000 years ago, and (c) stratified societies which characterised the development of 'civilisation' from around 5,000 years ago (Cohen 1998).

As population size increased, the sympathy and relationships that characterise 'egalitarian' societies were replaced by economic and political relationships, such that access to food for many depended increasingly on rights and obligations, rather than basic productivity itself. Around 5,000 years ago, large-scale 'civilisations' emerged, apparently independently, in Egypt, the Middle East, India, China, sub-Saharan Africa, Peru and Mexico, in which differential control of the means of production became extreme (Cohen 1998).

The precursors of social stratification are apparent in the animal kingdom, where many social species are characterised by a dominance ranking that is maintained through physical threat or force, or sometimes mediated by coalitions of allies as in chimpanzees (Wrangham and Peterson 1996). Access to mates may be determined through physical competition, whereas female access to resources may be likewise determined through a pecking order. High-ranking female primates monopolise the best resources and have significantly higher reproductive success as a consequence (Packer et al. 1995; Johnson 2003). However, it is also helpful to consider hierarchies from a positive perspective, taking into consideration the potential benefits to individuals not only of leadership, but also 'followership' (Van, Hogan, and Kaiser 2008). Some individuals may accept lower 'follower' status, as it may potentially reduce exposure to risks; but in doing so they may open themselves to exploitation by leaders. Changes in these risks and rewards may play out across generations, such that the penalties for adopting lower status may be encountered only when the ability to resist them has been lost.

Social species such as extant apes (and presumably ancestral hominins) face a number of scenarios in which group decisions may be required, such as foraging, defence, communal parenting or migration, or where cohesion within a large, dispersed group might be needed (Van, Hogan, and Kaiser 2008). In non-human apes, leadership is demonstrated by 'alpha' individuals, mostly males, and may involve a combination of despotic and democratic elements. Male common chimpanzees, for example, form coalitions through which the status hierarchy is contested and maintained. In contemporary human foraging societies, leadership accrues to 'big men' who may exercise a disproportionate influence on group decisions, but relations remain relatively egalitarian and consensual (Van, Hogan, and Kaiser 2008), and it is notable that many such societies appear to constrain the emergence of status inequalities (Wiessner 1997). Under these conditions, followership offers many benefits whilst imposing few costs.

The emergence of larger sedentary farming communities enabled a shift in the possible power relations, allowing a few individuals to consolidate their control of resources and individuals. This in turn altered the scale of social hierarchy towards large-scale coercive power. More powerful leaders could use favoured, self-interested supporters to boost their power base and exert greater control over those of lower rank. Although the benefits of followership might thereby decline, the lower-rank members of sedentary communities have little ability to escape such power relations (Van, Hogan, and Kaiser 2008), and therefore they remain available for exploitation. These hierarchical relations have major significance for the nutritional status for all members of the population. As Brown and Konner (1987) noted, an important function of lower-rank individuals in stratified societies is to insulate those with power from the threat of starvation. It is clear that famines have been common since the dawn of 'civilisation', and that social rank has been a dominant factor affecting survival (Shennan 2002).

The emergence of agriculture generates a displacement in time between the physical effort and the subsequent energy payoff. This displacement tends towards the concept of 'ownership' of land, technology and agricultural resources, invoking in turn the concept of property and descent rights. The utilisation of land changes under conditions of ownership, with food used for political and economic purposes beyond subsistence. Those not producing food are required to contribute economically in some other way, generating complex associations between agricultural productivity and other resources (Cohen 1989). Similarly, those producing food may have had limited ability to consume the products of their labour, as documented in nineteenth century India (Davis 2002).

Agricultural surplus effectively functions as 'extracorporeal fat depots', breaking the immediate physiological link between energy stores in body size. Individuals of higher social status would not only have had priority access to such external stores in times of famine, they would also have used control of these resources to manipulate the behaviour of others. Thus, the development of surplus is strongly implicated in the social inequality that exerts a strong effect on human health today. However, those societies adopting animal agriculture have historically been less exposed to famine than those relying entirely on crop agriculture (Kagawa et al. 2002), since stock animals represent a more mobile and flexible store of calories.

In the short-term, improved access to food benefits energy stores, leading to correlations between social status and levels of adiposity (though these vary, as described below). But *across* generations, greater energy stores translate into a greater capacity to buffer lean mass and the trajectory of growth from temporary insufficiency in dietary energy supply. Thus, except in extreme conditions such as famine, social status is more strongly associated with size and physique than with adiposity, not because it does not impact on energy supplies but because its effect is sufficiently powerful to transcend them to other functions. A wide variety of studies have reported reduced body size in those of low social status in diverse settings (Steckel 1979; Steckel 1998), indicative of chronic energy insufficiency relative to needs in previous generations. In contemporary Western populations, there is an opposite trend towards increased fatness in children of lower social status (Ness et al. 2006). Although this attracts most attention in the context of differential obesity risk, it may also indicate an adaptive strategy. Increased energy stores in the current generation may, across future generations, slowly resolve the loss of height by increasing birth weight or providing more energy for lactation. As national living standards improve, social disparities in stature slowly decrease (Komlos 1994; Komlos 1998; Steckel 1998). Though these shifts are ultimately driven by more equal access to adequate diet, energy stores are likely to play a key role in increasing the allocation to growth, and in the trans-generational strategy for regulating this.

The immediate link between food supply and social rank is reflected in changes in cultural values of body fatness (Brown and Konner 1987). As discussed in Chapter 6, when food is at a premium, those of higher rank can express their status through corpulence, whereas the poor remain thin and undernourished. I suggested in Chapter 6 that such corpulence may convey important information about health and immune status in relation to age, as well as gross energy stores. The twentieth century has witnessed extraordinary changes in these relationships. Food has become plentiful in industrialised societies, whereas leisure-time physical activity has become the scarce resource in an environment of mechanisation. Since large body size is no longer exclusive to a few, those of higher rank have come to value slimness, especially in young adult life, while the poor, with reduced access to a healthy diet and activity facilities, are more likely to become overweight (Brown and Konner 1987). Obesity was probably rare even in Europe prior to 1800, affecting first the elites and then the poor as economic factors systematically altered class exposure to dietary and physical activity changes (Trowell 1975).

In European history, famine has been one of the primary causes of large-scale migration, one recent example being the emigration of the Irish to the New World. Not only was famine the stress these migrants sought to leave behind, as the potato harvest failed, it was also the stress they encountered when they crossed the Atlantic, as they were marginalised in their new homeland. Large-scale migrations have generally been undertaken during conditions of energy stress or famine, for example, the transport of African slaves to the plantations of the Americas (Prentice 2001). This scenario generates the hypothesis that genes reaching such new environments may often have undergone selection for thriftiness in the process, and might hence have contributed to population variability in 'thrifty genes'. However, empirical evidence for this interpretation is currently lacking.

9.5   Re-evaluating the thrifty-genotype hypothesis

Given the evidence discussed above, it is now beneficial to reconsider the thrifty-genotype hypothesis of Neel (1962). In his original paper, Neel sought to explain unexpectedly high prevalences of diabetes in a few populations, notably Pima Indians in Mexico and the United States, some Polynesian populations, and Australian aborigines. Neel's hypothesis was that these populations had been exposed to regular cycles of feast and famine, favouring the selection of a sensitive metabolism. In his own words, he suggested that 'periods of gorging alternated with periods of greatly reduced food intake' (Neel 1962). Subsequently, he argued, 'the recency and suddenness of their transition from a hunting-gathering early agricultured life-style to a more settled and nutritionally assured existence might be 'telescoping' genetic adjustments which our own [European] ancestors spread over many generations'.

Native American, Polynesian and Australian aboriginal populations are still frequently referred to as possessing thrifty genotypes (Benyshek and Watson 2006), even though subsequent work has established that, relative to Europeans, almost all the world's populations show higher rates of type-2 diabetes (McMichael 2001). Furthermore, diabetes occurs spontaneously in captive primates, implying that the condition results from exposing animal physiology to a particular set of ecological factors rather than being the product of a specific 'thrifty' genotype (Campbell and Cajigal 2001). The finding that Europeans have lower rates of diabetes strongly contradicts the notion of cycles of feast and famine as the primary selective pressure favouring 'thrifty metabolism', given that Europeans with their long history of agriculture have if anything encountered more unstable circumstances and should therefore have undergone selection for the same traits (McMichael 2001). Despite this, the notion of feast and famine is frequently invoked when academics of diverse disciplines attempt to explain the human predisposition to obesity (Benyshek and Watson 2006).

To start with, it is helpful to consider humans as generically thrifty, demonstrated by the fact that insulin resistance can occur in all populations. Neel's initial theory proposed a 'quick insulin trigger', allowing rapid storage of energy following high energy intake. Subsequently, Reaven (1998) proposed that muscle insulin resistance was the primary element of thrifty metabolism. Whilst insulin resistance is commonly assumed to derive from metabolic thrift in response to energy scarcity, there are in fact a number of specific conditions or stresses associated with the condition, including puberty, pregnancy, trauma or sepsis as well as starvation (Swinburn 1996). In each case, insulin resistance redirects blood glucose away from skeletal muscle towards vital organs such as the brain and the placenta (Swinburn 1996), thus seemingly favouring survival or reproductive functions over physical activity.

On a similar theme, Chakravarthy and Booth (2004) have suggested that the impact of energy scarcity on metabolism varies according to the level of physical activity. Since the human body stores very little glycogen in muscle (approximately 4 MJ) compared to the energy contained in fat (37 MJ per kilogram), they have argued that humans generically have a thrifty metabolism in order to replenish muscle glycogen stores from triglyceride stores (given that post-digestive absorption and physical exertion are displaced in time). For example, they note that glycogen repletion occurs much faster in muscle tissue than in the liver after physical exertion, and oxidising greater quantities of fatty acids during exercise likewise allows the preservation of glycogen (Chakravarthy and Booth 2004). Studies of endurance training show an increased rate of fatty acid oxidation, along with an upregulation of enzymes that process free-fatty-acid oxidation in skeletal muscle (Chakravarthy and Booth 2004). Thus, according to this model, the capacity for exercise is preserved without diverting glucose primarily to muscle tissue.

This approach attributes a generically thrifty human metabolism to metabolic partitioning between physical activity and other functions during constrained energy supply, and it further implicates low levels of physical activity as a key element in the aetiology of insulin resistance and type-2 diabetes, though not necessarily causally. This perspective has much in common with other models of fuel partitioning which have proved successful in understanding the regulation of reproduction in mammals (Wade and Schneider 1992; Wade, Schneider, and Li 1996). Taubes (2008), for example, has argued that the insulin response to a high-carbohydrate diet upsets the balance of fatty acid supply and demand, and that it paradoxically induces lethargy (because of its lowering of blood sugar levels) whilst preventing lipolysis that would allow cellular energy demands to be met. Others have emphasized metabolic flexibility, the ability to shift readily between glucose and free fatty acids as a source of cellular fuel supply (Storlien et al. 2004). Whereas physical activity improves metabolic flexibility, a sedentary lifestyle reduces it, and hence predisposes to insulin resistance and diabetes (Corpeleijn et al. 2009).

The notion of human metabolism having been selected in order to balance the demands for physical activity against metabolic requirements for maintenance and breeding during chronic energy constraint seems much more plausible than the hypothesis that humans were shaped by regular cycles of starving and gorging. Significantly, this scenario implies the emergence of thrifty metabolism at some point during the evolutionary history of *Homo erectus*, though it still remains to explain why some populations should now show a greater vulnerability to diabetes. Native Americans, for example, show a substantially increased risk of diabetes compared to Europeans, despite the two populations having a similar epidemiology of risk factors such as overweight and sedentary lifestyle (Diamond 2003).

McMichael (2001) has emphasised the impact of a high-meat, low-carbohydrate diet prior to the emergence of agriculture, which would favour insulin insensitivity (i.e., insulin resistance) in order to maintain blood glucose supply. Although populations such as Native Americans and Polynesians have often been suggested to have endured starvation during their migrations, McMichael suggests that a more likely scenario is their restriction to a particularly low carbohydrate diet. For example, when early Amerindian populations spread from eastern Siberia into the North American continent, they would have encountered very little edible vegetation owing to the enlarged ice-sheets, and they would have consumed a diet almost entirely of animal products, as indeed do some polar populations today (VanDerMerwe 1992). McMichael (2001) has also suggested that Polynesians may likewise have consumed a diet high in meat and fish owing to their colonisation of islands that offered little capacity for cultivation. These low-glycaemic load diets would favour insulin resistance, and hence they would predispose to obesity and diabetes on re-exposure to a high-glycaemic load diet.

Decreased levels of physical activity also appear particularly important in decreasing the ability to tolerate variability in glycaemic load, as demonstrated by the extreme levels of body weight now observed in sedentary Polynesian populations (McGarvey 1991). The combination of a generically thrifty human metabolism, a high-glycaemic load diet, and low levels of physical activity offer a plausible model of excess weight gain that has substantially better capacity to explain the modern obesity epidemic than does the logic of the energy balance equation.

Finally, a lengthy history of dairy agriculture in Europeans and some African populations implies long-term exposure to a higher glycaemic load diet. In most non-European populations, the capacity to digest lactose (a primary energy source in breast-milk) is lost around the time of weaning (Kretchmer 1993); however, in populations which have practiced dairy agriculture, lactose tolerance has emerged through genetic mutation. European farmers, consuming a high-grain diet with dairy products, would have encountered substantially higher glycaemic load than other populations, which may have selected in favour of greater insulin sensitivity (McMichael 2001). Consistent with this hypothesis, Allen and Cheer (1996) found a negative correlation (r = −0.56) between the prevalences of diabetes and lactose tolerance in a range of the world's populations, with Europeans having the lowest prevalence of diabetes and the highest prevalence of lactose tolerance. Intriguingly, this scenario may account for apparent genetic variability in the risk of diabetes occurring within Polynesians. For example, although the population of Kosrae, a small Micronesian island in the Pacific, show extreme vulnerability to diabetes, those whose genomes contain contributions from European ancestry appear somewhat protected against this risk (Shell 2002).

Closer examination of the thrifty-genotype hypothesis therefore offers strong support for the notion of population variability in metabolism, but it detaches this from the idea of regular cycles of feast and famine as the primary selective pressure. Instead, partitioning energy between physical activity and other biological functions under conditions of energy constraint appears more important, with some interaction with the glycaemic load of the diet. In the following section, I suggest that variable disease load may have been a further factor favouring population variability in adipose tissue biology, indicated by ethnic variability in the disease consequences of overweight and obesity.

9.6   Variable disease load

Although different climates and diets exert subtly varying metabolic stresses, the energy requirements of the human body are broadly similar across different ecological environments. Why then should adipose tissue biology itself vary between populations? As discussed in Chapter 6, the main source of mortality in famines is infectious disease rather than negative energy balance itself. This implicates a differential exposure to infectious disease as a plausible selective pressure inducing population variability in the anatomical location and metabolic activity of adipose tissue depots.

The obligatory needs of energy for essential organs such as the brain, lungs, liver and kidney are common to all humans, whereas populations inhabiting different conditions have been exposed to different disease loads. Although visceral fat has received the most attention in the context of the metabolic syndrome, with Asians having proportionally greater visceral fat for a given level of BMI (Yajnik and Yudkin 2004; Park et al. 2001), recent research has identified deep-lying intra-muscular adipose tissue depots which also differed markedly between ethnic groups, with those of African ancestry having increased intra-muscular fat (Gallagher et al. 2005). It is therefore more appropriate to differentiate between peripheral adipose tissue depots, which appear to be more important in buffering longer term fluctuations between energy supply and demand, and competing deeper abdominal or limb depots which show stronger associations with metabolic risk. The location of energy stores close to target organs makes little sense in terms of long-term disparities between energy supply and demand, as there is sufficient time to mobilise energy from any adipose tissue depot (Pond 1998). Glycogen, a short-term fuel supply, is likewise unsuitable for sustaining immune response. In contrast, deep-lying fat depots are more appropriate for funding the immediate demands of the immune response and the local tissue-specific variability therein. Recent evidence for paracrine interactions between perinodal adipose depots and the lymph system supports the notion of a localised immune response regulated by adipose tissue (Pond 2003a; Mattacks, Sadler, and Pond 2004; Westcott et al. 2006).

Chapter 7 described a game theory perspective for energetics and adipose tissue, arguing that under conditions of energy constraint, maintenance and immune function were the prioritised functions of energy stores. Chapter 6 also described evidence that immune function exerts a significant energy cost. If we transpose the game-theoretical model into different ecological environments, immune function emerges as the most plausible target of local selective pressures, which could generate ethnic genetic variability in adipose tissue biology. This argument is based on the knowledge, as discussed below, that different diseases activate different components of immune system, and that these in turn impose different energetic costs.

The immune response is composed of several components, which differ in their energetic costs according to the particular disease invoking them. Such costs include immune defence of tissues, repair of damaged tissues, metabolic costs of fever, and the production and maintenance of lymphocytes, antibodies and other immune agents. Ironically, these costs also include the growth and metabolism of the pathogens themselves (Romanyukha, Rudnev, and Sidorov 2006). Several components of the immune response are adaptive and yet commonly considered indices of disease. Hypertriglyceridemia is one of the earliest metabolic responses to infection and may contribute not only to the mobilisation of energy stores but also to the host's defence (Long 1996). Fever is considered to provide a number of benefits (Kluger et al. 1997), but it imposes a high cost as each degree-Celsius rise in temperature increases metabolic rate by approximately 15% (Long 1996; Benhariz et al. 1997). Importantly, this effect is induced not directly by the external pathogen, but by the cytokines produced in response to the pathogen's appearance. Other diseases may induce prioritised defence of the mucosal lining. Thus, the overall energy costs of infectious disease depend on the sum of these different components.

Diseases vary in their site and level of infection, and hence in their relative demands on specific components of immunity, and therefore they are predicted to impose different energetic burdens on the organism. Infections of the gut such as Giardia or amoebic dysentery induce a different set of responses compared to plasmodium infections of erthrocytes. The immune response is also understood to be characterised by internal trade-offs, such that only some components are promoted in any given scenario (Long and Nanthakumar 2004).

The burden of disease is strongly associated with local ecosystems and climatic factors, and it is likely to have played an important role in genetic diversification throughout the evolutionary history of *Homo sapiens*. For example, malaria has long been one of the harshest pressures in Africa, but it is geographically specific in Asia, whereas cholera, a long-term stress in Asian populations, reached Africa only relatively recently (Kiple 1999). Diseases are often also seasonal in their distribution, reflecting ecological variability in temperature and rainfall. For example, the prevalence of diarrhoea in Gambia and Bangladesh tracks seasonal variability in such parameters (Rowland 1986), and its effects may therefore interact with seasonal variability in energy stores. There is little doubt that the infectious disease burden varies across continents and with latitude, season, habitat and local fauna.

However, many of the severest diseases that have dominated human morbidity and mortality in the last 10,000 years resulted from species jumps following the emergence of agriculture. Diamond (1998) has referred to the 'lethal gift of livestock': measles, tuberculosis and smallpox from cattle, influenza from pigs and ducks, pertussis (whooping cough) from pigs or dogs, and malaria from birds. Humans can also acquire a variety of other species of pathogen directly from domesticated- or wild-animal reservoirs. Some diseases appear to have jumped the species barrier but to have failed to persist in human populations over time (Diamond 1998). Most recently, HIV/AIDS jumped from wild primates to humans and is rapidly establishing itself as a new selective pressure. HIV/AIDS may have particular implications for human adiposity, given its manifestation as a severe wasting disease.

Many of these domesticated species were herd animals in their natural state, and the persistence of their diseases was dependent on a certain population density in order to allow continued transmission. The increase in human population size that followed the emergence of agriculture was therefore an important factor favouring the evolution of human versions of these diseases. Agriculture is capable of maintaining substantially greater population density than foraging, of an order of magnitude 10 to 100 times greater. For example, European plague tended to affect all cities, but not isolated villages (Cohen 1989), indicating the need for a certain population size for disease viability. Agricultural populations being sedentary furthermore often create fertile conditions for pathogens, such as allowing sewage to enter the supply of drinking water or using human forces, or those of domesticated animals, directly as fertiliser. (Diamond 1998). Similarly, large-scale irrigation networks provide ideal breeding conditions for other diseases such as schistosomiasis and malaria.

Once present, infectious diseases then moved between different global regions through human migration and trade networks. Cohen (1989) argues that three major population dispersals have made key contributions to the global disease distribution, namely, the link between China, India and the Mediterranean in the early Christian era, the expansion of the Mogol Empire in the thirteenth century AD, and the onset of European seaborne exploration in the fifteenth century AD. Other diseases spread in relation to agricultural practices and other forms of niche construction, and they have continued to be influenced by politico-economic change in recent centuries. It is notable that trade can also be considered a form of risk management regarding energy scarcity or micronutrient deficiencies, as proposed by Shennan (2002). For example, trade appears partially to have resolved the worsening of health following the early period of agricultural intensification along the Nile valley (Starling and Stock 2007). Thus, an activity that directly reduced energy stress may inadvertently have increased it again more indirectly by favouring the spread of diseases.

Recently, Paine and Boldsen (2006) have provided an important addition to this perspective by considering the tendency of epidemic diseases to evolve into childhood diseases, which may in turn have increased selective pressures on adiposity in younger age groups. Disease micro-organisms require a constant supply of hosts to ensure survival, and therefore they adapt to the demographic characteristics of their host organism. When diseases have an epidemic interval longer than 18 years, there is a limited capacity for those surviving the infection to benefit from any acquired immunity. As the cycle of infection shortens, and older individuals represent a pool of immunised survivors, the disease increasingly impacts on those in younger age categories, who have had no time to acquire such immunity. In doing so, the disease also tends to decline in virulence. In contemporary human populations, infectious diseases such as measles are responsible for millions of paediatric deaths annually but affect far larger numbers without causing death. This ecological pressure may be assumed to favour body fat stores during infancy and childhood in order to provide the energy required to maintain immune function, as considered by Kuzawa (1998).

I have hypothesised that the tendencies of African and Asian populations to prioritise the intra-muscular and visceral depots of adipose tissue, respectively, may therefore derive from contrasting exposures to fevers versus gastro-intestinal infectious diseases as the primary selective pressure (Wells 2009a). Such adaptive responses may then predispose to ethnic differences in the cytokine-induced burden of obesity and hence cardiovascular risk in contemporary populations (Wild and McKeigue 1997; McKeigue, Shah, and Marmot 1991; Forouhi and Sattar 2006; Zhu et al. 2005).

Previously, I suggested that the prioritised allocation of energy to visceral fat by Asians may have been favoured during chronic energy insufficiency (Wells 2007e). A key proximate cause of such energy insufficiency in South Asia comprises regular famines, induced by El Niño effects in global climate. However, there is little doubt that this proximate cause was greatly worsened by imperial economic policies (Davis 2002). A powerful indication of the impact of economics comprises an apparent increase in the proportion of deaths attributed directly to starvation as opposed to infectious diseases induced by poor immune status. In contrast to the general scenario proposed for famines (Mokyr and Ó Gráda 2002), the late Victorian age appears to have substantially increased the selective pressure of famine by manipulating food prices and access to food resources (Davis 2002). Detailed censuses indicate that the level of mortality frequently reached 30 to 40% in some areas of the Indian subcontinent, and in some cases was recorded at greater than 60% (Davis 2002). With several famines occurring within a single century and exerting such high mortality, economic policies themselves may plausibly have induced selection for particular components of adipose tissue biology.

Regular famines, imposing drastic mortality from starvation as well as disease, may therefore have selected for a more thrifty allocatory strategy (i.e., increased prioritisation of energy allocation to adipose rather than lean tissue).

On the one hand, such mortality may manifest as genetic selection since genetic variability in lean mass and body fat content is well established (see Chapter 2). On the other hand, selection may have favoured phenotypes deriving from developmental plasticity rather than genetic traits, for example, females exposed to famine in utero may have managed to survive and reproduce more successfully on exposure to subsequent famines during adulthood. Thus, the adipose tissue biology of contemporary Asians might represent the multigenerational accumulation of a thrifty developmental strategy. Both the biological models of thrift described in Chapter 7 may apply to this scenario, and more broadly, ethnic variability in adipose tissue biology should not be assumed to comprise a wholly genetic trait.

Disease and famine are notoriously interlinked, which would tend to increase local selective pressures on adipose tissue biology. The conserved link between nutrient-sensing and pathogen-sensing metabolic pathways suggests that this link is an important aspect of human biology (Hotamisligil 2006), further supported by the role of adipose tissue as the source of cytokines. Local adaptations to specific disease loads may account for differences between ethnic groups in the metabolic risks deriving from excess body weight.

This scenario may also have relevance for population variability in male preference for female body shape. First, given associations between infection exposure and insulin resistance and adiposity, with insulin resistance favouring central adiposity (Fernandez-Real et al. 2006; Fernandez-Real et al. 2007), body shape might transmit reliable signals of current immune status or disease history. This would predict a tendency of human populations to favour lower waist-hip ratio across diverse ecological environments, regardless of overall body size. Second, if specific disease burdens favour a different partitioning of lipid between competing adipose depots, then male preferences for female body shape might vary across ecological environments. These hypotheses are at present entirely speculative but merit further investigation.

9.7   Genetic variability and bet-hedging

Despite evidence that a variety of factors have acted on the human genome, as described above, recently published studies emphasise that the magnitude of such effects are small. There is little indication of substantial systematic genetic differences in adiposity, or in underlying metabolic traits, between populations, and hence little indication of marked adaptation to localized ecological conditions. Yet at the same time, studies repeatedly show a high degree of heritability in adiposity, with much of that heritability attributable to genetic rather than epigenetic factors.

This scenario can be attributed to the phenomenon of bet-hedging, whereby organisms within a population demonstrate variability as a strategy for risk management. Genetic factors relevant to adiposity have been discerned in five broad categories (Bouchard 2007), with numerous individual genes shown to exert statistically significant effects on adiposity, but with each individual magnitude of the effect very small. For example, one recent study of a western population (whose obesogenic environment would magnify any effect) showed that each risk allele for obesity increased average BMI by 0.15 kg/m^2, such that those having 10 such alleles had on average 1.5 kg/m^2 greater BMI than those with none of them (Willer et al. 2009). A similar scenario has been reported for other components of metabolism and development, such as the timing of puberty (Ong et al. 2009).

These data indicate that human metabolism is a carefully hedged bet, incorporating a substantial component of genetic variability without any single gene exerting a dominant effect. The consequence of such variability is that in any given environment, individuals will be distributed across a spectrum of adiposity, and some individuals will have greater reproductive fitness in consequence. Distributing genetic variability across so many genetic traits means that selection is unlikely to eradicate some genes whilst fixing others, ensuring that the variability is preserved across generations. This strategy is favoured in unstable environments, where committing to a single genetic strategy is inappropriate. This lack of genetic commitment is then further complemented by life-course plasticity, as discussed below.

9.8 The thrifty-phenotype hypothesis and population-metabolic variability

Whilst this chapter has reviewed evidence in favour of population genetic variability in metabolism and adipose tissue biology, population variability in the risk of obesity and diabetes need not be due only to this mechanism. As we improve our understanding of epigenetic effects, it is possible that variability in adiposity relates to differential epigenetic profiles, which could have emerged relatively recently, and which may exert only transient effects across generations. Other life-course induction mechanisms include the setting of hormonal axes in early life, and the induction of behavioural characteristics such as appetite. Just as bet-hedging generates random rather than systematic variability, so plasticity acts to buffer the genome from selective pressures. The effect of plasticity on adiposity in contemporary humans is illustrated by data from India.

In Chapter 5, the link between under-nutrition in early life and subsequent adiposity was discussed. Low birth-weight is associated with reduced lean mass in later life, and there are some indications that fat distribution is also influenced although the evidence remains weak. Low-birth-weight neonates from India have been reported in several studies to have a more central fat deposition at birth (Yajnik et al. 2003), whereas in later life, Indians appear to have higher levels of visceral fat for a given BMI value than Europeans (Yajnik and Yudkin 2004). Whether such characteristics reflect ethnic genetic adaptation, or are attributable to life-course adaptations to poor fetal growth, remains unclear. The typical Indian neonate is approximately 1 kg lighter than its European counterpart, plausibly due both to a reduced uterine size as well as a reduced fetal nutritional supply, and hence experiences a very different overall fetal environment. The increased adiposits is likely to be most important in terms of early life survival, but the low levels of lean mass may increase vulnerability to a high metabolic load in later life.

One factor associated with fetal growth variability is the thermal environment (Wells 2002; Wells and Cole 2002b); hence, one assumption might be that physical factors constrain the growth of Indian fetuses and alter adiposity accordingly. Whilst this factor is doubtless relevant, it is impossible to ignore the recent nutritional experience of the Indian population (Davis 2002), and this scenario may also apply to many other non-European populations. The effects of imperial economics described above were to increase the regularity and severity of famines, such that within the last three centuries famine became an inevitability experienced by each generation. In contrast to Europe, there is little evidence of secular trends in growth in the Indian population over the last two centuries, and some evidence even of a decline (Brennan, McDonald, and Shlomowitz 1997; Brennan, McDonald, and Shlomowitz 2004). Negative secular trends in height have also been recorded in some African populations (Tobias 1985), where trends in height are strongly associated with nutritional experience (Akachi and Canning 2007). Thus, the emergence of social stratification following the development of agriculture not only generated within-population disparities in access to food, but also led to between-population disparity as some global regions became bread-baskets or the source of raw materials for others. In the Victorian era, overseas populations coerced into supplying food for export buffered Europeans from regular, drastic El Nino-induced famines whose local effects were further exacerbated by Imperial economic policies.

Phenotypic plasticity is of course a fundamentally adaptive strategy, allowing the offspring to track maternal phenotype and thereby broader climatic and physical environmental conditions (Wells 2007f; Wells 2007a). However, chronic under-nutrition of the matriline acts to reduce fetal demand by reducing both uterine size across generations and the level of circulating nutrients.

I have previously referred to the effect of Imperialist economic policies on birth weight as the imposition of a 'metabolic ghetto' (Wells 2007f) in order to emphasise how the social inequality that occurs in small groups has often been enacted at the scale of entire populations. The phenotype of contemporary Asians (reduced height and lean mass but more fat, and in particular visceral fat, relative to Europeans) might therefore have accumulated in part through trans-generational plasticity over the last two centuries. Whilst the reduced lean mass is a clear indication of responding to reduced energy supplies, the increased adiposity may be adaptive not only in the short-term (greater insurance) but also in the longer-term, as a strategy for negating the current reduction in size and physique.

Low-birth-weight infants tend to undergo catch-up growth in order to recover their fetal deficit. Increased fat in the offspring may promote such catch-up growth. However, the faster rate of growth in turn increases energy demand on the mother during the period of lactation. It is plausible that the increased adi-posity observed in adult Indian women represents such an adaptation. Accord-ing to this hypothesis, poor growth during early life might promote subsequent fat accumulation in females in order to meet the increased energy demands of infants catching up. As described in the game-theory model presented in Chapter 7, maternal capital transfers would act to exploit improvements in ecological conditions in order to restore genetic potential in future generations. Examination of this hypothesis will require more rigorous testing of possible sex-differences in the ethnic variability in body composition for a given BMI value.

Improved nutrition in the future may therefore reverse multi-generational effects on body size and composition, though it may take a substantial period of time to do so, and growth during early life may be more beneficial than growth or weight gain at later time periods. Recently, I have suggested that it is beneficial to differentiate two contrasting aspects of the phenotypic induction of body composition (Wells 2009b). First, low birth weight appears to reduce 'metabolic capacity', which I define as the phenotype of organs such as the heart, liver, kidney and pancreas to tolerate variability in dietary intake and physical activity stimulus. The phenotype of these organs is closely associated with fetal growth, and hence birth weight, across the entire range of birth weight. This metabolic capacity must then tolerate the 'metabolic load' that emerges during post-natal growth and nutritional status. Metabolic load comprises the physiological stress of increased body mass and that occurs through postnatal growth, deriving from both greater physique (muscle mass) and adipose tissue mass, especially the deep-lying depots with greater metabolic activity. Broadly, physiological traits such as blood pressure and insulin sensitivity normalise the metabolic load for any given capacity, which makes possible secular trends in body size (strongly influenced by growth in early life). However, rapid catch-up growth appears to generate excess metabolic load and hence increases the risk of diseases such as type-2 diabetes, stroke and cardiovascular disease. This is discussed further in Chapter 10 regarding the effects of the global economy.

According to this perspective, incremental improvements in metabolic capacity may be fundamental to resolving the multi-generational under-nutrition that has occurred in the Indian population. Increased weight gain during childhood, adolescence and adulthood may merely increase metabolic load and, if superimposed on poor metabolic capacity, merely exert detrimental effects on the offspring via maternal diabetes and hypertension. However, the Indian population should not perhaps be singled out in this respect. Worldwide variability in body size has strong associations with economic history, and the notion that 'thrifty genotypes' and 'thrifty phenotypes' are as much about the consequences of imperialism as about adaptation to long-term climatic or agricultural stresses deserves serious consideration.

Summary

Within the last 200,000 years, humans have colonised the majority of the Earth's surface, and in doing so they have exposed themselves to a variety of local selective pressures. The impact of these local selective pressures would have been enhanced whenever population crashes occurred, inducing genetic bottlenecks. As discussed in Chapter 8, such population booms and busts may be integrally related to adiposity, as energy stores represent a store of capital capable of contributing both to rapid population growth and to lean periods following the over-exploitation of food resources. The same capital can fund an immune system similarly challenged by the consequences of aggressive niche probing (e.g., colonising) or niche construction (e.g., agriculture).

Within this broader model, earlier populations of *Homo sapiens* can be assumed to have adapted to different climatic conditions, although with increasing cultural and technological sophistication, varying diets are also likely to have generated selective pressures. Collectively, this is likely to have resulted in local genetic adaptation, evident today in the subtle variability in physique and metabolism that is correlated with a variety of polymorphisms. However, the magnitude of any such local adaptation appears remarkably modest, and human metabolism looks instead like a carefully hedged bet, whereby numerous different genes contribute cumulatively to phenotype. Metabolism and adiposity are highly heritable, but differences within populations are generally much greater than those between them, indicating lack of genetic commitment to any particular adaptive strategy.

Furthermore, it is clear that a significant proportion of metabolic variability can be attributed to the life-course induction of a range of traits including size, physique, body composition, appetite, adipose tissue biology and energy metabolism. Such plasticity reflects a human genotype that has been selected to buffer itself from changes in DNA content, allowing short-term adaptations to wash out should future environments not favour them.

Following the emergence of agriculture, dietary stresses are likely to have intensified, exacerbated by the emergence of a substantially higher burden of infectious disease. Agriculture also facilitated the emergence of social hierarchies, increasing the variance of within- and between-population exposure to energy stress and disease. Again, whilst some population adaptation to these stresses may be genetic, as suggested for some aspects of the role of adipose tissue in immune function, much of the variability appears to be induced by phenotypic plasticity. Whether generated by epigenetic mechanisms, hormonal effects or behavioural tendencies, humans appear to transmit strategies for 'capital exploitation' across generations flexibly. This has a clear evolutionary logic, allowing each generation to benefit from the local experience of immediate ancestors, particularly the matriline, and to transfer those benefits to future generations, without committing to any specific strategy long-term. The instability of the *Homo sapiens* niche, owing in part to cycles of colonisation and self-inflicted population booms and busts, does not favour genetic commitment. Rather, the optimal use of energy capital depends on the legacy of recent generations (body size, ecological productivity) as well as broader factors such as climate and ecosystem characteristics. Variability in adiposity is part of the dynamic of life-history variability, aiding adaptation to variable and changing niches.

Extant human populations therefore show substantial variability in adiposity and related traits. The differences between populations discussed in Chapter 2 offer ample evidence that body composition is fundamental to the human capacity to occupy niches as variable as the arctic, tropical forests, steppe, near-deserts and high altitude. Such adiposity variability is now compounded by diverse ways for obtaining and storing energy that have emerged from technological development and changing socio-economic environments. The final chapter of this book highlights how the genetically unified and highly plastic human phenotype has been variably influenced by the larger scale forces characteristic of the Western capitalist economic niche.

10   *The evolution of human obesity*

As stated earlier, this book was not intended to be about obesity. Nevertheless, much of the interest now directed to human body fat derives from biomedical interest in elucidating the causes and consequences of excess body fat. What can an evolutionary perspective contribute to this issue?

Chapters 6 considered a variety of beneficial functions fulfilled by adipose tissue in human biology, whereas Chapters 7 to 9 explored possible selective pressures that may have impacted on adipose tissue and other traits during hominin and human evolution. Historically, a suite of traits has been considered fundamental to human evolution. These traits include bipedalism, encephalisation, manual dexterity, culture and language. More recent perspectives have emphasised the importance of human life history – our slow pattern of growth and our unusual pattern of parental care (Bogin 2001). I would suggest that body fat is no less important than these other traits, and indeed it is integrally related to several of them. On the one hand, energy reserves have played a key role in buffering biological functions from fluctuations in energy supply. This has been particularly important in relation to the large human brain, and potentially to our colonising reproductive strategy. On the other hand, energy reserves are more than simply a fuel depot; they contribute to the regulation of these functions including life history variability. It is this regulatory role that is crucial for understanding how environmental changes can, over a relatively short period of time, generate profound alterations in the population profile of adiposity.

We may therefore consider humans to be a species of mammal in which adiposity is a critical dynamic component of biology, guiding our development and life history within the context of our energy-demanding brain and the niches it has led us into. Human adiposity is highly sensitive to environmental factors because in our evolutionary past, this sensitivity helped optimise the trade-off between survival versus growth and reproductive schedule across diverse ecological conditions. Not only is each individual adapted to be sensitive in this way, encapsulated in the human genome, but mechanisms also allow sensitivity to recent ancestral experience, such that adiposity reflects trans-generational influences.

It is this integrative role of adipose tissue in other biological functions that furthermore accounts for differences between humans and other species. In hamsters, adiposity is closely associated with cues of photoperiodicity, reflecting this animal's need to regulate energy stores in relation to seasonal changes in energy availability (Schneider 2004). In humans, as discussed in the earlier chapters, specific factors such as large brains, dietary energy availability, a colonising reproductive strategy and heavy infectious disease loads may have been particularly important selective pressures on adipose tissue biology during different evolutionary periods. However, energy is stored to be used, and humans experience high metabolic costs when they maintain large adipose tissue depots for long time periods.

It is this organism that has been exposed in the twentieth century to profound ecological changes deriving from the social and economic effects of industrialisation and urbanisation. These changes have impacted simultaneously on many aspects of human behaviour and phenotype, but in obesity they have not manufactured a new disease, rather they have only increased the prevalence of a condition which is discernible prior to and throughout the human historical record.

10.1   The evolutionary history of obesity

The evolutionary history of obesity is very different from that of body fat itself. In Chapter 1, I described how at the population level, under-nutrition has been the primary nutritional stress until the industrialised era. Within that broader pattern, however, there is substantial evidence for the emergence of obesity on an individual basis over many thousand years, as reviewed previously by Bray (1990) and Haslam (2007).

Archaeologists have recovered a number of Stone Age statues portraying extreme corpulency of the female form. The well-known Venus of Willendorf, for example, dating from around 25,000 years ago, expresses a large abdomen and breasts, and other statues display increased abdominal and thigh girths. Interpretation of such artefacts is difficult, as they may at least partially express ideals. Often-cited theories are that these figures represent fertility symbols (a function that Haslam (2007) notes is ironic, given the association between extreme obesity and female infertility), or Mother Goddess figures (Gimbutas 1974). Nevertheless, their accurate portrayal of body fat distribution associated with female obesity strongly implies familiarity with the reality of high female body weight. Gynoid obesity is less detrimental than android obesity for fertility, and the statues are likely to express awareness of the generic value of energy reserves in female reproductive success.

Both obesity and its main comorbidity, diabetes, are described in the early historical literature. In the Ebers papyrus, dated to the start of the New Kingdom in Egyptian history at around 1550 BC, but possibly reflecting earlier knowledge, reference is made to 'excessive urination', a classic symptom of diabetes (Haslam 2007), and ancient Hindu writings likewise referred to extreme thirst, high urine output and wasting of the body (Haslam 2007). However, it was only in the late eighteenth century that the association between excess body weight and a risk of diabetes appears explicitly to have been recognised (Thomas 1811, in Haslam 2007).

Obesity itself is mentioned on numerous occasions in ancient Greek literature. Hippocrates noted an increased risk of sudden death in those fat compared to those lean (Hippocrates Transl. Adams 2008), and showed sophisticated understanding of the principles of energy balance: 'it is very injurious to health to take in more food than the constitution will bear, when, at the same time one uses no exercise to carry off this excess' (Hippocrates 2008). He recommended that weight loss could be achieved by taking exercise prior to meals, consuming a high-fat diet which would induce satiety, restricting food intake to one meal a day, and walking naked for as long as possible (Bray 1990) which would have increased energy expenditure by increasing heat loss. All of these propositions now have a scientific basis in the principles of appetite regulation or thermodynamics. Herodotus likewise recorded a tendency of Egyptians to vomit and purge themselves on a regular basis, on the assumption that such practices benefited health, and Pythagoras recommended constraints of food intake to prevent excess weight (Haslam 2007).

The ancient Greeks were likewise aware of a number of adverse consequences of obesity. Hippocrates observed that excess weight gain caused restlessness during the night, with 'sleep ... disturbed with frightful dreams of battles', while Dionysius, himself obese, employed attendants to waken him periodically during sleep to prevent suffocation (Haslam 2007). Hippocrates may also have been referring to angina when he described obesity as the cause of 'pain and distempers', particularly in those 'who, from a long habit of idleness, come, of a sudden, to use exercise' (Haslam 2007).

Hippocrates' views exerted a strong influence on the second-century-AD physician Galen, who in turn became the dominant medical authority for well over the following millennium. Galen's model of disease was based on the four elements or humours described by Hippocrates. Galen considered obesity to arise from an excess of 'bad humours', specifically blood (Papavramidou, Papavramidis, and Christopoulou-Aletra 2004). This model directly implicated energy intake as a key cause of excess weight gain; however, idleness and laziness were also considered predisposing factors. Galen further considered weight gain to increase body fat out of proportion to any increase in flesh, that is, lean mass (Papavramidou, Papavramidis, and Christopoulou-Aletra 2004).

Galen proposed a number of methods, including diet, exercise, massage and medication, by which weight loss could be attained (Papavramidou, Papavramidis, and Christopoulou-Aletra 2004). For example, in his treatise on hygiene (*De Sanitate Tuenda*), he described combining a number of behaviours, each favouring negative energy balance:

> Now, I have made any sufficiently stout patient moderately thin in a short time by compelling him to do rapid running, then wiping off his perspiration with very soft or very rough muslin, and then massaging him maximally with diaphoretic inunctions, which the younger doctors customarily call restoratives, and after such massage leading him to the bath, after which I did not give him nourishment immediately, but bade him rest for a while or do something to which he was accustomed, then led him to the second bath and then gave him abundant food of little nourishment, so as to fill him up but distribute little of it to the entire body (Galen 2001).

The ideas of Hippocrates and Galen were taken up by the Persian physician Avicenna (980–1037 AD). His *Canon of Medicine*, which was translated into Latin in the twelfth century and remained highly influential for several hundred years afterwards, maintained emphasis on behaviours promoting negative energy balance, such as hindering complete digestion, consuming bulky non-nutritious foods, and engaging in physical exercise (Bray 1990). The twelfth-century Jewish physician Maimonides similarly endorsed Galen's opinions, recommending both physical exercise and dietary restraint (Papavramidou, Papavramidis, and Christopoulou-Aletra 2004).

The first monographs focusing specifically on obesity emerged in the late sixteenth century (Bray 1990) and began to incorporate a growing understanding of the physical and chemical basis of physiology. In 1765, the Italian anatomist Morgagni demonstrated the preponderance of abdominal fat in obese individuals through post-mortem dissection (Haslam 2007), a finding subsequently confirmed by Wadd (1839). This focus on pathological anatomy would prove compatible with the work of the English clinician Thomas Sydenham, who initiated the systematic cataloguing of diseases on the basis of careful description of symptoms (Bray 1990).

Subsequent scientific understanding of obesity emerged from a succession of European schools of medicine (Bray 1990). In 1660, Robert Boyle had demonstrated life to be a chemical combustion process. He showed that when isolated in an airtight chamber, a mouse died at the same time that a candle expired (Boyle 1660). In 1783, Lavoisier and Laplace directly demonstrated the link between heat production and respiratory gas exchange in their celebrated experiment on guinea pigs, where the melting of ice surrounding the animal's container was proportional to the carbon dioxide produced (Lavoisier and

Laplace 1783). In post-revolutionary France, progress was also made in linking pathological anatomy to physical symptoms, giving rise, for example, to the recognition of different types of obesity. The first use of the term 'angina' is attributed to Heberden (1772), with the condition subsequently proposed 'to attack men much more frequently the women, particularly those who have short necks, who are inclinable to corpulency, and who at the same time lead an inactive or sedentary life' (Thomas 1811). Thomas likewise noted the tendency for diabetics to have fat 'within the thorax, abdomen, and pelvis', whereas 'subcutaneous fat is found in general much diminished' (Thomas 1811).

In 1847, Magnus had shown an increased oxygen content and decreased carbon dioxide content of the arteries relative to veins, demonstrating the transport of respiratory gases between body tissues (Magnus 1847). Nineteenth-century German medicine further introduced cell theory, a range of physiological measurement devices, and a comprehensive theory of thermodynamics in the form of von Helmhotz's law of energy conservation (von Helmholtz 1847). These theoretical principles subsequently gave rise to the science of calorimetry, fundamental to the experimental investigation of energy balance.

Although the Flemish statistician Quetelet is widely credited with the concept of adjusting weight for height to compare relative weight (Quetelet 1871), using the index now known as the BMI, similar work probing the concept of 'normal weight' versus 'overweight' was conducted by Chambers (1850). According to Chambers, greater weight in relation to other individuals of similar height was not due to muscle or bone, but to adipose tissue.

Following treatment for his own obesity, William Banting (1864) published a pamphlet that Bray (1990) considers the first popular diet book, 'A letter on corpulence, addressed to the public', advocating a dietary regime not dissimilar to the contemporary Atkins diet. This publication is indicative of growing nineteenth-century interest in the management of obesity in individuals, but it is the twentieth century that has seen the formal identification of obesity as a public health problem, invoking an ever-increasing volume of scientific research into its aetiology and treatment, and efforts by public health and government authorities to constrain its development.

What this brief history illustrates is that obesity and diabetes are far from new conditions, though angina (and by inference cardiovascular disease) appears to have been very rare prior to the mid-eighteenth century (Michaels 2001). The current obesity epidemic may be broadly attributed to two interrelated factors: first, the development of novel environmental exposures which more readily induce excess weight gain, and second, the exposure of increased numbers of individuals to the range of these obesogenic factors. These processes are both complex, and the following part of this chapter explores in some detail the emergence of the modern obesogenic niche.

10.2   The creation of the obesogenic niche

The first point to make about the emergence of the obesogenic niche is that the contribution of genetic factors to any trend in obesity is at best modest. This issue may appear controversial, given the strong association of genetic factors with adiposity within and between populations, but it is vital to distinguish between cross-sectional and longitudinal dimensions. Although at any given time point, individual rankings in fatness have a strong correlation with genetic profile, population changes over time are driven primarily by environmental change. A similar scenario applies to secular trends in intelligence. As documented in detail by Flynn (2007), despite IQ appearing to have high heritability, secular trends in IQ can be attributed to environmental effects concerning changes in the stimulatory environment. In similar manner, changes in adiposity within the lifespan of individuals must clearly derive from environmental factors, even if they impact on genetic expression.

There is some evidence of assortative mating for both physique and adiposity in some populations (Speakman et al. 2007), but this effect is likely to have been of limited significance prior to the obesity epidemic itself, simply because recognition of varying phenotypes would have been difficult when the range of weight was narrower. Those migrating from developing countries to industrialised countries may also contribute both particular genotypes, and particular phenotypes, each of which may react differently to exposure to the obesogenic environment. In the United States, the proportion of adults of Hispanic American background increased from below 5% in 1972 to around 13% in the year 2000 (Keith et al. 2006). In the United Kingdom, the proportion of adults of South Asian ancestry has also increased over the twentieth century. These populations appear to have a greater tendency to obesity than Europeans (McKeigue 1996). However, elucidating the contribution of genetics to these effects is extremely difficult given the fact that apparent ethnic variability in adipose tissue biology may derive from trans-generational induction rather than direct genetic variability. Furthermore, so-called 'natural experiments' on whole populations highlight the emergence of obesity in association with environmental change (Poston and Foreyt 1999).

Thus, despite multiple contributions of genetic factors to adiposity in every individual, the contemporary obesity epidemic can be attributed primarily to the emergence of the obesogenic niche, consisting of a variety of pressures, behaviours and physical factors which collectively influence the energy balance of individuals. The emergence of this niche reflects numerous secular trends, some with an extensive history and some which have emerged only recently through technological innovation. As will become clear, many of these trends have some association with the Western economic model of capitalism, which acts to manipulate the behaviour of individuals and thereby renders them more passive in their exposure to ecological stresses. These exposures constitute both 'push' and 'pull' factors, impacting at a variety of different levels of biology. Reflecting this complexity, we might think of the obesity epidemic as a number of upward steps in prevalence, as each new obesogenic factor is added to the overall scenario and adds to the intensity of the niche.

10.3   Secular trends in diet

Changes in dietary intake are discernible across lengthy time periods. For industrialised populations, it is clear that these have occurred both in the food available and in the manner in which it is consumed. Mintz (1985) described how the industrial revolution engineered substantial changes in the British diet, whilst also constructing a novel pattern of eating based around factory-working practices. However, these changes built on an earlier and longer trend towards increasing consumption of products containing sucrose, at the expense of other more nutritious foodstuffs.

Prior to agriculture, humans are assumed to have eaten a diet high in meat and low in carbohydrate (Colagiuri and Brand 2002; McMichael 2001). The likely Palaeolithic diet doubtless had many other features that differed from diets eaten in agricultural populations (Eaton and Konner 1985), but human diets did, and continue to, vary substantially (Milton 2000), and caution is required regarding the confidence with which past diets can be reconstructed (Milton 2000). For example, others consider underground tubers to have been a key resource in many populations (Conklin-Brittain, Wrangham, and Smith 2002), especially following the development of cooking (O'Connell, Hawkes, and Blurton Jones 2002). Nevertheless, the available evidence suggests that regardless of the ratio of protein to carbohydrate in different diets, the glycaemic load of agricultural diets tended to be higher than that of pre-agricultural diets. Most wild foods are high in fibre and bulk, and they release energy into the bloodstream relatively slowly (Milton 2000). Hence, the emphasis on grains in early agricultural diets initiated a shift towards a higher glycaemic load.

Historically, most agricultural societies have consumed a diet based around one or other form of starch, such as rice, millet, potato, maize or wheat (Mintz 1985). Other foods, such as oils, meats, fish, fruits, nuts, vegetables and seasonings have then been used to add flavour and texture, and to provide supplementary nutrients, but a central carbohydrate base appears almost universal, and the supplements have rarely been consumed in large quantities relative to the carbohydrate base. This generalised dietary pattern has facilitated adaptation to a variety of local ecosystems distributed throughout the Earth's tropical and temperate regions. Prior to the industrialised era, small elite populations were able to escape from such dietary niches, and their greater consumption of richer foodstuffs is reflected in reports of obesity in privileged populations as discussed above. Over the last two to three centuries, however, the diets consumed by entire populations have changed in several ways, including a shift from this essential starch/flavour combination to substantially greater consumption of meat, fats and refined sugars (Mintz 1985). These changes have been brought about by 'revolutionary pressures in food processing and consumption and by adding new foods, rather than simply cutting back on old ones' (Mintz 1985).

The history of the British diet provides an important example of such changes. Prior to the mainstream consumption of sugar, the primary dietary constituent was wheat or other grains, such that the British diet was remarkably similar to that consumed in most global regions. In 1650, English sugar consumption was restricted to the wealthy. By the eighteenth century, it was considered a dietary essential for all, and this increase in demand was, by no coincidence, the central driving force for the slave trade. By 1900, sucrose accounted for approximately one-fifth of all calories in the British diet (Mintz 1985). The trend to greater sugar consumption was integrally entwined with complementary trends in the consumption of tea, and also coffee and chocolate. By the late nineteenth century, white bread and jam had become a dietary staple, and those unable to access these foodstuffs were considered to be below the poverty line. Sugar also played a central role in the creation of novel foodstuffs such as pastries, preserves and puddings, products which also enabled the ritualisation of the diet (Mintz 1985). Sugar-rich products such as biscuits and cakes, ideal for out-of-home consumption, aided the creation of the work break and fuelled the ever-increasing trend in sugar consumption.

The effect of such dietary shifts was to reverse the relationship between the dietary core and its fringe, such that consumption of processed fats and sugars came to exceed that of grain and vegetables. The new British diet of white bread, jam and sweetened tea was cheap and ideal for feeding the new proletariat at minimal cost, but the 'quick energy' came at the expense of a worsening of overall nutrition (Mintz 1985).

In addition to its effect on the diet of individuals, this burgeoning contribution of sugar to the British diet had significant political and economic effects. Global trade in sugar was one of the primary sources of government revenue, such that control of this trade played a key role in Imperial economic policies. Equally, the contribution of sugar to manufactured food products initiated the trend for commercial companies to manipulate the choices and behaviour of their consumers. Indeed, Mintz (1985) argues convincingly that sugar and capitalism are structurally embedded within one another. The New World slave plantations of the sixteenth century that produced sugar acted as the model for full capitalism, and the capitalist economic model then exploited sugar production over successive centuries for national and individual profit (Mintz 1985). Technological innovation led to new food products such as hard chocolate, creating entire new markets and food-consumption patterns based around them.

Sugar likewise aided directly in the creation and maintenance of the modern urban proletariat that underpins profit in the capitalist system (Mintz 1985). Per acre, the calorie productivity of sugar plantations is substantially greater than that for other starch products. Population growth could therefore be met without substantial increases in the production of other food items such as meat and vegetables. As the growing factory industry absorbed this increased population, increasing numbers of individuals consumed their diet without any direct contribution to food production. Whilst in the short-term this practice merely altered the kind of physical effort required by work, the stage was set for profound changes in physical-activity patterns as technology increasingly replaced human labour (see below).

With the development of the commercialised food industry through the twentieth century, the final component of dietary change has been for decreased direct household consumption of specific foodstuffs, and instead the consumption, whether in or out of the home, of factory-produced products (Mintz 1985). These products have detached food consumption not only from physical effort, but also from the concept of meals, generally considered by anthropologists to represent the primary daily social event across human societies. By replacing meals with foods which require minimal preparation prior to eating, apparent individual control is increased at the expense of social participation. As Mintz writes, 'when one is serving oneself from a serving plate, the helpings must be adjusted to the desires of others who are eating'. In contrast, the consumption of discrete products makes it possible for everyone to eat exactly what they want, when and where they want, and as much as they want. Food is effortlessly available in industrialised societies 24 hours a day, from commercial outlets or refrigerators. The net effect of these trends is that they have 'desocialised eating' (Mintz 1985).

Within these broader trends, others more subtle in nature but perhaps no less significant for obesity are also apparent. One such trend comprises the replacement of sucrose with glucose fructose syrup, a product containing equivalent calories to sucrose which nevertheless appears to increase the likelihood of excess weight gain by stimulating triglyceride synthesis in the liver (Bray, Nielsen, and Popkin 2004). Other trends include the altered fat content of meat, as preferences have altered in relation to both taste and health issues.

As individuals have become consumers of mass-produced food, rather than the direct producer and preparer of meals, they have become subject to a range of economic forces that act to maintain behaviour within patterns that are sufficiently predictable to maintain food industry profits (Mintz 1985). These forces, concealed within the guise of apparent greater convenience, are paradoxically responsible for a narrowing of choice, constraining the capacity for individuals to resist market influences (Mintz 1985; Shell 2002). Sugar was initially claimed to be healthy, to the extent that it was even suggested a beneficial addition to breast-milk. Tobacco, sugar and tea were furthermore the first products created by the capitalist approach that conveyed the notion that one could become different by consuming differently (Mintz 1985), a concept that remains central to the modern food industry with its hyperbolic advertising. Now, modern retailers further target particular portions of the population with particular products, for example, promoting cheap energy-dense products in poorer neighbourhoods where the pressure to maximise 'energy-value for money' may be greatest (Shell 2002). These activities are strongly implicated in the differing prevalences of obesity according to socio-economic status (Drewnowski 2009).

Dietary change is strongly associated with urbanisation, discussed further below. As individuals move from rural environments, where they were often food producers, to cities, they change both the types of food consumed and the schedule of taking meals. Commercial foods are designed to maximise shelf-life and contain high energy content at the expense of other nutrients which rapidly deteriorate. The food industry has a strong motivation to increase the fat and sugar content of foods because these ingredients simultaneously enhance shelf life, reduce storage volume, and maximise profits in relation to production costs, while further appearing to promote convenience and palatability to the consumer.

Today's supermarkets are therefore stocked with products which have an energy density substantially greater than most traditional foodstuffs (Prentice and Jebb 2003). This property, along with a high refined-carbohydrate content which impacts on insulin levels, reduces any 'natural' capacity of human physiology to regulate energy intake in relation to energy expenditure. Products with similar characteristics are also fundamental to the fast food industry that has proliferated in industrialised cities during the second half of the twentieth century, equivalent to a real economic growth of 75% between 1980 and 1995 alone in the United States (Binkley, Eales, and Jekanowski 2000). The frequency of the consumption of fast food is directly associated with increased body weight in American adults (Jeffery and French 1998; Binkley, Eales, and Jekanowski 2000). Energy-dense foods have also entered the domestic home following the mass distribution of refrigerators and freezers (Cannon 2008).

Thus, whether people eat in or out, the energy density of their diet tends to be greater than it was formerly.

Whatever the impact of other factors, dietary intake trends lie at the heart of the contemporary obesity epidemic, not least because commercial companies have taken inadequate steps to change their products and marketing practices as the problem has emerged. It is perhaps ironic that what is finally motivating multi-national corporations to take obesity seriously appears to be the recognition by commercial companies in general that their own health benefit funds are increasingly directed towards overweight employees (Shell 2002). Just as with the tobacco industry, the main motivating force may derive from the fear of mass-litigation, with test cases already probing whether food manufacturers can be sued for the sale of unhealthy products (Shell 2002).

10.4   Secular trends in physical activity

Changes in human activity patterns relate to a wide variety of factors operating over a variety of different timescales. Whilst much attention is directed towards technological developments in recent decades, the earliest relevant changes in physical activity may be dated back to the emergence of a sexual division of labour prior to agriculture. It was arguably this that initiated the detachment of energy consumption from energy acquisition in some adult individuals.

In non-human animal species, there tends to be a direct association between the physical effort of foraging and the resulting returns. Ecologists use optimal foraging theory to predict how much time an animal should direct to foraging, and within that total, how much time to direct to specific resources (Kelly 1995; Shennan 2002). Increasing foraging returns allows the allocation of time to other activities such as predator surveillance, courting, reproducing and sleep. Reconstruction of the diet of early *Homo* is notoriously difficult, but evidence suggests some degree of a sexual division of labour. Whilst both sexes are likely to have hunted, large game appears to have been pursued by parties of males, and small game by females who also gathered vegetable resources (O'Connell, Hawkes, and Blurton Jones 2002). Data from contemporary foraging societies are consistent with this general perspective, with the disproportionate contribution of females to offspring care, not least the carrying of infants, impacting on the type of foraging activities that can be undertaken. Few other animal species share food outside the content of parental care, although chimpanzees and bonobos are known to do so (Hohmann and Fruth 1997).

This mode of food acquisition starts to break the inherent link between effort and reward in any individual, generating instead a social energy budget in which the sum of several inputs balances several outputs. Likewise, the tendency for humans to process foodstuffs introduces a delay between their procurement and their consumption, which may further distort effort-reward associations. Small-scale societies tend to be egalitarian, such that all individuals are required to contribute to the diet. The sharing of food between family groups, offering the opportunity for some to acquire calories they did not directly capture from the environment, constitutes an important social aspect of risk management (Wiessner 1997).

This is particularly evident with regards to younger age groups, where there is greater consistency between humans and other species. All mammals and birds provision their offspring, such that the costs of growth are funded by parental rather than offspring activity. However, a connection between offspring effort and dietary reward is maintained through the behavioural system whereby offspring express demand. Studies of birds have shown that auditory begging signals are themselves energetically costly, such that excessive begging impacts adversely on growth rate (Godfray 1991; Godfray 1995). Humans show consistency with this mechanism, as infant crying is extremely expensive metabolically during early life (Wells 2003a). Only towards the end of infancy do the costs of growth become so low that the integrity of this relationship is lost, allowing infants to 'blackmail' their parents. Under 'natural ecosystem conditions', human infant weight gain is a function of external ecological conditions, but strongly mediated by maternal foraging effort and energy stores. Maternal resource-capture and activity patterns likewise constrain the rate of reproduction, such that non-sedentary populations typically have a birth interval of around four years (Galdikas and Wood 1990), though this is still shorter than that of other extant apes.

The capacity to detach energy intake from physical effort was clearly increased following the emergence of agriculture, in particular through the development of complex societies where individual elites obtained their resources through political rather than physical power. Records from early societies provide ample evidence that those controlling the productivity of others were able to achieve opulent surroundings and a rich diet at the expense of little physical effort, reflected in reports of excess weight and obesity in diverse historical populations (Brown and Konner 1987). This scenario has persisted throughout the history of agriculture, with the only constraint on the emergence of excess weight comprising limitations on the numbers of individuals who could achieve such a lifestyle. It is clear that many such civilisations were not sustainable over long time periods because of a disparity between the nutritional needs of an increasing population size and the ecological stochasticity attributable in part to farming practices (Fagan 1999). Within these limits, prior to industrialisation, obesity effectively represented a condition of the affluent, whether in Western or non-Western populations.

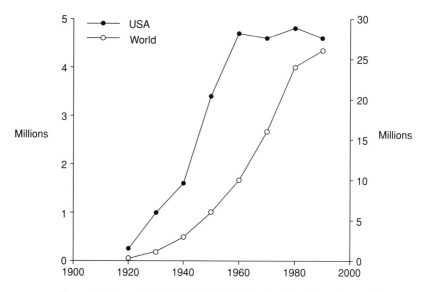

Figure 10.1. Trends in the United States (left-hand axis) and the entire world (right-hand axis) over the twentieth century in the number of tractors used in agriculture. Mechanised power replaced human muscle power, which had been a primary limiting factor of agricultural productivity, as well as a significant component of human energy balance prior to this century. Data from McNeill (2000).

The most profound transformation of physical activity patterns was initiated by the industrial revolution. Initially, industrialisation often required high levels of physical activity from individual workers, contributing long working hours and high physical effort. In Europe around 1800, for example, over 70% of the mechanical power required for human activities was derived directly from human muscular activity (McNeill 2000). As technological innovation spread, physical effort began to be replaced by mechanisation. Whilst the industrial revolution is commonly connected with the nineteenth century, its full impact on population-activity patterns emerged only during the twentieth century (Komlos 1998). A major contributing factor here has been the shift from physical agricultural work to urban employment. In the United States, over half the population worked in agriculture in 1920, but only 2 to 3% by 1990 (McNeill 2000). Figure 10.1 illustrates the mechanisation of agriculture through trends in the number of tractors in the United States and in the entire world. As the case has so often been, the United States merely spearheaded a broader shift in human behaviour.

Within this shift towards non-agricultural activities, a number of other trends have emerged. First, even within the agricultural sector, human labour has increasingly been replaced by machinery, with financial capital rather than physical labour driving productivity. Second, the geographical locus of industry has changed as the cost of labour has become incorporated into global financial systems. Heavy industry still persists, but it has often been transferred away from Western populations to other global regions where the costs of physical labour are reduced. Third, Western economies have shifted from manufacturing physical products to providing services, resulting in information rather than materials being produced, exchanged and consumed. As a result, fewer people, especially in Western populations, require physical effort in their work, and leisure-time activity dominates the energy budget. This in turn predicts new associations between physical activity and social status.

Urbanisation, closely associated with industrialisation in the modern world, is a further critical factor impacting on physical activity levels. Those migrating from rural to urban environments rarely maintain their activity levels, as whatever employment is available in the proliferating shanty towns typically involves commerce or service industry activities rather than physical labour. Cities are also increasingly dominated by vehicular transport, such that the entire environment has shifted towards a discouragement of walking in favour of private or public vehicles. US cities in particular were designed around the concept of the private car (McNeill 2000). Car use in the United Kingdom has escalated 10-fold over a 40-year period (Haines et al. 2000). In the United States, each additional hour per day spent in a car was associated with a 6% increase in the risk of obesity, whereas each hour of walking was associated with a 4.8% reduction in risk (Frank, Andresen, and Schmid 2004). Such trends impact in particular on children, who are increasingly discouraged from any outdoor activity. In the United Kingdom, the proportion of road use attributable to cycling fell from around a third in the 1940s to less than 1% in the 1990s (Economist 26/4/08). Economic development has also reduced activity levels in developing countries such as Brazil (Hallal et al. 2003) and rural South Africa (Cook, Alberts, and Lambert 2008). Yet in Holland, where walking and cycling remain common forms of travel, the prevalence of obesity is substantially lower than elsewhere in Europe (Haines et al. 2000).

The extraordinarily rapid advent of computer technology clearly represents a key component of this final trend. Those whose work is primarily computer-based need display only the minimum level of physical activity, remaining sedentary at a desk throughout the working day. These trends further interact with an exposure to stress, as new working environments maintain many of the hierarchical structures that initially emerged in relation to agriculture-oriented political systems (see below). Children have no need to work at computers, but they have been led to their own niche of children's television and computer games (see below). These trends contribute to the strong association between sedentary behaviour and a risk of obesity in diverse populations, as reviewed in Chapter 3.

Despite profound changes in the nature of physical activity in industrialized populations, its significance for obesity remains contentious. There is ample evidence that physical activity stimulates appetite, but little direct evidence for the popular notion that physical activity has become detached from appetite through behavioural means. An alternative explanation is that obesity is associated with lower physical activity levels because high circulating insulin levels inhibit cellular energy balance and induce lethargy (Taubes 2008). Thus, declines in physical activity may accompany the obesity epidemic without driving it.

10.5   Changes in circadian rhythms

Changes in physical-activity patterns comprise a great deal more than reductions in physical effort per se. Since the industrial revolution, major changes have occurred in the distribution of activities across the 24-hour cycle. A physically active lifestyle is generally associated with physical effort during daylight hours, and little effort during the hours of darkness. The advent of modern technology has impacted on this norm in several different ways, both by providing new behavioural opportunities and by making them available regardless of external conditions.

Widespread access to television emerged in Western populations in the second half of the twentieth century and is currently close to saturation. Television viewing has been proposed to act on body-weight regulation in a number of ways, including a lowering of metabolic rate, an exposure to food advertisements, and a displacing of physical activity or sleep (see Chapter 3 and below). Recent studies have identified the presence of television in the bedroom as a significant risk factor for excess weight gain in children (Delmas et al. 2007), and television viewing in childhood predicts obesity status in adulthood (Viner and Cole 2005).

Cross-sectional studies have identified consistent inverse associations between sleep duration and body fatness, both in Western and non-Western populations (Patel and Hu 2008). There are currently very few longitudinal investigations of this issue, but those that are available support the hypothesis that reduced baseline sleep duration predicts increased weight gain subsequently (Al et al. 2007). Other studies have described secular decreases in the duration of sleep in Western populations (National Sleep Foundation 2008;

Iglowstein et al. 2003). Importantly, some studies have demonstrated that this effect is independent of the contributions both of television viewing and other physical activities, suggesting that sleep might impact on body fatness through the disruption of circadian rhythms regardless of other component of physical activity (Wells et al. 2008b). Nevertheless, a study that intervened to increase sleep duration found only limited evidence of changes in the endocrine profile (Littman et al. 2007) and more generally, is remains unclear if sleep patterns disrupt metabolism, or vice versa.

The relationship between behavioural activities stemming from recent technological innovation and body-weight regulation remains a critical area for research. The notion that obesity derives from a simple energy imbalance, through a mismatch between energy intake and physical activity, is increasingly considered over-simplistic, and an improved understanding of the role of circadian rhythms in body-weight regulation (Bray and Young 2006) represents a major opportunity for behavioural intervention, particularly in children.

10.6 Secular trends in social stress

Prior to the emergence of agriculture, the available evidence suggests humans may have been relatively egalitarian in their social structure (Cohen 1989; Wiessner 1997), although variability in rank would certainly have existed given similar characteristics in primate populations. With the development of civilisations based on agricultural productivity, those of lower social status would typically have been obliged to show the highest levels of physical activity, similar to those of contemporary farmers in non-industrialised populations (Ulijaszek 2000), whilst simultaneously being the most vulnerable to energy uncertainty (Brown and Konner 1987). This association might have impacted on subsequent generations in two different ways.

First, if social rank were highly heritable, high- and low-ranked individuals might have consistently undergone differing selective pressures, favouring different metabolic traits in the two sub-populations, which would then predispose to genetic variability in the risk of obesity according to socio-economic status in contemporary populations. Whilst theoretically plausible, this scenario is nonetheless unlikely. The uncertainty of history, such that both families' social status and ecological conditions varied over time, along with genetic exchange within regional populations, would have constrained any such genetic differentiation. More likely therefore is a second scenario, in that all humans have a common physiological basis whereby social stress impacts on metabolism and health (Siervo, Wells, and Cizza 2008). At any given time, those exposed to higher stress therefore respond in terms of cortisol secretion, associated in turn with increased abdominal fat deposition as discussed in Chapter 3.

Social inequality has been associated with an obesity risk in many populations (Molarius et al. 2000), and when comparing between populations, the same trend is apparent (Pickett et al. 2005). Such associations may be generated through more than one causal pathway, and at present our understanding of this issue remains limited. Human history shows ample evidence of a variety of types of stress, attributable to plagues, famines, invasions and wars, brutal political regimes or anarchic insecurity, acting over and above any more local social dynamics. Reconstructing the evolution of stress is therefore difficult, although some evidence from contemporary populations suggests that social stress, rather than physical disasters, exerts the longest effects (Flinn and England 1997).

In developing countries, social inequality may contribute to differential obesity risk through the pathway of under-nutrition in early life. Those of poorer social status typically work in more labour-intensive activities, whilst furthermore having reduced access to adequate food. These stresses act in particular on women, who perform a wide range of agricultural or other activities demanding physical effort and often work long hours. A number of studies have linked heavy physical activity during pregnancy to detrimental effects on fetal growth (Huffman 1988; Dwarkanath et al. 2007; Rao et al. 2003), through mechanisms such as reduced uterine blood flow or reduced energy availability. Maternal psychosocial stress may likewise be transmitted to the offspring (Kuzawa and Sweet 2009), as suggested by animal studies (Mueller and Bale 2006). Low birth weight and stunting remain major risk factors for obesity in such populations, particularly those rapidly modernising so that childhood weight gain is excessive relative to birth or infant size.

As modern urban communities become less family oriented, new forms of social stress, in particular work practices, may emerge (Siervo, Wells, and Cizza 2008). Recent evidence suggests that hierarchical inequality in the workplace is associated with metabolic risk and abdominal adiposity (Nomura et al. 2007; Brunner, Chandola, and Marmot 2007; Lallukka et al. 2008; Purslow et al. 2008). These effects may be worsened by the decreasing physical nature of modern work, with low activity levels exacerbating the obesogenic impact of social stress.

As with dietary intake and physical activity behaviour, social stress may have a deeper structural association with the capitalist economic model. The generation of ever greater profits requires the market continually to increase its consumption of products. Those of high status not only show the highest levels of consumption, but also appear as a symbol of success, inspiring emulation by others. Given the greater reproductive success of high-status individuals in the past, though not in modern populations,[1] the attributes of such individuals appear desirable to others. Commercial companies use high-status individuals to advertise the desirability of their products, with two main consequences. First, sales are indeed driven higher, and second, the gap between actual and ideal circumstances becomes itself a source of stress. For example, data from 21 developed countries showed that income inequality, a marker for increased stress in those of lower socio-economic status, is associated with the proportion of obese adults, and with the prevalence of diabetes (Pickett et al. 2005). In women, this association between income inequality and obesity remained after adjustment for variability in energy intake.

Through its impacts both on the working environment, and on the 'chase for status', capitalism is an important source of psycho-social stress. Changes in the social environment attributable to the evolution of hierarchical divisions of labour therefore may represent an important contributing factor to the obesity epidemic, although it is worth bearing in mind that alternative social structures may also have generated significant stress and that capitalism is also often associated with malnutrition.

10.7   Secular trends in reproductive behaviour

Economic transformations of society have altered the profile of female repro-duction, both decreasing family size and increasing average maternal age at first conception (Hicks and Allen 1999). Humans have used a variety of approaches for contraception over millennia; however, infanticide is likely to have been the primary mode of population control, simply because prior to the inven-tion of pharmacological contraceptives and surgical methods for abortion, the opportunities for manipulating conception and pregnancy must be assumed to have been limited. The introduction of the contraceptive pill, followed by other methods in the latter half of the twentieth century, has profoundly altered the rate of reproduction in Western women, though sex-specific abortion remains common in populations such as India and China (Fathalla 1998). Whereas most female primates in the wild are continuously either pregnant or lactating, many women in Western populations either control or prevent entirely the conception of offspring. Given the importance of energy stores in meeting the costs of pregnancy and lactation, albeit reduced when the diet is unrestricted, a major source of energy stress has been removed from such women.

---

[1] The low reproductive success of those of high social status in Western populations has long puzzled evolutionary biologists. Recently, Mace (2008) has suggested that high-status individuals *perceive* the costs of additional offspring as much higher than do low-status individuals, even though they have substantially greater resources in absolute terms.

The emergence of contraception has therefore contributed to population variability body fatness, but in a complex way. If cycles of pregnancy involve redistributions of body fat as proposed (Lassek and Gaulin 2006), women who undergo few or no pregnancies may preserve a less central adipose tissue distribution into later life. However, acting in opposition to such effects, age itself induces a more central adipose tissue distribution. Several studies have now described increasing maternal age as a risk factor for childhood obesity. For example, in a sample of girls aged 9 to 10 years, the risk of obesity increased by around 15% for every five-year increment in maternal age (Patterson et al. 1997). The mechanism whereby increasing maternal age may contribute to increased fatness in the offspring may thus relate to changes in metabolism or fat distribution; however, this needs further investigation.

The other component of reproductive function relevant to adiposity and sensitive to secular trends is breast-feeding, which may have implications for both mother and offspring. Formula-feeding was initiated at the start of the twentieth century, when the first commercial formulae were produced. Their uptake increased steadily until research raised doubts about possible health costs, and the promotion of breast-feeding has been a major public health exercise in both developed and developing countries in recent decades. Despite this, many mothers in both settings use formula-milk, often owing to economic pressures which prevent them from breast-feeding.

The evidence regarding possible associations between breast-feeding and obesity has been contradictory, perhaps because of inconsistency in the ways in which both breast-feeding and childhood obesity have been assessed. Despite meta-analyses suggesting a protective effect of breast-feeding for subsequent obesity risk (Owen et al. 2005; Arenz et al. 2004), the direct reduction in adiposity was extremely small in the large ALSPAC study and mostly attributable to confounding factors (Toschke et al. 2007). A similar lack of effect on adulthood body composition was reported in Brazil (Victora et al. 2003). The issue is notoriously difficult to research, since breast-feeding mothers differ from those formula-feeding in many background variables besides the content and manner of their nutritional intakes. However, there are several ways in which formula-feeding might be associated with obesity, and these require further work. Specific issues meriting investigation include variability in formula-milk energy density and glycaemic load, effects of the hormone leptin present in breast-milk, and associations between initial formula-feeding and the time of introduction and energy-density of complementary food. Improved characterisation of both breast-feeding and formula-feeding is required to test these ideas further.

More robust data are available for maternal outcomes in developed countries, where a systematic review showed that lactation is associated with a reduced risk of type-2 diabetes, as well as a reduced risk of breast and ovarian cancer and postpartum depression (Ip et al. 2007). Thus, the emergence of the formula-milk industry appears to be associated with a deleterious metabolic impact on both mother and offspring; however, the full nature of these associations requires elucidation.

10.8   Secular trends in exposure to pharmacological agents, toxins and disease

The individual toxin most studied in relation to obesity is tobacco, with many datasets providing high-quality data on variability in exposure. In general, smoking is associated with reduced appetite and hence with lower body weight (Chiolero et al. 2008). However, heavy smoking is associated with insulin resistance and increased central adiposity (Chiolero et al. 2008). With increasing evidence for associations between smoking and disease, increased public health campaigns, the prohibition of advertising, and litigation against tobacco manufacturers, the prevalence of smoking in industrialised populations is beginning to fall. In response, tobacco companies increasingly seek their profits outside Western populations, and the prevalence of smoking in modernising countries is increasing (West 2006). Furthermore, even as the prevalence of smoking reduces in industrialised populations, longer-term impacts on obesity may still occur through trans-generational mechanisms.

Smoking in pregnancy has been associated in several studies with an increased risk of obesity in the offspring (Oken, Levitan, and Gillman 2008), although whether such associations are due to physiological causation, acting, for example, through low birth weight, or merely reflect statistical associations between smoking and other obesogenic behaviour, remains unclear (Leary et al. 2006b). The tendency for cessation of smoking to induce weight gain (Filozof, Fernandez Pinilla, and Fernandez-Cruz 2004) may be particularly important in accounting for secular trends in birth weight, in turn associated with obesity in the offspring. In countries including the United States, Canada, the United Kingdom, Finland, Norway and India, birth weight has increased significantly in recent decades, although data from France conflict with this general pattern (Wells 2007f). This trend cannot be attributed to increases in average gestational age, as preterm births have in general increased during the same period (Joseph et al. 1998; Kramer et al. 2002), nor to a reduction in post-term births following induction, as the effect is apparent after adjustment for gestational age. Kramer and colleagues (2002) found an increase of 0.22 z-scores over the period 1978 to 1996 in a Canadian hospital, which became non-significant after adjustment for confounders. Amongst these confounders was a secular decline in maternal smoking, although changes in maternal body mass index and gestational age were also important contributing factors.

More broadly, increasing exposure to two types of chemical may be implicated in increasing obesity rates (Keith et al. 2006). First, endocrine disrupters generated by industry may predispose to increasing body fat, while a variety of medications such as antidepressants, anti-diabetics, anti-hypertensives, contraceptives and anti-histamines may also induce weight gain. Exposure to these chemicals has increased both through clinical practice and through commercial activities. More recently, treatments for the HIV/AIDS virus are known to induce altered fat distribution (Kotler 2008), which may transmit effects to the next generation.

The effect of secular trends in disease exposure on adiposity is difficult to evaluate, since whilst infectious diseases demand energy through the immune response, and have historically been associated with weight loss, they have also been associated with increased adiposity (Fernandez-Real et al. 2007). Broadly, there has been a decline in infectious disease and trauma since the industrial revolution consolidated, owing to improvements in living conditions, sanitation, nutrition and the development of vaccines. In the United Kingdom, for example, infectious and parasitic diseases accounted for one-third of all deaths in 1880, but only 17% in 1997 (Hicks and Allen 1999). The decline in infant mortality has been particularly notable, falling from 140 per 1000 in 1900 to fewer than 6 per 1000 in 1997 (Hicks and Allen 1999). Given the trade-off between immune function and growth (Prentice and Darboe 2008), it is plausible that national vaccination programmes, by drastically reducing the incidence of many childhood diseases, have contributed to faster growth rates, which in turn may contribute to the potential for overweight, but empirical data for this hypothesis are lacking. An infection previously common in industrialised populations, H pylori, has been associated with decreased levels of ghrelin, the hormone signalling hunger (Shiotani et al. 2005). Logic therefore suggests that a reducing disease burden might promote appetite, and this generic hypothesis merits further attention.

10.9   The global obesity epidemic

Despite being the focus of a massive quantity of research in the last two decades, the global obesity epidemic could still be said to be taking the biomedical community by surprise. The Western biomedical model is primarily pathogen-oriented and focused at reducing the transmission of disease vectors through vaccination or the promotion of hygiene, and the treatment of infection within the body.

Lifestyle diseases such as the metabolic syndrome, cardiovascular disease and cancers have a very different biological basis, emerging through long-term behavioural patterns and being sensitive to trans-generational factors. The level of obesity that we see today reflects in part the exposure of previous generations to the obesogenic niche or paradoxically to undernutrition. Rose (1982) referred to the incubation period of cardiovascular disease, describing an improved ability of prior, compared to current, physiological traits to predict the likelihood of death. In contrast to this 'hidden' scenario, obesity represents a more visible manifestation of ill-health, although its deleterious effects may also take time to emerge. Global trends in obesity therefore offer a stark warning as to the future burden of disease. Type-2 diabetes, previously termed 'adult onset diabetes', is increasingly recorded in overweight and obese children (Haines et al. 2007). Whilst the concept of obesity as a disease requires careful examination (see below), at the population level the obese show increased risk of the metabolic syndrome with implications both for the health of individuals and the costs of treatment.

The secular trend in obesity can be described only with a degree of impre-cision because of population inconsistencies in the relationship between the primary obesity index (BMI) and body fatness. Subject to these limitations, there is nevertheless ample evidence of an extraordinarily rapid increase in the prevalence of overweight and obesity. The sheer speed of the epidemic in the American population is striking (Mokdad et al. 1999). There is little need to present any data here, in part because the phenomenon is well established, and in part because any data will rapidly become out-of-date. Nor is the obe-sity epidemic restricted to Western industrialised populations. Excess weight is rapidly becoming as significant a public health problem as malnutrition in many developing countries, and the number of overweight or obese individuals worldwide now exceeds the number underweight (Popkin 2007).

From a health-economics perspective, the outlook looks bleak. Obesity once developed is difficult to treat, and at the present time pharmacological and behavioural management have failed to make a significant impact. Bariatric surgery is currently the most successful treatment; however, it is likely that improved pharmacological strategies and novel approaches such as vaccination (Zorrilla et al. 2006) will emerge in the future. Efforts to prevent obesity appear equally unsuccessful at the present time, which can be attributed largely to the lack of willingness of governments and commercial companies to alter the constraints which act on the behaviour of individuals. This chapter has highlighted the way in which a number of secular trends, operating above the level of the individual, impact on energy balance, and given the sensitivity of energy metabolism to such ecological factors, excess weight gain is inevitable in the majority of individuals.

Yet, from another perspective, our understanding of this interaction is improving. This book has aimed to contribute by elucidating the evolutionary biology of human adiposity. If this knowledge can be converted into strategies, there is no reason why alterations to the Western industrialised niche might not be achieved, leading to reduced obesity prevalence. Realistically, sociological changes need to occur over more than one generation, given that adiposity in each generation partly reflects ecological exposures in the previous one.

10.10   Obesity and capitalism

The obesity epidemic offers a powerful reminder of the intricate relationship between physiology and human ecology. We are perhaps a species 'designed' for excess, with our extraordinarily sophisticated but expensive brains that allow us to manipulate both our physical environment and our fellow humans, and our profligate colonising reproductive strategy. Prior to the emergence of agriculture, a set of factors limited the capture of energy from the environment. Since the industrial revolution these factors have been not only eroded but replaced by others acting on groups as well as individuals that proactively promote energy transfer. In the twenty-first century, there is much similarity between the obesity epidemic and another major problem confronting our species, global warming. Both challenges have in common an excessive utilisation of energy within the ecosystems that humans occupy, and because humans occupy the majority of the planet's ecosystems, the effects are being felt at a global level. In both cases, if the response is aimed primarily at the level of the individual, success is likely to be limited and long in coming. Many of the 'choices' that people might make have, in reality, already been made for them by governments and commercial companies.

What emerges from the history of obesity is the integral role of capitalism in manipulating behaviour. Capitalism takes many forms and involves numerous dimensions, such as the supposedly 'free market' economy, private enterprise and profit, and the feedback of market forces on trade interactions, but my emphasis here is on the current obsession with continual economic growth, its fundamental role in manipulating consumers' behaviour, and on the unequal distribution of power and wealth that it enables. Individuals are influenced at many biological levels by capitalism, and variably so according to their social and economic status. Many of these influences translate directly into differential exposure to the obesogenic niche. Obesity might therefore be considered the message of capitalism written across the body – a visible symbol of how corporate profits have been maximised by a number of interest groups focusing on food, entertainment and travel (Nestle 2003). Today's children are encountering these economic forces before they have even been born, through the impact

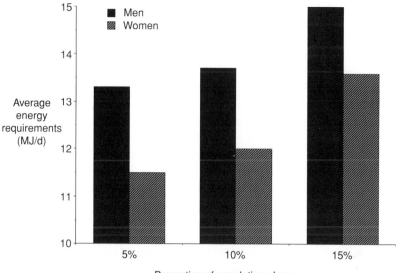

Figure 10.2. Simple simulation of the effect of increasing obesity prevalence on population energy requirements. The proportions of normal weight (<25 kg/m^2), overweight (25 to 29.99 kg/m^2), grade-1 obese (30 to 34.99 kg/m^2) and grade-2 obese (>35 kg/m^2) individuals were modelled as (a) 75, 10, 5 and 0 %, (b) 60, 15, 10 and 5%, and (c) 55, 20, 15 and 10%. Using data on energy requirements of these four BMI categories (Prentice et al. 1996), the average per capita daily energy requirement was calculated. This simulation demonstrates the greater quantity of food required as obesity prevalence increases.

of maternal pregnancy physiology. Profits are maximised through predictable behaviour, and the food and leisure industries in combination with other working practices have steadily altered when, where, how and what we eat, and our physical activity patterns. Profits are also maximised by converting individuals into a docile population of passive consumers of experience (Mintz 1985), who are nevertheless encouraged to aspire to a lifestyle of conspicuous consumption.

Capitalism emerged from the foundations of the sugar plantations (Mintz 1985), and it is no accident that the contemporary obesogenic niche is constructed from the manipulative interaction of economic forces, calories and carbohydrate. Sucrose and profit have been linked for centuries and today's overweight and obese people with their higher energy expenditures and hence increased needs are a reliable and growing source of financial income for those selling food. Numerous reports of the diet of those obese suggests a high intake of refined carbohydrate foodstuffs (Taubes 2008). Figure 10.2 presents a simple simulation of the number of calories consumed by a population of fixed size as the prevalence of obesity increases, based on the data of Prentice and colleagues (1996). The increased energy requirements translate directly into increased food sales. A second fortuitous source of income then derives from the diet industry, which is increasingly suggested to have contributed to, rather than ameliorated, obesity. Responding to the promotion of low-fat diets, dieters have switched to high-carbohydrate diets which often have a high glycaemic load (La Berge 2008), a critical factor predisposing to weight gain. The food industry has thus developed two self-reinforcing markets, while mitigating criticism by pointing to the wide choice of products available. More broadly, 'it is hard to think of any major industry that might benefit if people ate less food; certainly not the agriculture, food product, grocery, restaurant, diet or drug industries. All flourish when people eat more, and all employ armies of lobbyists to discourage governments from doing anything to inhibit overeating' (Nestle 2003).

One might ask how companies manage consistently to sell people more food than they actually need. Economic theory predicts that individuals buy a product for a price that seems reasonable, and that they should refuse to purchase products they do not want or need. However, the food industry outflanks this prediction in two ways. First, individuals no longer know the absolute value of food, because they no longer participate in its production. They are therefore influenced by notions of value, and by promotions such as 'two-for-the-price-of-one' or a better-value larger portion size. Second, the food industry has created an entire dietary niche that by-passes natural appetite regulation – energy-containing drinks. There is a limit to how much solid food that can be consumed, because stomach capacity acts as an inherent limitation. Energy-containing drinks are not constrained in this way, and the explosion of the sugar-based drinks market represents a coherent out-manoeuvring of appetite control. Systematic reviews show associations of soft drink consumption and obesity in children, adolescents and adults (Malik, Schulze, and Hu 2006; Harrington 2008), translating into increased cardiovascular risk in middle-aged adults (Dhingra et al. 2007). These two mechanisms are only two amongst a general pattern of behavioural manipulation by commercial companies. The US food supply equates to approximately twice the average daily energy need, and to get rid of the excess, companies compete for consumers, especially children, through adverts, new products, larger portions and health claims (Nestle 2003).

Highlighting the structural association between our current model of capitalism and contemporary ill-health is not an extreme ideological assault. From a purely economic perspective, capitalism has performed well in comparison with other economic models, which has contributed to its historical 'success' in recent centuries. Moreover, capitalism is neither good nor bad for health in a simplistic sense. Improved living conditions in some populations since the industrial revolution can be attributed at a number of levels to the benefits of private enterprise. However, benefits to some populations have been obtained at the expense of costs to others, and the economic development of Europe went hand in hand with the underdevelopment of Africa and other colonial regions (Rodney 1972). The childhood stunting so prevalent in ex-colonial countries, and now a risk factor for obesity as these countries urbanise and industrialise, is partly a direct legacy of those former economic imbalances. Within populations, the tobacco industry is well established to have a conflict of interest between population health and profit, and the infant-formula industry is another well-known example. What is good for profit is often bad for the health of individuals or populations, and yet part of the success of Western capitalism has been its capacity to avoid confronting this issue. Multi-national corporations operate outside national boundaries, and national public health policies appear readily outflanked by globalised economic influences.

Historically, humans have been affected most by infectious diseases, and the Western biomedical model evolved in response. Today's main sources of morbidity and mortality, not only in industrialised but also in modernising populations, are the so-called lifestyle diseases – cardiovascular disease, diabetes, stroke, hypertension, cancer and physical accidents associated with vehicles. The biomedical model is still coming to terms with the implications of these secular trends, whereby the risk factors for disease are behaviours and the social vectors that underlie their spread amongst populations. Western medicine has a century of experience tackling the role of the mosquito in transmitting malaria, but very little expertise in tackling the corporate strategies that prop up the obesogenic niche. When appropriate biomedical evidence is available, governments have been slow to regulate industry because they benefit from corporate taxation.

The market forces of capitalism continually incorporate more and more of the world's population. In recent decades, large multi-national food companies are turning to modernising countries as a new source of profit. A scan of such company's websites typically reveals a description of specific energy-dense products high in refined carbohydrate targeted at the enormous populations of countries such as India, Brazil and China. The number of private vehicles is likewise escalating rapidly in the cities of developing country, driven by the manufacturers' pursuit of sales opportunities generated by the status accorded to such luxury items. Just as early private enterprise was originally conducted 'offshore' and out of sight in the slave plantations, so contemporary profits of multi-national corporations are increasingly generated somewhat invisibly, in the growing cities of Brazil, China and India. Much of the profit extracted from modernising countries will derive from the rapidly expanding urban slums (Davis 2006), where newly arrived migrants turn for the first time to commercial food products whilst simultaneously entering the industrialised economy.

Capitalism is particularly potent in its effects on female reproductive biology. The high energy burden of offspring care has impacted on female biology throughout human evolution, resulting in an unusually sensitive pregnancy physiology (Haig 1993), an unusual sexual division of labour, and an unprecedented level of cooperative breeding relative to other mammals. Economic factors target female biology at many levels, impacting on the schedule of reproduction, pregnancy metabolism, and the likelihood of breast-feeding. In doing so, they contribute directly to the physiological induction of obesity in the next generation. Less directly, economic factors disrupt the transfer of women's knowledge and expertise in the care and nutrition of offspring. For example, the spread of formula-feeding in the United States induced a collective loss of practical experience regarding breast-feeding (Maher 1992), preventing the trans-generational transfer of expertise. This is turn reduces the success rate of breast-feeding in contemporary populations. From a historical perspective, the exposure of women to under-nutrition through imperial economic policies in previous generations contributes to growth patterns and increased obesity risk in contemporary populations (Wells 2010).

The inadvertent role of women in transmitting obesity risk to their offspring should not, however, detract from emphasis on themselves. Figure 10.3 illustrates sex differences in the prevalence of adult obesity according to several broad global regions. Whereas in relatively affluent populations such as Europe, North America, Australasia and several Asian populations the two sexes have similar obesity prevalences, obesity tends to be commoner in women compared to men in South American, Middle Eastern, African and Caribbean populations. In African and Caribbean populations, women are roughly twice as likely to be obese as men, and a similar trend is emerging in poorer Asian countries such as India and Pakistan, despite their lower absolute BMI values. These data indicate, as do those of Europe, an interaction between countries' socio-economic status and the disproportionate exposure of women to obesogenic factors. This in turn highlights that women are more vulnerable to the population inequalities that derive from the globalised economy. Poor rural women are not outside the global economy, they are merely the category with the least capacity to evade commercial manipulation of their behaviour. Reflecting the economics of agriculture and trade, the cheapest foods are often those based on refined carbohydrate. The Pima Indians of Arizona, notorious for their high rates of obesity today, do not appear to have suffered from this condition 150 years ago. Obesity arrived in combination with poverty, duly addressed by a United States government ration which (on the basis of data from similar scenarios elsewhere) provided around half its calories from sugar and flour (Taubes 2008).

Interacting with this effect of dietary composition, the higher obesity prevalence in women may be mediated by different factors in different global regions,

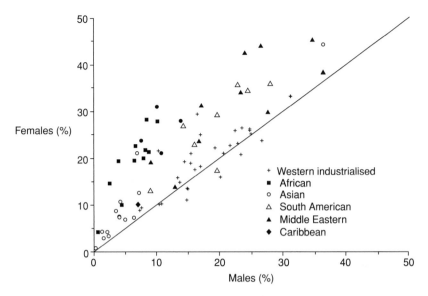

Figure 10.3. Sex differences in the prevalence of obesity categorised by BMI according to global region. Though BMI is an imperfect means of categorising obesity across populations, as discussed in Chapter 2 it has utility for indicating the approximate magnitude of such sex differences. In Western industrialised populations, such as Europe, North America and Australasia, the prevalence of obesity is similar between the sexes. There is also little difference in Asian populations. A moderately greater female prevalence is apparent in South American populations, and a substantially greater female prevalence in African, Middle Eastern and Caribbean populations. Data from http://www.iotf.org/database/documents/ GlobalPrevalenceofAdultObesity8thOctober08.pdf

relating variously to issues such as gender bias in children's nutrition,[2] fetal exposure to maternal work during pregnancy, or constraints on adult behaviour for religious reason. Thus, capitalism is by no means the only issue of relevance, and access to education and social independence as well as economic development are important. Nevertheless, the association of increased female obesity and economic factors strongly implies that addressing women's livelihoods will bring particular benefits to their health, whilst further passing these benefits on to subsequent generations. For many reasons, therefore, the impact of capitalism on women is of especial concern.

Just as capitalism has an integral association with calories, so has obesity become structurally embedded in the same web. For the clinician, obesity may represent a problem, but for several global industries, obesity represents a

[2] The greater prevalence of obesity in women may derive in part form their greater vulnerability to early-life under-nutrition owing to a preferential feeding of male children.

rewarding opportunity (Cannon 2008). Whilst those overweight consume more food, they may also receive expensive pharmacological treatments, fuelling the profits of the pharmaceutical industry. The simplicity of the categorisation of obesity is now well established. Many professional sportsmen have a BMI in the overweight or obese range owing to their high muscle mass rather than extreme adiposity. A comprehensive study of over 27,000 adults from 52 countries showed that waist girth is a far more sensitive predictor of cardiovascular mortality than BMI (Yusuf et al. 2005). The BMI category of overweight has been suggested to capture those 'pre-obese' and bring them into the market for treatments regardless of whether their cardiovascular risk warrants weight loss (Cannon 2008). This point is made not to belittle the health risks associated with the condition of obesity, which are well established,[3] but to probe the nature of this association. If abdominal fat, physical inactivity and energy-dense diets are more closely related to cardiovascular risk than BMI itself, then it may be those traits and behaviours, over and above weight loss, that merit clinical management (Cannon 2008). The obesogenic niche is best considered one in which individuals' behaviour and physiology is altered with consequences for metabolism, rather than simply one in which 'people get heavy or fat'.

Individuals can try to resist the impact of this niche. Many are aware of the benefits of doing so, and they promote different lifestyles and diets while attempting to reject market influences. The reality is that most face significant physical, social or economic impediments to such behaviours and lack the resources or coordination to oppose the power of multi-national corporations. The growing urban populations, not least those in the rapidly expanding slums of many developing countries, are available for economic manipulation simply because they have already lost most control over their food supply and activity patterns. However much governments hope to address obesity by promoting behavioural change in individuals, it is likely that only efforts to tackle the obesogenic niche itself will make a significant impact.

10.11   The future of obesity

Humans evolved as an animal in which fuel supply and energy stores integrate diverse functions – a combination of thrift and control. Like a tug-of-war when

---

[3] For example, one in four Australians aged 25 years or more is predicted to develop diabetes in the next 5–10 years (Frankish 2001), a risk associated directly with overweight and obesity prevalences of 40 and 20%, respectively. Obese adolescents with type-2 diabetes are at high risk of limb amputation and kidney failure (Ludwig 2007). Obesity is already increasing the risk of premature death in adolescents (Ludwig 2007), and it is implicated in falls in life expectancy (Ezzati et al. 2008).

everyone stops pulling at the same time, humans in an obesogenic environment no longer maintain coherent physiology, as the metabolic pathways that evolved to integrate homeostasis, physical activity, appetite, immune function and reproductive function are disrupted by contradictory influences. Plentiful energy availability is not the sum total of the obesogenic niche, but it does aid the manifestation of high levels of adiposity. Yet dietary energy is not an infinite resource, and there are signs that counterbalancing factors constraining global energy availability are emerging.

Today's obesity epidemic has been enabled in part by the mechanisation of agriculture, replacing human labour with petroleum-dependent machinery, resulting in cheap food being available throughout industrialised populations (McNeill 2000). More recently, the green revolution was essentially a nitrogen revolution – developing high-productivity crop strains and then enabling their implementation through nitrogen-based fertilisers, generated from natural gas supplies. This technology has led to a seven-fold increase in the application of nitrogen fertilisers since the 1960s (Tilman 1998). Yet, once again, agricultural productivity cannot be considered outside of the context of capitalism. Within countries, the economics of agriculture may directly contradict those of health. For example, even as biomedical practitioners have attempted to promote reduced food consumption, US economic policy has encouraged ever higher agricultural productivity (Tillotson 2004). At an international level, the supposedly free market is beset by national regulation, regional subsidies that distort trade economics, and export agriculture at the expense of local food production. At the start of the twenty-first century, a number of factors are beginning to stress this global food production system.

In the first decade of the twenty-first century, agriculture is being targeted in a new direction, producing biofuels to reduce fossil fuel consumption (Lancet 2008). This strategy, diverting land away from food production, is already implicated in rising food prices and is contributing to the re-emergence of food insecurity on the global agenda. It is, however, increasingly discredited as a strategy for addressing climate change (Lancet 2008). Global warming is also challenging agricultural productivity in many countries by increasing climatic volatility. For example, crop yields in developing countries have fallen substantially for at least a decade (Lancet 2008). Until recently, famines tended to be local and attributable to specific political events, but the new globalised economy links every geographical region, and the economic policies of industrialised populations impact rapidly on those of less-developed populations. Current tensions may be resolved by new policies, but globalisation is increasingly linking the prevalence of over- and under-nutrition in different parts of the world.

In the 1970s, global food insecurity was relatively successfully addressed by the green revolution, though more so in Asia than in Africa owing to the emphasis on rice and wheat strains (McNeill 2000). In response to this new food supply, the world's population has continued to grow at, from a long-term view, a phenomenal rate. We could be said to be colonising the modern agricultural niche in the way that our distant ancestors colonised new territory (Wells and Stock 2007). Now, however, there is little new land available for cultivation, especially as the world undergoes continued urbanisation, and hence increased productivity is required within existing areas of farmland. India manages to feed 17% of the world's population using only 3% of the world's farmland (Economist 19/04/2008), but the challenge is stark. Agricultural technological progress takes time, and improved farm yields cannot emerge overnight. As this book goes to press in 2009, India is experiencing another failed monsoon and poor harvests.

The food crisis emerging in 2008 may prove to be short-lived, addressed in the short-term by humanitarian programmes while economic policies adapt to the longer-term challenge. As always, the poor will take the strain, with the 1 billion people living on less than $1 per day most vulnerable to increased food prices (Lancet 2008). As discussed by Brown and Konner in their pioneering article on evolution and obesity (1987), the 'function' of the poor in agricultural societies is to insulate the rich, and this relationship is now being played out at an international level.

Global warming and climate instability may, however, make this crisis more fundamental. The world's population continues to grow, the supply of farmland is limited, and the main route to increasing agricultural productivity involves the very activities (intensive use of machinery and fertilisers) that are also driving greenhouse emissions and making agricultural yields more unpredictable. Some have suggested that humans adopted agriculture only when the climate became sufficiently stable for this subsistence mode to generate reliable food supplies (Richerson, Boyd, and Bettinger 2001). The destabilising effects of the capitalist economic model on energy utilisation may ultimately prove so profound that the seemingly unlimited food supply experienced by many in the late twentieth century might prove merely a temporary state, an illusion of feast with a genuine global famine still to come.

This book has focused on the evolutionary biology of human body fat, but in doing so it has tried to show that the kind of animal we are makes us vulnerable to our current economic niche. Over-nutrition and under-nutrition, both major manifestations of ill-health, might appear opposite sides of the spectrum, but in reality they are structurally linked. Both are associated with high rates of energy turnover in industrialised countries, which in turn is driven by an economic model that generates wealth by manipulating the behaviour of individuals and populations. Capturing energy from the environment and manipulating its allocation to survival and breeding has been the hallmark of human evolutionary success and recent global colonisation, but the scale and manner of contemporary human energy use will ultimately prove unsustainable. The epidemic of human obesity acts as a marker of the increasingly disruptive impact of our economic system on human biology, and its greater prevalence in less-affluent women highlights both the disproportionate role of the maternal energy budget during hominin evolution, and the disproportionate vulnerability of contemporary women to economic manipulation.

References

Aagaard-Tillery KM, Grove K, Bishop J, Ke X, Fu Q, McKnight R, and Lane RH (2008) Developmental origins of disease and determinants of chromatin structure: maternal diet modifies the primate fetal epigenome. *Journal of Molecular Endocrinology* 41 (2):91–102.

Abdullah M and Wheeler EF (1985) Seasonal variations, and the intra-household distribution of food in a Bangladeshi village. *American Journal of Clinical Nutrition* 41 (6):1305–1313.

Adair LS (1992) Postpartum nutritional status of Filipino women. *American Journal of Human Biology* 4:635–646.

Adair LS and Cole TJ (2003) Rapid child growth raises blood pressure in adolescent boys who were thin at birth. *Hypertension* 41 (3):451–456.

Adams AM (1995) Seasonal variations in energy balance among agriculturalists in central Mali: compromise or adaptation? *European Journal of Clinical Nutrition* 49 (11):809–823.

Agras WS, Hammer LD, McNicholas F, and Kraemer HC (2004) Risk factors for childhood overweight: a prospective study from birth to 9.5 years. *Journal of Pediatrics* 145 (1):20–25.

Agras WS, Kraemer HC, Berkowitz RI, Korner AF, and Hammer LD (1987) Does a vigorous feeding style influence early development of adiposity? *Journal of Pediatrics* 110 (5):799–804.

Ahima RS (2006) Adipose tissue as an endocrine organ. *Obesity (Silver.Spring)* 14 Suppl 5:242S–249S.

Ahmed SM, Adams A, Chowdhury AM, and Bhuiya A (1998) Chronic energy deficiency in women from rural Bangladesh: some socioeconomic determinants. *Journal of Biosocial Science* 30 (3):349–358.

Aiello LC and Key C (2002) Energetic consequences of being a Homo erectus female. *American Journal of Human Biology* 14 (5):551–565.

Aiello LC and Wells JC (2002) Energetics and the evolution of the genus *Homo*. *Annual Review of Anthropology* 31:323–338.

Aiello LC and Wheeler P (1995) The expensive-tissue hypothesis: the brain and the digestive-system in human and primate evolution. *Current Anthropology* 36 (2):199–221.

Akachi Y and Canning D (2007) The height of women in Sub-Saharan Africa: the role of health, nutrition, and income in childhood. *Annals of Human Biology* 34 (4):397–410.

Al Mamun, Lawlor DA, Cramb S, O'Callaghan M, Williams G, and Najman J (2007) Do childhood sleeping problems predict obesity in young adulthood? Evidence

302

from a prospective birth cohort study. *American Journal of Epidemiology* 166 (12):1368–1373.

Alam, DS, Van Raaij JM, Hautvast JG, Yunus M, and Fuchs GJ (2003) Energy stress during pregnancy and lactation: consequences for maternal nutrition in rural Bangladesh. *European Journal of Clinical Nutrition* 57 (1):151–156.

Allen JS and Cheer SM (1996) The non-thrifty genotype. *Current Anthropology* 37:831–842.

Allison DB, Paultre F, Heymsfield SB, and Pi-Sunyer FX (1995) Is the intra-uterine period really a critical period for the development of adiposity? *International Journal of Obesity and Related Metabolic Disorders* 19 (6):397–402.

Allman J, Hakeem A, and Watson K (2002) Two phylogenetic specializations in the human brain. *Neuroscience* 8:335–346.

Altmann J, Schoeller D, Altmann SA, Muruthi P, and Sapolsky RM (1993) Body size and fatness of free-living baboons reflect food availability and activity levels. *American Journal of Primatology* 30:149–161.

Ancel A, Visser H, Handrich Y, Masman D, and Maho YL (1997) Energy saving in huddling penguins. *Nature* 385:304–305.

Andersen RE, Crespo CJ, Bartlett SJ, Cheskin LJ, and Pratt M (1998) Relationship of physical activity and television watching with body weight and level of fatness among children: results from the Third National Health and Nutrition Examination Survey. *Journal of the American Medical Association* 279 (12):938–942.

Anderson J, Osborn SB, Tomlinson RW, Newton D, Rundo J, Salmin L, and Smith JW (1964) Neutron-activation analysis in man in vivo: a new technique in medical investigation. *Lancet* 2 (7371):1201–1205.

Anton SC, Leonard WR, and Robertson ML (2002) An ecomorphological model of the initial hominid dispersal from Africa. *Journal of Human Evolution* 43 (6):773–785.

Arenz S, Ruckerl R, Koletzko B, and von KR (2004) Breast-feeding and childhood obesity: a systematic review. *International Journal of Obesity and Related Metabolic Disorders* 28 (10):1247–1256.

Arfai K, Pitukcheewanont PD, Goran MI, Tavare CJ, Heller L, and Gilsanz V (2002) Bone, muscle, and fat: sex-related differences in prepubertal children. *Radiology* 224 (2):338–344.

Armstrong E (1983) Relative brain size and metabolism in mammals. *Science* 220 (4603):1302–1304.

Astrup A (2001) The role of dietary fat in the prevention and treatment of obesity: efficacy and safety of low-fat diets. *International Journal of Obesity and Related Metabolic Disorders* 25 Suppl 1:S46–S50.

Astrup A, Astrup A, Buemann B, Flint A, and Raben A (2002) Low-fat diets and energy balance: how does the evidence stand in 2002? *Proceedings of the Nutrition Society* 61 (2):299–309.

Atanassova P, Tonchev AB, Peneva VN, Chaldakov GN, Valchanov KP, Fiore M, and Aloe L (2007) What are subcutaneous adipocytes really good for? Viewpoint 3. *Experimental Dermatology* 16:56–59.

Atkin LM and Davies PS (2000) Diet composition and body composition in preschool children. *American Journal of Clinical Nutrition* 72 (1):15–21.

Atwater WO and Benedict FG (1903) Experiments on the metabolism of energy and matter in the human body: Bulletin 136. Office of Experimental Studies: United States Department of Agriculture.

Badman MK and Flier JS (2007) The adipocyte as an active participant in energy balance and metabolism. *Gastroenterology* 132 (6):2103–2115.

Bailey KV (1965) Quantity and composition of breastmilk in some New Guinean populations. *Journal of Tropical Pediatrics and Environmental Child Health* 11 (2):35–49.

Baird J, Fisher D, Lucas P, Kleijnen J, Roberts H, and Law C (2005) Being big or growing fast: systematic review of size and growth in infancy and later obesity. *British Medical Journal* 331 (7522):929.

Ballew C and Haas JD (1986) Altitude differences in body composition among Bolivian newborns. *Human Biology* 58 (6):871–882.

Bandini LG, Schoeller DA, and Dietz WH (1990) Energy expenditure in obese and nonobese adolescents. *Pediatric Research* 27 (2):198–203.

Banting W (1864) *Letter on corpulence*. Harrison: London.

Barac-Nieto M, Spurr GB, Lotero H, and Maksud MG (1978) Body composition in chronic undernutrition. *American Journal of Clinical Nutrition* 31 (1):23–40.

Barbosa L, Butte NF, Villalpando S, Wong WW, and Smith EO (1997) Maternal energy balance and lactation performance of Mesoamerindians as a function of body mass index. *American Journal of Clinical Nutrition* 66 (3):575–583.

Barker DJ (1998) *Mothers, babies and health in later life*. Churchill: Edinburgh.

Barker DJ, Osmond C, Forsen TJ, Kajantie E, and Eriksson JG (2005) Trajectories of growth among children who have coronary events as adults. *New England Journal of Medicine* 353 (17):1802–1809.

Barker G, Barton H, Beavitt P, Bird M, Daly P, and et al. (2002) Prehistoric foragers and farmers in Southeast Asia: renewed investigations at Niah Cave, Sarawak. *Proceedings of the Prehistoric Society* 68:147–164.

Barker M, Robinson S, Osmond C, and Barker DJ (1997) Birth weight and body fat distribution in adolescent girls. *Archives of Diseases in Childhood* 77 (5):381–383.

Barraclough DJ, Conroy ML, and Lee D (2004) Prefrontal cortex and decision making in a mixed-strategy game. *Nature Neuroscience* 7 (4):404–410.

Barreiro LB, Laval G, Quach H, Patin E, and Quintana-Murci L (2008) Natural selection has driven population differentiation in modern humans. *Nature Genetics* 40 (3):340–345.

Bateson P (2001) Fetal experience and good adult design. *International Journal of Epidemiology* 30 (5):928–934.

Bateson P, Barker D, Clutton-Brock T, Deb D, D'Udine B, Foley RA, Gluckman P, Godfrey K, Kirkwood T, Lahr MM, McNamara J, Metcalfe NB, Monaghan P, Spencer HG, and Sultan SE (2004) Developmental plasticity and human health. *Nature* 430 (6998):419–421.

Bateson P and Martin PC (1999) *Design for a life: how behaviour develops*. Cape: London.

Batterham RL, Cowley MA, Small CJ, Herzog H, Cohen MA, Dakin CL, Wren AM, Brynes AE, Low MJ, Ghatei MA, Cone RD, and Bloom SR (2002) Gut hormone PYY(3–36) physiologically inhibits food intake. *Nature* 418 (6898):650–654.

Bavdekar A, Yajnik CS, Fall CHD, Bapat S, Pandit AN, Deshpande V, Bhave S, Kellingray SD, and Joglekar C (1999) Insulin resistance syndrome in 8-year-old Indian children: small at birth, big at 8 years, or both? *Diabetes* 48 (12):2422–2429.

Beall CM and Goldstein MC (1992) High prevalence of excess fat and central fat patterning among Mongolian pastoral nomads. *American Journal of Human Biology* 4:747–756.

Beaton GH (1989) Small but healthy? Are we asking the right question? *European Journal of Clinical Nutrition* 43 (12):863–875.

Behar DM, Villems R, Soodyall H, Blue-Smith J, Pereira L, Metspalu E, Scozzari R, Makkan H, Tzur S, Comas D, Bertranpetit J, Quintana-Murci L, Tyler-Smith C, Wells RS, and Rosset S (2008) The dawn of human matrilineal diversity. *American Journal of Human Genetics* 82 (5):1130–1140.

Behnke AR, Feen BG, and Welham WC (1942) The specific gravity of healthy men. *Journal of the American Medical Association* 118:495–498.

Bell SJ and Sears B (2003) Low-glycemic diets: impact on obesity and chronic diseases. *Critical Reviews in Food Science and Nutrition* 43:357–377.

Belsky J, Steinberg L, and Draper P (1991) Childhood experience, interpersonal development, and reproductive strategy: an evolutionary theory of socialization. *Child Development* 62 (4):647–670.

Benhariz M, Goulet O, Salas J, Colomb V, and Ricour C (1997) Energy cost of fever in children on total parenteral nutrition. *Clinical Nutrition* 16 (5):251–255.

Benn RT (1971) Some mathematical properties of weight-for-height indices used as measures of adiposity. *British Journal of Preventive and Social Medicine* 1971 Feb;25(1):42–50.

Benyshek DC and Watson JT (2006) Exploring the thrifty genotype's food-shortage assumptions: a cross-cultural comparison of ethnographic accounts of food security among foraging and agricultural societies. *American Journal of Physical Anthropology* 131 (1):120–126.

Berg AH and Scherer PE (2005) Adipose tissue, inflammation, and cardiovascular disease. *Circulation Research* 96 (9):939–949.

Bergmann C (1847) Über die Verhältnisse der wärmeökonomie der Thiere zu ihrer Grösse. *Göttinger Studien* 3:595–708.

Bernard A, Zwingelstein G, Meister R, and Wild TF (1988) Hyperinsulinemia induced by canine distemper virus infection of mice and its correlation with the appearance of obesity. *Comparative Biochemistry and Physiology B* 91 (4):691–696.

Bernstein IM, Goran MI, Amini SB, and Catalano PM (1997) Differential growth of fetal tissues during the second half of pregnancy. *American Journal of Obstetrics and Gynecology* 176 (1 Pt 1):28–32.

Bhadra M, Mukhopadhyay A, and Bose K (2005) Differences in body composition between pre-menarcheal and menarcheal Bengalee Hindu girls of Madhyamgram, West bengal, India. *Anthropological Science* 113:141–145.

Billewicz WZ and McGregor IA (1981) The demography of two West African (Gambian) villages, 1951–75. *Journal of Biosocial Science* 13:219–240.

Binh TQ, Davis TM, Johnston W, Thu LT, Boston R, Danh PT, and Anh TK (1997) Glucose metabolism in severe malaria: minimal model analysis of the intravenous glucose tolerance test incorporating a stable glucose label. *Metabolism* 46 (12):1435–1440.

Binkley JK, Eales J, and Jekanowski M (2000) The relation between dietary change and rising US obesity. *International Journal of Obesity and Related Metabolic Disorders* 24 (8):1032–1039.

Bjorntorp P (1997) Hormonal control of regional fat distribution. *Human Reproduction* 12 Suppl 1:21–25.

Blaxter, KL (1989) *Energy metabolism in animals and man.* Cambridge University Press: Cambridge.

Blundell JE and Greenough A (1994) Pharmacological aspects of appetite: implications for the treatment of obesity. *Biomedical Pharmacotherapy* 48 (3–4):119–125.

Bogin B (1988) *Patterns of human growth.* Cambridge University Press: Cambridge.

Bogin B (2001) *The growth of humanity.* Wiley-Liss: New York.

Bogin B and Varela-Silva MIO (2006) Life history trade-offs in human growth. *American Journal of Physical Anthropology*: 66–67.

Bonneaud C, Mazuc J, Gonzalez G, Haussy C, Chastel O, Faivre B, and Sorci G (2003) Assessing the cost of mounting an immune response. *American Naturalist* 161 (3):367–379.

Bonner JT (1965) *Size and cycle.* Princeton University Press: Princeton, NJ.

Boserup E (1965) *The conditions of agricultural growth.* Aldine: Chicago.

Botton J, Heude B, Maccario J, Ducimetiere P, and Charles MA (2008) Postnatal weight and height growth velocities at different ages between birth and 5 y and body composition in adolescent boys and girls. *American Journal of Clinical Nutrition* 87 (6):1760–1768.

Bouchard C (2007) The biological predisposition to obesity: beyond the thrifty genotype scenario. *International Journal of Obesity (London).*

Bouchard C, Tremblay A, Despres JP, Nadeau A, Lupien PJ, Theriault G, Dussault J, Moorjani S, Pinault S, and Fournier G (1990) The response to long-term overfeeding in identical twins. *New England Journal of Medicine* 322 (21):1477–1482.

Bouchard C, Tremblay A, Despres JP, Theriault G, Nadeau A, Lupien PJ, Moorjani S, Prudhomme D, and Fournier G (1994) The response to exercise with constant energy intake in identical twins. *Obesity Research* 2 (5):400–410.

Bouchard C, Tremblay A, Despres JP, Nadeau A, Lupien PJ, Moorjani S, Theriault G, and SY Kim (1996) Overfeeding in identical twins: 5-year postoverfeeding results. *Metabolism* 45 (8):1042–1050.

Bowler JM, Johnston H, Olley JM, Prescott JR, Roberts RG, Shawcross W, and Spooner NA (2003) New ages for human occupation and climatic change at Lake Mungo, Australia. *Nature* 421 (6925):837–840.

Boyle R (1660) *New Experiments Physico-Mechanicall, Touching the Spring of the Air, and its Effects (Made, for the Most Part, in a New Pneumatical Engine).* H. Hall: Oxford.

Bray GA (1990) Obesity: historical development of scientific and cultural ideas. *International Journal of Obesity* 14 (11):909–926.

Bray GA, Nielsen SJ, and Popkin BM (2004) Consumption of high-fructose corn syrup in beverages may play a role in the epidemic of obesity. *American Journal of Clinical Nutrition* 79 (4):537–543.

Bray MS and Young ME (2006) Circadian rhythms in the development of obesity: potential role for the circadian clock within the adipocyte. *Obesity Reviews* 8:169–181.

Brennan L, McDonald J, and Shlomowitz R (1997) Towards an anthropometric history of Indians under British rule. *Research in Economic History* 17:185–246.

Brennan L, McDonald J, and Shlomowitz R (2004) A long run decline in final adult female height in India? *Man in India* 84:9–13.

Bribiescas RG (2001) Serum leptin levels and anthropometric correlates in Ache Amerindians of eastern Paraguay. *American Journal of Physical Anthropology* 115 (4):297–303.

Bronson FH (1989) *Mammalian reproductive biology*. University of Chicago Press: Chicago.

Brooke OG, Harris M, and Salvosa CB (1973) The response of malnourished babies to cold. *Journal of Physiology* 233 (1):75–91.

Brown JE, Jacobson HN, Askue LH, and Peick MG (1981) Influence of pregnancy weight gain on the size of infants born to underweight women. *Obstetrics and Gynecology* 57 (1):13–17.

Brown JE, Potter JD, Jacobs DR, Jr., Kopher RA, Rourke MJ, Barosso GM, Hannan PJ, and Schmid LA (1996) Maternal waist-to-hip ratio as a predictor of newborn size: Results of the Diana Project. *Epidemiology* 7 (1):62–66.

Brown JE, Murtaugh MA, Jacobs DR, Jr., and Margellos HC (2002) Variation in newborn size according to pregnancy weight change by trimester. *American Journal of Clinical Nutrition* 76 (1):205–209.

Brown KH, Akhtar NA, Robertson AD, and Ahmed MG (1986) Lactational capacity of marginally nourished mothers: relationships between maternal nutritional status and quantity and proximate composition of milk. *Pediatrics* 78 (5):909–919.

Brown PJ and Konner M (1987) An anthropological perspective on obesity. *Annals of the New York Academy of Sciences* 499:29–46.

Brozek J, Grande F, Anderson JT, and Keys A (1963) Densitometric analysis of body composition: revision of some quantitative assumptions. *Annals of the New York Academy of Sciences* 110:113–140.

Brunner EJ, Chandola T, and Marmot MG (2007) Prospective effect of job strain on general and central obesity in the Whitehall II Study. *American Journal of Epidemiology* 165 (7):828–837.

Bryden MM (1972) Body size and composition of elephant seals (Mirounga leonina): absolute measures and estimates from bone dimensions. *Journal of Zoology* 167:265–276.

Bulik CM and Allison DB (2001) The genetic epidemiology of thinness. *Obesity Reviews* 2:107–115.

Bunn HT (1994) Early pleistocene hominid foraging strategies along the ancestral Omo river at Koobi Fora, Kenya. *Journal of Human Evolution* 27:247–266.

Buss DM (1989) Sex differences in human mate preferences: evolutionary hypotheses tested in 37 cultures. *Behavioral and Brain Sciences* 12:1–49.

Butler C, Tull ES, Chambers EC, and Taylor J (2002) Internalized racism, body fat distribution, and abnormal fasting glucose among African-Caribbean women in Dominica, West Indies. *Journal of the National Medical Association* 94 (3):143–148.

Butte N, Heinz C, Hopkinson J, Wong W, Shypailo R, and Ellis K (1999) Fat mass in infants and toddlers: comparability of total body water, total body potassium, total body electrical conductivity, and dual-energy X-ray absorptiometry. *Journal of Pediatric Gastroenterology and Nutrition* 29 (2):184–189.

Butte NF and Calloway DH (1981) Evaluation of lactational performance of Navajo women. *American Journal of Clinical Nutrition* 34 (10):2210–2215.

Butte NF, Wong WW, Fiorotto M, Smith EO, and Garza C (1995) Influence of early feeding mode on body composition of infants. *Biology of the Neonate* 67 (6):414–424.

Butte NF, Hopkinson JM, Wong WW, Smith EO, and Ellis KJ (2000) Body composition during the first 2 years of life: an updated reference. *Pediatric Research* 47 (5):578–585.

Byrne CD and Phillips DI (2000) Fetal origins of adult disease: epidemiology and mechanisms. *Journal of Clinical Pathology* 53 (11):822–828.

Cameron N, Pettifor J, De WT, and Norris S (2003) The relationship of rapid weight gain in infancy to obesity and skeletal maturity in childhood. *Obesity Research* 11 (3):457–460.

Cameron N, Preece MA, and Cole TJ (2005) Catch-up growth or regression to the mean? Recovery from stunting revisited. *American Journal of Human Biology* 17 (4):412–417.

Campbell BC and Cajigal A (2001) Diabetes: energetics, development and human evolution. *Medical Hypotheses* 57 (1):64–67.

Campbell PT, Katzmarzyk PT, Malina RM, Rao DC, Perusse L, and Bouchard C (2001) Stability of adiposity phenotypes from childhood and adolescence into young adulthood with contribution of parental measures. *Obesity Research* 9 (7):394–400.

Campos DB, Palin MF, Bordignon V, and Murphy BD (2008) The 'beneficial' adipokines in reproduction and fertility. *International Journal of Obesity (London)* 32 (2):223–231.

Cann RL, Stoneking M, and Wilson AC (1987) Mitochondrial DNA and human evolution. *Nature* 325 (6099):31–36.

Cannon B and Nedergaard J (2004) Brown adipose tissue: function and physiological significance. *Physiological Reviews* 84 (1):277–359.

Cannon G (2008) Out of the box: why do we all now seem to agree that obesity is a disease; and what's wrong with being overweight? *Public Health Nutrition* 11 (4):331–334.

Carey WB (1985) Temperament and Increased Weight-Gain in Infants. *Journal of Developmental and Behavioral Pediatrics* 6 (3):128–131.

Carey WB, Hegvik RL, and McDevitt SC (1988) Temperamental factors associated with rapid weight gain and obesity in middle childhood. *Journal of Developmental and Behavioral Pediatrics* 9 (4):194–198.

Casey VA, Dwyer JT, Coleman KA, and Valadian I (1992) Body mass index from childhood to middle age: a 50-y follow-up. *American Journal of Clinical Nutrition* 56 (1):14–18.

Caspersen CJ, Powell KE, and Christenson GM (1985) Physical activity, exercise, and physical fitness: definitions and distinctions for health-related research. *Public Health Reports* 100 (2):126–131.

Catalano PM, Thomas AJ, Avallone DA, and Amini SB (1995) Anthropometric estimation of neonatal body composition. *American Journal of Obstetrics and Gynecology* 173 (4):1176–1181.

Catalano PM, Tyzbir ED, Allen SR, Mcbean JH, and Mcauliffe TL (1992) Evaluation of fetal growth by estimation of neonatal body-composition. *Obstetrics and Gynecology* 79 (1):46–50.

Cavagnini F, Croci M, Putignano P, Petroni ML, and Invitti C (2000) Glucocorticoids and neuroendocrine function. *International Journal of Obesity and Related Metabolic Disorders* 24 Suppl 2:S77–S79.

Ceesay SM, Prentice AM, Cole TJ, Foord F, Weaver LT, Poskitt EM, and Whitehead RG (1997) Effects on birth weight and perinatal mortality of maternal dietary supplements in rural Gambia: 5 year randomised controlled trial. *British Medical Journal* 315 (7111):786–790.

Chakravarthy MV and Booth FW (2004) Eating, exercise, and "thrifty" genotypes: connecting the dots toward an evolutionary understanding of modern chronic diseases. *Journal of Applied Physiology* 96 (1):3–10.

Chambers EC, Tull ES, Fraser HS, Mutunhu NR, Sobers N, and Niles E (2004) The relationship of internalized racism to body fat distribution and insulin resistance among African adolescent youth. *Journal of the National Medical Association* 96 (12):1594–1598.

Chambers TL (1850) On corpulence. *Lancet* i:557–560.

Chehab FF, Qiu J, Mounzih K, Ewart-Toland A, and Ogus S (2002) Leptin and reproduction. *Nutrition Reviews* 60 (10 Pt 2):S39–S46.

Chen LC, Alauddin Chowdhury AK, and Huffman SL (1979) Seasonal dimensions of energy protein malnutrition in rural Bangladesh: the role of agriculture, dietary practices, and infection. *Ecology of Food and Nutrition* 8:175–187.

Cheung CC, Thornton JE, Kuijper JL, Weigle DS, Clifton DK, and Steiner RA (1997) Leptin is a metabolic gate for the onset of puberty in the female rat. *Endocrinology* 138 (2):855–858.

Chiolero A, Faeh D, Paccaud F, and Cornuz J (2008) Consequences of smoking for body weight, body fat distribution, and insulin resistance. *American Journal of Clinical Nutrition* 87 (4):801–809.

Chiolero R, Revelly JP, and Tappy L (1997) Energy metabolism in sepsis and injury. *Nutrition* 13 (9 Suppl):45S–51S.

Chomtho S, Wells JC, Williams JE, Davies PS, Lucas A, and Fewtrell MS (2008) Infant growth and later body composition: evidence from the 4-component model. *American Journal of Clinical Nutrition* 87 (6):1776–1784.

Christakis NA and Fowler JH (2007) The spread of obesity in a large social network over 32 years. *New England Journal of Medicine* 357 (4):370–379.

Clayton PE, Gill MS, Hall CM, Tillmann V, Whatmore AJ, and Price DA (1997) Serum leptin through childhood and adolescence. *Clinical Endocrinology (Oxford)* 46 (6):727–733.

Clutton-Brock J (1989) *The Walking Larder: Patterns of Domestication, Pastoralism, and Predation*. Unwin Hyman: London.

Clutton-Brock TH, Albon SD, and Guinness FE (1989) Fitness costs of gestation and lactation in wild mammals. *Nature* 337 (6204):260–262.

Cockburn TA (1971) Infectious diseases in ancient populations. *Current Anthropology* 12:45–62.

Coelho R, Wells J, Symth J, Semple R, O'Rahilly S, Eaton S, and Hussain K (2007) Severe hypoinsulinaemic hypoglycaemia in a premature infant associated with poor weight gain and reduced adipose tissue. *Hormone Research* 68 (2):91–98.

Cohen MN (1989) *Health and the rise of civilisation*. Yale University Press: New Haven.

Cohen MN (1998) The emergence of health and social inequalities in the archaeological record. In: Strickland SS and Shetty PS (eds) *Human biology and social inequality*. Cambridge University Press Cambridge, pp 249–271.

Cohen MN (1977) *The food crisis in prehistory: overpopulation and the origins of agriculture*. New Haven, Yale University Press.

Cohen MN and Armelagos GJ (1984) *Palaeopathology and the origins of agriculture*. Academic Press: Orlando, Florida.

Cohen S, Doyle WJ, Turner RB, Alper CM, and Skoner DP (2004) Childhood socioeconomic status and host resistance to infectious illness in adulthood. *Psychosomatic Medicine* 66 (4):553–558.

Cohn SH (1987) New concepts of body composition. In: Ellis KJ, Yasumura S, and Morgan WD (eds) *In vivo body composition studies*. Plenum Press: New York, pp 1–14.

Colagiuri S and Brand MJ (2002) The 'carnivore connection' – evolutionary aspects of insulin resistance. *European Journal of Clinical Nutrition* 56 Suppl 1:S30–S35.

Cole TJ (1986) Weight/height^p compared to weight/height^2 for assessing adiposity in childhood: influence of age and bone age on p during puberty. *Annals of Human Biology* 13 (5):433–451.

Cole TJ (2000) Secular trends in growth. *Proceedings of the Nutrition Society* 59 (2):317–324.

Cole TJ (2004) Children grow and horses race: is the adiposity rebound a critical period for later obesity? *BMC Pediatrics* 4:6.

Cole TJ, Bellizzi MC, Flegal KM, and Dietz WH (2000) Establishing a standard definition for child overweight and obesity worldwide: international survey. *British Medical Journal* 320 (7244):1240–1243.

Cole TJ, Freeman JV, and Preece MA (1995) Body mass index reference curves for the UK, 1990. *Archives of Diseases in Childhood* 73 (1):25–29.

Collier G and Johnson DF (2000) Sucrose intake as a function of its cost and the cost of chow. *Physiology and Behavior* 70 (5):477–487.

Collins KJ and Roberts DF (1988) *The Capacity for Work in the Tropics*. Cambridge University Press: Cambridge.

Collins S (1995) The limit of human adaptation to starvation. *Nature Medicine* 1 (8):810–814.

Comuzzie AG, Cole SA, Martin L, Carey KD, Mahaney MC, Blangero J, and VandeBerg JL (2003) The baboon as a nonhuman primate model for the study of the genetics of obesity. *Obesity Research* 11 (1):75–80.

Conklin-Brittain NL, Wrangham RW, and Smith CC (2002) A two-stage model of increased dietary quality in the early hominin evolution: the role of fibre. In: Ungar PS, Teaford MF (ed) *Human diet: its origins and evolution.* Bergin and Harvey: Westport, CT, pp 61–76.

Cook I, Alberts M, and Lambert EV (2008) Relationship between adiposity and pedometer-assessed ambulatory activity in adult, rural African women. *International Journal of Obesity (London)* 32(8):1327–1330.

Cooney CA, Dave AA, and Wolff GL (2002) Maternal methyl supplements in mice affect epigenetic variation and DNA methylation of offspring. *Journal of Nutrition* 132 (8 Suppl):2393S–2400S.

Cooper C, Kuh D, Egger P, Wadsworth M, and Barker D (1996) Childhood growth and age at menarche. *British Journal of Obstetrics and Gynaecology* 103 (8):814–817.

Corvalan C, Gregory CO, Ramirez-Zea M, Martorell R, and Stein AD (2007) Size at birth, infant, early and later childhood growth and adult body composition: a prospective study in a stunted population. *International Journal of Epidemiology* 36 (3):550–557.

Crompton AW, Taylor CR, and Jagger JA (1978) Evolution of homeothermy in mammals. *Nature* 272 (5651):333–336.

Dabelea D, Hanson RL, Lindsay RS, Pettitt DJ, Imperatore G, Gabir MM, Roumain J, Bennett PH, and Knowler WC (2000) Intrauterine exposure to diabetes conveys risks for type 2 diabetes and obesity: a study of discordant sibships. *Diabetes* 49 (12):2208–2211.

Dabelea D, Knowler WC, and Pettitt DJ (2000) Effect of diabetes in pregnancy on offspring: follow-up research in the Pima Indians. *Journal of Maternal-Fetal Medicine* 9 (1):83–88.

Dabelea D and Pettitt DJ (2001) Intrauterine diabetic environment confers risks for type 2 diabetes mellitus and obesity in the offspring, in addition to genetic susceptibility. *Journal of Pediatric Endocrinology and Metabolism* 14 (8):1085–1091.

Dall SR and Boyd IL (2004) Evolution of mammals: lactation helps mothers to cope with unreliable food supplies. *Proceedings of the Royal Society B: Biological Sciences* 271 (1552):2049–2057.

Dallman MF, Pecoraro N, Akana SF, La Fleur SE, Gomez F, Houshyar H, Bell ME, Bhatnagar S, Laugero KD, and Manalo S (2003) Chronic stress and obesity: a new view of "comfort food". *Proceedings of the National Academy of Sciences of the United States of America* 100 (20):11696–11701.

Dando WA (1980) *The geography of famine.* Edward Arnold: London.

Dark J (2005) Annual lipid cycles in hibernators: integration of physiology and behaviour. *Annual Review of Nutrition* 25:469–497.

Davies PS (1992) Estimates of body fat in infancy and childhood. *American Journal of Human Biology* 4:621–624.

Davis M (2002) *Late Victorian holocausts: El Nino and the making of the third world.* Verso: London.

Davis M (2006) *Planet of slums.* Verso: London.

Davison AN and Dobbing J (1968) The developing brain. In: Davison AN and Dobbing J (eds) *Applied neurochemistry.* Blackwell: Oxford, pp 253–286.

Dawber TR, Meadors GF, and Moore FE, Jr. (1951) Epidemiological approaches to heart disease: the Framingham Study. *American Journal of Public Health and the Nation's Health* 41 (3):279–281.

de Bruin NC, van Velthoven KA, Stijnen T, Juttmann RE, Degenhart HJ, and Visser HK (1995a) Quantitative assessment of infant body fat by anthropometry and total-body electrical conductivity. *American Journal of Clinical Nutrition* 61 (2):279–286.

de Bruin NC, Westerterp KR, Degenhart HJ, and Visser HK (1995b) Measurement of fat-free mass in infants. *Pediatric Research* 38 (3):411–417.

de Ridder CM, de Boer RW, Seidell JC, Nieuwenhoff CM, Jeneson JA, Bakker CJ, Zonderland ML, and Erich WB (1992a) Body fat distribution in pubertal girls quantified by magnetic resonance imaging. *International Journal of Obesity and Related Metabolic Disorders* 16 (6):443–449.

de Ridder CM, Thijssen JH, Bruning PF, Van den Brande JL, Zonderland ML, and Erich WB (1992b) Body fat mass, body fat distribution, and pubertal development: a longitudinal study of physical and hormonal sexual maturation of girls. *Journal of Clinical Endocrinology and Metabolism* 75 (2):442–446.

De Castro JM (1990) Social facilitation of duration and size but not rate of the spontaneous meal intake of humans. *Physiology and Behavior* 47:1129–1135.

De Castro JM (1997) Inheritance of social influences on eating and drinking in humans. *Nutrition Research* 17:631–648.

De Garine I (1993) Culture, seasons and stress in two traditional African cultures (Massa and Mussey). In: Ulijaszek SJ and Strickland SS (eds) *Seasonality and human ecology.* Cambridge University Press: Cambridge, pp 184–201.

De Garine I, Koppert G (1988) *Coping with seasonal fluctuations in food supply among savanna populations: the Massa and Mussey of Chad and Cameroon.* In: DeGarine I and Harrison GA (eds) Coping with uncertainty in food supply. Oxford University Press: Oxford, pp 210–259.

De Lany JP, Harsha DW, Kime JC, Kumler J, Melancon L, and Bray GA (1995) Energy expenditure in lean and obese prepubertal children. *Obesity Research* 3 Suppl 1:67–72.

Delgado HL, Martorell R, and Klein RE (1982) Nutrition, lactation, and birth interval components in rural Guatemala. *American Journal of Clinical Nutrition* 35 (6):1468–1476.

Delmas C, Platat C, Schweitzer B, Wagner A, Oujaa M, and Simon C (2007) Association between television in bedroom and adiposity throughout adolescence. *Obesity (Silver Spring)* 15 (10):2495–2503.

Del Prado M, Villapando S, Lance A, Alfonso E, Demmelmar H, and Koletzko B (2000) Contribution of dietary and newly formed arachidonic acid to milk secretion in women in low fat diets. *Advances in Experimental Medicine and Biology* 478:407–408.

Demas GE, Chefer V, Talan MI, and Nelson RJ (1997) Metabolic costs of mounting an antigen-stimulated immune response in adult and aged C57BL/6J mice. *American Journal of Physiology* 273 (5 Pt 2):R1631–R1637.

Demas GE, Drazen DL, and Nelson RJ (2003) Reductions in total body fat decrease humoral immunity. *Proceedings of the Royal Society B: Biological Sciences* 270 (1518):905–911.

Demerath EW, Choh AC, Czerwinski SA, Lee M, Sun SS, Chumlea WC, Duren D, Sherwood RJ, Blangero J, Towne B, and Siervogel RM (2007) Genetic and environmental influences on infant weight and weight change: the Fels Longitudinal Study. *American Journal of Human Biology* 19 (5):692–702.

Dempster P and Aitkens S (1995) A new air displacement method for the determination of human body composition. *Medicine and Science in Sports and Exercise* 27 (12):1692–1697.

Denisova DV, Nikitin YP, Zavjalova LG, and Burakova SV (2007) Trends in cardiovascular risk factors of Siberian adolescents during socioeconomic reforms in Russia (1989–2003). *Alaska Medicine* 49 (2 Suppl):110–116.

Denny MJ and Dawson TJ (1975) Comparative metabolism of tritiated water by macropodid marsupials. *American Journal of Physiology* 228 (6):1794–1799.

Deshmukh-Taskar P, Nicklas TA, Morales M, Yang SJ, Zakeri I, and Berenson GS (2006) Tracking of overweight status from childhood to young adulthood: the Bogalusa Heart Study. *European Journal of Clinical Nutrition* 60 (1):48–57.

Dettwyler KA and Fishman C (1992) Infant feeding practices and growth. *Annual Review of Anthropology* 21:171–204.

Deurenberg P, Deurenberg-Yap M, and Guricci S (2002) Asians are different from Caucasians and from each other in their body mass index/body fat per cent relationship. *Obesity Reviews* 3 (3):141–146.

Deurenberg P, Yap M, and van Staveren WA (1998) Body mass index and percent body fat: a meta analysis among different ethnic groups. *International Journal of Obesity and Related Metabolic Disorders* 22 (12):1164–1171.

Dewey KG, Heinig MJ, Nommsen LA, Peerson JM, and Lonnerdal B (1993) Breast-fed infants are leaner than formula-fed infants at 1 y of age: the DARLING study. *American Journal of Clinical Nutrition* 57 (2):140–145.

Dhillo WS (2007) Appetite regulation: an overview. *Thyroid* 17 (5):433–445.

Dhingra R, Sullivan L, Jacques PF, Wang TJ, Fox CS, Meigs JB, D'Agostino RB, Gaziano JM, and Vasan RS (2007) Soft drink consumption and risk of developing cardiometabolic risk factors and the metabolic syndrome in middle-aged adults in the community. *Circulation* 116 (5):480–488.

Diamond J (1998) *Guns, germs and steel.* Vintage: London.

Diamond J (2003) The double puzzle of diabetes. *Nature* 423 (6940):599–602.

Dietz WH, Jr. and Gortmaker SL (1985) Do we fatten our children at the television set? Obesity and television viewing in children and adolescents. *Pediatrics* 75 (5):807–812.

Di Meglio DP and Mattes RD (2000) Liquid versus solid carbohydrate: effects on food intake and body weight. *International Journal of Obesity and Related Metabolic Disorders* 24 (6):794–800.

Dionne I, Almeras N, Bouchard C, and Tremblay A (2000) The association between vigorous physical activities and fat deposition in male adolescents. *Medicine and Science in Sports and Exercise* 32 (2):392–395.

Dirks R (1993) Starvation and famine: cross-cultural codes and some hypothesis tests. *Cross-Cultural Research* 27:28–69.

Doak CM, Adair LS, Bentley M, Monteiro C, and Popkin BM (2005) The dual burden household and the nutrition transition paradox. *International Journal of Obesity (London)* 29 (1):129–136.

dos Santos Silva I, De Stavola BL, Mann V, Kuh D, Hardy R, and Wadsworth ME (2002) Prenatal factors, childhood growth trajectories and age at menarche. *International Journal of Epidemiology* 31 (2):405–412.

Dowse GK, Zimmet PZ, Finch CF, and Collins VR (1991) Decline in incidence of epidemic glucose intolerance in Nauruans: implications for the "thrifty genotype". *American Journal of Epidemiology* 133 (11):1093–1104.

Drazen DL, Demas GE, and Nelson RJ (2001) Leptin effects on immune function and energy balance are photoperiod dependent in Siberian hamsters (Phodopus sungorus). *Endocrinology* 142 (7):2768–2775.

Drewnowski A (2009) Obesity, diets, and social inequalities. *Nutrition Reviews* 67 Suppl 1:S36–S39.

Dufour DL and Sauther ML (2002) Comparative and evolutionary dimensions of the energetics of human pregnancy and lactation. *American Journal of Human Biology* 14 (5):584–602.

Dugdale AE and Payne PR (1987) A model of seasonal changes in energy balance. *Ecology of Food and Nutrition* 19:231–245.

Dulloo AG (1997) Regulation of body composition during weight recovery: integrating the control of energy partitioning and thermogenesis. *Clinical Nutrition* 16 Suppl 1:25–35.

Dunger DB, Ahmed ML, and Ong KK (2006) Early and late weight gain and the timing of puberty. *Molecular Cell Endocrinology* 254–255:140–145.

Du Pasquier L (1993) Evolution of the immune system. In: Paul WE (ed) *Fundamental immunology*. Raven: New York, pp 199–233.

Duran-Tauleria E, Rona RJ, and Chinn S (1995) Factors associated with weight for height and skinfold thickness in British children. *Journal of Epidemiology and Community Health* 49 (5):466–473.

Durham WH (1991) *Coevolution: genes, culture and human diversity*. Stanford University Press: Stanford.

Durnin JV (1987a) Energy requirements of pregnancy. an integrated study in five countries: background and methods. *Lancet* 2 (8564):895–896.

Durnin JV (1987b) Energy requirements of pregnancy: an integration of the longitudinal data from the five-country study. *Lancet* 2 (8568):1131–1133.

Durnin JV and Womersley J (1974) Body fat assessed from total body density and its estimation from skinfold thickness: measurements on 481 men and women aged from 16 to 72 years. *British Journal of Nutrition* 32 (1):77–97.

Dwarkanath P, Muthayya S, Vaz M, Thomas T, Mhaskar A, Mhaskar R, Thomas A, Bhat S, and Kurpad A (2007) The relationship between maternal physical activity during pregnancy and birth weight. *Asia Pacific Journal of Clinical Nutrition* 16 (4):704–710.

Eaton SB and Konner M (1985) Paleolithic nutrition: a consideration of its nature and current implications. *New England Journal of Medicine* 312 (5):283–289.

Eaton SB, Konner M, and Shostak M (1988) Stone agers in the fast lane: chronic degenerative diseases in evolutionary perspective. *American Journal of Medicine* 84 (4):739–749.

Egger G and Swinburn B (1997) An "ecological" approach to the obesity pandemic. *British Medical Journal* 315 (7106):477–480.

Eibl-Eibesfelt I (1997) The evolution of nurturant dominance. In: Wiessner P and Schiefenhovel W (eds) *Food and the status quest: an interdisciplinary perspective*. Bergahn Books: Providence, RI, pp 33–45.

Ekelund U, Aman J, Yngve A, Renman C, Westerterp K, and Sjostrom M (2002) Physical activity but not energy expenditure is reduced in obese adolescents: a case-control study. *American Journal of Clinical Nutrition* 76 (5):935–941.

Ekelund U, Ong K, Linne Y, Neovius M, Brage S, Dunger DB, Wareham NJ, and Rossner S (2006) Upward weight percentile crossing in infancy and early childhood independently predicts fat mass in young adults: the Stockholm Weight Development Study (SWEDES). *American Journal of Clinical Nutrition* 83 (2):324–330.

Ellis KJ (2000) Human body composition: in vivo methods. *Physiological Reviews* 80 (2):649–680.

Ellison PT (1981) Threshold hypotheses, development age, and menstrual function. *American Journal of Physical Anthropology* 54 (3):337–340.

Ellison PT (1982) Skeletal growth, fatness and menarcheal age: A comparison of two hypotheses. *Human Biology* 54:269–281.

Ellison PT (1990) Human ovarian function and reproductive ecology: new hypotheses. *American Anthropology* 92:933–952.

Ellison PT (2001) *On fertile ground*. Harvard University Press: Cambridge.

Ellison PT (2003) Energetics and reproductive effort. *American Journal of Human Biology* 15 (3):342–351.

Emanuel I, Filakti H, Alberman E and Evans SJ (1992) Intergenerational studies of human birthweight from the 1958 birth cohort. 1. Evidence for a multigenerational effect. *British Journal of Obstetrics and Gynaecology* 99(1):67–74.

Eriksson M, Tynelius P, and Rasmussen F (2008) Associations of birthweight and infant growth with body composition at age 15: the COMPASS study. *Paediatric Perinatal Epidemiology* 22 (4):379–388.

Ettyang GA, van Marken Lichtenbelt WD, Esamai F, Saris WH, and Westerterp KR (2005) Assessment of body composition and breast milk volume in lactating mothers in pastoral communities in Pokot, Kenya, using deuterium oxide. *Annals of Nutrition and Metabolism* 49 (2):110–117.

Euser AM, Finken MJ, Keijzer-Veen MG, Hille ET, Wit JM, and Dekker FW (2005) Associations between prenatal and infancy weight gain and BMI, fat mass, and fat distribution in young adulthood: a prospective cohort study in males and females born very preterm. *American Journal of Clinical Nutrition* 81 (2):480–487.

Evans KC, Evans RG, Royal R, Esterman AJ, and James SL (2003) Effect of caesarean section on breast milk transfer to the normal term newborn over the first week of life. *Archives of Diseases in Childhood. Fetal and Neonatal Edition* 88 (5):F380–F382.

Ewing WG, Studier EH, and O'Farrell JJ (1970) Autumn fat deposition and gross body composition in three species of Myotis. *Comparative Biochemistry and Physiology* 36:119–129.

Ezzahir N, Alberti C, Deghmoun S, Zaccaria I, Czernichow P, Levy-Marchal C, and Jaquet D (2005) Time course of catch-up in adiposity influences adult anthropometry in individuals who were born small for gestational age. *Pediatric Research* 58 (2):243–247.

Ezzati M, Friedman AB, Kulkarni SC, and Murray CJ (2008) The reversal of fortunes: trends in county mortality and cross-county mortality disparities in the United States. *PLoS Medicine* 5 (4):e66.

Fagan B (1999) *Floods, famines and emperors*. Basic Books: New York.

Fan J, Liu F, Wu J, and Dai W (2004) Visual perception of female physical attractiveness. *Proceedings of the Royal Society B: Biological Sciences* 271 (1537):347–352.

Fathalla M (1998) The missing millions. *People and the Planet* 7 (3):10–11.

Ferguson NS and Gous RM (1997) The influence of heat production on voluntary food intake of growing pigs given protein-deficient diets. *Animal Science* 64 (365):378.

Fernandez-Real JM, Lopez-Bermejo A, Vendrell J, Ferri MJ, Recasens M, and Ricart W (2006) Burden of infection and insulin resistance in healthy middle-aged men. *Diabetes Care* 29 (5):1058–1064.

Fernandez-Real JM, Ferri MJ, Vendrell J, and Ricart W (2007) Burden of infection and fat mass in healthy middle-aged men. *Obesity (Silver Spring)* 15 (1):245–252.

Fernandez-Real JM and Ricart W (1999) Insulin resistance and inflammation in an evolutionary perspective: the contribution of cytokine genotype/phenotype to thriftiness. *Diabetologia* 42 (11):1367–1374.

Ferro-Luzzi A (1990) Seasonal energy stress in marginally nourished rural women: interpretation and integrated conclusions of a multicentre study in three developing countries. *European Journal of Clinical Nutrition* 44 Suppl 1:41–46.

Ferro-Luzzi A and Branca F (1993) Nutritional seasonality: the dimensions of the problem. In: Ulijaszek SJ and Strickland SS (eds) *Seasonality and human ecology*. Cambridge University Press: Cambridge, pp 149–165.

Ferro-Luzzi A, Scaccini C, Taffese S, Aberra B, and Demeke T (1990) Seasonal energy deficiency in Ethiopian rural women. *European Journal of Clinical Nutrition* 44 Suppl 1:7–18.

Fewtrell MS, Lucas A, Cole TJ, and Wells JC (2004) Prematurity and reduced body fatness at 8–12 y of age. *American Journal of Clinical Nutrition* 80 (2):436–440.

Fidler N, Sauerwald T, Pohl A, Demmelmair H, and Koletzko B (2000) Docosahexaenoic acid transfer into human milk after dietary supplementation: a randomized clinical trial. *Journal of Lipid Research* 41 (9):1376–1383.

Filozof C, Fernandez Pinilla MC, and Fernandez-Cruz A (2004) Smoking cessation and weight gain. *Obesity Reviews* 5 (2):95–103.

Fink B, Manning JT, and Neave N (2006) The 2nd-4th digit ratio (2D:4D) and neck circumference: implications for risk factors in coronary heart disease. *International Journal of Obesity (London)* 30 (4):711–714.

Fink B, Neave N, and Manning JT (2003) Second to fourth digit ratio, body mass index, waist-to-hip ratio, and waist-to-chest ratio: their relationships in heterosexual men and women. *Annals of Human Biology* 30 (6):728–738.

Fiorotto ML, Cochran WJ, and Klish WJ (1987) Fat-free mass and total body water of infants estimated from total body electrical conductivity measurements. *Pediatric Research* 22 (4):417–421.

Fleming PJ, Azaz Y, and Wigfield R (1992) Development of thermoregulation in infancy: possible implications for SIDS. *Journal of Clinical Pathology* 45 (11 Suppl):17–19.

Flinn MV and England BG (1997) Social economics of childhood glucocorticoid stress response and health. *American Journal of Physical Anthropology* 102:33–53.

Flynn JR (2007) *What is intelligence?* Cambridge University Press: Cambridge.

Fogelholm M and Kukkonen-Harjula K (2000) Does physical activity prevent weight gain – a systematic review. *Obesity Reviews* 1:95–111.

Foley R (2001) The evolutionary consequences of increased carnivory in humans. In: Stanford CB, Bunn HT (eds) *Meat-eating and human evolution*. Oxford University Press: Oxford, pp 305–331.

Foley R (1987) *Another unique species*. Harlow, Longmans.

Foley RA (1993) *The influence of seasonality on human evolution*. Ulijaszek SJ and Strickland SS. Seasonality and human ecology. 17–37. Cambridge, Cambridge University Press.

Foley RA and Elton S (1998). Time and energy: the ecological context for the evolution of bipedalism. In: Strasser, E. (ed.) *Strasser, E. Primate locomotion: recent advances*. 419–433. New York, Plenum Press.

Foley RA and Lee PC (1991b) Ecology and energetics of encephalisation in homind evolution. *Philosophical Transactions of the Royal Society Series B* 334, 223–232.

Foley RA and Lee PC (1991a) Ecology and energetics of encephalisation in hominid evolution. *Philosophical Transactions of the Royal Society Series B* 334:223–232.

Folinsbee KE and Brooks DR (2007) Miocene hominoid biogeography: pulses of dispersal and differentiation. *Journal of Biogeography* 34:383–397.

Fomon SJ, Haschke F, Ziegler EE, and Nelson SE (1982) Body composition of reference children from birth to age 10 years. *American Journal of Clinical Nutrition* 35 (5 Suppl):1169–1175.

Forbes GB (1989) Changes in body composition. In: Ross Laboratories (ed) Report of the 98th Ross conference on pediatric research. Columbus, pp 112–118.

Forbes GB and Hursh JB (1961) Estimation of total body fat from potassium-40 content. *Science* 133:1918.

Forbes GB, Sauer EP, and Weitkamp LR (1995) Lean body mass in twins. *Metabolism* 44 (11):1442–1446.

Forouhi NG and Sattar N (2006) CVD risk factors and ethnicity–a homogeneous relationship? *Atherosclerosis. Suppl* 7 (1):11–19.

Forsum E, Sadurskis A, and Wager J (1989) Estimation of body fat in healthy Swedish women during pregnancy and lactation. *American Journal of Clinical Nutrition* 50 (3):465–473.

Foster MA, Hutchison JM, Mallard JR, and Fuller M (1984) Nuclear magnetic resonance pulse sequence and discrimination of high- and low-fat tissues. *Magnetic Resonance Imaging* 2 (3):187–192.

Foster-Powell K, Holt SH, and Brand-Miller JC (2002) International table of glycemic index and glycemic load values: 2002. *American Journal of Clinical Nutrition* 76 (1):5–56.

Fraga MF, Ballestar E, Paz MF, Ropero S, Setien F, Ballestar ML, Heine-Suner D, Cigudosa JC, Urioste M, Benitez J, Boix-Chornet M, Sanchez-Aguilera A, Ling C, Carlsson E, Poulsen P, Vaag A, Stephan Z, Spector TD, Wu YZ, Plass C, and Esteller M (2005) Epigenetic differences arise during the lifetime of monozygotic twins. *Proceedings of the National Academy of Sciences of the United States of America* 102 (30):10604–10609.

Frank LD, Andresen MA, and Schmid TL (2004) Obesity relationships with community design, physical activity, and time spent in cars. *American Journal of Preventive Medicine* 27 (2):87–96.

Frankish H (2001) Obesity and diabetes epidemics show no sign of abating. *Lancet* 358 (9285):896.

Freitak D, Ots I, Vanatoa A, and Horak P (2003) Immune response is energetically costly in white cabbage butterfly pupae. *Proceedings of the Royal Society B: Biological Sciences* 270 Suppl 2:S220–S222.

Friedl KE, Moore RJ, Martinez-Lopez LE, Vogel JA, Askew EW, Marchitelli LJ, Hoyt RW, and Gordon CC (1994) Lower limit of body fat in healthy active men. *Journal of Applied Physiology* 77 (2):933–940.

Frisancho AR (2000) Prenatal compared with parental origins of adolescent fatness. *American Journal of Clinical Nutrition* 72 (5):1186–1190.

Frisancho AR, Klayman JE, and Matos J (1977) Influence of maternal nutritional status on prenatal growth in a Peruvian urban population. *American Journal of Physical Anthropology* 46 (2):265–274.

Frisch RE (1985) Fatness, menarche, and female fertility. *Perspective in Biololgy and Medicine* 28 (4):611–633.

Frisch RE (1990) The right weight: body fat, menarche and ovulation. *Baillieres Clinical Obstetrics and Gynaecology* 4 (3):419–439.

Frisch RE and McArthur JW (1974) Menstrual cycles: fatness as a determinant of minimum weight for height necessary for their maintenance or onset. *Science* 185 (4155):949–951.

Froguel P and Boutin P (2001) Genetics of pathways regulating body weight in the development of obesity in humans. *Experimental Biology and Medicine (Maywood.)* 226 (11):991–996.

Frongillo EA, Jr., de Onis M, and Hanson KM (1997) Socioeconomic and demographic factors are associated with worldwide patterns of stunting and wasting of children. *Journal of Nutrition* 127 (12):2302–2309.

Fuentes RM, Notkola IL, Shemeikka S, Tuomilehto J, and Nissinen A (2003) Tracking of body mass index during childhood: a 15-year prospective population-based family study in eastern Finland. *International Journal of Obesity and Related Metabolic Disorders* 27 (6):716–721.

Fuller NJ, Fewtrell MS, Dewit O, Elia M, and Wells JC (2002) Segmental bioelectrical impedance analysis in children aged 8–12 y: 1. The assessment of whole-body composition. *International Journal of Obesity and Related Metabolic Disorders* 26 (5):684–691.

Fuller NJ, Jebb SA, Laskey MA, Coward WA, and Elia M (1992) Four-component model for the assessment of body composition in humans: comparison with alternative methods, and evaluation of the density and hydration of fat-free mass. *Clinical Science (London)* 82 (6):687–693.

Furnham A, McClelland A, and Omer L (2003) A cross-cultural comparison of ratings of perceived fecundity and sexual attractiveness as a function of body weight and waist-to-hip ratio. *Psychology, Health, and Medicine.* 8 (2):219–230.

Gabrielsson BG, Johansson JM, Lonn M, Jernas M, Olbers T, Peltonen M, Larsson I, Lonn L, Sjostrom L, Carlsson B, and Carlsson LM (2003) High expression of complement components in omental adipose tissue in obese men. *Obesity Research* 11 (6):699–708.

Galdikas BM and Wood JW (1990) Birth spacing patterns in humans and apes. *American Journal of Physical Anthropology* 83 (2):185–191.

Gale CR, Martyn CN, Kellingray S, Eastell R, and Cooper C (2001) Intrauterine programming of adult body composition. *Journal of Clinical Endocrinology and Metabolism* 86 (1):267–272.

Galen (2001) *De sanitate tuenda*. Translated by Olms. Hildesheim: New York.

Galgani JE, Moro C, and Ravussin E (2008) Metabolic flexibility and insulin resistance. *American Journal of Physiology. Endocrinology and Metabolism* 295 (5):E1009–E1017.

Gallagher D, Kuznia P, Heshka S, Albu J, Heymsfield SB, Goodpaster B, Visser M, and Harris TB (2005) Adipose tissue in muscle: a novel depot similar in size to visceral adipose tissue. *American Journal of Clinical Nutrition* 81 (4):903–910.

Gamboa JA and Garcia FD (2007) Impact of seasonal scarcity on energy balance and body composition in peasant adolescents from Calakmul, Campeche Mexico. *American Journal of Human Biology* 19 (6):751–762.

Ganong WF (1999) *Review of medical physiology, 19th edition*. Appleton and Lange: Stamford, CT.

Garby L, Garrow JS, Jorgensen B, Lammert O, Madsen K, Sorensen P, and Webster J (1988) Relation between energy expenditure and body composition in man: specific energy expenditure in vivo of fat and fat-free tissue. *European Journal of Clinical Nutrition* 42 (4):301–305.

Garnett SP, Cowell CT, Baur LA, Fay RA, Lee J, Coakley J, Peat JK, and Boulton TJ (2001) Abdominal fat and birth size in healthy prepubertal children. *International Journal of Obesity and Related Metabolic Disorders* 25 (11):1667–1673.

Garrow JS and Webster J (1985) Quetelet's index (W/H2) as a measure of fatness. *International Journal of Obesity* 9 (2):147–153.

Gaskin PS and Walker SP (2003) Obesity in a cohort of black Jamaican children as estimated by BMI and other indices of adiposity. *European Journal of Clinical Nutrition* 57 (3):420–426.

Ghazanfar AA and Santos LR (2004) Primate brains in the wild: the sensory bases for social interactions. *Nature Reviews. Neuroscience* 5 (8):603–616.

Gibson RS, Ferguson EL, and Lehrfeld J (1998) Complementary foods for infant feeding in developing countries: their nutrient adequacy and improvement. *European Journal of Clinical Nutrition* 52 (10):764–770.

Gigante DP, Victora CG, Horta BL, and Lima RC (2007) Undernutrition in early life and body composition of adolescent males from a birth cohort study. *British Journal of Nutrition* 97 (5):949–954.

Gill GJ (1991) *Seasonality and agriculture in the developing world: a problem of the poor and powerless*. Cambrige University Press: Cambridge.

Gimbutas M (1974) *The goddesses and gods of old Europe. 6500–3500 B.C. Myths and cult images*. Thames and Hudson: London.

Girod JP and Brotman DJ (2003) The metabolic syndrome as a vicious cycle: does obesity beget obesity? *Medical Hypotheses* 60 (4):584–589.

Gluckman PD and Hanson MA (2006) Evolution, development and timing of puberty. *Trends in Endocrinology and Metabolism* 17 (1):7–12.

Gluckman PD, Hanson MA, and Spencer HG (2005) Predictive adaptive responses and human evolution. *Trends in Ecology and Evolution* 20 (10):527–533.

Godfray HC (1995) Evolutionary theory of parent-offspring conflict. *Nature* 376 (6536):133–138.

Godfray HCJ (1991) Signalling of need by offspring to their parents. *Nature* 352:328–330.

Godfrey K, Robinson S, Barker DJ, Osmond C, and Cox V (1996) Maternal nutrition in early and late pregnancy in relation to placental and fetal growth. *British Medical Journal* 312 (7028):410–414.

Goldman AS (2002) Evolution of the mammary gland defense system and the ontogeny of the immune system. *Journal of Mammary Gland Biology and Neoplasia* 7 (3):277–289.

Gordon ES (1970) Metabolic aspects of obesity. *Advances in Metabolic Disorders* 4:229–296.

Goulding A, Taylor RW, Jones IE, Lewis-Barned NJ, and Williams SM (2003) Body composition of 4- and 5-year-old New Zealand girls: a DXA study of initial adiposity and subsequent 4-year fat change. *International Journal of Obesity and Related Metabolic Disorders* 27 (3):410–415.

Grammer K (1997) Systems of power: the function and evolution of social status. In: Wiessner P and Schiefenhovel W (eds) *Food and the status quest: an interdisciplinary perspective*. Bergahn Books: Providence, RI, pp 69–85.

Grillol LP, Siqueira AF, Silva AC, Martins PA, Verreschi IT, and Sawaya AL (2005) Lower resting metabolic rate and higher velocity of weight gain in a prospective study of stunted vs nonstunted girls living in the shantytowns of Sao Paulo, Brazil. *European Journal of Clinical Nutrition* 59 (7):835–842.

Grunfeld C, Adi S, Soued M, Moser A, Fiers W, and Feingold KR (1990a) Search for mediators of the lipogenic effects of tumor necrosis factor: potential role for interleukin 6. *Cancer Research* 50 (14):4233–4238.

Grunfeld C, Soued M, Adi S, Moser AH, Dinarello CA, and Feingold KR (1990b) Evidence for two classes of cytokines that stimulate hepatic lipogenesis: relationships among tumor necrosis factor, interleukin-1 and interferon-alpha. *Endocrinology* 127 (1):46–54.

Guihard-Costa AM, Papiernik E, Grange G, and Richard A (2002) Gender differences in neonatal subcutaneous fat store in late gestation in relation to maternal weight gain. *Annals of Human Biology* 29 (1):26–36.

Guihard-Costa AM, Papiernik E, and Kolb S (2004) Maternal predictors of subcutaneous fat in the term newborn. *Acta Paediatrica* 93 (3):346–349.

Guillaume M, Lapidus L, and Lambert A (1998) Obesity and nutrition in children. The Belgian Luxembourg Child Study IV. *European Journal of Clinical Nutrition* 52 (5):323–328.

Guillermo-Tuazon MA, Barba CV, Van Raaij JM, and Hautvast JG (1992) Energy intake, energy expenditure, and body composition of poor rural Philippine women throughout the first 6 mo of lactation. *American Journal of Clinical Nutrition* 56 (5):874–880.

Gunnarsdottir I, Birgisdottir BE, Benediktsson R, Gudnason V, and Thorsdottir I (2004) Association between size at birth, truncal fat and obesity in adult life and its contribution to blood pressure and coronary heart disease; study in a high birth weight population. *European Journal of Clinical Nutrition* 58 (5):812–818.

Guo SS and Chumlea WC (1999) Tracking of body mass index in children in relation to overweight in adulthood. *American Journal of Clinical Nutrition* 70 (1):145S–148S.

Guo SS, Zeller C, Chumlea WC, and Siervogel RM (1999) Aging, body composition, and lifestyle: the Fels Longitudinal Study. *American Journal of Clinical Nutrition* 70 (3):405–411.

Gurven M and Walker R (2006) Energetic demand of multiple dependents and the evolution of slow human growth. *Proceedings of the Royal Society B: Biological Sciences* 273 (1588):835–841.

Haas JD (1976) Prenatal and infant development. In: Baker PT and Little MA (eds) *Man in the Andes: a multidisciplinary study of the high altitude Quechua.* Dowden, Hutchinson and Ross: Stroudsburg, pp 161–179.

Haas JD, Baker PT, and Hunt EE (1977) The effects of high altitude on body size and composition of the newborn infant in southern Peru. *Human Biology* 49:611–628.

Haas JD, Moreno-Black G, Frongillo EA, Jr., Pabon J, Pareja G, Ybarnegaray J, and Hurtado L (1982) Altitude and infant growth in Bolivia: a longitudinal study. *American Journal of Physical Anthropology* 59 (3):251–262.

Haig D (1992) Intragenomic conflict and the evolution of eusociality. *Journal of Theoretical Biology* 156 (3):401–403.

Haig D (1993) Genetic conflicts in human pregnancy. *Quarterly Review of Biology* 68 (4):495–532.

Haig D and Wharton R (2003) Prader-Willi syndrome and the evolution of human childhood. *American Journal of Human Biology* 15 (3):320–329.

Hainer V, Stunkard AJ, Kunesova M, Parizkova J, Stich V, and Allison DB (2000) Intrapair resemblance in very low calorie diet-induced weight loss in female obese identical twins. *International Journal of Obesity and Related Metabolic Disorders* 24 (8):1051–1057.

Haines A, McMichael T, Anderson R, and Houghton J (2000) Fossil fuels, transport, and public health. *British Medical Journal* 321 (7270):1168–1169.

Haines L, Wan KC, Lynn R, Barrett TG, and Shield JP (2007) Rising incidence of type 2 diabetes in children in the U.K. *Diabetes Care* 30 (5):1097–1101.

Hales CN and Barker DJ (1992) Type 2 (non-insulin-dependent) diabetes mellitus: the thrifty phenotype hypothesis. *Diabetologia* 35 (7):595–601.

Hallal PC, Victora CG, Wells JC, and Lima RC (2003) Physical inactivity: prevalence and associated variables in Brazilian adults. *Medicine and Science in Sports and Exercise* 35 (11):1894–1900.

Hancock AM, Witonsky DB, Gordon AS, Eshel G, Pritchard JK, Coop G, and Di Rienzo A (2008) Adaptations to Climate in Candidate Genes for Common Metabolic Disorders. *PLoS Genet* 4:e32.

Harding S, Rosato MG and Cruickshank JK (2004) Lack of change in birthweights of infants by generational status among Indian, Pakistani, Bangladeshi, Black Caribbean, and Black African mothers in a British cohort study. *International Journal of Epidemiology* 33(6):1279–1285.

Harpending H and Rogers A (2000) Genetic perspectives on human origins and differentiation. *Annual Review of Genomics and Human Genetics* 1:361–385.

Harrington S (2008) The role of sugar-sweetened beverage consumption in adolescent obesity: a review of the literature. *Journal of School Nursing* 24 (1):3–12.

Harrington TA, Thomas EL, Frost G, Modi N, and Bell JD (2004) Distribution of adipose tissue in the newborn. *Pediatric Research* 55 (3):437–441.

Harris HE, Ellison GT, Holliday M, and Lucassen E (1997) The impact of pregnancy on the long-term weight gain of primiparous women in England. *International Journal of Obesity and Related Metabolic Disorders* 21 (9):747–755.

Harshman LG and Zera AJ (2007) The cost of reproduction: the devil in the details. *Trends in Ecology and Evolution* 22:80–86.

Haschke F (1989) *Body composition during adolescence.* Columbus, Ohio.

Haslam D (2007) Obesity: a medical history. *Obesity Reviews* 8 Suppl.1:31–36.

Hattori K, Tatsumi N, and Tanaka S (1997) Assessment of body composition by using a new chart method. *American Journal of Human Biology* 9:573–578.

Hawkes K (2006) Slow life histories and human evolution. In: Hawkes K, Paine RR (eds) The evolution of human life history. James Currey Ltd: Oxford, pp 95–126.

Hawkes K and Bliege Bird R (2002) Showing off, handicap signaling, and the evolution of men's work. *Evolutionary Anthropology* 11:58–67.

Hayden B (1981) Subsistence and ecological adaptations of modern hunter/gatherers. In: Harding RS and Teleki G (eds) *Omnivorous primates.* Columbia University Press: New York, pp 344–421.

Heberden W (1772) *Some account of a disorder of the breast. Vol. II of medical transactions of the College of Physicians.* Royal College of Physicians: London.

Hediger ML, Overpeck MD, Kuczmarski RJ, McGlynn A, Maurer KR, and Davis WW (1998) Muscularity and fatness of infants and young children born small- or large-for-gestational-age. *Pediatrics* 102 (5):E60.

Heding LG, Persson B, and Stangenberg M (1980) B-cell function in newborn infants of diabetic mothers. *Diabetologia* 19 (5):427–432.

Hellgren EC, Vaughan MR, Kirkpatrick RC, and Scanlon PF (1990) Serial changes in metabolic correlates of hibernation in female black bears. *Journal of Mammalogy* 1990:291–300.

Hellin K and Waller G (1992) Mothers' mood and infant feeding: prediction of problems and practices. *Journal of Reproductive and Infant Psychology* 10:39–51.

Helmchen LA and Henderson RM (2004) Changes in the distribution of body mass index of white US men, 1890–2000. *Annals of Human Biology* 31 (2):174–181.

Hemachandra AH and Klebanoff MA (2006) Use of serial ultrasound to identify periods of fetal growth restriction in relation to neonatal anthropometry. *American Journal of Human Biology* 18 (6):791–797.

Henry CJ (1990) Body mass index and the limits of human survival. *European Journal of Clinical Nutrition* 44 (4):329–335.

Henry CJ and Rees DG (1991) New predictive equations for the estimation of basal metabolic rate in tropical peoples. *European Journal of Clinical Nutrition* 45 (4):177–185.

Henry CJ, Rivers JP, and Payne PR (1988) Protein and energy metabolism in starvation reconsidered. *European Journal of Clinical Nutrition* 42 (7):543–549.

Henss R (2000) Waist-to-hip ratio and attractiveness of the female figure. Evidence from photographic stimuli and methodological considerations. *Personality and Individual Differences* 28, 501–513.

Hess GH (1838) The evolution of heat in multiple proportions. *Poggendorf Ann Chemie Physik* 47:210–212.

Heymsfield SB and McManus CB (1985) Tissue components of weight loss in cancer patients. A new method of study and preliminary observations. *Cancer* 55 (1 Suppl):238–249.

Heymsfield SB, Olafson RP, Kutner MH, and Nixon DW (1979) A radiographic method of quantifying protein-calorie undernutrition. *American Journal of Clinical Nutrition* 32 (3):693–702.

Heymsfield SB, Gallagher D, Mayer L, Beetsch J and Pietrobelli A (2007) Scaling of human body composition to stature: new insights into body mass index. *American Journal of Clinical Nutrition* 86(1):82–91.

Hicks J and Allen GA (1999) A century of change: trends in UK statistics since 1990. Research paper 99/111. London, House of Commons Library.

Hill K and Hurtado AM (1996) *Ache life history: the ecology and demography of a foraging people*. Aldine de Gruyter: New York.

Hippocrates (2008) *The genuine works of Hippocrates translated from the Greek with a preliminary discourse and annotations*. Translated by Adams. The Sydenham Society: London.

Hoffman DJ, Sawaya AL, Coward WA, Wright A, Martins PA, de NC, Tucker KL, and Roberts SB (2000a) Energy expenditure of stunted and nonstunted boys and girls living in the shantytowns of Sao Paulo, Brazil. *American Journal of Clinical Nutrition* 72 (4):1025–1031.

Hoffman DJ, Sawaya AL, Verreschi I, Tucker KL, and Roberts SB (2000b) Why are nutritionally stunted children at increased risk of obesity? Studies of metabolic rate and fat oxidation in shantytown children from Sao Paulo, Brazil. *American Journal of Clinical Nutrition* 72 (3):702–707.

Hohmann G and Fruth B (1997) Food sharing and status in unprovisioned bonobos. In: Wiessner P and Schiefenhovel W (eds) *Food and the status quest: an interdisciplinary perspective*. Bergahn Books: Providence, RI, pp 47–67.

Hold-Cavell B (1997) The ecological bases of status hierarchies. In: Wiessner P and Schiefenhovel W (eds) *Food and the status quest: an interdisciplinary perspective*. Bergahn Books: Providence, RI, pp 19–31.

Holliday MA (1978) Body composition and energy needs during growth. In: Falkner F and Tanner JM (eds) *Human growth*. Plenum: New York, pp 101–117.

Holliday MA (1971) Metabolic rate and organ size during growth from infancy to maturity and during late gastation and early infancy. *Pediatrics* 47 (1):Suppl 2:169–179.

Hosoi S, Honma K, Daimatsu T, Kiyokawa M, Aikawa T, and Watanabe S (2005) Lower energy content of human milk than calculated using conversion factors. *Pediatrics International* 47 (1):7–9.

Hotamisligil GS (2006) Inflammation and metabolic disorders. *Nature* 444 (7121):860–867.

Houston AI and Mcnamara JM (1999) *Models of adaptive behaviour: an approach based on state*. Cambridge University Press: Cambridge.

Hrdy SB (2000) *Mother nature*. Vintage: London.

Huffman S (1988) Women, work and pregnancy outcome. *Mothers and Children* 7 (2):1–3.

Hughes VA, Frontera WR, Roubenoff R, Evans WJ, and Singh MA (2002) Longitudinal changes in body composition in older men and women: role of body weight change and physical activity. *American Journal of Clinical Nutrition* 76 (2):473–481.

Hultquist GT and Olding LB (1975) Pancreatic-islet fibrosis in young infants of diabetic mothers. *Lancet* 2 (7943):1015–1016.

Humphrey N (1986) *The inner eye*. Faber and Faber: London.

Hypponen E, Power C, and Smith GD (2004) Parental growth at different life stages and offspring birthweight: an intergenerational cohort study. *Paediatric and Perinatal Epidemiology* 18 (3):168–177.

Hytten F (1991) Nutrition. In: Hytten F and Chamberlain G (eds) *Clinical physiology in obstetrics*. Blackwell Scientific: Oxford, pp 150–172.

Hytten F and Leitch I (1971) *The physiology of human pregnancy. 2nd ed*. Blackwell Scientific: Oxford.

Iacobellis G, Pond CM, and Sharma AM (2006) Different "weight" of cardiac and general adiposity in predicting left ventricle morphology. *Obesity (Silver Spring)* 14 (10):1679–1684.

Ibanez L, Ong K, Dunger DB, and de Zegher, F (2006) Early development of adiposity and insulin resistance after catch-up weight gain in small-for-gestational-age children. *Journal of Clinical Endocrinology and Metabolism* 91 (6):2153–2158.

Ibanez L, Lopez-Bermejo A, Suarez L, Marcos MV, Diaz M, and de Zegher, F (2008a) Visceral adiposity without overweight in children born small-forgGestational-age. *Journal of Clinical Endocrinology and Metabolism* 93(6):2079–83.

Ibanez L, Suarez L, Lopez-Bermejo A, Diaz M, Valls C, and de ZF (2008b) Early development of visceral fat excess after spontaneous catch-up growth in children with low birth weight. *Journal of Clinical Endocrinology and Metabolism* 93 (3):925–928.

Iglowstein I, Jenni OG, Molinari L, and Largo RH (2003) Sleep duration from infancy to adolescence: reference values and generational trends. *Pediatrics* 111 (2):302–307.

Iliadou A, Cnattingius S, and Lichtenstein P (2004) Low birthweeight and type 2 diabetes: a study on 11162 Swedish twins. *International Journal of Epidemiology* 33:948–953.

Ip S, Chung M, Raman G, Chew P, Magula N, DeVine D, Trikalinos T, and Lau J (2007) Breastfeeding and maternal and infant health outcomes in developed countries. *Evidence Report/Technology Assessment (Full Rep)* (153):1–186.

James WP, Ferro-Luzzi A, and Waterlow JC (1988) Definition of chronic energy deficiency in adults. Report of a working party of the International Dietary Energy Consultative Group. *European Journal of Clinical Nutrition* 42 (12):969–981.

Jasienska G, Ziomkiewicz A, Ellison PT, Lipson SF, and Thune I (2004) Large breasts and narrow waists indicate high reproductive potential in women. *Proceedings. Biological Sciences* 271 (1545):1213–1217.

Jeffery RW and French SA (1998) Epidemic obesity in the United States: are fast foods and television viewing contributing? *American Journal of Public Health* 88 (2):277–280.

Jelliffe DB (1959) Protein-calorie malnutrition in tropical preschool children: a review of recent knowledge. *Journal of Pediatrics* 54 (2):227–256.

Jenkins JM, Brook PF, Sargeant S, and Cooke ID (1995) Endocervical mucus pH is inversely related to serum androgen levels and waist to hip ratio. *Fertility and Sterility* 63 (5):1005–1008.

Jequier E and Tappy L (1999) Regulation of body weight in humans. *Physiological Reviews* 79 (2):451–480.

Jinabhai CC, Taylor M, and Sullivan KR (2003) Implications of the prevalence of stunting, overweight and obesity amongst South African primary school children: a possible nutritional transition? *European Journal of Clinical Nutrition* 57 (2):358–365.

Jobling MA, Hurles ME, and Tyler-Smith C (2008) *Human evolutionary genetics: origins, peoples and disease*. Garland Science: New York.

Johannsen DL, Welk GJ, Sharp RL, and Flakoll PJ (2008) Differences in daily energy expenditure in lean and obese women: the role of posture allocation. *Obesity (Silver Spring)* 16 (1):34–39.

Johnson SE (2003) Life history and the competitive environment: trajectories of growth, maturation, and reproductive output among chacma baboons. *American Journal of Physical Anthropology* 120 (1):83–98.

Johnstone RA and Grafen A (1993) Dishonesty and the handicap principle. *Animal Behaviour* 46, 759–764.

Jones CG, Lawton JH and Shachak M (1994) Organisms as ecosystem engineers. *Oikos* 69:373–386.

Jones M (2007) *Feast: why humans share food*. Oxford University Press: Oxford.

Jönsson KI (1997) Capital and income breeding as alternative tactics of resource use in reproduction. *Oikos* 78:57–66.

Joseph KS, Kramer MS, Marcoux S, Ohlsson A, Wen SW, Allen A, and Platt R (1998) Determinants of preterm birth rates in Canada from 1981 through 1983 and from 1992 through 1994. *New England Journal of Medicine* 339 (20):1434–1439.

Jovanovic-Peterson L, Crues J, Durak E, and Peterson CM (1993) Magnetic resonance imaging in pregnancies complicated by gestational diabetes predicts infant birthweight ratio and neonatal morbidity. *American Journal of Perinatology* 10 (6):432–437.

Kagawa Y, Yanagisawa Y, Hasegawa K, Suzuki H, Yasuda K, Kudo H, Abe M, Matsuda S, Ishikawa Y, Tsuchiya N, Sato A, Umetsu K, and Kagawa Y (2002) Single nucleotide polymorphisms of thrifty genes for energy metabolism: evolutionary origins and prospects for intervention to prevent obesity-related diseases. *Biochemical and Biophysical Research Communications* 295 (2):207–222.

Kahn HS, Narayan KM, Williamson DF, and Valdez R (2000) Relation of birth weight to lean and fat thigh tissue in young men. *International Journal of Obesity and Related Metabolic Disorders* 24 (6):667–672.

Kamel EG, McNeill G, and Van Wijk MC (2000) Change in intra-abdominal adipose tissue volume during weight loss in obese men and women: correlation between magnetic resonance imaging and anthropometric measurements. *International Journal of Obesity and Related Metabolic Disorders* 24 (5):607–613.

Kamis AB and Latif NB (1981) Turnover and total-body water in macaque (Macaca fascicularis) and gibbon (Hylobates lar). *Comparative Biochemistry and Physiology* 70:45–46.

Kaplan H, Hill K, Lancaster J, and Hurtado AM (2000) A theory of human life history evolution: diet, intelligence, and longevity. *Evolutionary Anthropology* 2000 9 (4):156–185.

Karaolis-Danckert N, Buyken AE, Bolzenius K, Perim de FC, Lentze MJ, and Kroke A (2006) Rapid growth among term children whose birth weight was appropriate for gestational age has a longer lasting effect on body fat percentage than on body mass index. *American Journal of Clinical Nutrition* 84 (6):1449–1455.

Kardjati S, Kusin JA, Schofield WM, and de WC (1990) Energy supplementation in the last trimester of pregnancy in East Java, Indonesia: effect on maternal anthropometry. *American Journal of Clinical Nutrition* 52 (6):987–994.

Kashyap S, Schulze KF, Forsyth M, Zucker C, Dell RB, Ramakrishnan R, and Heird WC (1988) Growth, nutrient retention, and metabolic response in low birth weight infants fed varying intakes of protein and energy. *Journal of Pediatrics* 113 (4):713–721.

Katch VL, Campaigne B, Freedson P, Sady S, Katch FI, and Behnke AR (1980) Contribution of breast volume and weight to body fat distribution in females. *American Journal of Physical Anthropology* 53 (1):93–100.

Katz J (1896) Die mineralischen Bestandtheile des Muskelfleisches. *Archiv für der Gesammte Physiologie des Menschen und der Tiere* 63:1–85.

Katzmarzyk PT and Leonard WR (1998) Climatic influences on human body size and proportions: ecological adaptations and secular trends. *American Journal of Physical Anthropology* 106 (4):483–503.

Katzmarzyk PT, Perusse L, Malina RM, and Bouchard C (1999) Seven-year stability of indicators of obesity and adipose tissue distribution in the Canadian population. *American Journal of Clinical Nutrition* 69 (6):1123–1129.

Kaye W (2008) Neurobiology of anorexia and bulimia nervosa. *Physiology and Behavior* 94 (1):121–135.

Keith NM, Rowntree LG, and Gerachty JT (1915) A method for the determination of plasma and blood volume. *Archives of Internal Medicine* 16:547–576.

Keith SW, Redden DT, Katzmarzyk PT, Boggiano MM, Hanlon EC, Benca RM, Ruden D, Pietrobelli A, Barger JL, Fontaine KR, Wang C, Aronne LJ, Wright SM, Baskin M, Dhurandhar NV, Lijoi MC, Grilo CM, DeLuca M, Westfall AO, and Allison DB (2006) Putative contributors to the secular increase in obesity: exploring the roads less traveled. *International Journal of Obesity (London)* 30 (11):1585–1594.

Kelly JL, Stanton WR, McGee R, and Silva PA (1992) Tracking relative weight in subjects studied longitudinally from ages 3 to 13 years. *Journal of Paediatrics and Child Health* 28 (2):158–161.

Kelly RL (1995) *The foraging spectrum.* Smithsonian Institution Press: Washington.

Kensara OA, Wootton SA, Phillips DI, Patel M, Jackson AA, and Elia M (2005) Fetal programming of body composition: relation between birth weight and body composition measured with dual-energy X-ray absorptiometry and anthropometric methods in older Englishmen. *American Journal of Clinical Nutrition* 82 (5):980–987.

Keppel KG and Taffel SM (1993) Pregnancy-related weight gain and retention: implications of the 1990 Institute of Medicine guidelines. *American Journal of Public Health* 83 (8):1100–1103.

Kerr DS, Stevens MC, and Robinson HM (1978) Fasting metabolism in infants. I. Effect of severe undernutrition on energy and protein utilization. *Metabolism* 27 (4):411–435.

Kershaw EE and Flier JS (2004) Adipose tissue as an endocrine organ. *Journal of Clinical Endocrinology and Metabolism* 89 (6):2548–2556.

Keys A and Brozek J (1953) Body fat in adult man. *Physiological Reviews* 33 (3):245–325.

Keys A, Brozek J, Henschel A, Mickelsen O, and Taylor HL (1950) *The biology of human starvation.* University of Minnesota Press: Minneapolis.

Kilner RM (2001) A growth cost of begging in captive canary chicks. *Proceedings of the National Academy of Sciences of the United States of America* 98 (20):11394–11398.

Kimm SY, Barton BA, Obarzanek E, McMahon RP, Sabry ZI, Waclawiw MA, Schreiber GB, Morrison JA, Similo S, and Daniels SR (2001) Racial divergence in adiposity during adolescence: the NHLBI Growth and Health Study. *Pediatrics* 107 (3):E34.

Kiple KF (1999) *Cambridge world history of human diseases.* Cambridge University Press: Cambridge.

Kleiber M (1961) *The fire of life: an introduction to animal energetics.* Krieger: Huntingdon, NY.

Klein J and Fasshauer M (2007) What are subcutaneous adipocytes really good for? Viewpoint 1. *Experimental Dermatology* 16:50–53.

Kluger MJ, Kozak W, Conn CA, Leon LR, and Sosszynski D (1997) The adaptive value of fever. In: Mackowiak PA (ed) *Fever: basic mechanisms and management*, 2nd edition. Raven-Lippincott: New York, pp 255–266.

Knott CD (1998) Changes in orangutan caloric intake, energy balance, and ketones in response to fluctuating fruit availability. *International Journal of Primatology* 19:1061–1079.

Knott CD (2005) Energetic responses to food availability in the great apes: implications for hominin evolution. In: Brockman DK and van Schaik CP (eds) *Seasonality in primates: studies of living and extinct human and non-human primates*. Cambridge University Press: Cambridge, pp 351–378.

Komlos J (1998) Shrinking in a growing economy? The mystery of physical stature during the industrial revolution. *Journal of Economic History* (58):779–802.

Komlos J (1994) On the significance of anthropometric history. In: Komlos J (ed) *Stature, living standards, and economic development*. Chicago University Press: Chicago, pp 210–220.

Koo WW, Walters JC, and Hockman EM (2000) Body composition in human infants at birth and postnatally. *Journal of Nutrition* 130 (9):2188–2194.

Kopp-Woodroffe SA, Manore MM, Dueck CA, Skinner JS, and Matt KS (1999) Energy and nutrient status of amenorrheic athletes participating in a diet and exercise training intervention program. *International Journal of Sport Nutrition* 9 (1):70–88.

Korkeila M, Kaprio J, Rissanen A, Koshenvuo M, and Sorensen TI (1998) Predictors of major weight gain in adult Finns: stress, life satisfaction and personality traits. *International Journal of Obesity and Related Metabolic Disorders* 22 (10):949–957.

Kotani K, Tokunaga K, Fujioka S, Kobatake T, Keno Y, Yoshida S, Shimomura I, Tarui S, and Matsuzawa Y (1994) Sexual dimorphism of age-related changes in whole-body fat distribution in the obese. *International Journal of Obesity and Related Metabolic Disorders* 18 (4):207–2.

Kotler DP (2008) HIV and antiretroviral therapy: lipid abnormalities and associated cardiovascular risk in HIV-infected patients. *Journal of Acquired Immune Deficiency Syndrome* 49 Suppl 2:S79–S85.

Kramer MS, Morin I, Yang H, Platt RW, Usher R, McNamara H, Joseph KS, and Wen SW (2002) Why are babies getting bigger? Temporal trends in fetal growth and its determinants. *Journal of Pediatrics* 141 (4):538–542.

Kretchmer N (1993) Lactose tolerance and malabsorption. In: Kiple KF (ed) *The Cambridge world history of human disease*. Cambridge University Press: Cambridge, pp 813–817.

Kreymann G, Grosser S, Buggisch P, Gottschall C, Matthaei S, and Greten H (1993) Oxygen consumption and resting metabolic rate in sepsis, sepsis syndrome, and septic shock. *Critical Care Medicine* 21 (7):1012–1019.

Krishnaveni GV, Hill JC, Veena SR, Leary SD, Saperia J, Chachyamma KJ, Karat SC, and Fall CH (2005) Truncal adiposity is present at birth and in early childhood in South Indian children. *Indian Pediatrics* 42 (6):527–538.

Kromeyer-Hauschild K and Zellner K (2007) Trends in overweight and obesity and changes in the distribution of body mass index in schoolchildren of Jena, East Germany. *European Journal of Clinical Nutrition* 61 (3):404–411.

Ksiazek A, Konarzewski M, Chadzinska M, and Cichon M (2003) Costs of immune response in cold-stressed laboratory mice selected for high and low basal metabolism rates. *Proceedings of the Royal Society B: Biological Sciences* 270:2025–2031.

Kuk JL, Lee S, Heymsfield SB, and Ross R (2005) Waist circumference and abdominal adipose tissue distribution: influence of age and sex. *American Journal of Clinical Nutrition* 81 (6):1330–1334.

Kulin HE, Bwibo N, Mutie D, and Santner SJ (1982) The effect of chronic childhood malnutrition on pubertal growth and development. *American Journal of Clinical Nutrition* 36 (3):527–536.

Kushner RF, Schoeller DA, Fjeld CR, and Danford L (1992) Is the impedance index (ht2/R) significant in predicting total body water? *American Journal of Clinical Nutrition* 56 (5):835–839.

Kuzawa CW (1998) Adipose tissue in human infancy and childhood: an evolutionary perspective. *American Journal of Physical Anthropology* Suppl 27:177–209.

Kuzawa CW (2005) Fetal origins of developmental plasticity: are fetal cues reliable predictors of future nutritional environments? *American Journal of Human Biology* 17 (1):5–21.

Kuzawa CW, Quinn EA, and Adair LS (2007) Leptin in a lean population of Filipino adolescents. *American Journal of Physical Anthropology* 132 (4):642–649.

Kuzawa CW and Sweet E (2009) Epigenetics and the embodiment of race: developmental origins of US racial disparities in cardiovascular health. *American Journal of Human Biology* 21(1):2–15.

La Berge AF (2008) How the ideology of low fat conquered America. *Journal of the History of Medicine and Allied Sciences* 63(2):139–177.

Labayen I, Moreno LA, Blay MG, Blay VA, Mesana MI, Gonzalez-Gross M, Bueno G, Sarria A, and Bueno M (2006) Early programming of body composition and fat distribution in adolescents. *Journal of Nutrition* 136 (1):147–152.

Lahr MM (1996) *The evolution of modern human diversity*. Cambridge University Press: Cambridge.

Lahr MM and Foley R (1994) Multiple dispersals and modern human origins. *Evolutionary Anthropology* 3:48–60.

Lahr MM and Foley R (1998) Towards a theory of modern human origins: geography, demography, and diversity in recent human evolution. *Yearbook of Physical Anthropology* 41:137–176.

Lallukka T, Lahelma E, Rahkonen O, Roos E, Laaksonen E, Martikainen P, Head J, Brunner E, Mosdol A, Marmot M, Sekine M, Nasermoaddeli A, and Kagamimori S (2008) Associations of job strain and working overtime with adverse health behaviors and obesity: evidence from the Whitehall II Study, Helsinki Health Study, and the Japanese Civil Servants Study. *Social Science and Medicine* 66 (8):1681–1698.

Lancet (2008) Finding long-term solutions to the world food crisis. *Lancet* 371: 1389.

Lassek WD and Gaulin SJ (2006) Changes in body fat distribution in relation to parity in American women: a covert form of maternal depletion. *American Journal of Physical Anthropology* 131 (2):295–302.

Lassek WD and Gaulin SJ (2007a) Brief communication: menarche is related to fat distribution. *American Journal of Physical Anthropology* 133 (4):1147–1151.

Lassek WD and Gaulin SJ (2007b) Waist-hip ratio and cognitive ability: is gluteofemoral fat a privileged store of neurodevelopmental resources? *Evolution and Human Behavior* 29:26–34.

Laugero KD and Moberg GP (2000) Summation of behavioural and immunological stress: metabolic consequences to the growing mouse. *American Journal of Physiology.* 279:E44–E49.

Lavoisier AL and Laplace PS (1783) Mémoire sur la chaleur. *Mémoire de l'Académie Royale des Sciences.* Académie des Sciences: Paris pp 355–408.

Law CM, Barker DJ, Osmond C, Fall CH, and Simmonds SJ (1992) Early growth and abdominal fatness in adult life. *Journal of Epidemiology and Community Health* 46 (3):184–186.

Lawrence M, Coward WA, Lawrence F, Cole TJ, and Whitehead RG (1987a) Fat gain during pregnancy in rural African women: the effect of season and dietary status. *American Journal of Clinical Nutrition* 45 (6):1442–1450.

Lawrence M, Lawrence F, Coward WA, Cole TJ, and Whitehead RG (1987b) Energy requirements of pregnancy in The Gambia. *Lancet* 2 (8567): 1072–1076.

Le Stunff C, Fallin D, and Bougneres P (2001) Paternal transmission of the very common class I INS VNTR alleles predisposes to childhood obesity. *Nature Genetics* 29 (1):96–99.

Leary SD, Fall C, Osmond C, Lovel H, Campbell D, Eriksson J, Forrester T, Godfrey K, Hill J, Jie M, Law C, Newby R, Robinson S, and Yajnik C (2006a) Geographical variation in neonatal phenotype. *Acta Obstetricia et Gynecologica Scandinavica* 85 (9):1080–1089.

Leary SD, Smith GD, Rogers IS, Reilly JJ, Wells JC, and Ness AR (2006b) Smoking during pregnancy and offspring fat and lean mass in childhood. *Obesity (Silver Spring)* 14 (12):2284–2293.

Lechtig A, Delgado H, Yarbrough C, Habicht JP, Martorell R, and Klein RE (1976) A simple assessment of the risk of low birth weight to select women for nutritional intervention. *American Journal of Obstetrics and Gynecology* 125 (1):25–34.

Lee MO and Schaffer NK (1934) Anterior pituitary growth hormone and the composition of growth. *Journal of Nutrition* 7:337–363.

Lee PC, Majluf P, and Gordon IJ (1991) Growth, weaning and maternal investment from a comparative perspective. *Journal of ZoologyLond.* 225:99–114.

Le Magne J (1971) Advances in studies on the physiological control and regulation of food intake. In: Stellar E and Sprague JM (eds) *Progress in physiological psychology.* Academic Press: New York, pp 203–261.

Le Magne J (1985) *Hunger.* Cambridge University Press: Cambridge.

Leon DA, Koupilova I, Lithell HO, Berglund L, Mohsen R, Vagero D, Lithell UB and McKeigue PM (1996) Failure to realise growth potential in utero and adult obesity in relation to blood pressure in 50 year old Swedish men. *British Medical Journal* 312(7028):401–406.

Leonard WR and Robertson ML (1994) Evolutionary perspectives on human nutrition: the influence of brain and body size on diet and metabolism. *American Journal of Human Biology* 6:77–88.

Leonard WR and Robertson ML (1997) Comparative primate energetics and honinid evolution. *American Journal of Physical Anthropology* 102:265–281.

Leonard WR, Robertson ML, Snodgrass JJ, and Kuzawa CW (2003) Metabolic correlates of hominid brain evolution. *Comparative Biochemistry and Physiology. Part A: Molecular and Integrative Physiology* 136 (1):5–15.

Leonard WR and Thomas BR (1989) Biosocial responses to seasonal food stress in highland Peru. *Human Biology* 61:65–85.

Lewin R (1998) *Principles of human evolution.* Blackwell Scientific Inc: Malden, MA.

Lewin R and Foley RA (2004) *Principles of human evolution.* Blackwell Science Ltd: Oxford.

Ley RE, Turnbaugh PJ, Klein S, and Gordon JI (2006) Microbial ecology: human gut microbes associated with obesity. *Nature* 444 (7122):1022–1023.

Leyton GB (1946) The effects of slow starvation. *Lancet* i:73–79.

Li H, Stein AD, Barnhart HX, Ramakrishnan U, and Martorell R (2003) Associations between prenatal and postnatal growth and adult body size and composition. *American Journal of Clinical Nutrition* 77 (6):1498–1505.

Li R, O'Connor L, Buckley D, and Specker B (1995) Relation of activity levels to body fat in infants 6 to 12 months of age. *Journal of Pediatrics* 126 (3):353–357.

Lindsay RS, Dabelea D, Roumain J, Hanson RL, Bennett PH, and Knowler WC (2000) Type 2 diabetes and low birth weight: the role of paternal inheritance in the association of low birth weight and diabetes. *Diabetes* 49 (3):445–449.

Little MA, Leslie PW, and Campbell KL (1992) Energy reserves and parity of nomadic Turkana pastoralists. *American Journal of Human Biology* 4:729–738.

Littman AJ, Vitiello MV, Foster-Schubert K, Ulrich CM, Tworoger SS, Potter JD, Weigle DS, and McTiernan A (2007) Sleep, ghrelin, leptin and changes in body weight during a 1-year moderate-intensity physical activity intervention. *International Journal of Obesity (London)* 31 (3):466–475.

Livi-Bacci M (1992) *A concise history of world population.* Blackwell: Oxford.

Lochmiller RL and Deerenberg C (2000) Trade-offs in evolutionary immunology: just what is the cost of immunity? *Oikos* 88:87–98.

Locke R (2002) Preventing obesity: the breast milk-leptin connection. *Acta Paediatrica* 91 (9):891–894.

Long KZ and Nanthakumar N (2004) Energetic and nutritional regulation of the adaptive immune response and trade-offs in ecological immunology. *American Journal of Human Biology* 16 (5):499–507.

Long NC (1996) Evolution of infectious disease: how evolutionary forces shape physiological responses to pathogens. *News in Physiological Sciences* 11:83–90.

Loos RJ, Beunen G, Fagard R, Derom C, and Vlietinck R (2001) Birth weight and body composition in young adult men: a prospective twin study. *International Journal of Obesity and Related Metabolic Disorders* 25 (10):1537–1545.

Loos RJ, Beunen G, Fagard R, Derom C, and Vlietinck R (2002) Birth weight and body composition in young women: a prospective twin study. *American Journal of Clinical Nutrition* 75 (4):676–682.

Lord G (2002) Role of leptin in immunology. *Nutrition Reviews* 60 (10 Pt 2):S35–S38.

Loutan L and Lamotte JM (1984) Seasonal variations in nutrition among a group of nomadic pastoralists in Niger. *Lancet* i:945–947.

Lucas A (1991) Programming by early nutrition in man. *Ciba Foundation Symposium* 156:38–50.

Lucas A, Fewtrell MS, and Cole TJ (1999) Fetal origins of adult disease: the hypothesis revisited. *British Medical Journal* 319 (7204):245–249.

Ludwig DS (2007) Childhood obesity: the shape of things to come. *New England Journal of Medicine* 357 (23):2325–2327.

Ludwig DS, Peterson KE, and Gortmaker SL (2001) Relation between consumption of sugar-sweetened drinks and childhood obesity: a prospective, observational analysis. *Lancet* 357 (9255):505–508.

Lukmanji Z (1992) Women's workload and its impact on their health and nutritional status. *Progress in Food and Nutrition Science* 16 (2):163–179.

Lumey LH (1998) Compensatory placental growth after restricted maternal nutrition in early pregnancy. *Placenta* 19 (1):105–111.

Lynch SM and Zellner DA (1999) Figure Preferences in two generations of men: the use of figure drawings illustrating differences in muscle mass. *Sex Roles* 40:833–843.

Lyons MJ, Faust IM, Hemmes RB, Buskirk DR, Hirsch J, and Zabriskie JB (1982) A virally induced obesity syndrome in mice. *Science* 216 (4541):82–85.

Mace R (2008) Reproducing in cities. *Science* 319 (5864):764–766.

Maffeis C, Zaffanello M, and Schutz Y (1997) Relationship between physical inactivity and adiposity in prepubertal boys. *Journal of Pediatrics* 131 (2):288–292.

Magnus G (1847) Über die im Blute enthaltenen Gase, Sauerstoffe, Stickstoff und Kohlensaure. *Annalen der Physik und Chemie* 40:583–606.

Maher V (1992) Breast-feeding in cross-cultural perspective: paradoxes and proposals. In: Maher V (ed) *The anthropology of breast-feeding: natural law or social constraint*. Berg Publishers Ltd: Providence, RI, pp 1–32.

Maisey DS, Vale EL, Cornelissen PL, and Tovee MJ (1999) Characteristics of male attractiveness for women. *Lancet* 353 (9163):1500.

Malik VS, Schulze MB, and Hu FB (2006) Intake of sugar-sweetened beverages and weight gain: a systematic review. *American Journal of Clinical Nutrition* 84 (2):274–288.

Malina RM (1996) Tracking of physical activity and physical fitness across the lifespan. *Research Quarterly for Exercise and Sport* 67 (3 Suppl):S48–S57.

Malina RM (2008) Regional body composition: age, sex, and ethnic variation. In: Roche AF, Heymsfield SB, and Lohman TG (eds) *Human body composition*. Human Kinetics: Champaign, IL, pp 217–255.

Malina RM and Bouchard C (1991) *Growth, maturation, and physical activity*. Human Kinetics: Champaign, IL.

Malina RM, Katzmarzyk PT, and Beunen G (1996) Birth weight and its relationship to size attained and relative fat distribution at 7 to 12 years of age. *Obesity Research* 4 (4):385–390.

Malina RM and Little BB (2008) Physical activity: the present in the context of the past. *American Journal of Human Biology* 20 (4):373–391.

Manco M, Fernandez-Real JM, Equitani F, Vendrell J, Valera Mora ME, Nanni G, Tondolo V, Calvani M, Ricart W, Castagneto M, and Mingrone G (2007) Effect of massive weight loss on inflammatory adipocytokines and the innate immune system in morbidly obese women. *Journal of Clinical Endocrinology and Metabolism* 92 (2):483–490.

Mannino MA and Thomas KD (2002) Depletion of a resource? The impact of prehistoric human foraging on intertidal mollusc communities and its significance for human settlement, mobility and dispersal. *World Archaeology* 33:452–474.

Marin Spring PC, Amancio OM, Nobriga F, Araujo G, Koppel SM, and Dodge JA (1985) Fat and energy content of breast milk of malnourished and well nourished women, Brazil 1982. *Annals of Tropical Paediatrics* 5 (2):83–87.

Martin-Gronert MS and Ozanne SE (2005) Programming of appetite and type 2 diabetes. *Early Human Development* 81 (12):981–988.

Martinez-Cordero C, mador-Licona N, Guizar-Mendoza JM, Hernandez-Mendez J, and Ruelas-Orozco G (2006) Body fat at birth and cord blood levels of insulin, adiponectin, leptin, and insulin-like growth factor-I in small-for-gestational-age infants. *Archives of Medical Research* 37 (4):490–494.

Martin II LB, Scheuerlein A, and Wikelski M (2002) Immune activity elevates energy expenditure of house sparrows: a link between direct and indirect costs? *Proceedings of the Royal Society B: Biological Sciences* 270:153–158.

Mathews F, Youngman L, and Neil A (2004) Maternal circulating nutrient concentrations in pregnancy: implications for birth and placental weights of term infants. *American Journal of Clinical Nutrition* 79 (1):103–110.

Mathews F, Yudkin P, and Neil A (1999) Influence of maternal nutrition on outcome of pregnancy: prospective cohort study. *British Medical Journal* 319 (7206):339–343.

Mattacks CA, Sadler D, and Pond CM (2004) Site-specific differences in fatty acid composition of dendritic cells and associated adipose tissue in popliteal depot, mesentery, and omentum and their modulation by chronic inflammation and dietary lipids. *Lymphatic Research and Biology* 2 (3):107–129.

Matthes JW, Lewis PA, Davies DP, and Bethel JA (1996) Body size and subcutaneous fat patterning in adolescence. *Archives of Diseases in Childhood* 75 (6):521–523.

May RM and Rubenstein DI (1984) Reproductive strategies. In: Austin CR and Short RV (eds) *Reproductive fitness*. Cambridge University Press: London, pp 1–23.

Mayer L, Walsh BT, Pierson RN, Jr., Heymsfield SB, Gallagher D, Wang J, Parides MK, Leibel RL, Warren MP, Killory E, and Glasofer D (2005) Body fat redistribution after weight gain in women with anorexia nervosa. *American Journal of Clinical Nutrition* 81 (6):1286–1291.

Mayes PA (1993) Intermediary metabolism of fructose. *American Journal of Clinical Nutrition* 58(5 Suppl):754S–765S.

Mayo-Smith W, Hayes CW, Biller BM, Klibanski A, Rosenthal H, and Rosenthal DI (1989) Body fat distribution measured with CT: correlations in healthy subjects, patients with anorexia nervosa, and patients with Cushing syndrome. *Radiology* 170 (2):515–518.

Mazess RB, Cameron JR, and Sorenson JA (1970) Determining body composition by radiation absorption spectrometry. *Nature* 228 (5273):771–772.

McArdle WD, Katch FI, and Katch VL (1991) *Exercise physiology: energy, nutrition and human performance*. Lea and Febiger: Philadelphia.

McBrearty S and Jablonski NG (2005) First fossil chimpanzee. *Nature* 437 (7055):105–108.

McCance DR, Pettitt DJ, Hanson RL, Jacobsson LT, Knowler WC, and Bennett PH (1994) Birth weight and non-insulin dependent diabetes: thrifty genotype, thrifty phenotype, or surviving small baby genotype? *British Medical Journal* 308 (6934):942–945.

McCance RA (1962) Food, growth, and time. *Lancet* 2 (7258):671–676.

McCarthy A, Hughes R, Tilling K, Davies D, Smith GD, and Ben-Shlomo Y (2007) Birth weight; postnatal, infant, and childhood growth; and obesity in young adulthood: evidence from the Barry Caerphilly Growth Study. *American Journal of Clinical Nutrition* 86 (4):907–913.

McDade TW, Reyes-Garcia V, Tanner S, Huanca T, and Leonard WR (2008) Maintenance versus growth: investigating the costs of immune activation among children in lowland Bolivia. *American Journal of Physical Anthropology* 136 (4):478–484.

McDougall I, Brown FH, and Fleagle JG (2005) Stratigraphic placement and age of modern humans from Kibish, Ethiopia. *Nature* 433 (7027):733–736.

McGarvey ST (1991) Obesity in Samoans and a perspective on its etiology in Polynesians. *American Journal of Clinical Nutrition* 53 (6 Suppl):1586S–1594S.

McGloin AF, Livingstone MB, Greene LC, Webb SE, Gibson JM, Jebb SA, Cole TJ, Coward WA, Wright A, and Prentice AM (2002) Energy and fat intake in obese and lean children at varying risk of obesity. *International Journal of Obesity and Related Metabolic Disorders* 26 (2):200–207.

McGrew WC (1997) Dominant status, food sharing, and reproductive success in chimpanzees. In: Wiessner P and Schiefenhovel W (eds) *Food and the status quest: an interdisciplinary perspective*. Bergahn Books: Providence, RI, pp 39–45.

McHenry HM (1992a) Body size and proportions in early hominids. *American Journal of Physical Anthropology* 87:407–431.

McHenry HM (1992b) How big were early hominids? *Evolutionary Anthropology* 1:15–20.

McKeigue PM (1996) Metabolic consequences of obesity and body fat pattern: lessons from migrant studies. *Ciba Foundation Symposium* 201:54–64.

McKeigue PM, Shah B, and Marmot MG (1991) Relation of central obesity and insulin resistance with high diabetes prevalence and cardiovascular risk in South Asians. *Lancet* 337 (8738):382–386.

McMichael AJ (2001) Diabetes, ancestral diets and dairy foods. In: Macbeth H, Sheety P (eds) *Health and ethnicity*. Taylor and Francis: London, pp 133–146.

McNeely MJ, Fujimoto WY, Leonetti DL, Tsai EC, and Boyko EJ (2007) The association between birth weight and visceral fat in middle-age adults. *Obesity (Silver Spring)* 15 (4):816–819.

McNeill G, Payne PR, Rivers JP, Enos AM, deBritto J, and Mukarji DS (1988) Socio-economic and seasonal patterns of adult energy nutrition in a south Indian village. *Ecology of Food and Nutrition* 22:85–95.

McNeill J (2000) *Something new under the sun: an environmental history of the twentieth century*. Penguin Press: London.

Mead JG (1989) Shepherd's beaked whale – *Tasmacetus shepherdi*. In: Ridgway SH and Harrison SR (eds) *Handbook of marine mammals, volume 4: river dolphins and larger toothed whales*. Academic: London, pp 309–320.

Mela DJ and Catt S (1996) Ontogeny of human taste and smell preferences and their implications for food selection. In: Henry CJK and Ulijaszek SJ (eds) *Long-term consequences of early environment: growth, development and the lifespan developmental persepctive*. Cambridge University Press: Cambridge, pp 139–154.

Mellars P (2006a) A new radiocarbon revolution and the dispersal of modern humans in Eurasia. *Nature* 439 (7079):931–935.

Mellars P (2006b) Why did modern human populations disperse from Africa ca. 60,000 years ago? A new model. *Proceedings of the National Academy of Sciences of the United States of America* 103 (25):9381–9386.

Menken J and Cambpell C (1992) Forum: on the demography of South Asian famines. *Health Transition Review* 2:91–108.

Merchant AT, Anand SS, Vuksan V, Jacobs R, Davis B, Teo K, and Yusuf S (2005) Protein intake is inversely associated with abdominal obesity in a multi-ethnic population. *Journal of Nutrition* 135 (5):1196–1201.

Merchant K, Martorell R, and Haas JD (1990) Consequences for maternal nutrition of reproductive stress across consecutive pregnancies. *American Journal of Clinical Nutrition* 52 (4):616–620.

Mericq V, Ong KK, Bazaes R, Pena V, Avila A, Salazar T, Soto N, Iniguez G, and Dunger DB (2005) Longitudinal changes in insulin sensitivity and secretion from birth to age three years in small- and appropriate-for-gestational-age children. *Diabetologia* 48 (12):2609–2614.

Michaels L (2001) *The eighteenth-century origins of angina pectoris: predisposing causes, recognition and aftermath*. Wellcome Trust: London.

Mills JL, Shiono PH, Shapiro LR, Crawford PB, and Rhoads GG (1986) Early growth predicts timing of puberty in boys: results of a 14-year nutrition and growth study. *Journal of Pediatrics* 109 (3):543–547.

Milton K (2000) Hunter-gatherer diets-a different perspective. *American Journal of Clinical Nutrition* 71 (3):665–667.

Mintz SW (1985) *Sweetness and power: the place of sugar in modern history*. Viking Penguin Inc: New York.

Modi N, Thomas EL, Uthaya SN, Umranikar S, Bell JD and Yajnik C (2009) Whole body magnetic resonance imaging of healthy newborn infants demonstrates increased central adiposity in Asian Indians. *Pediatric Research* 65(5):584–587.

Mokdad AH, Serdula MK, Dietz WH, Bowman BA, Marks JS, and Koplan JP (1999) The spread of the obesity epidemic in the United States, 1991–1998. *Journal of the American Medical Association* 282 (16):1519–1522.

Mokyr J and Ó Gráda C (2002) What do people die of during famines: the Great Irish Famine in comparative perspective. *European Review of Economic History* 6:339–363.

Molarius A, Seidell JC, Sans S, Tuomilehto J, and Kuulasmaa K (1999) Waist and hip circumferences, and waist-hip ratio in 19 populations of the WHO MONICA Project. *International Journal of Obesity and Related Metabolic Disorders* 23 (2):116–125.

Molarius A, Seidell JC, Sans S, Tuomilehto J, and Kuulasmaa K (2000) Educational level, relative body weight, and changes in their association over 10 years: an international perspective from the WHO MONICA Project. *American Journal of Public Health* 90 (8):1260–1268.

Mondloch CJ (1995) Chcik hunger and begging effect parental allocation of feeding in pigeons. *Animal Behavior* 49:601–613.

Moore SE, Morgan G, Collinson AC, Swain JA, O'Connell MA, and Prentice AM (2002) Leptin, malnutrition, and immune response in rural Gambian children. *Archives of Diseases in Childhood* 87 (3):192–197.

Moran C, Hernandez E, Ruiz IE, Fonseca ME, Bermubez JA, and Zarate A (1999) Upper body obesity and hyperinsulinemia are associated with anovulation. *Gynecologic and Obstetric Investigation* 47:1–5.

Moret Y and Schmid-Hempel P (2000) Survival for immunity: the price of immune system activation for bumblebee workers. *Science* 290 (5494):1166–1168.

Mori A (1979) Analysis of population changes by measurement of body weight in the Koshima group of Japanese monkeys. *Primates* 20:371–397.

Morrison CD and Berthoud HR (2007) Neurobiology of nutrition and obesity. *Nutrition Review* 65 (12 Pt 1):517–534.

Moses RG, Luebcke M, Davis WS, Coleman KJ, Tapsell LC, Petocz P, and Brand-Miller JC (2006) Effect of a low-glycemic-index diet during pregnancy on obstetric outcomes. *American Journal of Clinical Nutrition* 84 (4):807–812.

Motil KJ, Sheng HP, Kertz BL, Montandon CM, and Ellis KJ (1998) Lean body mass of well-nourished women is preserved during lactation. *American Journal of Clinical Nutrition* 67 (2):292–300.

Mueller BR and Bale TL (2006) Impact of prenatal stress on long term body weight is dependent on timing and maternal sensitivity. *Physiology and Behavior* 88 (4–5):605–614.

Mueller WH, Dai S, and Labarthe DR (2001) Tracking body fat distribution during growth: using measurements at two occasions vs one. *International Journal of Obesity and Related Metabolic Disorders* 25 (12):1850–1855.

Mulligan J, Betts P, and Elia M (2005) Programming of body composition: studies in children aged 6.6 to 9.1 years. *International Journal of Body Composition Research* 3:97.

Muthayya S, Dwarkanath P, Thomas T, Vaz M, Mhaskar A, Mhaskar R, Thomas A, Bhat S, and Kurpad A (2006) Anthropometry and body composition of south Indian babies at birth. *Public Health Nutrition* 9 (7):896–903.

National Sleep Foundation (2008) *Sleep in America poll 2001*. National Sleep Foundation: Washington, DC.

Nedergaard J, Bengtsson T, and Cannon B (2007) Unexpected evidence for active brown adipose tissue in adult humans. *American Journal of Physiology Endocrinology and Metabolism* 293 (2):E444–E452.

Neel V (1962) Diabetes mellitus: a "thrifty" genotype rendered detrimental by "progress"? *American Journal of Human Genetics* 14:353–362.

Nelson LD and Morrison EL (2005) The symptoms of resource scarcity: judgments of food and finances influence preferences for potential partners. *Psychological Science* 16 (2):167–173.

Ness AR, Leary SD, Reilly J, Wells J, Tobias J, Clark E, and Smith GD (2006) The social patterning of fat and lean mass in a contemporary cohort of children. *International Journal of Pediatrics and Obstetrics* 1 (1):59–61.

Ness AR, Leary SD, Mattocks C, Blair SN, Reilly JJ, Wells J, Ingle S, Tilling K, Smith GD, and Riddoch C (2007) Objectively measured physical activity and fat mass in a large cohort of children. *PLoS Medicine* 4 (3):e97.

Nestle M (2003) The ironic politics of obesity. *Science* 299 (5608):781.

Newman LF, Boegehold A, Herlihy D, Kates RW, and Raaflaub K (1990) Agricultural intensification, urbanisation, and hierarchy. In: Newman LF (ed) *Hunger in history*. Blackwell: Cambridge, MA, pp 101–125.

Nicholls D, Wells JC, Singhal A, and Stanhope R (2002) Body composition in early onset eating disorders. *European Journal of Clinical Nutrition* 56 (9):857–865.

Nielsen JN, O'Brien KO, Witter FR, Chang SC, Mancini J, Nathanson MS, and Caulfield LE (2006) High gestational weight gain does not improve birth weight in a cohort of African American adolescents. *American Journal of Clinical Nutrition* 84 (1):183–189.

Nindl BC, Scoville CR, Sheehan KM, Leone CD, and Mello RP (2002) Gender differences in regional body composition and somatotrophic influences of IGF-I and leptin. *Journal of Applied Physiology* 92 (4):1611–1618.

Nommsen LA, Lovelady CA, Heinig MJ, Lonnerdal B, and Dewey KG (1991) Determinants of energy, protein, lipid, and lactose concentrations in human milk during the first 12 mo of lactation: the DARLING Study. *American Journal of Clinical Nutrition* 53 (2):457–465.

Nomura K, Nakao M, Sato M, Ishikawa H, and Yano E (2007) The association of the reporting of somatic symptoms with job stress and active coping among Japanese white-collar workers. *Journal of Occupational Health* 49 (5):370–375.

Norgan NG (1990) Body mass index and body energy stores in developing countries. *European Journal of Clinical Nutrition* 44 Suppl 1:79–84.

Norgan NG (1994a) Interpretation of low body mass indices: Australian aborigines. *American Journal of Physical Anthropology* 94 (2):229–237.

Norgan NG (1994b) Population differences in body composition in relation to the body mass index. *European Journal of Clinical Nutrition* 48 Suppl 3:S10–S25.

Norgan NG (1994c) Relative sitting height and the interpretation of the body mass index. *Annals of Human Biology* 21 (1):79–82.

Norgan NG (1997) The beneficial effects of body fat and adipose tissue in humans. *International Journal of Obesity and Related Metabolic Disorders* 21 (9):738–746.

Norgan NG, Ferro-Luzzi A, and Durnin JV (1982) The body composition of New Guinean adults in contrasting environments. *Annals of Human Biology* 9 (4):343–353.

O'Connell J, Hawkes K, and Blurton Jones N (2002) Meat-eating, grandmothering, and the evolution of early human diets. In: Ungar PS, Teaford MF (eds) *Human diet: its origin and evolution*. Bergin and Garvey: Westport, CT, pp 49–60.

O'Rahilly S, Farooqi IS, Yeo GS, and Challis BG (2003) Minireview: human obesity-lessons from monogenic disorders. *Endocrinology* 144 (9):3757–3764.

Odling-Smee FJ, Laland K, and Feldman MW (2003) *Niche construction*. Princeton University Press: Princeton.

Oftedal OT (1984) Milk composition, milk yield and energy output at peak lactation: a comparative review. *Symposia of the Zoological Society of London* 51:33–85.

Oftedal OT (2000) Use of maternal reserves as a lactation strategy in large mammals. *Proceedings of the Nutrition Society* 59 (1):99–106.

Oftedal OT and Iverson SJ (1995) Phylogenetic variation in the gross composition of milks. In: Jensen RG (ed) *Handbook of milk composition*. Academic Press: New York, pp 749–789.

Oja L and Jürimäe T (2002) Changes in anthropometrical characteristics during two years in 6 year old children. *Anthropologischer Anzeiger* 60 (3):299–308.

Oken E, Levitan EB, and Gillman MW (2008) Maternal smoking during pregnancy and child overweight: systematic review and meta-analysis. *International Journal of Obesity (London)* 32 (2):201–210.

Okosun IS, Liao Y, Rotimi CN, Dever GE, and Cooper RS (2000) Impact of birth weight on ethnic variations in subcutaneous and central adiposity in American children aged 5–11 years. A study from the Third National Health and Nutrition Examination Survey. *International Journal of Obesity and Related Metabolic Disorders* 24 (4):479–484.

Olhager E, Flinke E, Hannerstad U, and Forsum E (2003) Studies on human body composition during the first 4 months of life using magnetic resonance imaging and isotope dilution. *Pediatric Research* 54 (6):906–912.

Olivieri F, Semproli S, Pettener D and Toselli S (2008) Growth and malnutrition of rural Zimbabwean children (6–17 years of age). *American Journal of Physical Anthropology* 136(2):214–222.

Ong KK, Ahmed ML, and Dunger DB (1999) The role of leptin in human growth and puberty. *Acta Paediatrica. Supplement* 88 (433):95–98.

Ong KK, Ahmed ML, Emmett PM, Preece MA, and Dunger DB (2000) Association between postnatal catch-up growth and obesity in childhood: prospective cohort study. *British Medical Journal* 320 (7240):967–971.

Ong KK, Kratzsch J, Kiess W, and Dunger D (2002) Circulating IGF-I levels in childhood are related to both current body composition and early postnatal growth rate. *Journal of Clinical Endocrinology and Metabolism* 87 (3):1041–1044.

Ong KK, Northstone K, Wells JC, Rubin C, Ness AR, Golding J, and Dunger DB (2007) Earlier mother's age at menarche predicts rapid infancy growth and childhood obesity. *PLoS Medicine* 4 (4):e132.

Ong KK and Loos RJ (2006) Rapid infancy weight gain and subsequent obesity: systematic reviews and hopeful suggestions. *Acta Paediatrica* 95 (8):904–908.

Onland-Moret NC, Peeters PH, van Gils CH, Clavel-Chapelon F, Key T, Tjonneland A, Trichopoulou A, Kaaks R, Manjer J, Panico S, Palli D, Tehard B, Stoikidou M, Bueno-De-Mesquita HB, Boeing H, Overvad K, Lenner P, Quiros JR, Chirlaque MD, Miller AB, Khaw KT, and Riboli E (2005) Age at menarche in relation to adult height: the EPIC study. *American Journal of Epidemiology* 162 (7):623–632.

Orphanidou CI, McCargar LJ, Birmingham CL, and Belzberg AS (1997) Changes in body composition and fat distribution after short-term weight gain in patients with anorexia nervosa. *American Journal of Clinical Nutrition* 65 (4):1034–1041.

Owen CG, Martin RM, Whincup PH, Davey-Smith G, Gillman MW, and Cook DG (2005) The effect of breastfeeding on mean body mass index throughout life: a quantitative review of published and unpublished observational evidence. *American Journal of Clinical Nutrition* 82 (6):1298–1307.

Owen GM, Filer LJ, Maresh M, Fomon SJ (1966) Body composition of the infant. Part II. Sex-related differences in body composition in infancy. In: Falkner F (ed) *Human development*. Saunders: Philadelphia, pp 246–253.

Pace N and Rathburn EN (1945) Studies on body composition. III. The body water and chemically combined nitrogen content in relation to fat content. *Journal of Biological Chemistry* 158:685–691.

Packer C, Collins DA, Sindimwo A, and Goodall J (1995) Reproductive constraints on aggressive competition in female baboons. *Nature* 373 (6509):60–63.

Pagezy H (1984) Seasonal hunger as experienced by the Oto and the Twa women of a Ntomba village in the Equatorial forest (Lake Tumba, Zaire). *Ecology of Food and Nutrition* 15:13–27.

Paine RR and Boldsen JL (2006) Paleodemographic data and why understanding Holocene demography is essential to understanding human life history evolution in the pleistocene. In: Hawkes KK and Paine RR (eds) *The evolution of human life history*. James Currey Ltd.: Oxford, pp 307–330.

Pannacciulli N, Le DS, Chen K, Reiman EM, and Krakoff J (2007) Relationships between plasma leptin concentrations and human brain structure: a voxel-based morphometric study. *Neuroscience Letters* 412 (3):248–253.

Panter-Brick C (1993) Seasonality of energy expenditure during pregnancy and lactation for rural Nepali women. *American Journal of Clinical Nutrition* 57 (5):620–628.

Papavramidou NS, Papavramidis ST, and Christopoulou-Aletra H (2004) Galen on obesity: etiology, effects, and treatment. *World Journal of Surgery* 28 (6):631–635.

Parent AS, Teilmann G, Juul A, Skakkebaek NE, Toppari J, and Bourguignon JP (2003) The timing of normal puberty and the age limits of sexual precocity: variations around the world, secular trends, and changes after migration. *Endocrinology Review* 24 (5):668–693.

Parizkova J and Eiselt E (1980) Longitudinal changes in body build and skinfolds in a group of old men over a 16 year period. *Human Biology* 52 (4):803–809.

Park YW, Allison DB, Heymsfield SB, and Gallagher D (2001) Larger amounts of visceral adipose tissue in Asian Americans. *Obesity Research* 9 (7):381–387.

Parretti E, Carignani L, Cioni R, Bartoli E, Borri P, La TP, Mecacci F, Martini E, Scarselli G, and Mello G (2003) Sonographic evaluation of fetal growth and body composition in women with different degrees of normal glucose metabolism. *Diabetes Care* 26 (10):2741–2748.

Parsons TJ, Power C, Logan S, and Summerbell CD (1999) Childhood predictors of adult obesity: a systematic review. *International Journal of Obesity and Related Metabolic Disorders* 23 Suppl 8:S1–107.

Pasquet P, Brigant L, Froment A, Koppert GA, Bard D, de I, G, and Apfelbaum M (1992) Massive overfeeding and energy balance in men: the Guru Walla model. *American Journal of Clinical Nutrition* 56 (3):483–490.

Patel SR and Hu FB (2008) Short sleep duration and weight gain: a systematic review. *Obesity (Silver Spring)* 16 (3):643–653.

Pathak KA and Kumar DK (2000) Bamboo flowering and rodent out-break in North Eastern hill region of India. *Indian Journal of Hill Farming* 13:1–7.

Patterson ML, Stern S, Crawford PB, McMahon RP, Similo SL, Schreiber GB, Morrison JA, and Waclawiw MA (1997) Sociodemographic factors and obesity in preadolescent black and white girls: NHLBI's Growth and Health Study. *Journal of the National Medical Association* 89 (9):594–600.

Pawlowski B (1998) Why are newborns so big and fat? *Human Evolution* 13:65–72.

Peeters MW, Beunen GP, Maes HH, Loos RJ, Claessens AL, Vlietinck R, and Thomis MA (2007) Genetic and environmental determination of tracking in subcutaneous fat distribution during adolescence. *American Journal of Clinical Nutrition* 86 (3):652–660.

Pembrey ME, Bygren LO, Kaati G, Edvinsson S, Northstone K, Sjostrom M, and Golding J (2006) Sex-specific, male-line transgenerational responses in humans. *European Journal of Human Genetics* 14 (2):159–166.

Pereira ME and Pond CM (1995) Organisation of white adipose tissue in Lemuridae. *American Journal of Primatology* 35:1–13.

Permana PA and Reardon CL (2007) What are subcutaneous adipocytes really good for? Viewpoint 2. *Experimental Dermatology* 16:53–55.

Perry GH, Dominy NJ, Claw KG, Lee AS, Fiegler H, Redon R, Werner J, Villanea FA, Mountain JL, Misra R, Carter NP, Lee C, and Stone AC (2007) Diet and the evolution of human amylase gene copy number variation. Nature Genetics 39(10):1256–1260.

Pettitt DJ, Baird HR, Aleck KA, Bennett PH, and Knowler WC (1983) Excessive obesity in offspring of Pima Indian women with diabetes during pregnancy. *New England Journal of Medicine* 308 (5):242–245.

Pettitt DJ, Aleck KA, Baird HR, Carraher MJ, Bennett PH, and Knowler WC (1988) Congenital susceptibility to NIDDM. Role of intrauterine environment. *Diabetes* 37 (5):622–628.

Philipi T and Seger JH (1989) Hedging evolutionary bets, revisited. *Trends in Ecology and Evolution* 4:41–44.

Phillips DI and Young JB (2000) Birth weight, climate at birth and the risk of obesity in adult life. *International Journal of Obesity and Related Metabolic Disorders* 24 (3):281–287.

Phinney SD, Stern JS, Burke KE, Tang AB, Miller G, and Holman RT (1994) Human subcutaneous adipose tissue shows site-specific differences in fatty acid composition. *American Journal of Clinical Nutrition* 60 (5):725–729.

Pickett KE, Kelly S, Brunner E, Lobstein T, and Wilkinson RG (2005) Wider income gaps, wider waistbands? An ecological study of obesity and income inequality. *Journal of Epidemiology and Community Health* 59 (8):670–674.

Pierce MB and Leon DA (2005) Age at menarche and adult BMI in the Aberdeen children of the 1950s cohort study. *American Journal of Clinical Nutrition* 82 (4):733–739.

Piers LS, Diggavi SN, Thangam S, Van Raaij JM, Shetty PS, and Hautvast JG (1995) Changes in energy expenditure, anthropometry, and energy intake during the course of pregnancy and lactation in well-nourished Indian women. *American Journal of Clinical Nutrition* 61 (3):501–513.

Pietrobelli A, Faith MS, Allison DB, Gallagher D, Chiumello G, and Heymsfield SB (1998) Body mass index as a measure of adiposity among children and adolescents: a validation study. *Journal of Pediatrics* 132 (2):204–210.

Pigliucci M (2007) Do we need an extended evolutionary synthesis? *Evolution: International Journal of Organic Evolution* 61 (12):2743–2749.

Pine DS, Cohen P, Brook J, and Coplan JD (1997) Psychiatric symptoms in adolescence as predictors of obesity in early adulthood: a longitudinal study. *American Journal of Public Health* 87 (8):1303–1310.

Pine DS, Goldstein RB, Wolk S, and Weissman MM (2001) The association between childhood depression and adulthood body mass index. *Pediatrics* 107 (5):1049–1056.

Piperata BA, Dufour DL, Reina JC, and Spurr GB (2002) Anthropometric characteristics of pregnant women in Cali, Colombia and relationship to birth weight. *American Journal of Human Biology* 14 (1):29–38.

Pitts GC and Bullard TR (1968) Some interspecific aspects of body composition in mammals. Body composition in animals and man. National Academy of Science: Washington, DC, Publ. No. 1598, pp 45–70.

Poehlman E (2002) Menopause, energy expenditure, and body composition. *Acta Obstetricia and Gynecologica Scandinavica* 81:603–611.

Polychronakos C and Kukuvitis A (2002) Parental genomic imprinting in endocrinopathies. *European Journal of Endocrinology* 147 (5):561–569.

Pond CM (1984) Physiological and ecological importance of energy storage in the evolution of lactation: evidence for a common pattern of anatomical organisation of adipose tissue in mammals. *Symposia of the Zoological Society of London* 51:1–32.

Pond CM (1998) *The fats of life*. Cambridge University Press: Cambridge.

Pond CM (2003a) Paracrine interactions of mammalian adipose tissue. *Journal of Experimental Zoology Part A: Comparative Experimental Biology* 295 (1):99–110.

Pond CM (2003b) Paracrine relationships between adipose and lymphoid tissues: implications for the mechanism of HIV-associated adipose redistribution syndrome. *Trends in Immunology* 24 (1):13–18.

Pond CM (2007) What are subcutaneous adipocytes really good for? Viewpoint 6. *Experimental Dermatology* 16:64–67.

Pond CM and Mattacks CA (1985) Anatomical organisation of mammalian adipose tissue. *Fortschritte der Zoologie* 30:445–448.

Pond CM, Mattacks CA, and Ramsay MA (1994) The anatomy and chemical composition of adipose tissue in wild wolverines (*Gulo gulo*) in northern Canada. *Journal of Zoology* 232:603–616.

Pond CM and Ramsay MA (1992) Allometry of the distribution of adipose tissue in Carnivora. *Canadian Journal of Zoology* 70:342–347.

Popkin BM (2007) The world is fat. *Scientific American* 297 (3):88–95.

Popkin BM, Richards MK, and Montiero CA (1996) Stunting is associated with overweight in children of four nations that are undergoing the nutrition transition. *Journal of Nutrition* 126 (12):3009–3016.

Poppitt SD, Prentice AM, Goldberg GR, and Whitehead RG (1994) Energy-sparing strategies to protect human fetal growth. *American Journal of Obstetrics and Gynecology* 171 (1):118–125.

Poston WS and Foreyt JP (1999) Obesity is an environmental issue. *Atherosclerosis* 146 (2):201–209.

Prentice A, Prentice AM, and Whitehead RG (1981) Breast-milk fat concentrations of rural African women. 2. Long-term variations within a community. *British Journal of Nutrition* 45 (3):495–503.

Prentice A, Stubbs J (1999) Aetiology of obesity VI: appetite control, physiological factors. In: British Nutrition Foundation (ed) *Obesity: report of the British Nutrition Foundation Task Force*. Blackwell Science: Oxford, pp 72–82.

Prentice AM (2001) Fires of life: the struggles of an ancient metabolism in a modern world. *BNF Nutrition Bulletin* 26:13–27.

Prentice AM, Whitehead RG, Roberts SB, and Paul AA (1981) Long-term energy balance in child-bearing Gambian women. *American Journal of Clinical Nutrition* 34 (12):2790–2799.

Prentice AM, Whitehead RG, Watkinson M, Lamb WH, and Cole TJ (1983) Prenatal dietary supplementation of African women and birth-weight. *Lancet* 1 (8323):489–492.

Prentice AM, Black AE, Coward WA, Davies HL, Goldberg GR, Murgatroyd PR, Ashford J, Sawyer M, and Whitehead RG (1986) High levels of energy expenditure in obese women. *British Medical Journal (Clinical Research Edition)* 292 (6526):983–987.

Prentice AM, Poppitt SD, Goldberg GR, Murgatroyd PR, Black AE, and Coward WA (1994) Energy balance in pregnancy and lactation. *Advances in experimental medicine and biology* 352:11–26.

Prentice AM, Black AE, Coward WA, and Cole TJ (1996) Energy expenditure in overweight and obese adults in affluent societies: an analysis of 319 doubly-labelled water measurements. *European Journal of Clinical Nutrition* 50 (2):93–97.

Prentice AM, Moore SE, Collinson AC, and O'Connell MA (2002) Leptin and undernutrition. *Nutrition Review* 60 (10 Pt 2):S56–S67.

Prentice AM and Cole TJ (1994) Seasonal changes in growth and energy status in the Third World. *Proceedings of the Nutrition Society* 53 (3):509–519.

Prentice AM and Darboe MK (2008) Growth and host-pathogen interactions. In: Barker DJP, Bergmann RL and Ogra PL (eds) *The window of opportunity: pre-pregnancy to 24 months of age*. Nestlé Ltd and S. Karger AG: Vevey/Basel, pp 197–210.

Prentice AM and Goldberg GR (2000) Energy adaptations in human pregnancy: limits and long-term consequences. *American Journal of Clinical Nutrition* 71 (5 Suppl):1226S–1232S.

Prentice AM, Goldberg GR, and Prentice A (1994) Body mass index and lactation performance. *European Journal of Clinical Nutrition* 48 Suppl 3:S78–S86.

Prentice AM and Jebb SA (1995) Obesity in Britain: gluttony or sloth? *British Medical Journal* 311 (7002):437–439.

Prentice AM and Jebb SA (2003) Fast foods, energy density and obesity: a possible mechanistic link. *Obesity Reviews* 4 (4):187–194.

Price K and Ydenberg R (1995) Begging and provisioning of broods of asynchronously-hatched yellow-headed blackbird nestlings. *Behavorial Ecology and Sociobiology* 37:201–208.

Prokopec M and Bellisle F (1993) Adiposity in Czech children followed from 1 month of age to adulthood: analysis of individual BMI patterns. *Annals of Human Biology* 20 (6):517–525.

Puente XS, Sanchez LM, Gutierrez-Fernandez A, Velasco G, and Lopez-Otin C (2005) A genomic view of the complexity of mammalian proteolytic systems. *Biochemical SocietyTransactions* 33 (Pt 2):331–334.

Pulkki-Raback L, Elovainio M, Kivimaki M, Raitakari OT, and Keltikangas-Jarvinen L (2005) Temperament in childhood predicts body mass in adulthood: the cardiovascular risk in Young Finns Study. *Health Psychology* 24 (3):307–315.

Purslow LR, Young EH, Wareham NJ, Forouhi N, Brunner EJ, Luben RN, Welch AA, Khaw KT, Bingham SA, and Sandhu MS (2008) Socioeconomic position and risk of short-term weight gain: prospective study of 14,619 middle-aged men and women. *BMC. Public Health* 8 (1):112.

Quetelet LAJ (1871) *Anthropometrie ou measure des differentes facultes de l'homme*. C Marquardt: Brussels.

Raberg L, Vestberg M, Hasselquist D, Holmdahl R, Svensson E, and Nilsson JA (2002) Basal metabolic rate and the evolution of the adaptive immune system. *Proceedings of the Roayl Society B: Biological Sciences* 269:817–821.

Raikkonen K, Keltikangas-Jarvinen L, Adlercreutz H, and Hautanen A (1996) Psychosocial stress and the insulin resistance syndrome. *Metabolism* 45 (12):1533–1538.

Raikkonen K, Matthews KA, Kuller LH, Reiber C, and Bunker CH (1999) Anger, hostility, and visceral adipose tissue in healthy postmenopausal women. *Metabolism* 48 (9):1146–1151.

Raikkonen K, Matthews KA, and Salomon K (2003) Hostility predicts metabolic syndrome risk factors in children and adolescents. *Health Psychology* 22 (3):279–286.

Ramakrishnan U, Martorell R, Schroeder DG and Flores R. Role of intergenerational effects on linear growth. J Nutr 1999 Feb;129(2S Suppl):544S–549S.

Ramsay MA, Mattacks CA, and Pond CM (1992) Seasonal and sex differences in the cellular structure and chemical composition of adipose tissue in wild polar bears (*Ursus maritimus*). *Journal of Zoology* 228:533–544.

Randle PJ, Garland PB, Hales CN, and Newsholme EA (1963) The glucose fatty-acid cycle. Its role in insulin sensitivity and the metabolic disturbances of diabetes mellitus. *Lancet* 1 (7285):785–789.

Rao S, Kanade A, Margetts BM, Yajnik CS, Lubree H, Rege S, Desai B, Jackson A, and Fall CH (2003) Maternal activity in relation to birth size in rural India. The Pune Maternal Nutrition Study. *European Journal of Clinical Nutrition* 57 (4):531–542.

Ravaja N and Keltikangas-Jarvinen L (1995) Temperament and metabolic syndrome precursors in children: a three-year follow-up. *Preventive Medicine* 24 (5):518–527.

Ravelli AC, van Der Meulen JH, Osmond C, Barker DJ, and Bleker OP (1999) Obesity at the age of 50 y in men and women exposed to famine prenatally. *American Journal of Clinical Nutrition* 70 (5):811–816.

Ravelli GP, Stein ZA, and Susser MW (1976) Obesity in young men after famine exposure in utero and early infancy. *New England Journal of Medicine* 295 (7):349–353.

Ravussin E, Lillioja S, Knowler WC, Christin L, Freymond D, Abbott WG, Boyce V, Howard BV, and Bogardus C (1988) Reduced rate of energy expenditure as a risk factor for body-weight gain. *New England Journal of Medicine* 318 (8):467–472.

Reaven GM (1998) Hypothesis: muscle insulin resistance is the ("not-so") thrifty genotype. *Diabetologia* 41 (4):482–484.

Rebuffe-Scrive M, Enk L, Crona N, Lonnroth P, Abrahamsson L, Smith U, and Bjorntorp P (1985) Fat cell metabolism in different regions in women. Effect of menstrual cycle, pregnancy, and lactation. *Journal of Clinical Investigation* 75 (6):1973–1976.

Reik W, Davies K, Dean W, Kelsey G, and Constancia M (2001) Imprinted genes and the coordination of fetal and postnatal growth in mammals. *Novartis Foundation Symposium* 237:19–31.

Reilly JJ and McDowell ZC (2003) Physical activity interventions in the prevention and treatment of paediatric obesity: systematic review and critical appraisal. *Proceedings of the Nutrition Society* 62 (3):611–619.

Rennie DW, Covino BG, Howell BJ, Song SH, Kang BS, and Hong SK (1962) Physical insulation of Korean diving women. *Journal of Applied Physiology* 17:961–966.

Rennie KL, Jebb SA, Wright A, and Coward WA (2005) Secular trends in under-reporting in young people. *British Journal of Nutrition* 93 (2):241–247.

Richerson PJ, Boyd R, and Bettinger RL (2001) Was agriculture impossible during the pleistocene but mandatory during the holocene? *American Anthropology* 66:387–411.

Ridley M (1993) *The red queen: sex and the evolution of human nature*. Penguin: London.

Rigo J, Nyamugabo K, Picaud JC, Gerard P, Pieltain C, and De CM (1998) Reference values of body composition obtained by dual energy X-ray absorptiometry in preterm and term neonates. *Journal of Pediatric Gastroenterology and Nutrition* 27 (2):184–190.

Ritchie SA and Connell JM (2007) The link between abdominal obesity, metabolic syndrome and cardiovascular disease. *Nutrition, Metabolism, and Cardiovascular Disease* 17 (4):319–326.

Rivers JP (1988) The nutritional biology of famine. In: Harrison GA (ed) *Famine*. Oxford University Press: Oxford, pp 57–106.

Roberts DF (1953) Body weight, race and climate. *American Journal of Physical Anthropology* 11:533–558.

Roberts SB, Cole TJ, and Coward WA (1985) Lactational performance in relation to energy intake in the baboon. *American Journal of Clinical Nutrition* 41 (6):1270–1276.

Roberts SB, Savage J, Coward WA, Chew B, and Lucas A (1988) Energy expenditure and intake in infants born to lean and overweight mothers. *New England Journal of Medicine* 318 (8):461–466.

Roberts SB and Young VR (1988) Energy costs of fat and protein deposition in the human infant. *American Journal of Clinical Nutrition* 48 (4):951–955.

Robson SL, vanSchaik CP, and Hawkes K (2006) The derived features of human life history. In: Hawkes K and Paine RR (eds) *The evolution of human life history*. James Currie Ltd: Oxford, pp 17–44.

Rockson SG (2004) The elusive adipose connection. *Lymphatic Research and Biology* 2 (3):105–106.

Rodney W (1972) *How Europe underdeveloped Africa*. Bogle-L'Ouverture Publications: London.

Rodrigues ML and Da Costa TH (2001) Association of the maternal experience and changes in adiposity measured by BMI, waist:hip ratio and percentage body fat in urban Brazilian women. *British Journal of Nutrition* 85 (1):107–114.

Rodriguez G and Moreno LA (2006) Is dietary intake able to explain differences in body fatness in children and adolescents? *Nutrition, Metabolism, and Cardiovascular Disease* 16 (4):294–301.

Rodriguez G, Ventura P, Samper MP, Moreno L, Sarria A, and Perez-Gonzalez JM (2000) Changes in body composition during the initial hours of life in breast-fed healthy term newborns. *Biology of the Neonate* 77 (1):12–16.

Rodriguez G, Samper MP, Ventura P, Moreno LA, Olivares JL, and Perez-Gonzalez JM (2004) Gender differences in newborn subcutaneous fat distribution. *European Journal of Pediatrics* 163 (8):457–461.

Rodriguez-Girones MA, Enquist M, and Cotton PA (2001) Effects of begging on growth rates of nestling chicks. *Proceedings of the National Academy of Sciences of the United States of America* 95:4453–4457.

Rogers AR and Jorde LB (1995) Genetic evidence on modern human origins. *Human Biology* 67 (1):1–36.

Rogers I (2003) The influence of birthweight and intrauterine environment on adiposity and fat distribution in later life. *International Journal of Obesity and Related Metabolic Disorders* 27 (7):755–777.

Rogers IS, Ness AR, Steer CD, Wells JC, Emmett PM, Reilly JR, Tobias J, and Smith GD (2006) Associations of size at birth and dual-energy X-ray absorptiometry measures of lean and fat mass at 9 to 10 y of age. *American Journal of Clinical Nutrition* 84 (4):739–747.

Rolland-Cachera MF, Bellisle F, Deheeger M, Pequignot F, and Sempe M (1990) Influence of body fat distribution during childhood on body fat distribution in adulthood: a two-decade follow-up study. *International Journal of Obesity* 14 (6):473–481.

Rolland-Cachera MF, Deheeger M, Guilloud-Bataille M, Avons P, Patois E, and Sempe M (1987) Tracking the development of adiposity from one month of age to adulthood. *Annals of Human Biology* 14 (3):219–229.

Rolland-Cachera MF, Deheeger M, Akrout M, and Bellisle F (1995) Influence of macronutrients on adiposity development: a follow up study of nutrition and growth from 10 months to 8 years of age. *International Journal of Obesity and Related Metabolic Disorders* 19 (8):573–578.

Romanyukha AA, Rudnev SG, and Sidorov IA (2006) Energy cost of infection burden: an approach to understanding the dynamics of host-pathogen interactions. *Journal of Theoretical Biology* 241 (1):1–13.

Roosevelt AC (1984) Population, health, and the evolution of subsistence: conclusions from the conference. In: Cohen MN, Armelagos GJ (eds) *Palaeopathology at the origins of agriculture*. Academic Press: Orlando, FL, pp 559–583.

Rose G (1982) Incubation period of coronary heart disease. *British Medical Journal (Clinical Research Edition)* 284 (6329):1600–1601.

Rosenbaum M and Leibel RL (1999) Clinical review 107: Role of gonadal steroids in the sexual dimorphisms in body composition and circulating concentrations of leptin. *Journal of Clinical Endocrinology and Metabolism* 84 (6):1784–1789.

Rosetta L (1986) Sex differences in seasonal variations of the nutritional status of Serere adults in Senegal. *Ecology of Food and Nutrition* 18:231–244.

Rowland MG (1986) The Gambia and Bangladesh: the seasons and diarrhoea. *Dialogue on Diarrhoea* (26):3.

Rowlands AV, Ingledew DK, and Eston RG (2000) The effect of type of physical activity measure on the relationship between body fatness and habitual physical activity in children: a meta-analysis. *Annals of Human Biology* 27 (5):479–497.

Roy K, Valentine JW, Jabolnski D, and Kidwell SM (1996) Scales of climatic variability and time averaging in Pleistocene biotas: implications for ecology and evolution. *Trends in Ecology and Evolution* 11:458–463.

Rubner M (1894) Quelle der Thierschen warme. *Zeitschrift der Biologie* 30:73–142.

Ruff C (2002) Variation in human body size and shape. *Annual Review of Anthropology* 31:211–232.

Rush D (1981) Nutritional services during pregnancy and birthweight: a retrospective matched pair analysis. *Canadian Medical Association Journal* 125 (6):567–576.

Rutenberg GW, Coelho AM, Lewis DS, Carey KD, and McGill HC (1987) Body composition in baboons: evaluating a morphometirc method. *American Journal of Primatology* 12:275–285.

Ryg M, Lydersen C, Markussen NH, Smith TG, and Oritsland NA (1990) Estimating the blubber content of phocid seals. *Canadian Journal of Fisheries and Aquatic Sciences* 47:1223–1237.

Sachdev HS, Fall CH, Osmond C, Lakshmy R, Dey Biswas SK, Leary SD, Reddy KS, Barker DJ, and Bhargava SK (2005) Anthropometric indicators of body composition in young adults: relation to size at birth and serial measurements of body mass index in childhood in the New Delhi birth cohort. *American Journal of Clinical Nutrition* 82 (2):456–466.

Sampei MA, Novo NF, Juliano Y, Colugnati FA, and Sigulem DM (2003) Anthropometry and body composition in ethnic Japanese and Caucasian adolescent girls: considerations on ethnicity and menarche. *International Journal of Obesity and Related Metabolic Disorders* 27 (9):1114–1120.

Savino F, Costamagna M, Prino A, Oggero R, and Silvestro L (2002) Leptin levels in breast-fed and formula-fed infants. *Acta Paediatrica* 91 (9):897–902.

Savino F, Liguori SA, Oggero R, Silvestro L, and Miniero R (2006) Maternal BMI and serum leptin concentration of infants in the first year of life. *Acta Paediatrica* 95 (4):414–418.

Sayer AA, Syddall HE, Dennison EM, Gilbody HJ, Duggleby SL, Cooper C, Barker DJ, and Phillips DI (2004) Birth weight, weight at 1 y of age, and body composition in older men: findings from the Hertfordshire Cohort Study. *American Journal of Clinical Nutrition* 80 (1):199–203.

Schaible UE and Kaufmann SH (2007) Malnutrition and infection: complex mechanisms and global impacts. *PLoS Medicine* 4 (5):e115.

Schieve LA, Cogswell ME, and Scanlon KS (1998) An empiric evaluation of the Institute of Medicine's pregnancy weight gain guidelines by race. *Obstetrics and Gynecology* 91 (6):878–884.

Schlichting CD and Pigliucci M (1998) Phenotypic evolution: a reaction norm perspective. Sinauer: Sunderland.

Schneider JE (2004) Energy balance and reproduction. *Physiology and Behavior* 81 (2):289–317.

Schoeller DA (1996) Hydrometry. In: Roche AF, Heymsfield SB, and Lohman TG (eds) *Human body composition*. Human Kinetics: Champaign, IL, pp 25–43.

Schoenemann PT (2004) Brain size scaling and body composition in mammals. *Brain, Behavior and Evolution* 63 (1):47–60.

Schousboe K, Visscher PM, Erbas B, Kyvik KO, Hopper JL, Henriksen JE, Heitmann BL, and Sorensen TI (2004) Twin study of genetic and environmental influences on adult body size, shape, and composition. *International Journal of Obesity and Related Metabolic Disorders* 28 (1):39–48.

Schroeder DG, Martorell R, and Flores R (1999) Infant and child growth and fatness and fat distribution in Guatemalan adults. *American Journal of Epidemiology* 149 (2):177–185.

Schultink WJ, Klaver W, Van WH, Van Raaij JM, and Hautvast JG (1990) Body weight changes and basal metabolic rates of rural Beninese women during seasons with different energy intakes. *European Journal of Clinical Nutrition* 44 Suppl 1:31–40.

Schultz W, Tremblay L, and Hollerman JR (2000) Reward processing in primate orbitofrontal cortex and basal ganglia. *Cerebral Cortex* 10 (3):272–284.

Schutz Y, Kyle UU, and Pichard C (2002) Fat-free mass index and fat mass index percentiles in Caucasians aged 18–98 y. *International Journal of Obesity and Related Metabolic Disorders* 26 (7):953–960.

Schutz Y, Lechtig A, and Bradfield RB (1980) Energy expenditures and food intakes of lactating women in Guatemala. *American Journal of Clinical Nutrition* 33 (4):892–902.

Schwanz LE (2006) Schistosome infection in deer mice (Peromyscus maniculatus): impacts on host physiology, behavior and energetics. *Journal of Experimental Biology* 209 (Pt 24):5029–5037.

Schwartz MW and Morton GJ (2002) Obesity: keeping hunger at bay. *Nature* 418 (6898):595–597.

Seidell JC, Oosterlee A, Deurenberg P, Hautvast JG, and Ruijs JH (1988) Abdominal fat depots measured with computed tomography: effects of degree of obesity, sex, and age. *European Journal of Clinical Nutrition* 42 (9):805–815.

Sellen DW (2006) Lactation, complementary feeding, and human life history. In: Hawkes K and Paine RR (eds) *The evolution of human life history*. James Currey Ltd: Oxford, pp 155–196.

Semproli S and Gualdi-Russo E (2007) Childhood malnutrition and growth in a rural area of Western Kenya. *American Journal of Physical Anthropology* 132(3):463–469.

Sewell MF, Huston-Presley L, Super DM, and Catalano P (2006) Increased neonatal fat mass, not lean body mass, is associated with maternal obesity. *American Journal of Obstetrics and Gynecology* 195 (4):1100–1103.

Sharrock KC, Kuzawa CW, Leonard WR, Tanner S, Reyes-Garcia VE, Vadez V, Huanca T, and McDade TW (2008) Developmental changes in the relationship between leptin and adiposity among Tsimane children and adolescents. *American Journal of Human Biology* 20 (4):392–398.

Shell ER (2002) *The hungry gene: the inside story of the obesity industry*. Grove Press: New York.

Shelley HJ (1966) Glycogen reserves and their changes at birth and in anorexia. *British Medical Bulletin* 17:137–143.

Shennan S (2002) *Genes, memes and human history: Darwinian archaeology and cultural evolution*. Thames and Hudson: London.

Shephard RJ (1985) Adaptation to exercise in the cold. *Sports Medicine* 2:59–71.

Shields BM, Knight BA, Powell RJ, Hattersley AT, and Wright DE (2006) Assessing newborn body composition using principal components analysis: differences in the determinants of fat and skeletal size. *BMC Pediatrics* 6:24.

Shiono PH, Klebanoff MA, Graubard BI, Berendes HW, and Rhoads GG (1986) Birth weight among women of different ethnic groups. *Journal of the American Medical Association* 255 (1):48–52.

Shiotani A, Miyanishi T, Uedo N, and Iishi H (2005) Helicobacter pylori infection is associated with reduced circulating ghrelin levels independent of body mass index. *Helicobacter* 10 (5):373–378.

Shoelson SE, Lee J, and Goldfine AB (2006) Inflammation and insulin resistance. *Journal of Clinical Investigation* 116 (7):1793–1801.

Sibly R, Calow P, and Nichols N (1985) Are patterns of growth adaptive? *Journal of Theoretical Biology* 112:553–574.

Sidebottom AC, Brown JE, and Jacobs DR, Jr. (2001) Pregnancy-related changes in body fat. *European Journal of Obstetrics, Gynecology, and Reproductive Biology* 94 (2):216–223.

Siervo M, Wells JCK, and Cizza G (2008) Evolutionary theories, psychosocial stress and the modern obesity epidemic. *Obesity and Metabolism* 4:131–142.

Silverman BL, Rizzo T, Green OC, Cho NH, Winter RJ, Ogata ES, Richards GE, and Metzger BE (1991) Long-term prospective evaluation of offspring of diabetic mothers. *Diabetes* 40 Suppl 2:121–125.

Simmen B and Hladik CM (1998) Sweet and bitter taste discrimination in primates: scaling effects across species. *Folia Primatologica (Basel)* 69 (3):129–138.

Simondon KB, Ndiaye T, Dia M, Yam A, Ndiaye M, Marra A, Diallo A, and Simondon F (2007) Seasonal variations and trends in weight and arm circumference of non-pregnant rural Senegalese women, 1990–1997. *European Journal of Clinical Nutrition* 62(8):997–1004.

Singh D (1993) Adaptive significance of female physical attractiveness: role of waist-to-hip ratio. *Journal of Personality and Social Psychology* 65 (2):293–307.

Singh D and Young RK (1995) Body weight, waist-to-hip ratio, breasts, and hips: role in judgements of female attractiveness and desirability for relationships. *Ethology and Sociobiology* 16:483–507.

Singh J, Prentice AM, Diaz E, Coward WA, Ashford J, Sawyer M, and Whitehead RG (1989) Energy expenditure of Gambian women during peak agricultural activity measured by the doubly-labelled water method. *British Journal of Nutrition* 62 (2):315–329.

Singhal A, Cole TJ, and Lucas A (2001) Early nutrition in preterm infants and later blood pressure: two cohorts after randomised trials. *Lancet* 357 (9254):413–419.

Singhal A, Fewtrell M, Cole TJ, and Lucas A (2003a) Low nutrient intake and early growth for later insulin resistance in adolescents born preterm. *Lancet* 361 (9363):1089–1097.

Singhal A, Wells J, Cole TJ, Fewtrell M, and Lucas A (2003b) Programming of lean body mass: a link between birth weight, obesity, and cardiovascular disease? *American Journal of Clinical Nutrition* 77 (3):726–730.

Siri WE (1961) Body composition from fluid spaces and density. In: Brozek J and Henschel A (eds) *Techniques for measuring body composition*. National Academy of Sciences: Washington, DC, pp 223–244.

Smink A, Ribas-Fito N, Garcia R, Torrent M, Mendez MA, Grimalt JO, and Sunyer J (2008) Exposure to hexachlorobenzene during pregnancy increases the risk of overweight in children aged 6 years. *Acta Paediatrica* 97(10):1465–1469.

Smith DE, Lewis CE, Caveny JL, Perkins LL, Burke GL, and Bild DE (1994) Longitudinal changes in adiposity associated with pregnancy. The CARDIA Study. Coronary Artery Risk Development in Young Adults Study. *Journal of the American Medical Association* 271 (22):1747–1751.

Smith DW, Truog W, Rogers JE, Greitzer LJ, Skinner AL, McCann JJ, and Harvey MA (1976) Shifting linear growth during infancy: illustration of genetic factors in growth from fetal life through infancy. *Journal of Pediatrics* 89 (2):225–230.

Snodgrass JJ, Leonard WR, Tarskaia LA, Alekseev VP, and Krivoshapkin VG (2005) Basal metabolic rate in the Yakut (Sakha) of Siberia. *American Journal of Human Biology* 17 (2):155–172.

Snodgrass JJ, Sorensen MV, Tarskaia LA, and Leonard WR (2007) Adaptive dimensions of health research among indigenous Siberians. *American Journal of Human Biology* 19 (2):165–180.

Sorensen TI, Price RA, Stunkard AJ, and Schulsinger F (1989) Genetics of obesity in adult adoptees and their biological siblings. *British Medical Journal* 298 (6666):87–90.

Soto N, Bazaes RA, Pena V, Salazar T, Avila A, Iniguez G, Ong KK, Dunger DB, and Mericq MV (2003) Insulin sensitivity and secretion are related to catch-up growth in small-for-gestational-age infants at age 1 year: results from a prospective cohort. *Journal of Clinical Endocrinology and Metabolism* 88 (8):3645–3650.

Speakman JR (2007) A nonadaptive scenario explaining the genetic predisposition to obesity: the "predation release" hypothesis. *Cell Metabolism* 6 (1):5–12.

Speakman JR (2006) Thrifty genes for obesity and the metabolic syndrome–time to call off the search? *Diabetes and Vascular Disease Research* 3 (1):7–11.

Speakman JR, Djafarian K, Stewart J, and Jackson DM (2007) Assortative mating for obesity. *American Journal of Clinical Nutrition* 86 (2):316–323.

Spencer T and Heywood P (1983) Seasonality, subsistence agriculture and nutrition in a lowland community of Papua New Guinea. *Ecology of Food and Nutrition* 13:221–229.

Speth JD (1987) Early hominid subsistence strategies in seasonal habitats. *Journal of Archaeological Science* 14:13–29.

Speth JD and Spielmann KA (1983) Energy source, protein metabolism, and hunter-gatherer subsistence strategies. *Journal of Anthropological Archaeology* 2:1–31.

Stanford C and Bunn HT (2001) *Meat-eating and human evolution*. Oxford University Press: Oxford.

Stanner SA and Yudkin JS (2001) Fetal programming and the Leningrad Siege study. *Twin Research* 4 (5):287–292.

Starling AP and Stock JT (2007) Dental indicators of health and stress in early Egyptian and Nubian agriculturalists: a difficult transition and gradual recovery. *American Journal of Physical Anthropology* 134 (4):520–528.

Stearns SC (1992) *The evolution of life histories.* Oxford University Press: Oxford.

Steckel RH (1998) The formative period of the new anthropometric history. In: Komlos J and Cuff T (eds) *Classics in anthropometric history.* Scripta Mercaturae Verlag: St Katherinen, Germany.

Steckel RH (1979) Slave height profiles from coastwise manifests. *Explorations in Economic History* 16:363–380.

Stein AD, Zybert PA, van de BM, and Lumey LH (2004) Intrauterine famine exposure and body proportions at birth: the Dutch Hunger Winter. *International Journal of Epidemiology* 33 (4):831–836.

Stein AD, Kahn HS, Rundle A, Zybert PA, van der Pal-de Bruin, and Lumey LH (2007) Anthropometric measures in middle age after exposure to famine during gestation: evidence from the Dutch famine. *American Journal of Clinical Nutrition* 85 (3):869–876.

Stein Z, Susser M, Saenger G, and Marolla F (1975) *Famine and human development: the Dutch Hunger Winter of 1944–1945.* Oxford University Press: New York.

Stephenson TR, Hundertmark KJ, Schwartz CC, and Ballenberghe V (1998) Predicting body fat and body mass in moose with ultrasonography. *Canadian Journal of Zoology* 76:717–722.

Stettler N, Stallings VA, Troxel AB, Zhao J, Schinnar R, Nelson SE, Ziegler EE, and Strom BL (2005) Weight gain in the first week of life and overweight in adulthood: a cohort study of European American subjects fed infant formula. *Circulation* 111 (15):1897–1903.

Stettler N, Zemel BS, Kumanyika S, and Stallings VA (2002) Infant weight gain and childhood overweight status in a multicenter, cohort study. *Pediatrics* 109 (2):194–199.

Stini WA (1978) Malnutrition, body size and proportion. *Ecolology of Food and Nutrition* 1:125–132.

Stratz CH (1909) Wachstum und Proportionen des Menschen vor und nach der Geburt. *Archiv für Anthropologie* 8:287–297.

Strickland SS and Ulijaszek SJ (1994) Body mass index and illness in rural Sarawak. *European Journal of Clinical Nutrition* 48 Suppl 3:S98–108.

Stuart HC, Hill P, and Shaw C (1940) The growth of bone, muscle and overlying tissue as revealed by studies of roentgenograms of the leg areas. *Monograph of the Society for Research in Child Development* 5:1–90.

Stubbs RJ and Tolkamp BJ (2006) Control of energy balance in relation to energy intake and energy expenditure in animals and man: an ecological perspective. *British Journal of Nutrition* 95 (4):657–676.

Studier EH, Sevivk SH, and Wilson DE (1994) Proximate, caloric, nitrogen and mineral composition of bodies of some tropical bats. *Comparative Biochemistry and Physiology* 109A:601–610.

Stunkard AJ, Harris JR, Pedersen NL, and McClearn GE (1990) The body-mass index of twins who have been reared apart. *New England Journal of Medicine* 322 (21):1483–1487.

352   *References*

Stunkard AJ, Sorensen TI, Hanis C, Teasdale TW, Chakraborty R, Schull WJ, and
    Schulsinger F (1986) An adoption study of human obesity. *New England Journal
    of Medicine* 314 (4):193–198.
Suwa G, Kono RT, Katoh S, Asfaw B, and Beyene Y (2007) A new species of great
    ape from the late Miocene epoch in Ethiopia. *Nature* 448 (7156):921–924.
Swami V and Tovee MJ (2006) Does hunger influence judgments of female physical
    attractiveness? *British Journal of Psychology* 97 (Pt 3):353–363.
Swinburn BA (1996) The thrifty genotype hypothesis: how does it look after 30 years?
    Diabetic Medicine 13 (8):695–699.
Symmonds ME, Bryant MJ, Clarke L, Darby CJ, and Lomax MA (1992) Effect of
    maternal cold exposure on brown adipose tissue and thermogenesis in the
    neonatal lamb. *Journal of Physiology* 455:487–502.
Symons, D. *The evolution of human sexuality.* 1979. Oxford, Oxford University Press.
Taheri S, Lin L, Austin D, Young T, and Mignot E (2004) Short sleep duration is
    associated with reduced leptin, elevated ghrelin, and increased body mass index.
    PLoS Medicine 1 (3):e62.
Takahata N, Satta Y, and Klein J (1995) Divergence time and population size in the
    lineage leading to modern humans. *Theoretical Population Biology* 48:198–221.
Tanner JM (1955) Relation between age at puberty and adult physique in man. *Journal
    of Physiology* 127 (1):17P.
Taubes G (2008) *The diet delusion.* Vermillion: London.
Thame M, Osmond C, Bennett F, Wilks R, and Forrester T (2004) Fetal growth is
    directly related to maternal anthropometry and placental volume. *European
    Journal of Clinical Nutrition* 58 (6):894–900.
Thomas EL, Saeed N, Hajnal JV, Brynes A, Goldstone AP, Frost G, and Bell JD
    (1998) Magnetic resonance imaging of total body fat. *Journal of Applied
    Physiology* 85 (5):1778–1785.
Thomas R (1811) *The modern practice of physic.* Collins and Co.: New York.
Thongprasert K, Tanphaichitre V, Valyasevi A, Kittigool J, and Durnin JV (1987)
    Energy requirements of pregnancy in rural Thailand. *Lancet* 2 (8566):1010–1012.
Thorpe SK, Holder RL, and Crompton RH (2007) Origin of human bipedalism as an
    adaptation for locomotion on flexible branches. *Science* 316 (5829):1328–1331.
Thureen PJ, Phillips RE, Baron KA, DeMarie MP, and Hay WW, Jr. (1998) Direct
    measurement of the energy expenditure of physical activity in preterm infants.
    Journal of Applied Physiology 85 (1):223–230.
Tienboon P and Wahlqvist ML (2002) A prospective study of weight and height going
    from infancy to adolescence. *Asia Pacific Journal of Clinical Nutrition* 11
    (1):42–47.
Tilg H and Moschen AR (2006) Adipocytokines: mediators linking adipose tissue,
    inflammation and immunity. *Nature Reviews. Immunology* 6 (10):772–783.
Tillotson JE (2004) America's obesity: conflicting public policies, industrial economic
    development, and unintended human consequences. *Annual Review of Nutrition*
    24:617–643.
Tilman D (1998) The greening of the green revolution. *Nature* 396:211–212.
Tinbergen N (1963) On aims and methods of ethology. *Zeitschrift für Tierpsychologie*
    20:410–433.

Tobias PV (1985) The negative secular trend. *Journal of Human Evolution* 14:347–356.

Torrence R (1983) Time budgeting and hunter-gatherer technology. In: Bailey GN (ed) *Hunter-gatherer economy in prehistory: a European perspective*. Cambridge University Press: Cambridge, pp 11–22.

Torun B and Viteri FE (1994) Influence of exercise on linear growth. *European Journal of Clinical Nutrition* 48 Suppl 1:S186–S189.

Toschke AM, Martin RM, von KR, Wells J, Smith GD, and Ness AR (2007) Infant feeding method and obesity: body mass index and dual-energy X-ray absorptiometry measurements at 9–10 y of age from the Avon Longitudinal Study of Parents and Children (ALSPAC). *American Journal of Clinical Nutrition* 85 (6):1578–1585.

Tovee MJ and Cornelissen PL (1999) The mystery of female beauty. *Nature* 399 (6733):215–216.

Tovee MJ, Reinhardt S, Emery JL, and Cornelissen PL (1998) Optimum body-mass index and maximum sexual attractiveness. *Lancet* 352 (9127):548.

Tovee MJ, Maisey DS, Emery JL, and Cornelissen PL (1999) Visual cues to female physical attractiveness. *Proceedings of the Royal Society B: Biological Sciences* 266 (1415):211–218.

Tovee MJ, Hancock PJ, Mahmoodi S, Singleton BR, and Cornelissen PL (2002) Human female attractiveness: waveform analysis of body shape. *Proceedings of the Royal Society B: Biological Sciences* 269 (1506):2205–2213.

Tovee MJ, Swami V, Furnham A, and Mangalparsad R (2006) Changing percpetions of attractiveness as observers are exposed to a different culture. *Evolution and Human Behavior* 27:443–456.

Towne B, Czerwinski SA, Demerath EW, Blangero J, Roche AF, and Siervogel RM (2005) Heritability of age at menarche in girls from the Fels Longitudinal Study. *American Journal of Physical Anthropology* 128 (1):210–219.

Treuth MS, Figueroa-Colon R, Hunter GR, Weinsier RL, Butte NF, and Goran MI (1998) Energy expenditure and physical fitness in overweight vs non-overweight prepubertal girls. *International Journal of Obesity and Related Metabolic Disorders* 22 (5):440–447.

Tribe DE and Peel L (1963) Body composition of the kangaroo (*Macrotus* sp.). *Australian Journal of Zoology* 11:273–285.

Trivers RL (1972) Parental investment, and sexual selection. In: Campbell B (ed) *Sexual selection and the descent of man*. Aldine: Chicago, pp 139–179.

Troiano RP, Frongillo EA, Jr., Sobal J, and Levitsky DA (1996) The relationship between body weight and mortality: a quantitative analysis of combined information from existing studies. *International Journal of Obesity and Related Metabolic Disorders* 20 (1):63–75.

Trowell H (1975) Obesity in the western world. *Plant Foods Man* 1:157–165.

Turnbaugh PJ, Ley RE, Mahowald MA, Magrini V, Mardis ER, and Gordon JI (2006) An obesity-associated gut microbiome with increased capacity for energy harvest. *Nature* 444 (7122):1027–1031.

Turnbull CM (1972) *The mountain people*. Simon & Schuster: New York.

Tyler ER, Adams S, and Mallon EB (2006) An immune response in the bumblebee, Bombus terrestris leads to increased food consumption. *BMC Physiology* 6:6.

Uehara S and Nishida T (1987) Body weights of wild chimpanzees (*Pan troglodytes schweinfurthii*) of the Mahale Mountains National Park, Tanzania. *American Journal of Physical Anthropology* 72:315–321.

Ulijaszek SJ (1993) Seasonality of reproductive performance in rural Gambia. In: Ulijaszek SJ and Strickland SS (eds) *Seasonality and human ecology*. Cambridge University Press: Cambridge, pp 76–88.

Ulijaszek SJ (2002) Human eating behaviour in an evolutionary ecological context. *Proceedings of the Nutrition Society* 61:517–526.

Ulijaszek SJ (2000) Work and energetics. In: Stinson S, Bogin B, Huss-Ashmore R, O'Rourke D (eds) *Human biology: an evolutionary, biocultural perspective.* Wiley-Liss: New York, pp 345–376.

Urlando A, Dempster P, and Aitkens S (2003) A new air displacement plethysmograph for the measurement of body composition in infants. *Pediatric Research* 53 (3):486–492.

Uthaya S, Thomas EL, Hamilton G, Dore CJ, Bell J, and Modi N (2005) Altered adiposity after extremely preterm birth. *Pediatric Research* 57 (2):211–215.

van Lenthe FJ, Kemper HC, van MW, and Twisk JW (1996) Development and tracking of central patterns of subcutaneous fat in adolescence and adulthood: the Amsterdam Growth and Health Study. *International Journal of Epidemiology* 25 (6):1162–1171.

van Steenbergen WM, Kusin JA, de WC, Lacko E, and Jansen AA (1983) Lactation performance of mothers with contrasting nutritional status in rural Kenya. *Acta Paediatrica Scandinavica* 72 (6):805–810.

Van Vugt M, Hogan R, and Kaiser RB (2008) Leadership, followership, and evolution: Some lessons from the past. *American Psychologist* 63 (3):182–196.

Van DerMerwe RJ (1992) Reconstructing prehistoric diets. In: Jones S, Martin R, and Pilbeam D (eds) *The Cambridge encyclopaedia of human evolution.* Cambridge University Press: Cambridge, pp 369–372.

Van Itallie TB, Yang MU, Heymsfield SB, Funk RC, and Boileau RA (1990) Height-normalized indices of the body's fat-free mass and fat mass: potentially useful indicators of nutritional status. *American Journal of Clinical Nutrition* 52 (6):953–959.

Verkauskiene R, Beltrand J, Claris O, Chevenne D, Deghmoun S, Dorgeret S, Alison M, Gaucherand P, Sibony O, and Levy-Marchal C (2007) Impact of fetal growth restriction on body composition and hormonal status at birth in infants of small and appropriate weight for gestational age. *European Journal of Endocrinology* 157 (5):605–612.

Vernon RG and Pond CM (1997) Adaptations of maternal adipose tissue to lactation. *Journal of Mammary Gland Biology and Neoplasia* 2 (3):231–241.

Victora CG, Barros FC, Huttly SR, Teixeira AM, and Vaughan JP (1992) Early childhood mortality in a Brazilian cohort: the roles of birthweight and socioeconomic status. *International Journal of Epidemiology* 21 (5):911–915.

Victora CG, Barros F, Lima RC, Horta BL, and Wells J (2003) Anthropometry and body composition of 18 year old men according to duration of breast feeding: birth cohort study from Brazil. *British Medical Journal* 327 (7420):901.

Victora CG, Sibbritt D, Horta BL, Lima RC, Cole T, and Wells J (2007) Weight gain in childhood and body composition at 18 years of age in Brazilian males. *Acta Paediatrica* 96 (2):296–300.

Victora CG, Adair L, Fall C, Hallal PC, Martorell R, Richter L, and Sachdev HS (2008) Maternal and child undernutrition: consequences for adult health and human capital. *Lancet* 371 (9609):340–357.

Viegas OA, Scott PH, Cole TJ, Eaton P, Needham PG, and Wharton BA (1982a) Dietary protein energy supplementation of pregnant Asian mothers at Sorrento, Birmingham. I: Unselective during second and third trimesters. *British Medical Journal (Clinical Research Edition)* 285 (6342):589–592.

Viegas OA, Scott PH, Cole TJ, Mansfield HN, Wharton P, and Wharton BA (1982b) Dietary protein energy supplementation of pregnant Asian mothers at Sorrento, Birmingham. II: Selective during third trimester only. *British Medical Journal (Clinical Research Edition)* 285 (6342):592–595.

Villalpando S, Butte NF, Wong WW, Flores-Huerta S, Hernandez-Beltran Md, O'Brian Smith E, and Garza C (1991) Lactation performance of Mesoamerindians. *European Journal of Clinical Nutrition* 46:337–348.

Villar J, Cogswell M, Kestler E, Castillo P, Menendez R, and Repke JT (1992) Effect of fat and fat-free mass deposition during pregnancy on birth weight. *American Journal of Obstetrics and Gynecology* 167 (5):1344–1352.

Viner RM and Cole TJ (2005) Television viewing in early childhood predicts adult body mass index. *Journal of Pediatrics* 147 (4):429–435.

Visser M, Bouter LM, McQuillan GM, Wener MH, and Harris TB (1999) Elevated C-reactive protein levels in overweight and obese adults. *Journal of the American Medical Association* 282 (22):2131–2135.

Visser M, Bouter LM, McQuillan GM, Wener MH, and Harris TB (2001) Low-grade systemic inflammation in overweight children. *Pediatrics* 107 (1):E13.

von Helmholtz H (1847) *Über die warmeenwicklung bei der muskelaction.* G Reiner: Berlin.

von Hevesy G and Hofer E (1934) Die Verweilzeit des Wassers im menschlichen Korper, untersucht mit Hilfe von "schwerem" Wasser als Indicator. *Klinische Wochenschrift* 13:1524–1526.

Vorbach C, Capecchi MR, and Penninger JM (2006) Evolution of the mammary gland from the innate immune system? *Bioessays* 28 (6):606–616.

Wadd W (1839) *Comments on corpulency, lineaments on leanness.* Ebers and Co.: London.

Wadden TA and Stunkard AJ (1987) Psychopathology and obesity. *Annals of the New York Academy of Sciences* 499:55–65.

Waddington CH (1966) *Development and differentiation.* Macmillan: New York.

Wade GN and Schneider JE (1992) Metabolic fuels and reproduction in female mammals. *Neuroscience and Biobehavorial Reviews* 16 (2):235–272.

Wade GN, Schneider JE, and Li HY (1996) Control of fertility by metabolic cues. *American Journal of Physiology* 270 (1 Pt 1):E1–19.

Walker R, Gurven M, Hill K, Migliano A, Chagnon N, De SR, Djurovic G, Hames R, Hurtado AM, Kaplan H, Kramer K, Oliver WJ, Valeggia C, and Yamauchi T (2006) Growth rates and life histories in twenty-two small-scale societies. *American Journal of Human Biology* 18 (3):295–311.

Walker SP, Gaskin PS, Powell CA, and Bennett FI (2002) The effects of birth weight and postnatal linear growth retardation on body mass index, fatness and fat distribution in mid and late childhood. *Public Health Nutrition* 5 (3):391–396.

Walter J and Paulsen M (2003) Imprinting and disease. *Seminars in Cell and Developmental Biology* 14 (1):101–110.

Wang Y, Ge K, and Popkin BM (2000) Tracking of body mass index from childhood to adolescence: a 6-y follow-up study in China. *American Journal of Clinical Nutrition* 72 (4):1018–1024.

Wang Y, Monteiro C, and Popkin BM (2002) Trends of obesity and underweight in older children and adolescents in the United States, Brazil, China, and Russia. *American Journal of Clinical Nutrition* 75 (6):971–977.

Wang Z, Deurenberg P, Wang W, Pietrobelli A, Baumgartner RN, and Heymsfield SB (1999) Hydration of fat-free body mass: review and critique of a classic body-composition constant. *American Journal of Clinical Nutrition* 69 (5):833–841.

Wang Z, Wang Z-M, and Heymsfield SB (1999) History of the study of human body composition: a brief review. *American Journal of Human Biology* 11:157–165.

Wang ZM, Pierson RN, Jr., and Heymsfield SB (1992) The five-level model: a new approach to organizing body-composition research. *American Journal of Clinical Nutrition* 56 (1):19–28.

Warbrick-Smith J, Behmer ST, Lee KP, Raubenheimer D, and Simpson SJ (2006) Evolving resistance to obesity in an insect. *Proceedings of the National Academy of Sciences of the United States of America* 103 (38):14045–14049.

Wardle J (1999) Aetiology of obesity VIII: psychological factors. In: British Nutrition Foundation (ed) *Obesity: report of the British Nutrition Foundation Task Force*. Blackwell Science: Oxford, pp 83–91.

Wareham NJ, van Sluijs EM, and Ekelund U (2005) Physical activity and obesity prevention: a review of the current evidence. *Proceedings of the Nutrition Society* 64 (2):229–247.

Washburn SL (1960) Tools and human evolution. *Scientific American* 203:63–75.

Wass P, Waldenstrom U, Rossner S, and Hellberg D (1997) An android body fat distribution in females impairs the pregnancy rate of in-vitro fertilization-embryo transfer. *Human Reproduction* 12 (9):2057–2060.

Waterland RA and Garza C (1999) Potential mechanisms of metabolic imprinting that lead to chronic disease. *American Journal of Clinical Nutrition* 69 (2):179–197.

Watkins SC and Menken J (1985) Famines in historical perspective. *Population and Development Review* 11:647–675.

Watson E, Forster P, Richards M, and Bandelt HJ (1997) Mitochondrial footprints of human expansions in Africa. *American Journal of Human Genetics* 61 (3):691–704.

Watson KK and Platt ML (2008) Review. Neuroethology of reward and decision making. *Philosophical Transactions of the Royal Society B: Biological Sciences* 363(1511): 3825–3835.

Watve MG and Yajnik CS (2007) Evolutionary origins of insulin resistance: a behavioral switch hypothesis. *BMC. Evolutionary Biology* 7:61.

Weary DM and Fraser D (1995) Calling by domestic puglets: reliable signals of need? *Animal Behavior* 50:1047–1055.

Weast RC (1975) *Handbook of chemistry and physics* 56th edition. 1975. Cleveland, Ohio, CRC Press.

Webster JD, Hesp R, and Garrow JS (1984) The composition of excess weight in obese women estimated by body density, total body water and total body potassium. *Human Nutrition Clinical Nutrition* 38 (4):299–306.

Weinsier RL, Hunter GR, Zuckerman PA, and Darnell BE (2003) Low resting and sleeping energy expenditure and fat use do not contribute to obesity in women. *Obesity Research* 11 (8):937–944.

Weits T, van der Beek EJ, Wedel M, and Ter Haar Romeny BM (1988) Computed tomography measurement of abdominal fat deposition in relation to anthropometry. *International Journal of Obesity* 12 (3):217–225.

Wells JC (1998a) Child distress and parental response in two year old children: implications for energy intake. *Annals of Human Biology* 25:392–393.

Wells JC (1998b) Is obesity really due to high energy intake or low energy expenditure? *International Journal of Obesity and Related Metabolic Disorders* 22 (11):1139–1140.

Wells JC (2000) A Hattori chart analysis of body mass index in infants and children. *International Journal of Obesity and Related Metabolic Disorders* 24 (3):325–329.

Wells JC (2002) Thermal environment and human birth weight. *Journal of Theoretical Biology* 214 (3):413–425.

Wells JC (2003a) Parent-offspring conflict theory, signaling of need, and weight gain in early life. *Quarterly Review of Biology* 78 (2):169–202.

Wells JC (2003b) The thrifty phenotype hypothesis: thrifty offspring or thrifty mother? *Journal of Theoretical Biology* 221 (1):143–161.

Wells JC (2006) The evolution of human fatness and susceptibility to obesity: an ethological approach. *Biological Reviews of the Cambridge Philosophical Society* 81 (2):183–205.

Wells JC (2007a) Flaws in the theory of predictive adaptive responses. *Trends in Endocrinology and Metabolism* 18 (9):331–337.

Wells JC (2007b) Review of methods for body composition assessment in children. In: Ranke MB, Price DA, and Reiter EO (eds) *Growth hormone therapy in pediatrics – 20 years of KIGS*. Karger: Basel, pp 461–476.

Wells JC (2007c) Sexual dimorphism of body composition. *Best Practice and Research. Clinical Endocrinology and Metabolism* 21 (3):415–430.

Wells JC (2007d) The programming effects of early growth. *Early Human Development* 83 (12):743–748.

Wells JC (2007e) Commentary: Why are South Asians susceptible to central obesity?–the El Nino hypothesis. *International Journal of Epidemiology* 36 (1):226–227.

Wells JC (2007f) The thrifty phenotype as an adaptive maternal effect. *Biological Reviews of the Cambridge Philosophical Society* 82 (1):143–172.

Wells JC (2009a) Ethnic variability in adiposity and cardiovascular risk: the variable disease selection hypothesis. *International Journal of Epidemiology* 38(1):63–71.

Wells JC and Cole TJ (2002a) Adjustment of fat-free mass and fat mass for height in children aged 8 y. *International Journal of Obesity and Related Metabolic Disorders* 26 (7):947–952.

Wells JC and Cole TJ (2002b) Birth weight and environmental heat load: a between-population analysis. *American Journal of Physical Anthropology* 119 (3):276–282.

Wells JC and Davies PS (1998) Estimation of the energy cost of physical activity in infancy. *Archives of Diseases in Childhood* 78 (2):131–136.

Wells JC and Stock JT (2007) The biology of the colonizing ape. *American Journal of Physical Anthropology* Suppl 45:191–222.

Wells JC and Victora CG (2005) Indices of whole-body and central adiposity for evaluating the metabolic load of obesity. *International Journal of Obesity (London)* 29 (5):483–489.

Wells JC, Stanley M, Laidlaw AS, Day JM, and Davies PS (1996) The relationship between components of infant energy expenditure and childhood body fatness. *International Journal of Obesity and Related Metabolic Disorders* 20 (9):848–853.

Wells JC, Stanley M, Laidlaw AS, Day JM, Stafford M, and Davies PS (1997) Investigation of the relationship between infant temperament and later body composition. *International Journal of Obesity and Related Metabolic Disorders* 21 (5):400–406.

Wells JC, Fuller NJ, Dewit O, Fewtrell MS, Elia M, and Cole TJ (1999) Four-component model of body composition in children: density and hydration of fat-free mass and comparison with simpler models. *American Journal of Clinical Nutrition* 69 (5):904–912.

Wells JC, Coward WA, Cole TJ, and Davies PS (2002) The contribution of fat and fat-free tissue to body mass index in contemporary children and the reference child. *International Journal of Obesity and Related Metabolic Disorders* 26 (10):1323–1328.

Wells JC, Hallal PC, Wright A, Singhal A, and Victora CG (2005) Fetal, infant and childhood growth: relationships with body composition in Brazilian boys aged 9 years. *International Journal of Obesity (London)* 29 (10):1192–1198.

Wells JC, Fewtrell MS, Williams JE, Haroun D, Lawson MS, and Cole TJ (2006) Body composition in normal weight, overweight and obese children: matched case-control analyses of total and regional tissue masses, and body composition trends in relation to relative weight. *Internatonal Journal of Obesity (London)* 30 (10):1506–1513.

Wells JC, Cole TJ, Bruner D, and Treleaven P (2008a) Body shape in American and British adults: between-country and inter-ethnic comparisons. *International Journal of Obesity (London)* 32 (1):152–159.

Wells JC, Cole TJ, and Treleaven P (2008b) Sleep patterns and television viewing in relation to obesity and blood pressure: evidence from an adolescent Brazilian birth cohort. *International Journal of Obesity (London)* 32(7):1042–1049.

Wells JC, Chomtho S, and Fewtrell MS (2007) Programming of body composition by early growth and nutrition. *Proceedings of the Nutrition Society* 66 (3):423–434.

Wells JC, Cole TJ, and Davies PS (1996) Total energy expenditure and body composition in early infancy. *Archives of Diseases in Childhood* 75 (5):423–426.

Wells JC, Cole TJ, and Treleaven P (2008) Age-variability in body shape associated with excess weight: the UK National Sizing Survey. *Obesity (Silver Spring)* 16 (2):435–441.

Wells JC, Treleaven P, and Cole TJ (2007) BMI compared with 3-dimensional body shape: the UK National Sizing Survey. *American Journal of Clinical Nutrition* 85 (2):419–425.

Wells JCK (2009b) Historical cohort studies and the early origins of disease hypothesis: making sense of the evidence. *Proceedings of the Nutrition Society* 68: 179–188.

Wells JC (2009c) Maternal capital and the metabolic ghetto: an evolutionary perspective on the trans-generational basis of health inequalities. *American Journal of Human Biology* – in press.

Wendorf M (1989) Diabetes, the ice free corridor, and the Paleoindian settlement of North America. *American Journal of Physical Anthropology* 79 (4):503–520.

West R (2006) Tobacco control: present and future. *British Medical Bulletin* 77–78:123–136.

West-Eberhard MJ (2003) *Developmental plasticity and evolution*. Oxford University Press: Oxford.

Westcott ED, Mattacks CA, Windsor AC, Knight SC, and Pond CM (2006) Perinodal adipose tissue and fatty acid composition of lymphoid tissues in patients with and without Crohn's disease and their implications for the etiology and treatment of CD. *Annals of the New York Academy of Sciences* 1072:395–400.

Weststrate JA, Van KH, and Deurenberg P (1986) Changes in skinfold thicknesses and body mass index in 171 children, initially 1 to 5 years of age: a 5 1/2-year follow-up study. *International Journal of Obesity* 10 (4):313–321.

Wetsman A and Marlowe F (1999) How universal are preferences for female waist-to-hip ratio ratios? Evidence from the Hadza of Tanzania. *Evolution and Human Behavior* 20:219–228.

Weyer C, Pratley RE, Lindsay RS, and Tataranni PA (2000) Relationship between birth weight and body composition, energy metabolism, and sympathetic nervous system activity later in life. *Obesity Research* 8 (8):559–565.

Wheatley BP (1982) Energetics of foraging in *Macaca fascicularis* and *Pongo pygmaeus* and a selective advantage of large body size in the Orang-utan. *Primates* 23:348–363.

Wheeler PE (1992) The thermoregulatory advantages of large body size for hominids foraging in savanna envrionments. *Journal of Human Evolution* 23:351–62.

Wheeler PE (1993) The influence of stature and body form on hominid energy and water budgets: a comparison of Australopithecus and early Homo. *Journal of Human Evolution* 24:13–28.

Whitaker RC, Pepe MS, Seidel KD, Wright JA, and Knopp RH (1998) Gestational diabetes and the risk of offspring obesity. *Pediatrics* 101 (2):E9.

White CR, Phillips NF, and Seymour RS (2006) The scaling and temperature dependence of vertebrate metabolism. *Biolocial Letters* 2:125–127.

White TD, Asfaw B, DeGusta D, Gilbert H, Richards GD, Suwa G, and Howell FC (2003) Pleistocene Homo sapiens from Middle Awash, Ethiopia. *Nature* 423 (6941):742–747.

WHO (1985) *Energy and protein requirements*. WHO: Geneva.

Widdowson EM (1976) The response of the sexes to nutritional stress. *Proceedings of the Nutrition Society* 35 (2):175–180.

Widdowson EM (1950) Chemical composition of newly born mammals. *Nature* 166 (4224):626–628.

Widdowson EM and McCance RA (1960) Some effects of accelerating growth. I. General somatic development. *Proceedings of the Royal Society of London. Series B, Biological Sciences* 152:188–206.

Wiessner P (1997) Levelling the hunter: constraints on the social quest in foraging soceties. In: Wiessner P and Schiefenhovel W (eds) *Food and the status quest: food, status, culture, and nature*. Bergahn Books: Providence, RI, pp 171–191.

Wiessner P and Schiefenhovel W (1996) *Food and the status quest: an interdisciplinary perspective*. Berghahn Books: Providence, RI.

Wild S and McKeigue P (1997) Cross-sectional analysis of mortality by country of birth in England and Wales, 1970–92. *British Medical Journal* 314 (7082):705–710.

Wiley AS (1994b) Neonatal size and infant mortality at high altitude in the western Himalaya. *American Journal of Physical Anthropology* 94 (3):289–305.

Wiley AS (1994a) Neonatal and maternal anthropometric characteristics in a high altitude population of the western Himalaya. *American Journal of Human Biology* 6:499–510.

Williams GC (1966) *Adaptation and natural selection*. Princeton University Press: Princeton, NJ.

Wirminghaus JO and Perrin MR (1993) Seasonal changes in density, demography and body composition of small mammals in a southern temperate forest. *Journal of Zoology* 229:303–318.

Wisse BE (2004) The inflammatory syndrome: the role of adipose tissue cytokines in metabolic disorders linked to obesity. *Journal of the American Society of Nephrology* 15 (11):2792–2800.

Wlodeck D and Gonzalez M (2003) Decreased energy levels can cause and sustain obesity. *Journal of Theoretical Biology* 225:33–44.

Wolff GL, Kodell RL, Moore SR, and Cooney CA (1998) Maternal epigenetics and methyl supplements affect agouti gene expression in Avy/a mice. *FASEB Journal* 12 (11):949–957.

Wood B and Collard M (1999) The human genus. *Science* 284 (5411):65–71.

Woods SC and Seeley RJ (2000) Adiposity signals and the control of energy homeostasis. *Nutrition* 16 (10):894–902.

Wrangham R (1977) Feeding behaviour of chimpanzees in Gombe National Park, Tanzania. In: Clutton-Brock TH (ed) *Primate ecology*. Academic Press: London, pp 503–538.

Wrangham R and Peterson D (1996) *Demonic males. Apes and the origins of human violence*. Houghton Mifflin Co.: Boston.

Wright CM, Parker L, Lamont D, and Craft AW (2001) Implications of childhood obesity for adult health: findings from thousand families cohort study. *British Medical Journal* 323 (7324):1280–1284.

Wright CM and Parkinson KN (2004) Postnatal weight loss in term infants: what is normal and do growth charts allow for it? *Archives of Diseases in Childhood Fetal Neonatal Ed* 89 (3):F254–F257.

Wynn A (1987) Nutrition before conception and the outcome of pregnancy. *Nutrition and Health* 5:31–43.

Yajnik CS (2004) Obesity epidemic in India: intrauterine origins? *Proceedings of the Nutrition Society* 63 (3):387–396.

Yajnik CS, Fall CH, Coyaji KJ, Hirve SS, Rao S, Barker DJ, Joglekar C, and Kellingray S (2003) Neonatal anthropometry: the thin-fat Indian baby. The Pune Maternal Nutrition Study. *International Journal of Obesity and Related Metabolic Disorders* 27 (2):173–180.

Yajnik CS and Yudkin JS (2004) The Y-Y paradox. *Lancet* 363 (9403):163.

Yeung MY and Smyth JP (2003) Nutritionally regulated hormonal factors in prolonged postnatal growth retardation and its associated adverse neurodevelopmental outcome in extreme prematurity. *Biology of the Neonate* 84 (1):1–23.

Yliharsila H, Kajantie E, Osmond C, Forsen T, Barker DJ, and Eriksson JG (2008) Body mass index during childhood and adult body composition in men and women aged 56–70 y. *American Journal of Clinical Nutrition* 87 (6):1769–1775.

Young JB and Shimano Y (1998) Effects of rearing temperature on body weight and abdominal fat in male and female rats. *American Journal of Physiol* 274 (2 Pt 2):R398–R405.

Yssing M and Friis-Hansen B (1966) Body composition of newborn infants. *Acta Paediatrica Scandinavica* 159 Suppl:117–118.

Yu DW and Shepard GH (1998) Is beauty in the eye of the beholder? *Nature* 396:321–322.

Yusuf S, Hawken S, Ounpuu S, Bautista L, Franzosi MG, Commerford P, Lang CC, Rumboldt Z, Onen CL, Lisheng L, Tanomsup S, Wangai P, Jr., Razak F, Sharma AM, and Anand SS (2005) Obesity and the risk of myocardial infarction in 27,000 participants from 52 countries: a case-control study. *Lancet* 366 (9497):1640–1649.

Zaadstra BM, Seidell JC, Van Noord PA, te Velde ER, Habbema JD, Vrieswijk B, and Karbaat J (1993) Fat and female fecundity: prospective study of effect of body fat distribution on conception rates. *British Medical Journal* 306 (6876):484–487.

Zafon C (2007) Oscillations in total body fat content through life: an evolutionary perspective. *Obesity Reviews* 8:525–530.

Zahavi A (1975) Mate selection – a selection for handicap. *Journal of Theoretical Biology* 53:205–214.

Zahavi A (1981) Natural selection, sexual selection and the selection of signals. In: Scudder GGE and Reveal JL (eds) *Evolution today: proceedings of the second international congress of systematic and evolutionary biology*. Hunt Institute for Botanical Documentation: Pittsburgh, pp 133–138.

Zamboni M, Armellini F, Turcato E, Todisco P, Gallagher D, Dalle GR, Heymsfield S, and Bosello O (1997) Body fat distribution before and after weight gain in anorexia nervosa. *International Journal of Obesity and Related Metabolic Disorders* 21 (1):33–36.

Zhang Y, Proenca R, Maffei M, Barone M, Leopold L, and Friedman JM (1994) Positional cloning of the mouse obese gene and its human homologue. *Nature* 372 (6505):425–432.

Zhu S, Heymsfield SB, Toyoshima H, Wang Z, Pietrobelli A, and Heshka S (2005) Race-ethnicity-specific waist circumference cutoffs for identifying cardiovascular disease risk factors. *American Journal of Clinical Nutrition* 81 (2):409–415.

Ziegler EE, O'Donnell AM, Nelson SE, and Fomon SJ (1976) Body composition of the reference fetus. *Growth* 40 (4):329–341.

Zihlman AL and McFarland RK (2000) Body mass in lowland Gorillas: a quantitative analysis. *American Journal of Physical Anthropology* 113:61–78.

Zorrilla EP, Iwasaki S, Moss JA, Chang J, Otsuji J, Inoue K, Meijler MM, and Janda KD (2006) Vaccination against weight gain. *Proceedings of the National Academy of Sciences of the United States of America* 103 (35):13226–13231.

Index

abdominal fat
  assessment, 124
  cardiovascular risk, 297
  catch-up growth, 139
  cold stress, 171
  cortisol, 67
  disease load, 240
  ethnicity, **46**, **47**, 97, 259
  foetal growth, 97
  genetic factors, 240
  growth retardation, 137
  health risks, 6
  infant growth, 137
  infant weight gain, 138
  inflammation, 67
  lipoprotein lipase, 67
  neonate, 129, 130
  phenotypic induction, 133, 134
  social stress, 187, 286
  weight loss, **167**
abortion, 287
ache, 235
activity level, infant temperament, **86**
acute phase inflammatory proteins, 184
adipocyte, 169, 195
  storage capacity, 59
  thrifty genes, 204
adiponectin, 70
adipose tissue
  bet hedging, 264
  birth, 227
  colonising, 8, 238
  composition, 18, 196
  costs, 198
  cultural values, 255
  dissection, 7
  endocrine organ, 13, 72
  energy content, 160
  energy stores, 25
  epicardial, 71
  evolutionary history, 13
  genetic variation, 260
  geographic variability, 259
  hibernation, 199
  immune function, 13, 72, 262

insulin metabolism, 66
  intramuscular, 197, 259
  life course, 92–117
  maintenance costs, 198
  mammalian, 197
  perinodal, 197
  perinodal depot, 260
  receptors, 196
  regional distribution, 12, 21, 37, 43
  regulatory system, 8
  reproduction, 13
  reproductive strategy, 238
  sexual dimorphism, 43
  structural, 169
  structure, 196
  thermoregulation, 199
  thigh depot, 176
adiposity indices, 30, **38**, 123
  conceptual development, 274
adiposity rebound, 142
adiposity signals, 65
adolescence, evolution, 231
adoption studies, fat mass, 55
adrenarche, 69
advertising, 279, 284
aging
  body composition, 111
  fat mass index, 111, **112**
  lean mass index, 111, **112**
  sexual dimorphism, **112**
  skinfolds, **112**
  thigh girth, **192**
  waist-hip ratio, **124**, 191
agouti-related protein, 63
agriculture, 210
  ancient, 1
  dietary variability, 248
  emergence, 249, 250
  famine, 251
  heath impact, 2
  Nile Valley, 262
  physical effort, 281
  political systems, 254
  productivity, 254
  seasonality, 161, 252

363

alcohol, 74, 76
allometric scaling, 199, 201, 232
allometry, 224
altitude
    birth weight, 98
    infant body composition, 102
    neonate, 98, 99
amoebic dysentery, 260
amylin, 65, 66, 68
ancient Greece, 3
ancient Rome, 1
androgen receptors, 109
androgens, 69
Angelman syndrome, 60
angina, 272, 274
angiogenesis, 65
angiotensin, 70
animal domestication, 249, 250, 261
anorexia nervosa, 88, 156, 158, 168, 212
    body mass index, **157**
    neurobiology, 64
anteater, 201
anthropometry, 19
    digital, 45–47
    intrauterine growth retardation, **129**
antibodies, 184, 260
antidepressants, 290
apes, social organisation, 241
appetite, 5, 23, 62–64, 77, 265
    carbohydrate, 74
    gastric distension, 65
    genetic factors, 58, 59
    hypothalamus, 63
    imprinted genes, 60
    infection, 184
    insulin, 62
    leptin, 62, 68
    neurobiology, 62
    phenotypic induction, 206
    physical activity, 284
    protein, 74
    psychosocial stress, 87
    regulation, 82
    signalling pathways, 62
    smoking, 289
    social cues, 235
    soft drinks, 294
    thrifty genes, 204
appetite regulation
    diet, 76
    eating disorders, 64
    Hippocrates, 270
arachidonic acid, 71
Archimedes' principle. *See* densitometry
arcuate nucleus, 63
Aristotle, 10

army rangers, 157
    weight loss, 158
artificial selection, 250
assortative mating, 275
athletes, 173
Atkins diet, 75
Australian aborigines, 234, 256
Australopithecines, 215
australopithecines, 218, 236
    body composition, 222
    body size, 220
    diet, 233
    disease load, 239
    encephalisation, **221**
Avicenna, 273

baboon
    birth, 227
    breast milk composition, 229
    captive, 24
    diet, 218
    heritability of fatness, 57
    lactation, 177
    percent fat, 223
    wild, 24
bacteria, gut microbes, 61
Bacteroidetes, 61
bactrian camel, **24**
badger, **24**
bandwagon effect, 192
Bangladesh, 154
Banting, 274
basal metabolism, 239
    brain, **182**
    brain evolution, 226
    cold stress, 246
    energy balance, 54, 55
    fever, 184, 260
    genetic factors, 59
    glucose, **182**
    pregnancy, 114, 177
    sleep, 284
    television, 284
bats, body fat variability, 21, 22
bear, 17, 21, 202
    brown, **24**
Beckwith-Wiedemann syndrome, 60
begging signals, 281
begging theory, 83
benn index, 26
beta cell mass, 120
bet-hedging, 208, 209
bet hedging, 264, 265
bio-electrical impedance, 18
biofuels, 299
bipedalism, 14, 225, 270

birth interval, 281
birth weight, 93, 95, 114, 266
birthweight, 267
birth weight
   adult disease risk, 120
   altitude, 98
   body mass index, 127
   cold stress, 99, 183
   ethnicity, 97
   fat distribution, 265
   heat stress, 99, **246**
   Iceland, 102
   maternal diet, 130
   menarche, 126, 149
   seasonality, 130
   secular trend, 289
   supplementation, 130
   thermal environment, 102
   transgenerational effects, 207
   twin studies, 126
biscuit, 277
blood glucose, 65
   satiety, 82
blood glucose control, 122
blood pressure, 120, 267
   cortisol, 67
blood vessel, 70
   adipose tissue, 18
blubber, 170, 171
body cell mass, 111
body composition
   accuracy and precision, 16
   chemical composition, 17
   eating disorders, 159
   ethnicity, 29
   experiments in humans, 5
   hominins, 222, 223
   human age trends, 11
   human geographical variability, 11, 25–45
   infant, 100–103
   life course, 118–152
   methods, 3, 11, 16–20
   phenotypic induction, 118–152
   sexual dimorphism, 94, 223
   tracking, 122
   trade-offs, 263
body fat
   energy store, 10
   human geographical variability, 14
body girths, 45–47
body mass index
   adiposity index, 4, 25, 28, 30
   adiposity rebound, 142
   body shape, 123
   breast milk production, 177
   children, **34**

development, **27**
eating disorders, 156, 158
ethnicity, **29**
famine, **157**
fat distribution, **111**
genetic factors, 264
Hattori chart, **33–35**
heritability, **55–58**
hominins, 220
human geographical variability, **39**
infancy, **27**
lactation, 116
lactation performance, 178
limitations, 123
mortality, 156, 159
obesity categorisation, 6, 19, 26
percent fat, 28
physical activity, 36
physique, 28, **34**, **35**
seasonality, 163
secular trend, 5, 6, 27, 58
sexual dimorphism, **43**, 48
sexual selection, 190
standard deviation score, 26, 27
starvation, 156, **157**
tracking, 142, 143, **147**
underweight categorisation, 26
visceral fat, **111**
body proportions, 182
body shape, 123
   cultural preferences, 190
   cultural values, 255
   insulin resistance, 263
   IQ, 189
   pregnancy, 115
   sexual selection, 187
body size
   australopithecines, 220
   chimpanzee, 220
   hominins, 219, 224
   lactation, 224
   phenotypic induction, **136**
Bolivia, 98, 102, 213
bone marrow, 109
boom and bust, 247
boom bust dynamics, 237
bottleneck, 203, 228, 244, 247
Boyle, 273
brain, 257, 259
   appetite neurobiology, 62–64
   basal metabolism, **182**
   buffering, 227
   critical window, 119
   energy demands, 179
   energy expenditure, 181
   energy requirements, 66, 181, 271

brain (*cont.*)
　　energy supply, **211**
　　glucose, **182**
　　growth, 225
　　hominins, 225
　　human evolution, 270
　　imaging, 63
　　infant, 227
　　life course, 231
　　population density, 242
　　reproduction, 174
　　size, 225
　　specialisation, 235
　　starvation, 180
brain evolution, 226
brain size, 13, 14
　　imprinted genes, 60
brain space, starvation, 181
Brazil
　　activity patterns, 283
　　breast-feeding, 288
　　commercialisation, 295
　　phenotypic induction, 126
bread, 277
breast-feeding, 101, 116, 288, 296
　　Brazil, 288
　　childhood obesity, 288
　　energy costs, 176
　　obesity, 141
　　signalling, 84
breast milk, 99
　　composition, 176
　　cross species variability, 200
　　energy density, 177
　　leptin, 178, 180, 288
　　mammalian composition, 229
　　output, 212
　　weaning, 235
breast milk composition, IQ, 190
brown adipose tissue, 8, 25, 169
buffering, 153, 162, 168, 180, 183, 197, 230,
　　　234, 265, 266
　　brain, 66, 227
　　paracrine factors, 71
buffering space, 171
bumblebees, 184

cadaver analysis, 7, 16, 20
cake, 277
calorie, 51
calorimetry, 51
Cameroon, 165
canalisation, 12, 121
cancer, 289, 291, 295
canoe voyages, 247
capital breeding, 175, 200

capitalism, 2, 89, 275, 277, 295, 297
　　history, 293
　　ill-health, 294
　　psychosocial stress, 286
　　reproduction, 296
carbohydrate, dietary intake, 74–77
carbon dixoide production, 51
carcass analysis, 233
carcass dissection, obesity, 273
cardiovascular disease, 119, 267, 274, 291, 295
cardiovascular risk, 3, 5, 6
　　ethnicity, 262
　　toxic environment, 88
carnivores, body fat variability, **22**
car travel, 80
car use, 283
catch-up growth, 103, 136, **142**, 266
　　abdominal fat, 139
　　body mass index, 139
　　insulin resistance space, 139
caterpillar, 198
cattle, diseases, 261
cell theory, 274
cellular energy metabolism, 257
cellular metabolism, 64, 65
cemeteries, 7
central fat. *See* abdominal fat
chemical energy, 50
childhood, evolution, 231
childhood obesity
　　breast-feeding, 288
　　dietary protein, 74
　　fat distribution, 105, **106**
　　lean mass, 105
　　sleep, 284
　　soft drinks, 294
　　television, 284
　　toxins, 73
　　type 2 diabetes, 291
children
　　body composition, 84, 103–108
　　body mass index, **34**
　　television viewing, 283
chimpanzee
　　birth interval, 231
　　body size, 220
　　diet, 218, 233
　　disease load, 239
　　encephalisation, **221**
　　food sharing, 280
　　immune system, 239
　　life cycle, **231**
　　seasonality, 218
　　social organisation, 241
chimpanzees, 253
China, 253

chocolate, 277
cholecstokinin, 65
cholera, 240, 261
chronic energy deficiency, 176, 255, 262
  categorisation, 26
circadian rhythms
  hormones, 72
  secular trend, 284
  sleep, 80
cities, early, 261
civilisation, 253
climate
  adaptation, 14
  energetics, 7
  fat distribution, 171
  genetic factors, 203
  metabolism, 245
climate change, 247, 249, 251, 252, 292, 299, 300
  hominins, 217
coffee, 277
cold adaptation, 170
cold stress, 169
  basal metabolism, 246
  birth weight, 183
  energy stores, 202
  genetic adaptation, 245
  infant, 102
  neonate, 99
  seasonality, 219
Colombia, 159
colonisation, 201, 247, 258
  Homo erectus, 236
colonising, 270
colonising ape, 13, 235
colonising reproductive strategy, 292, 300
commercial companies, 277, 288, 291, formula milks,
  advertising, 287
  feeding behaviour, 82
  food industry, 278
  television, 283
complementary foods, 230, 235, 288
complex societies, 281
computed tomography, 4, 18, 109, 168
computer games, 284
computer technology, 283
concentration camps, 4
conception, 172–175, 212, 287
  body shape, 189
consumer behaviour, 292
contraception, 237, 287, 290
cooperative breeding, 230
corporate taxation, 295

corporative breeding, 296
corpulence, 255
cortisol, 67, 212, 241, 286
cotton rat, **24**
courting, 197
crab-eating macaque, **24**
crab-eating monkey, 218
critical window, 119, **121**
Crohn's disease, 71
crop failure, 1
crops, 250
crop yields, 299
cross-cultural studies, 189
crying
  begging signals, 281
  signalling, 84
cultural values, 255
culture, 270
cycling, 283
cytokines, 185, 260, 262
  inflammation, 70, 72, 73
  signals, 7, 72, 73

dairy agriculture, 258
dairy products, 250
dendritic cells, 71
densitometry, 3, 7, 16, 18
  skinfolds, **20**
density
  fat, 18
  lean, 18
depression, 289
  obesity, 87
developmental plasticity, 263, 266
  imprinted genes, 59, 60
developmental schedule, 13
diarrhoea, 261
diet
  agricultural, 276
  agriculture, 250
  Atkins, 274
  British in history, 277
  childhood, 85
  evolution, 234
  fish, 276
  foragers, 250
  Galen, 273
  hominin, 232, 233
  intake, 73–77
  restriction, 5
  ritualisation, 277
  secular trend, 276–280
  secular trends, 277
  toxic environment, 89
  urbanisation, 279
dietary carbohydrate, toxic environment, 89

dietary energy
  brain evolution, 226
  human evolution, 271
dietary energy density, 76
dietary fat, 75
dietary intake
  Guru Walla, **166**
  lactation, 190
diet-induced thermogenesis. *See*
    thermogenesis
diet industry, 294
dieting, 5, 9
digestion, 196, 226, 250
  gut microbes, 61
  satiety, 62, 63
digestive and, Avicenna, 273
direct calorimetry, 51
disease
  agriculture, 261
  children, 262
  cycles of infection, 262
  evolution, 262
  low birth weight, 120
  seasonality, 261
disease load, 14, 238
  fat distribution, 240
  genetic factors, 240
  human evolution, 271
dispersal, 236, 244, 262
dissection, lymphatic system, 70
divers, 171
dog, 229
dolphin, 170
drought, 250
dry seasons, 217
dual energy x-ray absorptiometry, 4
duck, 261
Dutch hunger winter, 128, 131
  rations, 155
dwarf hamster, **24**
DXA, 94, 96, 109, 133

early origins hypothesis, 119
eating disorders
  fat distribution, 159, 168
  neurobiology, 64
  refeeding, 158, 168
eating preferences, neurobiology, 63
eating style, 82
  twin studies, 82
Ebers papyrus, 271
ecological fluctuations, 2
ecological volatility, **236**
ecology, energetics, 7
economic development, 297
economic forces, 279
economic growth, 279, 292

economic policies, 299
  famine, 265
  Imperial, 263
  imperial, 277, 296
economics
  colonial, 4, 7
  global, 7
  imperialism, 88
  instability, 2
economic theory, 294
economic transition, 283
economic underdevelopment, 295
ecosystem engineers, 248
egalitarian societies, 253
Egypt, 253
elephant seal, 22, **24**
El Ni±o, 186, 252, 263, 266
emigration, 255
encephalisation, 221, 225, 270
endocrine disrupters, 289
endocrine factors, 64–72
energetic efficiency, 224
energetic effiiciency, 51, 77
energetics
  body size, 224
  lactation, 113, 115
  pregnancy, 113
energy balance, 49–54, 71, 77, 196,
    210
  circadian rhythms, 285
  Guru Walla, 165, **167**
  Hippocrates, 272
  reproduction, 174
  social cues, 64
energy balance equation, 49–54,
    73
energy density, 288, formula milk,
  food preferences, 87
  primate diet, 233
  secular trend, 280
energy expenditure, 51
  crying, 84
  Guru Walla, **166**
  Hippocrates, 270
  obese children, 79
  physical activity, 77
  regulation, 62
  signalling, 84
  tissue synthesis, 52
energy flux, reproductive function, 173
energy intake, 3, 52
  diet, 73
energy metabolism
  bet hedging, 264
  brain, 181
  genetic factors, 203
  trade-offs, **211**

energy requirements
  allometry, 199
  brain, 226
  elderly, 230
  food sales, 294
  foraging, 234
  immune function, 184, 185
  infants, 226
  muscle, 197
  obesity, **293**
  organ mass, 259
  organs, 181
  pregnancy, 113
  reproductive schedule, **207**
energy reserves, Venus figurines,
  271
energy sensing, 62
energy stores, 7, 195
  cold stress, 202
  extra somatic, 199
  growth, 232
  human evolution, 270
  lactation, 150
  malnutrition, 153
  mammals, 21
  reproduction, 173, 230, 287
  seasonality, 202
  signalling, 190, 192
  social status, 254
  strategy, 210
  survival, 161
energy, supply and demand, 9
epicardial adipose tissue, 71
epigenetic effects, 265
epigenetics, 49, 59–61, 148,
  204
essential fat, 160
estrogen, 109
ethnicity,
  abdominal fat, 97
  anthropometry, 46
  birth weight, 97
  body fat content, **29**
  body shape, **45–47**
  cardiovascular risk, 262
  genetic factors, 47
  intramuscular fat, 259
  phenotypic induction, 275
  visceral fat, 259
ethology, 10
evolutionary pyschology, 10
exercise
  Galen, 273
  Hippocrates, 272
exercise training, 257
expensive tissue hypothesis, 226
exploitation, 253

fall-back foods, 230
famine, 2, 252, 263, 286
  20th-century, 252
  agriculture, 251
  Bangladesh, 154, **155**
  birth weight, 128
  disease risk, 239
  emigration, 255
  Europe, 255
  fertility, 252
  genetic factors, 252
  history, 1, 252
  immune function, 213
  Imperial economics, 265
  India, 252, 263
  Irish potato, 154, 186, 239
  mortality, 154, 252, 263
  Somalia, 154
  survival, **155**
famine oedema, 156
fashion, 190
fast food, 279
fast foods, 76
fat
  density, 18
  energy content, 52
fat accretion, foetus, **94**
fat deposition,
  foetus, 93, **95**
  pregnancy, 114
  social stress, 187
fat distribution
  adult, 109, **110**
  childhood obesity, **106**
  children, 105
  cold stress, 170, 171
  disease load, 240
  eating disorders, 158, 159,
    168
  game theory, 212
  growth, 108
  heat stress, 245
  HIV/AIDS, 290
  immune function, 185
  lactation, 116
  lipoprotein lipase, 109
  low birth weight, 133
  menopause, 109, 113
  neonate, 96, 130, 212
  obesity, 274
  oestrogen, 69
  phenotypic induction, 133
  pregnancy, 115, 288
  psychosocial stress, 87
  puberty, 106, 108
  sex hormones, 69, 109
  sexual selection, 187

fat distribution (*cont.*)
   tracking, **147**
   Venus figurines, 271
   weight loss, 157
fat mass
   allometric scaling, 199
   birth, 227
   foetus, **95**
   Guru Walla, **166**
   infant temperament, **86**
   neonate, 95, **228**
   phenotypic induction, 134
   scaling with lean mass, **23**, 30, **31**, **39**
   scaling with size, 30, **31**, **38**
   social status, 255
   starvation, **165**
   tracking, 144, **146**
fat mass index
   adiposity index, 30, 32
   adult, 109
   aging, 111, **112**
   children, 103, **104**, **105**
   foetus, 93
   geographic variability, 40, **41**, **42**,
     48
   hominins, 222
   infant, 100
   neonate, 96
   obese children, **35**
   pregnancy, 114
   sexual dimorphism, **41**, **44**, 103, **104**
fat oxidation
   genetic factors, 246
   thrifty genes, 204
feast and famine, 2, 161, 203, 247, 251,
   256
feeding style, infant, 85
fermentation, 226
fertilisers, 299
fertility, famine, 252
fertility symbols, 271
fetal growth, 59
fetal life, phenotypic induction, 12
fever, 184, 260
Firmicutes, 61
foetal growth, 209, 267
   abdominal fat, 97
foetal nutrition, 120, 136
foetus, 113, 114
   body composition, 93–95
folivory, 232
followership, 253, 254
food hoard, 201
food industry, 278, 279, 294
food insecurity, 1, 2
food prices, 263

food-processing, 277
food sharing, 280, 281
   apes, 241
food shortages, 251
food storage, 250
food stores, 251
food supplies, 300
foragers, 2, 161, 250
   food shortages, 251
foraging, 249
   energy costs, 226
   social stress, 242
foraging returns, 238
formula feeding, 101, 288, 296
formula-feeding, signalling, 84
fossil record, 7, 9, 238
founder effects, 203
fox, arctic, 202
Framingham heart study, 5
free fatty acids, 66
free market, 299
free-market economy, 292
freezer, 279
Frisch hypothesis, 149, 172, 173
frugivory, 232
fruit, sweetness preferences, 233
fuel availability, 63
fuel depots, 197, **211**
fuel supply, 196

Galen, 272, 273
Gambia, 130
   immune function, 185
   leptin, 185
   reproduction, 176
   seasonality, 163, 252
game theory, 63, 209, 210, 239, 260, 266
   fat distribution, 212
game theory space, 213
gastric distension, 65
gene flow, 245
genetic admixture, 244
genetic factors, 11, 13
   abdominal fat, 240
   adipose tissue biology, 260
   adoption studies, 55
   agriculture, 248
   appetite, 58, 59
   basal metabolism, 59, 246
   bet hedging, 264
   body mass index, 41
   Dutch hunger winter, 131
   ethnicity, 47
   famine, 252
   fat oxidation, 246
   feast and famine, 256

heritability, 55, 56
human origins, 244
imprinted genes, 59–60
insulin, 59
leptin, 58
lipid oxidation, 59
maturation, 108
metagenome, 61
migration, 275
obesity, 264, 285
obesity epidemic, 275
physical activity, 59
thermogenesis, 59
thinness, 58
thrift, 13, 203, 208
twin studies, 55
type 2 diabetes space, 205
genetic polymorphisms, 248
genetic potential, 141
gestational diabetes, 127, 130
ghrelin, 63, 65, 290
giardia, 260
global economics, 295
global warming, 250, 292, 299, 300
glucagon, 66
glucose, 185
 brain use, **182**
 infant requirements, 181
glucose fructose syrup, 278
glucose intolerance, 122
glutamine, 185
glycaemic index, 75
 pregnancy, 130
glycaemic load, 75, 76, 288, formula
  milk
 agricultural diet, 276
 agriculture, 234, 247
 dieting, 294
 early Homo, 247
 Palaeolithic migration, 258
glycogen, 52, 54, 63, 66, 67, 99, 153, 195,
  196, 210, 260
 physical activity, 257
good genes hypothesis, 189
gorilla
 captive, 24
 encephalisation, **221**
 growth rate, 229
 seasonality, 217
 social organisation, 241
grandmothers, 230
green revolution, 299
grey kangaroo, 22, **24**
grey squirrel, **24**
ground squirrel, 200
growth, 179, 210, 212

abdominal fat, 137
catch up, 103, 208
foetus, 93
human evolution, 270
imprinted genes, 59
infancy, 84
insulin-like growth factor 1, 74
life history, 237
maturation, 108
metabolic capacity, **140**
metabolic load, **140**
obesity, 137
parasites, 239
parental care, 281
plasticity, 122
puberty, 69
seasonality, 163
sex hormones, 69
strategy, 231
growth adrenarche, 69
growth trajectory, **136**
Guatemala, 126
guinea pig, 227
 perinodal adipose tissue content, 71
Guru Walla, 165, **166**
gut, 226
gut microbes, 61–62
gut peptides, 63, 65

hamster, 201
hamsters, 271
harvest, 250
harvest season, 116, 162
 weight, **164**
Hattori chart, **33–35**
 adult geographic variability, **42**
 children, **34**, **104**
 infant, **100**
heart, 109, 122, 159, 267
heat stress, 224
 birth weight, **246**
 genetic adaptation, 245
 infant, 102
 insulation, 171
 neonate, 99
 pregnancy, 115
helminths, 238
hepatitis, 238
heritability
 adiposity, 264
 baboons, 57
 body mass index, 55–58
 fat mass, 55
 lean mass, 56
 obesity, 58
 social rank, 285

Herodotus, 272
herpes, 238
hibernation, 170, 197, 199
high carbohydrate diet, 198
high-fat diet, epigenetic effects, 61
Hindu writings, 272
Hippocrates, 272
HIV/AIDS, 261, 290
HIV infection, 71
holocene, 250
homeostasis, 17, 76, 122, 169
hominin evolution, 216
hominins, 215, 244
    body composition, 222
    body mass index, 220
    body size, 219
    diet, 232
    insulin, 234
    lactation, 226, 230
    life cycle, **231**
    migration, 218
    muscle mass, 223
    physical activity, 234
    social organisation, 241
Homo erectus, 215, 216
    body composition, 222
    body size, 220
    disease load, 239
    encephalisation, 221
    life cycle, **231**
    migration, 236
    thrifty genes, 258
hormonal axes, 265
hormonal programming, 132, 204
hormones, 64–72. *See also* insulin;
        leptin
    circadian rhythms, 72
    signals, 7
human evolution, 244–269
human origins, 244
humours, 272
hunger, 82
    signalling, 83
hungry season, 116, 162
    weight, **164**
hunting, 188, 210, 247, 248, 250,
        280
hydration, 3, 17
hydrodensitometry. *See* densitometry
hydrometry. *See* total body water
hygiene, 240
hypertension, 6, 119, 120, 122, 295
hypertriglyceridaemia, 260
hypothalamus, 174
    appetite, 63–64
    gut peptides, 65
    leptin, 68

Iceland, 102
Ik, 1
illness, 67
immune function, 67, 72, 183, 212, 228,
        246
    adaptive, 183
    cytokines, 186
    ecological load, 260
    energy costs, 184
    fat distribution, 185
    innate, 183
    insulin resistance, 73, 185
    social stress, 187
    weaning, 230
immune response, 290
    cytokines, 240
    energy requirements, 260
    paracrine factors, 70
immune system, 197
    transgenerational effects, 200
imprinted genes, parent-offspring conflict,
        59
income breeding, 114, 175, 200, 201
India, 253
    abortion, 287
    commercialisation, 295
    famine, 252
    famine mortality, 263
    famines, 4
    low birth weight, 133, 265
    neonatal body composition, 97, **98**
    neonate, 99
    phenotypic induction, 133
    secular trend, 265
indirect calorimetry, 51, 273
industrialisation, 271, 283
industrialised populations, 289
industrialised societies, 255, 276
    pollution, 73
    psychosocial stress, 88
industrial revolution, 276, 282, 292, 294
industrial societies, 2
industry
    infant formula, 295
    tobacco, 295
infancy, phenotypic induction, 12
infant,
    body composition, 100–103
    diet, 101
    energy requirements, 226
    fat mass index, 100
    lean mass index, 100
    sexual dimorphism, 101
    weight gain, 138
infant growth, menarche, 149, **150**
infanticide, 287
infants, mortality, 290

infant weight gain
  childhood adiposity, 74
  physical activity, 80
infection, 260
  appetite, 184
  weaning, 227
infectious disease, 154, 259, 290, 295
infectious diseases, 240
inflammation, 72–73, 185
  abdominal fat, 67
  cytokines, 70
  insulin resistance, 73
influenza, 240, 261
information, 240
insulation, 169, 170, 171
insulin, 196
  adiposity signal, 65, 68
  appetite, 62
  diet, 67, 75
  genetic factors, 59
  hunger, 82
  metabolism, hominin, 234
  physical activity, 284
  reproduction, 175
  resistance, 66, 67
  thrifty genes, 203
insulin-like growth factor 1, 74
insulin-like growth factor 2, imprinted genes, 59
insulin metabolism
  dairy agriculture, 258
  population density, 242
insulin resistance, 257
  abdominal fat, 139
  catch-up growth, 139
  female shape, 263
  functions, 196
  hominin, 234
  immune function, 185
  inflammation, 72
  meat eating, 247
  Palaeolithic diet, 258
  phenotypic induction, 206
  physical activity, 257
  population size, 242
  psychosocial stress, 87
  smoking, 289
  thrifty genes, 205, 256
insulin sensitivity, 67, 73
inter-birth interval, 230, 250
interleukins, 70
intestines, 109
intramuscular adipose tissue, 259
intrauterine growth retardation, 128
in vivo neutron activation analysis, 4

jam, 277
joule, 51
juvenile period, evolution, 231

kangaroo, 234
ketones, 181
kidney, 122, 267
kidneys, 259
kilojoule. *See* joule
kin, 241
koala, 201
Korea, 170
Kosrae, 259
k-strategy, 235
kwashiorkor, 5

lactation, 13, 212, 266
  baboon, 177
  bear, 202
  dietary intake, 190
  energetics, 7, 115
  energy costs, 176
  fat distribution, 116
  fat oxidation, 116
  hominins, 226, 230
  Homo erectus, 224
  leptin, 68
  maternal body mass index, 177
  orang utan, 218
  pig, 201
  primates, 237
  rat, 201
  seal, 202
  strategy, 200
  type 2 diabetes, 289
  whale, 202
lactose, 258
Ladakh, 99
landownership, 254
language, 270
Laplace, 273
Lavoisier, 273
leadership, 253, 254
lean mass
  dietary protein, 74
  heritability, 56
  leptin, 180
  phenotypic induction, 134
lean mass index, 32
  adult, 109
  aging, 111, **112**
  children, 103, **104**, **105**
  foetus, 93
  geographic variability, **40**, **42**, 48
  hominins, 222
  infant, 100
  neonate, 96

lean mass index (*cont.*)
    obese children, **35**
    sexual dimorphism, **40**, **44**, 103, **104**
lemur, 23
Leningrad siege, 128, 131
leptin, 194
    adiposity signal, 65, 68–69
    appetite, 62
    breast-milk, 68
    breast milk, 178, 180, 288
    discovery, 7
    Gambia, 185
    genetic factors, 58
    hypothalamus, 63
    immune function, 185
    lean mass, 180
    mice, 175, 185
    phenotypic induction, 206
    placenta, 68
    reproduction, 68
    reproductive energetics, 174
    sexual dimorphism, 68
    sleep, 80
    starvation signal, 68
    trade-offs, 67, 212
lethargy, 284
leukotrines, 71
life course, body composition, 118
life cycle, 153
    hominin, **231**
    hominins, 225
    human, **231**
life histories theory, 231
life history, growth, 237
life history theory, 122, 194, 270
    mammals, 25
lifestyle diseases, 9, 295
limb proportions, 223
limb system, 260
lipid deposition, 49, 52. *See also* fat deposition
lipid management system, 197
lipid oxidation, 49
    genetic factors, 59
lipogenesis, 75
lipolysis, 257
    perinodal adipose tissue, 71
lipoprotein lipase, 67, 109
    sex hormones, 69
litigation, 280
liver, 109, 122, 181, 196, 259, 267
    paracrine factors, 70
    starvation, 159
low birth weight, 120
    fat distribution, 133
    obesity, 286
    phenotypic induction, **142**

low-protein diet, 74
lungs, 109, 259
lymphatic system, 186
lymph nodes, 70
lymphocytes, 184
lymphoid tissue, 70

macrosomia, 127
magnetic resonance imaging, 4, 18, 98, 109, 110, 127, 129
maize, 276
malaria, 238, 246, 248, 261, 295
malnutrition,
    breast-feeding, 176
    energetics, 7
    infant, 179
    pregnancy, 131
mammals
    body composition at birth, **228**
    body fat variability, 16, 21, **22–24**, 25
    breast milk composition, 229
    lactation, 237
    primitive, 199
marasmus, 5
market, 286
market forces, 295
markets, 279, 299
marmoset, 229
Massas, 165
mate preferences, 189
maternal adiposity, 237
maternal body mass index, birth weight, 180
maternal diet, 129, 130
maternal investment, 232
maternal malnutrition, 128
maternal obesity, offspring body composition, 96
maturation, 148
mautam, 251
meals, social cues, 278
measles, 261, 262
meat, 250, 276
    composition, 278
    insulin metabolism, 247, 258
meat eating, 218
mechanical work, 51
mechanisation, 77, 299
    secular trend, **282**
menarche, 108, 173
    foetal growth, 126
    Frisch hypothesis, 172
    infant growth, 149
    waist-hip ratio, 189
menopause, fat distribution, 113
Mesopotamia, 1

metabolic capacity, 121, 122, 206, 267
  growth, **140**
metabolic flexibility, 66, 257
metabolic ghetto, 266
metabolic imprinting, 119
metabolic load, 121, 122, 267
  growth, **140**
  meat, 233
metabolic syndrome, 137, 291
Mexico, 253
mice
  epigenetic effects, 61
  gut microbes, 61
  immune function, 185
  leptin, 175, 185
  reproduction, 175
micronutrient deficiencies, 262
migration, 197, 237, 247, 255
  from Africa, 244
  birds, 200
  cities, 295
  famine, 2
  genetic factors, 275
  hominins, 218
  Homo erectus, 236
  rural-urban, 283
  seasonality, 13, 17
  starvation, 258
millet, 276
minerals, 3
Minnesota starvation study, 5, 158, 164
  weight, **165**
miocene, 217
mitochondrial DNA, 244
Mongol empire, 262
Mongolia, 171
moose, **24**
Morgagni, 273
mortality
  body mass index, 156
  famine, 252
  life history, 237
  starvation, 263
  statistics, 3
moth, 198
mother goddess figures, 271
mouse, respiration, 273
multinational corporations, 295
multinational food companies, 295
muscle,
  paracrine factors, 70
  population density, 242
muscle mass, 21, 109, 188, 193, 196, 210, 257, 267
  energy requirements, 181
  glucose uptake, 89, 208

hominins, 223
insulin resistance, 203
starvation, 159
muscles, energy supply, **211**

Nariokotome boy, 220
national health and nutrition examination
  survey, 6
natural disasters, 251
Neanderthals, 216
Neel, James, 2
neolithic revolution, 250
neonate
  abdominal fat, 129
  adiposity, **228**
  altitude, 99
  body composition, 95–99
  brain, 183
  brown adipose tissue, 169
  fat distribution, 212
  fat mass, 183
  India, 97, **98**
nephron number, 120
neurobiology, appetite, 62
neuropeptide Y, 63
niche, 197, **236**
  maternal metabolism, 237
  pregnancy, 237
niche construction, 14, 247, 248, 249, 262
Nile Valley, 262
Nisa, 228
nomads, 251
noradrenaline, 66

obesity, 203
  breast-feeding, 141
  cardiovascular risk, 6, 8
  categorisation, 19, 26, 27
  cold stress, 99
  depression, 87
  Dutch hunger winter, 131
  endocrine disrupters, 290
  energy expenditure, 77
  energy requirements, **293**
  environmental induction, 12
  epidemic, 14, 77
  epigenetics, 148
  evolution, 271
  genetic factors, 55–63, 264, 285
  growth, 137
  gut microbes, 61
  heritability, 58
  historical record, 281
  history, 255, 274
  inflammation, 72
  low birth weight, 131, 286

obesity (*cont.*)
  maternal age, 288
  measurement, 19
  pharmacological treatment, 297
  phenotypic induction, 137
  prevalence, 5, 6, 58
  prevalence and gender, 296
  psychological stress, 87
  secular trend, 6
  sedentary behaviour, 284
  sex difference, **297**
  sleep, 284
  sleep duration, 80
  smoking, 289
  social inequality, 286, 287
  social network, 89
  socioeconomic status, 279
  soft drinks, 294
  starting, 286
  stunting, 30, 140
  susceptibility, 54
  television viewing, 80
  thrifty genes, 256
  toxic environment, 88
  transport, 283
  treatment, 15
  viral infection, 73
  weight loss, 166
obesity epidemic, 275, 290–292
  physical activity, 284
obesogenic niche, 88, 274, 275–290, 291,
    292
  emergence, 275
  genetics, 58
oedema, 156
oestrogen, 69
omentum, 70
oncostatin, 70
ontogeny, 10–12
  imprinted genes, 60
optimal foraging theory, 280
orang utan, 199
  encephalisation, **221**
  fat metabolism, 24, 218
  lactation, 218
  seasonality, 218
organ mass, 21, 196, 210
  energy needs, 181
  energy requirements, 259
  starvation, 159, **160**
overfeeding, heritability, 56
oxidisable fuels, 174
  regulation by insulin, 68
  regulation by leptin, 68
oxygen consumption, 51
oxygen uptake, brain, 181

Palaeolithic diet, 258
palatability, 82, 276
  neurobiology, 63
  secular trend, 278
pancreas, 65, 122, 267
paracrine factors, 70–72
Paracrine regulation, 186
paracrine regulation, 201
Paraguay, 235
parasite, 239
parasites, 154, 238
parental care, 197, 280
parent-offspring conflict, imprinted genes, 59
parity, 97, 116
pathogen, 261
pathogens, 183, 184, 186, 239, 260
Penguin, 170
percent fat
  adult, 109
  body mass index, 28
  children, **104**
  hominins, 222
  infant, 100
  neonate, 95, 96
  statistical limitations, 11, 27, 30, 32
pertussis, 261
Peru, 189, 253
pharmaceutical industry, 9, 15
phenotypic induction, 12, 119, **121**, 207, 265
  abdominal fat, 134
  body size, 126, **136**, 180
  Brazil, 126
  ethnicity, 275
  infant, 138
  insulin resistance, 206
  maturation, 148
phenotypic plasticity, 204
photonic scanning, 45, **46**, **47**
photoperiodicity, 80, 202, 271
physical activity, 210
  body fat content, 78, 80
  body mass index, 36, 58
  cardiovascular risk, 297
  children, 78
  energy balance, 54
  energy expenditure, 77, **79**
  foraging, 234
  glycogen, 257
  hominins, 234
  infant weight gain, 80
  insulin resistance, 257
  leisure time, 283
  muscle deposition, 36, 80
  obesity, **79**
  pregnancy, 286
  secular trend, 280–284

social status, 285
technology, 278
thrifty genes, 204, 257
weight gain in children, **80**
physical effort, 2, 7
agriculture, 80, 281
foraging, 280
secular trend, 283
social status, 286
physique, 123, 267
tracking, 143
pig
breast milk composition, 229
dietary protein, 74
diseases, 261
lactation, 201
malnutrition, 154, 161
pigeon milk, 200
Pima Indians, 89, 256, 296
thrifty phenotype, 205
placenta, 113, 114, 257
placental nutrition, 227
plague, 261, 286
plantations, 278, 293, 295
plasmodium infections, 260
plasticity, 209, 232, 245, 252, 264, 265
adiposity, 11
developmental plasticity, 59
growth, 122
pregnancy, 113
pleistocene, 250
plethysmography. *See* densitometry
pliocene, 217
Plutella xylostella, 198
polar bear, 201, 202
adiposity, 170
political regimes, 286
pollution, 73
Polynesia, 256, 258, 259
polyunsaturated fatty acids, 71
Pond, Caroline, 7, 11
ponderal index, 129
population crash, 237, 238
population density, 261
insulin, 242
population growth, 250, 251, 278
population pressure, 249, 250
porpoise, 170
potassium counting, 3
potato, 276
potoroo, **24**
poverty, 4, 277, 296
power, 292
Prader-Willi syndrome, 60
p-ratio, 74
predator prey cycles, 237

predictive adaptive responses, 206
pregnancy, 179, 257, 287
Dutch hunger winter, 128
energetics, 7, 114
energy requirements, 115
fat distribution, 113, 288
Gambia, 113
glycaemic index, 130
heat stress, 115, 245
leptin, 68
malnutrition, 131
physical activity, 286
smoking, 289
type 2 diabetes, 205
weight gain, 113
preterm infant, 127, 132
primate, reproduction, 175
primates, 16
body fat variability, 23
brain-gut trade-off, 226
brain size, 227
Bristol composition, 229
diet, 232
dietary trends, 235
disease load, 238
epigenetic effects, 61
fertility, 189
HIV/AIDS, 261
mate preferences, 189
maternal rank, 241
neurobiology, 63
reproduction, 253, 287
social rank, 253
sucrose preferences, 233
type 2 diabetes, 256
private enterprise, 292
profit, 286, 292, 295
profits, 293
programming, 119
proletariat, 277, 278
proopiomelanocortin, 63
property rights, 254
prostaglandins, 71
protein
energy content, 52
intake, 3, 74
protein accretion, foetus, 93, **94**
protein-energy malnutrition, 5
protein synthesis, 184
proximate causation, 10, 11, 49
psychological factors, 63
psychological stress, 67
psychosocial stress, 285–287
anorexia nervosa, 88
appetite, 87
energy density, 87

psychosocial stress (*cont.*)
  fat distribution, 87
  industrialised societies, 88
  obesity, 87
  workplace, 286
puberty, 257
  body mass index, 27
  eating disorders, 9
  fat distribution, 106
  sex hormones, 69
public health, 2, 5, 9
  economic policy, 89
public health campaigns, smoking,
  289
public health policies, 295
Pythagoras, 272

Quetelet, 274

rabbit, 229
racism, 87
radiography, 3
rat
  breast milk composition, 229
  critical window, 119
  lactation, 201
  malnutrition, 119
  mautam, 251
  perinodal adipose tissue content, 71
  phenotypic induction, 119, 121
  reproduction, 175
rations, 155
rats, neurobiology, 62
refeeding, 165
refined carbohydrate, 293
refrigerator, 278, 279
reindeer, 202, 229
reproduction, 14, 172–179, 183
  energetics, 250
  energy balance, 174
  energy expenditure, 173
  energy flux, 173
  foraging theory, 280
  Frisch hypothesis, 173
  insulin, 175
  leptin, 174, 175
  mammals, 197
  metabolism, 174
  oxidisable fuels, 174
  primate, 175
  primates, 253, 287
  rat, 175
  secular trend, 287
reproductive rate, 232
  ape, 237
  human, 237

reproductive schedule, **207**
reproductive strategy, 235
resistin, 70
respiratory quotient, 199
rice, 276
risk management, 12, 208
  food sharing, 281
ritual fattening, 54, 165
rodents, body fat variability, 21, **22**
r-strategy, 235

sanitation, 290
satiation, 82
satiety, 82
  diet, 75
  digestion, 62, 63
  fluids, 76
satiety signals
  cholecstokinin, 65
  ghrelin, 65
schistosomiasis, 261
seal, 23, 202
  grey, **24**
  harp, 227
  ringed, **24**
seasonality, 13, 17, 198, **236**
  agriculture, 80, 161, 252
  australopithecines, 219
  birth rate, 168
  birth weight, 130
  body mass index, 163
  chimpanzee, 217
  cold stress, 219
  disease load, 261
  energy supply, 234
  Gambia, 252
  gorilla, 217
  growth, 153
  habitats, 217
  hominins, 216, 224
  lactation, 116
  orang utan, 218
  physical effort, 80
  primate diet, 232
  weight, **164**
  weight loss, 162, 163
secular trend
  birth weight, 289
  body mass index, 5, 11, 27
  body size, 267
  circadian rhythms, 284
  diet, 276–280
  in the diet, 288
  disease, 289
  eating disorders, 9
  energy density, 280

growth, 208
height, 2
hominin size, 220
India, 265
IQ, 275
mechanisation, **282**
obesity, 6, 12, 58
palatability, 278
pharmacological agents, 289–290
physical activity, 280–284
physical effort, 283
reproduction, 287
research on adiposity, **8**
sleep, 284
social stress, 285–287
sugar consumption, 277
type 2 diabetes, 291
Western Samoa, 7
secular trends, obesogenic niche, 275
sedentary behaviour, 77
sedentism, 250, 252
selective pressures, 195
senescence, 230
sepsis, 257
settlements, reproduction, 174
sewage, 261
sex difference, obesity prevalence, **297**
sex homone binding proteins, 69
sex hormones, 69
  fat distribution, 69
  fetal exposure, 69
sexual attraction, 13
sexual dimorphism, 12
  adipose tissue distribution, **43**
  adolescence, **104**
  adult, 108
  aging, **112**
  australopithecines, 225
  body mass index, **39**, **43**
  body shape, 46
  children, **104**, **105**, **107**
  children space, 103
  energetics, 211
  fat distribution, **107**, 116, 211
  fat mass index, **41**, **44**, 108
  foetus, 94
  height, 37
  hominin body composition, 223
  hominin height, 221
  infant, 101
  lean mass index, **40**, **44**, 108
  neonate, 96
  pig, 161
  skinfolds, **107**
  survival, 161
  trade-offs, 210

sexual dimrphism, leptin, 68
sexual division of labour, 280, 296
sexual selection, body shape, 187
sexual swelling, 189
shanty towns, 283
sheep, 229
shrew, 199, 201
Siberia, 88, 258
signalling, 290
  body shape, 263
  breast size, 192
  honest, 192
  immune function, 263
  leptin, 178
  parent-offspring, 83
  reproduction, 174
  sexual selection, 188
  waist-hip ratio, 188
signalling pathways, appetite, 62
signalling proteins, 70
skinfolds
  aging, 112
  altitude, 98
  children, 106, **107**
  fat distribution, **107**, 123, 124
  infant, 102
  infant growth, 179
  intrauterine growth retardation, 128, **129**
  phenotypic induction, 133
  ratios, **125**
  sexual dimorphism, 106, **107**
  tracking, 144, **147**
skinfold thickness, 4, 7, 19, 27, 36, 37
  densitometry, **20**
  fat distribution, **45**
  sexual dimorphism, **45**
slavery, 295
slave trade, 255, 277
sleep
  foraging theory, 280
  Hippocrates, 272
  obesity, 284
  secular trend, 284
  television, 284
sleep duration
  leptin, 80
  obesity, 80
slimness, 255
slums, 295, 297
smallpox, 261
smoking, 58, 137, 289
social cues, 82
  appetite, 235
  meals, 278
social energy budget, 280
social hierarchy, 254

social inequality, 266
  obesity, 287
  obesity risk, 286
sociality, 14, 64
social network, obesity, 89, **90**
social rank, 241
  heritability, 285
  primates, 253
  survival, 254
social status, 241, 283, 285
  adiposity, 255
  emergence, 253
  physical effort, 286
  physique, 255
social stratification, 253, 266
social stress
  fat deposition, 187
  foraging, 242
  hominins, 241
  immune function, 187
  immunosuppression, 241
  secular trend, 285–287
  transgenerational effects, 286
sociobiology, 10
socioeconomic status, obesity, 279
soft drinks, 75, 294
Somalia, 154
South Africa, activity patterns, 283
speed, 198
spiney mouse, **24**
spleen, 159
sportsmen, 297
stacking, 237
starch, 276
starvation, 1, 4, 159
  body composition, **165**
  body mass index, **157**
  brain, 180
  bumblebees, 184
  experimental, 5
  immune function, 184
  imperialism, 88
  migration, 258
  mortality, 263
  organ masses, **160**
  social effects, 254
Stele of famine, 1
stillbirths, 173
stillborn infant, 93, 95
stoat, **24**
stock animals, 162, 254
storage fat, 160
strategy, 9, 10, 14, 99, 151, 153, 179, 183, 199,
     200, 207, 231, 266
  energy stores, 210
  fat distribution, 211

stratified societies, 253
stress hormones, 66
stress, obesity, 87
stroke, 6, 119, 267, 295
stunting, 179, 286, 295
  obesity, 140
  waist girth, 141
sucrose, 75, 233, 276, 278, 293
  insulin response, 76
sugar consumption, 277
sugar, health claims, 279
supermarket, 279
supplementation, 130
surgery, 15
  bariatric, 291
survival, 161, 212, 254
  hosts/pathogens, 262
sweetness preferences, 233

tamarin, 229
taste, 82
tea, 277, 279
technology, 14, 248
  innovation, 282
television 284
  children, 283
television viewing
  obesity, 80
  physical activity, 80
temperament
  childhood adiposity, **86**
  children, 87
  infant, 84, **85**, 86
testosterone, 69, 109
thermal environment, 245
  birth weight, 265
  infant, 102
  pregnancy, 115
thermal load, energetics, 7
thermodynamics, 51
  Hippocrates, 272
  historical development, 274
thermogenesis, 52, 75
  thrifty genes, 204
thigh girth
  mate preferences, 191
  sexual selection, 191
  Venus figurine, 271
thin-fat phenotype, 97, 133
thinness, genetic factors, 58
thrift, 54, 55, 202, 203, 206
  birth weight, 246
  emigration, 255
  genetic basis, 208
  genetic variability, 13
thrifty genes, 224, 256

insulin resistance, 205
thrifty genotype hypothesis, 203, 248
thrifty phenotype hypothesis, 121, 204
thrifty phenotype, type 2 diabetes, 205
thymus gland, 70
tiger, **24**
Tinbergen, 153
  Niko, 10, 11, 13, 49
tissue defence, 184
tissue repair, 184, 186, 260
tissue synthesis, 52
tobacco, 279, 295
torpor, 199
total body water, 3, 17, 21
  neonate, 95
toxic environment, 9
  diet, 89
  obesity, 88
  refined carbohydrate, 89
toxins, 73, 289
tracking, 12, 119, **121**, 132
  body mass index, 142, 143
  fat distribution, **147**
  fat mass, 144
  fatness, **145**, **146**
  physique, 151
  skinfolds, 144, **145**, **147**
tractor, 282
trade, 261, 262, 277, 292, 296, 299
trade-off, 180, 183, 235, 257, 290
trade-offs, 12, 13, 210, 261, 263
  energy metabolism, **211**
  leptin, 67
trans-generational effects, 14
transgenerational effects, 151, 180, 204, 206,
    208, 209
  birth weight, 207
  epigenetic effects, 61
  immune system, 200
  stress, 286
transgenerational plasticity, 266
transport, 283
trauma, 67, 257, 290
triglycerides, 109, 195, 196, 197, 246, 257
  breast milk, 176
  synthesis, 66
tropics, 7, 23, 162
tuberculosis, 261
tumour necrosis factor, 70, 198
twin studies
  birth weight, 126
  fat mass, 55
  feeding behaviour, 82
  growth, 126
  overfeeding, 56
  type 2 diabetes, 205

underfeeding, 56
type 1 diabetes, 130, 205
type 2 diabetes, 6, 65, 119, 203, 267, 295
  history, 271
  lactation, 289
  non Europeans, 258
  physical activity, 257
  primates, 256
  thrifty genes, 205, 256
  thrifty phenotype, 205

ultimate causation, 10
ultrasound, 128
underfeeding, heritability, 56
under-musculation, 224
unsaturated fatty acids, 71
urbanisation, 249, 271, 300
  dietary change, 279
  employment, 282
uterine size, 151, 266
uterus, 113

vaccination, 291
vaccines, 290
vasoconstriction, 171
vehicles, 283, 295
velvety free-tailed bat, 23
Venus of Willendorf, 271
vertebrates, 13
viruses, 239, 240
visceral adipose tissue
  cortisol, 67
  gene expression, 60
  inflammation, 72
visceral fat
  adult, 110
  ethnicity, 259
  magnetic resonance imaging, **111**
  psychosocial stress, 87
vitamins, 3
VNTR polymorphism. *See* insulin, genetic
  factors

waist girth
  adiposity indices, 124
  adult, 110
  cardiovascular risk, 297
  dietary protein, 74
  health risks, 6
  stunting, 141
  Venus figurine, 271
  weight loss, **167**
waist-hip ratio, 35, 123
  aging, **124**, 191
  birth weight, 133
  cold stress, 171

waist-hip ratio (*cont.*)
  disease load, 264
  fertility, 188
  IQ, 189
  limitations, **125**
  phenotypic induction, 133
  reproduction, 191
walking, 283
war, 286
weaning, 227, 258
weight gain
  adolescent, 54
  children, 142
  disease risk, 137
  fat distribution, 133
  humours, 272
  infant, 53, 54, 138
  infant body composition, 228
  infant diet, 101
  infant temperament, 85
  lactation, 116
  maternal, 113
  menarche, 149
  Minnesota starvation study, 164
  obesity, 286
  phenotypic induction, 136
  pregnancy, 113, 115, 129, 130
  sleep, 284
  smoking, 289
weight loss, 54
  abdominal fat, **167**

fat distribution, 157, 158
lactation, 116
neonate, 99, 183
obesity, 166
seasonality, 162, 163
skinfolds, 157
visceral fat, 166
weight watchers, 5
Western Samoa, 7
whale, 23, 170, 202
  beaked, 24
wheat, 276
whooping cough, 261
wolverine, **24**
woodchuck, **24**
workplace, 286
world war II, 4, 5
World War II
  concentration camps, **155**
  Dutch hunger winter, 128
  ghettos, 198
  prisoner of war camp, 154
  rations, **155**
  survival, 156, 161
wound healing, 70, 186
writing, 251

yuma bat, 22, **24**

zoology, 9
Zulus, 190